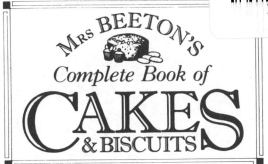

Mrs BEETON'S

Complete Book of

CAKES
& BISCUITS

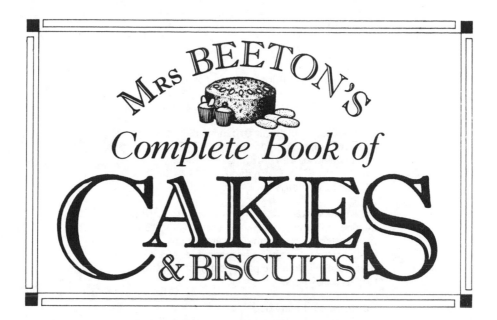

Mrs BEETON'S
Complete Book of
CAKES
& BISCUITS

Consultant Editor **Bridget Jones**

9/10

WARD LOCK

This paperback edition published 1993

© Text and illustrations Ward Lock Limited 1989

First published in Great Britain in 1989
by Ward Lock Limited
Villiers House, 41/47 Strand,
London WC2N 5JE, England
a Cassell Company

Editor: Jenni Fleetwood
Additional cake decorating material supplied by,
and cake designs created by, Jacqui Hine
Photography by Clive Streeter
Home Economist: Jacqui Hine
Stylist: Alison Meldrum
Illustration: Tony Randell
Text filmset in New Caledonia
by M & R Computerised Typesetting Limited
Printed and bound in Great Britain by The Bath Press, Avon

British Library Cataloguing in Publication Data

Beeton, Mrs, *1836-1865*
   Mrs Beeton's complete book of cakes and
   biscuits
   1.Cakes,   Recipes
   2.Biscuits,   Recipes
   641.8′653

   ISBN 0-7063-7150 X

**Mrs Beeton's is a registered trademark of
Ward Lock Ltd**

CONTENTS

USEFUL WEIGHTS AND MEASURES

USING METRIC OR IMPERIAL MEASURES

Throughout the book, all weights and measures are given first in metric, then in Imperial. For example 100 g/4 oz, 150 ml/¼ pint or 15 ml/1 tbsp.

When following any of the recipes use either metric or Imperial – do not combine the two sets of measures as they are not interchangeable.

EQUIVALENT METRIC/IMPERIAL MEASURES

Weights   The following chart lists some of the metric/Imperial weights that are used in the recipes.

METRIC	IMPERIAL
15 g	½ oz
25 g	1 oz
50 g	2 oz
75 g	3 oz
100 g	4 oz
150 g	5 oz
175 g	6 oz
200 g	7 oz
225 g	8 oz
250 g	9 oz
275 g	10 oz
300 g	11 oz
350 g	12 oz
375 g	13 oz
400 g	14 oz
425 g	15 oz
450 g	16 oz
575 g	1¼ lb
675 g	1½ lb
800 g	1¾ lb
900 g	2 lb
1 kg	2¼ lb
1.4 kg	3 lb
1.6 kg	3½ lb
1.8 kg	4 lb
2.25 kg	5 lb

Liquid Measures   The following chart lists some metric/Imperial equivalents for liquids. Millilitres (ml), litres and fluid ounces (fl oz) or pints are used throughout.

METRIC	IMPERIAL
50 ml	2 fl oz
125 ml	4 fl oz
150 ml	¼ pint
300 ml	½ pint
450 ml	¾ pint
600 ml	1 pint

Spoon Measures   Both metric and Imperial equivalents are given for all spoon measures, expressed as millilitres and teaspoons (tsp) or tablespoons (tbsp).

All spoon measures refer to British standard measuring spoons and the quantities given are always for level spoons.

Do not use ordinary kitchen cutlery instead of proper measuring spoons as they will hold quite different quantities.

METRIC	IMPERIAL
1.25 ml	¼ tsp
2.5 ml	½ tsp
5 ml	1 tsp
15 ml	1 tbsp

Length All linear measures are expressed in millimetres (mm), centimetres (cm) or metres (m) and inches or feet. The following list gives examples of typical conversions.

METRIC	IMPERIAL
5 mm	¼ inch
1 cm	½ inch
2.5 cm	1 inch
5 cm	2 inches
15 cm	6 inches
30 cm	12 inches (1 foot)

OVEN TEMPERATURES

Whenever the oven is used, the required setting is given as three alternatives: degrees Celsius (°C), degrees Fahrenheit (°F) and gas.

The temperature settings given are for conventional ovens. If you have a fan oven, then read the notes below and follow the manufacturer's instructions.

°C	°F	gas
110	225	¼
120	250	½
140	275	1
150	300	2
160	325	3
180	350	4
190	375	5
200	400	6
220	425	7
230	450	8
240	475	9

NOTE ON FAN OVENS AND CONTINENTAL OVENS

All the temperatures and timings given are for a conventional oven, with main heating sources located on both sides (in addition, some electric ovens may have a low-powered element located in the base).

Forced convection ovens – or fan ovens – have a built-in fan which re-circulates the hot air, providing even temperatures over a greater number of shelves. This is ideal for batch baking. This type of oven heats up very quickly and food cooks more quickly. It is the equivalent of between 10 and 20 degrees hotter than the conventional cooker. When using this type of oven always follow the manufacturer's instructions closely and adjust the cooking temperatures accordingly.

Continental electric ovens have the heating elements located in the top and bottom of the oven. These do give slightly different results and the manufacturer's instructions should be followed closely.

MICROWAVE INFORMATION

Occasional microwave hints and instructions are included for certain recipes, as appropriate. The information given is for microwave ovens rated at 650-700 watts.

The following terms have been used for the microwave settings: High, Medium, Defrost and Low. For each setting, the power input is as follows: High = 100% power, Medium = 50% power, Defrost = 30% power and Low = 20% power.

All microwave notes and timings are for guidance only: always read and follow the manufacturer's instructions for your particular appliance. The aim in providing microwave information is to indicate which recipes can be cooked successfully by that method, or short cuts which can be made by using the microwave for a small part of the preparation of a recipe.

Always remember to avoid putting any metal in the microwave and never operate the microwave empty.

INTRODUCTION

Baking cakes and biscuits is one of the more rewarding aspects of cookery and the results are always greatly appreciated. When *Beeton's Book of Household Management* was in its first edition, the selection of cakes was limited by comparison to what is expected of the subject today; however, it was taken for granted that cakes would be baked at home for everyday as well as for special occasions. Luncheon Cake, A Nice Plain Cake for Children, Holiday Cake and Saucer-cake for Tea are just a few examples of the cakes that were recommended as ordinary fare in the first edition. The same simple ingredients and methods used to make those economical cakes are to be found in many of the recipes throughout this edition.

Special-occasion cakes of that era included a rich cake for weddings or christenings, or a cake flavoured with both sweet and bitter almonds. All these traditional cakes are also included within the chapters that follow, along with other recipes that were introduced to later editions of Mrs Beeton's book.

Particular attention has been paid to the section on cake decorating and it has been revised and up-dated especially for this edition. The information has been brought up-to-date, in keeping with the traditional spirit of the book, providing all the basic guidance that the newcomer to cake decorating needs. The essential recipes and techniques are all clearly explained and step-by-step illustrations highlight any complicated methods.

One of the characteristics of Mrs Beeton's biscuit recipes is their simplicity and it is rewarding to re-test the most basic mixtures, consisting of little more than flour and water, and to discover the wonderful, crisp light results. The plain, savoury biscuits require the minimum of mixing and little in the way of skill, yet they are quite superior to the commercial alternatives and far cheaper to prepare.

By way of a contrast to these perfect examples of dry, unfermented bread, as they were termed in the original text, the section on biscuits includes a good variety of sweet recipes that range from spicy Ginger Snaps to tempting Almond Macaroons and richer chocolate concoctions.

Whether you are looking for a plain, mid-week cake, some savoury biscuits to complete a first-rate cheeseboard or an elaborate confection to complement aromatic morning coffee or a delicate cup of afternoon tea, you will find a suitable recipe in the chapters of *Mrs Beeton's Complete Book of Cakes and Biscuits*. As expected of a book of this title, the instructions are clear, the recipes easy to follow and the range of information is comprehensive by today's standards. Read through the recipes, take a look at the photographs and you will be inspired to exercise your knowledge of cake making or develop your baking skills.

FOLLOWING THE RECIPES

There are a few basic culinary rules that can be applied when following all recipes or preparing any food. Good kitchen practice, accuracy when following recipes and care when cooking food are the general principles which should be applied to all cooking processes. Certain cakes and biscuits are particularly delicate and special attention should be paid to their preparation. Follow these guidelines to ensure both kitchen safety and success.

BEFORE YOU START

The starting point for making any recipe is to read it through, checking that you have all the ingredients that are listed, in the right quantities, and all the cooking utensils that are needed. As well as checking these obvious points, make sure that you will have enough time to prepare and cook the recipe; this is particularly important if you are making a cake that may require lengthy cooking.

It may seem very obvious, but do clear the work surface before you start – it is all too easy to begin a baking session in enthusiasm when the kitchen is already crowded with dishes waiting to be washed after a meal, or from a previous cooking task. The lack of space and the mess suddenly become all too apparent when the tray of red-hot cakes is removed from the oven and there is not a space anywhere to put it down.

Assemble all the ingredients, utensils and baking tins. If you want to make any adjustments to the quantities – for example preparing a large batch of cakes – then work through the ingredients list, jotting down the quantities you intend to prepare, or noting any other changes so that you will be consistent as you weigh and prepare the recipe. It is very easy to forget to double up just one item when preparing a double quantity of mixture and it can be disastrous!

Lastly, make sure the oven is empty, ready for use and that the shelves are in position.

CHOICE OF INGREDIENTS

Information on basic ingredients is given on pages 19-27, but in general all ingredients should be fresh and of good quality. The rule for baking is to have foods such as butter, margarine, eggs and milk at room temperature unless otherwise stated in the recipe. Always wash eggs under cool water before cracking them open.

KITCHEN HYGIENE

Always make sure that areas where food is prepared are thoroughly clean, that all utensils are clean and dry and that dish cloths and tea-towels are scrupulously clean. And the same applies to your hands – do not handle raw food, then cooked food without washing your hands in between. Keep all utensils for raw and cooked food separate or washed between use.

WEIGHING AND MEASURING

It is important to follow the recipes closely for success. Use only one set of measures, either metric or Imperial. Use an accurate set of scales for weighing, a measuring jug for measuring quantities of fluid and British standard spoon measures.

Weigh all the ingredients before you begin to prepare the mixture so that they are all ready to be added as they are needed. It is a good idea to weigh dry ingredients, such as flour and sugar, before softer foods, like butter or margarine, as this saves having to wash the scoop or container on the scales in between weighing the items. Keep the prepared ingredients separate until they are ready to be mixed in the right order.

PREPARING TINS AND HEATING THE OVEN

Always make sure you have the correct size and shape of tin and prepare it in advance according to the instructions given in the recipe, or by following specific advice given by the bakeware manufacturer as appropriate. If you are unsure as to exactly how to line tins, then check with the chapter that explains and illustrates all the basics.

Prepare the oven, taking care to select the right temperature, at the stage suggested in the recipe.

MIXING THE INGREDIENTS

Follow the recipe method closely, taking note of any advice on the texture or colour of the mixture so that you know what you should be aiming for. If you are unsure of any term or process, then check it in the chapter on basics or in the glossary as appropriate.

The majority of cake mixtures should be baked as soon as they are prepared unless the recipe states otherwise. When preparing biscuits always observe suggested chilling times before baking.

COOKING TIMES

Check the cooking time before you put the cakes or biscuits into the oven, setting a timer as a reminder. Many recipes give a range of times within which the cake or biscuits should be cooked, so check on the cooking progress at the first suggested time. Before opening the oven door make sure that you know what you are looking for in the finished item, then you will be able to decide quickly whether it is cooked or not.

REMOVING FOOD FROM THE OVEN

Make sure that you have a clear space on which to put the baked goods as soon as they are removed from the oven. Have a heat-proof mat or stand on the work suface and always remember to use a thick oven glove to protect your hands.

Have a wire rack ready to receive the cooked food if the recipe suggests that it ought to be transferred to one. You may need a palette knife to slide biscuits off a baking sheet, or a small knife to loosen a cake around the sides of a tin. If you are removing a cake from a loose-bottomed tin, then have a suitable vessel ready to support the middle of the tin allowing the side to slide down. A storage jar with a heat-resistant top is ideal for this.

FINISHING THE RECIPE

Follow the advice given in the recipe for cooling and finishing the baked items. Some recipes offer guidance on storing the baked goods, otherwise follow the general instructions at the beginning of the sections on cakes and biscuits.

UTENSILS FOR MAKING AND BAKING CAKES AND BISCUITS

This section provides a guide to the essential and useful utensils for making cakes and biscuits. Specialist equipment for cake decorating and biscuit making is not included here but it is discussed in the relevant chapters. For preparing a simple cake, or a batch of small cakes, very little is needed in the way of equipment but if you bake regularly, or enjoy experimenting with more complicated recipes, then it is worth discovering the wide variety of utensils and baking tins which are available. One of the most important pieces of equipment for cooking cakes and biscuits is the oven. For good results you should have an oven which has a reliable thermostat, keeping the temperature constant and accurate, and which cooks evenly throughout the cavity. It is a good idea to have the oven professionally checked if you have doubts about its technical performance.

SMALL UTENSILS FOR PREPARING MIXTURES

Bowls and Basins One of the first items of equipment to consider has to be a container in which to mix all the ingredients. There are all sorts of mixing bowls and basins available, from glazed earthenware through to flimsy plastic. The size of bowl will depend on the amount of mixture which you are preparing and the method used to mix the ingredients; for example, if fat has to be rubbed into flour, then the bowl should be big enough to allow you to do this even if the quantities used are small. As well as the main mixing bowl you may have to use another container for beating eggs or for combining other ingredients.

Fairly heavy bowls are best for creaming ingredients together since they tend to be more stable. As well as glass and earthenware, the choice includes heavy plastic bowls which have a rubber strip on the base to prevent them from slipping on the surface. Some bowls have rims or handles to make them easy to hold with one hand while you are working.

If you bake frequently, then it is a good idea to invest in a set of basins and bowls of different sizes. Remember that those which are made of ovenproof glass can also be very useful for many other kitchen tasks, and make sure that you have some basins that will withstand the heat when placed over a saucepan of hot water.

After use wash bowls and basins in hot soapy water and rinse them under clean hot water. Drain and dry them thoroughly before storing, preferably in a closed cupboard, away from dust. Take care when stacking basins to avoid jamming them together.

Kitchen Scales More so than in any other area of cooking, when baking it is vital to weigh ingredients accurately and for this you will need a reliable set of kitchen scales. There are many types and a wide range of prices from which to select. Scales graduated in either metric or Imperial are available and many types provide the facility for measuring both.

Good quality balance scales are usually very accurate and they can be used with either metric or Imperial weights. They should always be used on a level work surface, with the correct scoop as supplied by the manufacturer.

A good beam scale also provides an accurate means of weighing ingredients. A sliding device is used to select the required weight before the ingredients are added to the scoop which should balance perfectly when the amount is correct. These tend to be more fiddly to use and they are not the most popular type of scales.

Digital scales vary in accuracy according to their type, and often according to cost. They are neat and clean, and they can be free standing or wall mounted. Always follow the manufacturer's instructions closely when using them and do make sure that batteries are replaced when necessary to ensure continued accuracy.

Spring scales indicate the weight on a dial. This is probably the least accurate type of scale but this is usually only a problem when weighing small quantities, or preparing very precise mixtures. Before buying this type of scale make sure that the dial registers small quantities as well as large ones. Instead of the traditional scoop, some scales of this type have mixing bowls, measuring jugs or neat streamlined containers to hold the ingredients. They can be free standing or wall mounted.

Whichever type you choose, always follow the manufacturer's instructions. If necessary check that the dial or digital indicator registers zero before adding ingredients. Keep the container for food scrupulously clean, washing and drying it after each use. All scales should be kept in a dry place and for convenience they are often positioned on the work surface, with the scoop (or its equivalent) inverted for cleanliness when not in use.

Measuring Spoons and Jugs It is vital to have a set of measuring spoons which comply with British Standard measures. All spoon measures given throughout the book refer to these, and serving spoons must not be used instead. Most kitchen shops, hardware stores and department stores stock spoon measures, often with metric equivalents, and these are usually quite inexpensive.

Measuring jugs are available in many shapes and sizes, and they should always be used for accuracy when using liquids.

Spoons and Spatulas A wooden spoon is used for beating fat with sugar (known as creaming) or for similar tasks. The spoon should have a handle which is long enough for the mixture to be beaten efficiently but it should not be too long for comfort. Firm, rigid plastic spoons which are as strong as wooden spoons are an alternative and these are preferable in terms of hygiene.

A large metal spoon is necessary for folding in dry ingredients, for example when making a sponge cake. Any suitable serving spoon can be used for this purpose.

A plastic spatula is useful for scraping all the mixture from the inside of a bowl; select one with a large, flexible end.

Knives A kitchen knife is used for cutting up and chopping ingredients. A round-bladed knife or small palette knife is used for smoothing mixture and easing cakes away from the edge of a tin. A large palette knife or metal spatula is used for lifting baked items off hot baking sheets.

Sieve and Sifter A fine metal or plastic sieve is used for sifting flour or a similar dry ingredient before adding it to a mixture.

A sifter is useful for sprinkling caster or icing sugar over finished cakes but it is not an essential piece of equipment.

Fine Grater A fine grater is usually used for grating lemon or orange rind which is added to mixtures. Most large graters have the facility for grating coarsely and finely. A very fine, small nutmeg grater is useful for grating whole nutmegs but the ground spice can be used for baking.

Citrus Squeezer Lemon or orange juice is sometimes added to cake or biscuit mixtures and a citrus squeezer is used to extract the juice from the fruit. A wide variety of types are available, some quite inexpensive, and it is a good idea to look for one which includes a strainer to prevent the pips from dropping in when the juice is measured.

Whisk A whisk is used for whisking egg whites or similar tasks. Either a balloon or coiled whisk is ideal for light tasks; a rotary whisk can be useful for heavier work.

Cutters Pastry cutters or biscuit cutters are available in metal or plastic, in fluted or plain rounds, squares or a variety of other shapes.

Pastry Brush Useful for greasing tins with a little oil. After use the brush should be washed in very hot soapy water, rinsed and thoroughly dried.

Oil Well A handy gadget for those who often need to grease tins: a small plastic container complete with brush and cover to hold oil ready for greasing tins.

Wire Racks Most cakes and biscuits are turned out of the tin and placed on a wire rack to cool. For making sandwich cakes it is wise to have two cooling racks.

ELECTRICAL APPLIANCES

Food Mixers These take the hard work out of beating and creaming cake mixtures. The smaller, hand-held mixers or beaters or those with an optional stand are ideal for making light cakes, for whisking eggs for a Swiss roll or sponge, or for whisking egg whites. The large, free-standing mixers are useful for preparing large quantities of heavy mixtures, for example fruit cakes. Although these appliances are used for creaming and beating they cannot be used for folding in.

Food Processors Most food processors have an optional attachment for mixing or beating, usually a plastic blade. They are ideal for preparing one-stage cake mixtures but it is important to avoid processing the ingredients for too long. Some food processors have the facility for whisking egg whites.

BAKING TINS

Baking Sheets These come in a variety of sizes, some with edges, others without. They can also have a non-stick coating. Many new ovens come complete with a baking sheet provided by the manufacturer. The sheets should always be cooled after cooking, then washed in hot, soapy water and dried thoroughly before storing in a dry cupboard. Do check that a large sheet will fit inside your oven before you buy one.

Plain Deep Cake Tins For baking large cakes, these can be square or round, in one piece or with a loose bottom. They are available with a variety of non-stick coatings. The loose-bottomed tins are useful for making semi-rich cakes or deep sponges which can be difficult to remove from one-piece tins. Very rich, heavy cakes are easy to remove from tins, and are often allowed to cool completely or partly cool in the tin before being transferred to a wire rack. All tins should be thoroughly washed and dried after use and before being stored in a dry cupboard. Follow the manufacturers' instructions for the treatment of specific non-stick coatings.

Springform Tins These are deep, round tins which have a spring clip to hold the side together and a loose base which is removed when the clip is loosened. They are ideal for light cakes which can be difficult to remove from tins. These tins usually have a choice of bases, including a ring-tin base.

Cake Forms Cake forms are useful for baking large, rich fruit cakes. The form consists of the sides for the tin and this is placed on a baking sheet. The 'tin' is then lined with greaseproof paper and greased before the mixture is added.

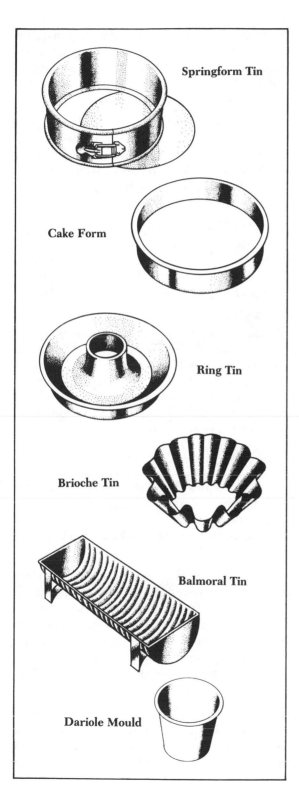

Springform Tin

Cake Form

Ring Tin

Brioche Tin

Balmoral Tin

Dariole Mould

Sandwich Tins Shallow, straight-sided tins, usually round, often with a non-stick coating, which are used to make cakes in pairs; for example Victoria sandwich. The tins can be base lined before use if the mixture is likely to stick during cooking.

Shallow Tins Available in various shapes, round, oblong or square with straight or slightly sloping sides. They can be plain or fluted, with or without a non-stick coating.

Swiss Roll Tins Large, very shallow tins, oblong in shape and usually in two sizes. They may have a non-stick coating but these tins are usually lined with greaseproof paper before use.

Loaf Tins Narrow, deep and long, these are used for making loaf cakes and semi-rich fruit cakes. They are available with non-stick coatings but are often lined before use. Tins which can have adjustable sides to make them larger or smaller are also available.

Ring Tins With rounded or square bottoms, good for making light cakes. Kugelhopf moulds are deep and highly decorated.

Brioche Tin A large, round fluted tin with sloping sides. Useful for baking light cakes as well as for the traditional rich bread.

Balmoral Tin A long, narrow tin, with a base which is semi-circular in shape and some-times supported by metal stands at both ends. This type of tin has decorative ridges from side to side all along its length and is not as deep as a loaf tin.

Patty Tins Usually in the form of a tray of six or twelve individual hollows, these are used for baking individual cakes and tartlets. They can be deep or shallow, patterned or plain, with or without a non-stick coating.

Dariole Moulds Also known as castle tins, these are small, deep tins which are usually about 150 ml/5 fl oz in capacity or slightly less. Used to make English-style Madeleines, plain cakes coated in jam and coconut.

Shaped Tins Cake tins are available in a wide variety of different shapes, from large and small heart-shaped tins to numeral shapes, hexagonal tins, oval shapes and so on. Many of these can be hired from cook shops and hardware stores to make special, one-off cakes.

OVENPROOF CAKE DISHES

With the development of microwave cooking, and particularly combination microwave cooking, more glassware cooking dishes are available in shapes suitable for baking cakes which can withstand the temperatures in the conventional oven. As well as ordinary ovenproof glassware, some dishes are available with a non-stick coating. They are available as deep round dishes, shallow round dishes, loaf dishes and fluted dishes similar to brioche tins. If you do want certain dishes for dual purpose use then these are suitable.

DISPOSABLE ITEMS

Greaseproof Paper This is widely used in baking. It is used for lining cake tins, for rolling up in cakes which are to be cooled before filling and for making icing bags to be used for intricate icing.

Non-stick Baking Parchment This is a non-stick paper which does not need greasing and which is particularly useful for items which tend to stick during cooking, for example very delicate biscuits or meringues. It can be used in place of greaseproof paper for base lining sandwich tins.

Paper Cake Cases These may be plain or patterned, and are used instead of patty tins for baking small cakes. The paper cases are stood on baking sheets or they can be placed in the patty tins for support. Large cake cases are available for putting inside tins when making semi-rich cakes or deep sponges. Small paper cake cases, of the type generally used for confectionery, may be used to make tiny cakes for small children, or petits fours.

Wax Paper This is not as widely used as greaseproof paper but it can be used for lining tins when making certain delicate cakes. It is similar to greaseproof paper but has a wax coating on one side.

Rice Paper A fine, opaque paper which is edible. It is used as a base for macaroons and similar mixtures which tend to stick during cooking. The edges are trimmed but the rice paper base bakes into the mixture and is eaten with it.

Cooking Foil Not widely used in baking but it is useful for loosely covering the top of cakes which are cooked for a long period of time, and which may begin to darken too much on top before the middle is cooked.

Brown Paper Although this is not used in direct contact with the food, it is wrapped neatly around the outside of tins when baking heavy, rich mixtures in a cool oven for long periods of time. By wrapping several thicknesses of paper around the outside of the tin the cake is prevented from forming a dry crust during cooking.

DECORATING EQUIPMENT

Specialist equipment for decorating cakes is listed in the chapter on cake decorating. A few items are useful for the preparation of certain mixtures; for example when piping biscuits.

Piping or Icing Bags Large piping bags are usually made of nylon or heavy cotton which is treated with a moisture-proof coating. They can be lightweight or firmer. They are useful for piping biscuits or sponge fingers. Bags should always be thoroughly washed, rinsed and dried after use and they should be boiled occasionally.

Large Piping Nozzles Large plain and fluted nozzles are used for piping uncooked, soft biscuit mixtures; also meringue-type mixtures as well as for piping cream and other fillings for cakes.

Classic Madeira Cake (page 85) and Weekend Walnut Loaf (page 52)

Mixed Fruit Loaf (page 65) and Cherry Cake (page 64)

A GUIDE TO INGREDIENTS

The basic ingredients for making both cakes and biscuits are the same but the proportions in which they are used vary greatly to produce different results. The cooked cake will only be as good as the ingredients that went into the mixture and it is important to use the right type of each ingredient to achieve the required result. The following notes outline the main ingredients which form the basis for many of the recipes, with information on the different types which are available and how they should be stored. Do take note of information supplied on packaging and take advantage of leaflets and advice which is offered by manufacturers. Remember, most manufacturers want to help you to achieve the best results when using their products and they can also be helpful in solving any particular problems which you may encounter.

FLOUR

There is a wide range of flours available and the choice depends on the purpose for which it is required. Flour is obtained by milling wheat. The wheat grain is made up of various parts: the *endosperm* which is the starchy part and which is intended to provide food for the growing plant; the *outer bran layers* which are the main source of fibre; the *aleurone* which is a layer between the bran and the endosperm, providing protein, vitamins and minerals; and the *germ*, or *wheatgerm*, which is rich in protein, oil and vitamins. (The germ is the part of the grain that will grow if it is planted.)

The grain is broken down by milling. During this process either all or part of the grain can be used to make the flour. Each type of flour has a different composition and they can be broadly grouped according to the percentage of the whole cleaned wheat grain which they contain; this is known as the extraction rate. The extraction rate is given on the packet and this is useful for checking the difference between the types of brown flour that are available.

Wholemeal or Wholewheat Flour This flour contains all the wheat grain with nothing added or taken away during processing and milling. This is known as 100% extraction flour and the preferred term is wholemeal, although both names are used. When 'whole' is included in the name of the flour it means it contains all the grain.

Brown Flour This type of flour usually contains about 85% of the wheat grain (85% extraction rate) and it is most often sold under particular brand names. The term 'wheatmeal' was at one time used for this type of flour but this was confusing and its use is now illegal.

White Flour This type of flour usually contains about 75% of the wheat grain although some white flours have a lower extraction rate. Most of the bran and wheatgerm are removed during the milling process in order to produce white flour.

81% Extraction Flour This is a flour which bridges the gap between brown and white flour and it is sold under various brand names. The extraction rate is given on the packets.

Stoneground Flour This term is used for wheat which is ground between two stones instead of by modern roller methods and it does not reflect the composition of the flour.

As well as the composition of the flour which depends on the amount of the grain which it contains, other processes go to make up the different types of flour we can buy.

Plain Flour This is flour which does not have any raising agent added. It is the common term used for plain white flour. It is used for certain types of cake mixture and for making biscuits. It is also used in pastry.

Self-raising Flour This is flour which has a raising agent added to it. When used in recipes the term usually relates to white flour but self-raising wholemeal or brown flours are also available. The amount of raising agent to flour is carefully balanced during the production process so that it gives perfect results in the majority of cake recipes. When self-raising brown flour is required this is stated in the ingredients list.

Soft Flour This is usually white. This flour has a low protein content and it is very light. It is manufactured for use in light cake or biscuit mixtures, for example Victoria sandwich cakes, Genoese sponge cake or piped Viennese biscuits, or for making pastry. It is one of the most 'modern' types of flour and many manufacturers offer guidance on its use and sample recipes.

Strong Flour This is usually white. It has a high protein content and it is used in yeast mixtures, particularly in bread making.

Malted Wheat Flour This is brown flour to which malted wheat is added to give a distinctive texture and flavour. Again the main use for this type of flour is in bread but it can be used in savoury biscuits.

STORING FLOUR

Flour should be kept in a cool, dry, airy place. The bag of flour can be placed in an airtight tin or the flour can be turned into a storage jar with a tight-fitting lid. The jar should always be thoroughly washed and dried before it is filled with a new batch of flour. Do not add new flour to the remains of an older batch.

Plain white flour can be stored for four to six months but self-raising flour does not keep as well and it should be stored for up to two or three months. Wholemeal and brown flours have a higher fat content than white flour so they may go rancid if they are not properly stored or if they are kept for too long. These should be kept for up to two months, so it is best to buy small quantities frequently. Store wholemeal and brown flours in a cool, dry place and keep them separate from white flour as they should be used sooner.

CORNFLOUR

Cornflour is produced from maize and it is quite different from wheat flour. It is very fine, almost pure starch, and it is sometimes combined with wheat flour in certain cake and biscuit recipes.

RAISING AGENTS

For the majority of cake mixtures a raising agent is added to make the cake rise during cooking. In the case of a whisked mixture, such as a whisked sponge, air is incorporated into the mixture during whisking and it acts as the raising agent since it expands as the mixture is heated in the oven. Self-raising flour is used in the majority of cake recipes and it is not usually necessary to add any additional raising agent, although there are exceptions to this rule.

A combination of acid and alkaline substances are used to make most cake mixtures rise. When they are moistened and heated in combination they produce a gas (carbon dioxide) and it is the gas bubbles which make the mixture rise. The heat of the oven sets the cake and this traps the bubbles in place. Alternatively, yeast can be used as a raising agent. Yeast ferments with sugar and moisture in the presence of warmth and it produces carbon dioxide, the bubbles of which are trapped during proving (or the rising process) and baking. Yeast is used mainly for bread making.

Baking Powder Baking powder is the most common leavening agent used in baking when self-raising flour is not used for a recipe. Baking powder is made up of bicarbonate of soda (alkaline), selected acids and a certain amount of starch. These ingredients are combined in the exact proportions required to produce a rise when the powder is both moistened and heated. It is important to use the correct amount of baking powder as suggested in the recipe because too much can cause failure just as too little will result in inadequate rising.

Bicarbonate of Soda Bicarbonate of soda is used in certain recipes, for example gingerbread. Once it is moistened the bicarbonate of soda quickly starts to produce the bubbles which result in a rise, so recipes which contain bicarbonate of soda must be cooked as soon as they are mixed.

Cream of Tartar This is an acid which can be combined with bicarbonate of soda and used instead of baking powder. To be used in this way, two parts of cream of tartar should be mixed with one part of bicarbonate of soda. This is not a common raising agent for cakes but it is used in certain recipes.

Yeast In warm conditions, when combined with moisture and sugar, yeast produces carbon dioxide to make doughs and selected cake mixtures rise. There are a few cakes which rely on yeast for their rise but it is used mainly for making bread and heavy doughs. Either fresh or dried yeast can be used successfully in cooking.

Fresh yeast is sometimes available from bakers. It should be creamy in colour, have a slightly beery smell, be cool to the touch and easy to break. It can be stored in a polythene bag in the refrigerator for up to a week or it can be frozen, well wrapped, for up to a month. Fresh yeast should be blended with warm liquid for use.

Dried yeast is available in packets and tins and it keeps very well if unopened (for up to one year). Once opened it keeps for about two to three months. Before use the dried yeast is reconstituted by sprinkling it over lukewarm liquid and leaving it, loosely covered, in a warm place until it has dissolved and the liquid is frothy. The yeast liquid should be stirred to make sure that all the grains of dried yeast have dissolved before it is mixed with other ingredients.

Easy-blend yeast is a dried yeast which must be added straight to the dry ingredients. When this is used the manufacturer's instructions should be followed closely for good results.

Storing Raising Agents All dry raising agents should be stored in an airtight container in a cool, dry place. Old, stale raising agents will not give the required results, so they should be stored for no more than two or three months, then discarded. Dried yeast should be stored in a cool, dry place in an airtight container. Fresh yeast wrapped in polythene can be kept for a short time in the refrigerator or it can be frozen.

FAT

The majority of cakes and biscuits include a certain amount of fat and the richer types have a high proportion of fat added. There are various fats which can be used but the majority of cakes and biscuits are made from butter or margarine.

Butter This gives an excellent flavour in cooking. If it is allowed to soften at room temperature, butter creams extremely well.

When taken straight from the refrigerator and rubbed into dry ingredients, it is ideal for making cakes and biscuits. It can also be melted with other ingredients before being added to the dry ingredients.

There are two types of butter to choose from: the first is sweet cream butter which is salted or slightly salted. The second is lactic butter which is slightly salted or unsalted and may be referred to as the continental type.

Traditionally, the sweet cream varieties are the most popular and they form the largest proportion of butter produced in the United Kingdom, the Republic of Ireland and New Zealand. This type of butter is produced by churning cream which has been allowed to stand for approximately twelve hours. The addition of salt produces the characteristic flavour and improves the keeping quality of the butter.

A certain amount of lactic butter is produced in the United Kingdom but the majority is imported. A culture of lactic acid is added to the cream before it is churned; this results in a slightly acidic flavour.

In addition a number of regional butters are produced in the United Kingdom. These have subtle individual flavour qualities that are appreciated on bread. These are not usually specified for use in recipes.

When buying butter always check the sell-by date which is given on the packet. (Remember that sell-by dates are for guidance only and they are not a compulsory feature.) Store butter in the refrigerator, neatly packed in its original wrapping. The keeping quality of butter does vary according to its type and packaging. Butter in foil packaging keeps slightly better than butter in parchment packing, and salted butter keeps nominally better than the unsalted type. The foil-wrapped butter can be kept for up to eleven weeks in the refrigerator; butter in parchment can be kept for seven weeks.

Butter can be frozen, when the unopened pack should be enclosed in a sealed polythene bag. The unsalted type will keep best in the freezer and it can be stored for up to six months. Salted butter can be frozen for up to three months.

All butter should be well wrapped during storage as it absorbs flavours and odours.

To clarify butter, heat gently until melted, then stand for 2–3 minutes. Pour off clear yellow liquid on top and allow to solidify. This is the clarified butter.

Margarine Margarine is probably the most popular fat used in baking as it is less expensive than butter and yet gives comparable results, although the flavour is not as good. Generally, it is made of 80% fat and a maximum of 16% water, with added flavouring, colouring and emulsifiers.

Margarine is produced from blended edible oils and soft fats and the type used is specified on the packet or tub. Fish oil and soft animal fats can be used in combination with vegetable oils; some margarines use vegetable oils only. There are two types, either hard, block margarine or soft, tub margarine. The texture of the margarine depends on type of oils or fats used and on the manufacturing process. For creaming, the block margarine should be allowed to soften at room temperature in the same way as butter. Soft margarine can be used straight from the refrigerator. The nature of the processing method results in soft margarine being whipped before packing so that it is particularly light and will cream easily with sugar. Soft margarine is particularly useful for making one-stage mixtures.

Lard Lard is white, melted and clarified pork fat which was once very popular for cooking. It contributes little colour or flavour and it is sometimes used with spices, treacle and syrup for making gingerbread or similar cakes. Otherwise it is not widely used in the preparation of cakes and biscuits.

Dripping This is melted down meat fat – usually beef – and it has a distinctive flavour. It is not an ingredient which is commonly used in making cakes and biscuits but it is used in a handful of traditional, and very economical, recipes.

When it is used in baking recipes, dripping obtained from meat should be clarified. To do this the fat is heated gently in a large saucepan with the same volume of cold water until the water just begins to boil. All scum must be removed as it rises to the surface and the dripping is allowed to simmer in the water for 5 minutes. The liquid is then strained through a muslin-lined sieve into a clean bowl. The bowl is covered and the fat allowed to solidify in a cool place. The lard is lifted off the water in one piece and any sediment on its underside is scraped off. Lastly, the lard is heated very gently until all spitting and bubbling ceases, to evaporate all the water.

Oil Some recipes are developed specifically to use oil in cakes and biscuit doughs but otherwise this fat is not used for baking. However, it is the most convenient form of fat for greasing baking tins.

Low-fat Spreads These spreads should not be confused with margarine. They are manufactured specifically for spreading and they are not recommended instead of margarine or butter for cooking cakes since they have a high water content and they contain little fat, as the term suggests. The fat content of the spread should be given on the container and this varies according to the product.

SUGAR

Sugar, in its many forms, is widely used in cooking and it is a vital ingredient in ensuring the success of many baking recipes. Its prime function is to sweeten, but certain types of sugar also add flavour to cake and biscuit mixtures. It is important that the correct proportion of sugar is used, as stated in the recipe, and that it is incorporated into the mixture correctly.

As well as sugar, syrup and treacle are used for certain recipes; these ingredients are derived from sugar.

Granulated Sugar This is probably the most common type of sugar and it should be used in recipes where the term 'sugar' is used in the ingredients list. It is used in recipes that contain enough liquid for it to dissolve completely or where the cooking temperature and time are adequate to ensure that it dissolves. For example, it is used in rubbed-in mixtures and for melted mixtures. It can be used for creamed mixtures but caster sugar gives better results.

Caster Sugar This is finer than granulated sugar, it dissolves more quickly and it is the most suitable sugar for creaming with fat or for use in whisked mixtures. It gives more volume and a lighter result than granulated sugar in these recipes. In addition, caster sugar can be sprinkled over cooked sponge cakes and plain biscuits to enhance their appearance.

Soft Light Brown Sugar The term used to describe this type of sugar varies according to the manufacturer; for example it may be sold as 'light golden soft sugar'. It is a fine-grained sugar which has cane molasses added, to provide flavour as well as darkening the colour. It is used in light fruit cakes or in other baking recipes and adds flavour as well as sweetening the mixture.

Soft Dark Brown Sugar Again the term used varies according to the manufacturer and this type of sugar may be sold as 'rich dark soft sugar'. It is similar to the soft light brown sugar but it contains more cane molasses, giving it a richer flavour and darker colour. It is used in rich fruit cakes or gingerbreads and it can be used to make certain biscuits.

Muscovado Sugar Muscovado sugar is very dark, moist and fairly fine-grained. It is unrefined cane sugar and it has a very dark, almost black, colour and strong flavour. It is not widely used in baking but it can be used in making rich fruit cakes to give a very dark colour and rich flavour to the mixture.

Raw Cane Sugar This is sugar which contains a certain amount of the impurities from sugar cane which are otherwise removed during the processing of white sugars. Some brown sugars are first refined, then molasses is added to contribute the characteristic flavour and colour. Raw cane sugars are not refined first – the darker varieties naturally contain the most impurities and molasses; the lighter types contain fewer impurities. The composition of the product is indicated on the packet and if the sugar has first been refined, then had molasses added (or caramel), then this will be indicated by an ingredients list.

Demerara Sugar Demerara sugar is light brown in colour, with a fairly rich flavour and large crystals. It is not widely used in baking but it can be sprinkled over the top of certain types of cakes (for example, loaf cakes) before cooking to give a crunchy topping.

Icing Sugar This is very fine, powdered sugar which is not commonly used in cake mixtures but which forms the basis for many different types of icing. It is ideal for sweetening whipped cream as it dissolves very rapidly. It is also useful for sprinkling over cooked cakes and biscuits once they are cooled.

Lump Sugar This is made from granulated sugar which is moistened with syrup and moulded. The lumps or cubes of sugar are dried and packed into boxes. It does not have a role to play in baking recipes other than for crushing and sprinkling over baked cakes and biscuits as decoration.

Preserving Sugar As its name implies this sugar is manufactured specifically for use in preserves. It has very large crystals and it can be sprinkled over loaf cakes before cooking.

Golden Syrup This is a blend of sugar syrup, caramel and flavourings. It is used in certain baking recipes instead of sugar. It can be used to glaze the top of light fruit cakes just before they are served.

Black Treacle This is made from molasses and sugar syrup. It has a very dark colour and strong flavour and it is used in certain baking recipes, for example gingerbread, or it is added to rich fruit cakes.

Molasses Molasses is the very dark, thick syrup which is drained from raw sugar cane. It is interchangeable with black treacle in cooking.

Storing Sugar All types of sugar, syrup and treacle should be stored in airtight containers and kept in a cool, dry place. Soft brown sugar may harden slightly during storage but it usually softens again if it is warmed briefly in a cool oven (or for a few seconds in the microwave). Icing sugar does not have a long shelf life as it does harden and it is vital that there are no lumps in it if it is used to prepare icings. Syrup and treacle tins should be wiped clean with absorbent kitchen paper after use and they must be stored in a dry place. Do not use the contents of old tins which may have rusted or been damaged.

EGGS

Eggs play a vital role in cake making. They are used to lighten cakes and to ensure that they rise and set during cooking. In some mixtures, where a high proportion of eggs are used, they are the only raising agent.

The eggs can be used whole or they may be separated before they are added to the mixture. Whisked with sugar, they may form the basis for the mixture and the other ingredients will be folded into them. For some recipes the egg yolks are incorporated first, then the whisked whites are folded into the mixture. In this case a little of the white should be stirred in first to soften the bulk of the mixture before the rest of the whites are folded in.

In some recipes just the whites or yolks are used; for example, meringues require the whites only and biscuits often use just yolks. Other recipes may call for more whites than yolks in order to produce a very light mixture.

Buying eggs Eggs come in different sizes and they are also categorised by quality. Two quality grades of whole eggs are sold, either A or B quality and this is clearly stated on the box. There are regulations that have to be observed for the sale of pre-packed eggs, and certain information has to be included on the outside of the box.

Firstly, the class of eggs must be clearly marked and the number of eggs in the box indicated. The size of the eggs must also be shown along with the registered number of the packing station, the name and address of those responsible for packing and the date on which the eggs were packed. In addition there may be a sell-by date, although this is optional – always look out for this and make sure that it has not expired if it is included.

Egg Sizes Class A eggs are graded in sizes from 1-7 and the sizes most commonly available are 2-4.

Size 1 – 70 g and over
Size 2 – 65 g and under 70 g
Size 3 – 60 g and under 65 g
Size 4 – 55 g and under 60 g
Size 5 – 50 g and under 55 g
Size 6 – 45 g and under 50 g
Size 7 – under 45 g

Size 3 are the most suitable for baking unless otherwise stated; for example if large eggs are called for then size 2 should be used.

Storing Eggs Eggs should be stored in the refrigerator, preferably in their box, and the pointed end of each egg should be kept downwards to help prevent breakage, reduce evaporation and help to prevent any odours being absorbed through the shell.

Using Eggs For many recipes it is best if eggs are used at room temperature so they should be removed from the refrigerator about 30 minutes before they are to be used. However this is not essential. It is very important that eggs are clean and they should be washed under cool water and dried before they are cracked, taking care not to break them, of course. It is best to crack eggs individually into a mug, cup or small basin before adding them to mixtures and any traces of broken shell should be removed.

Eggs are a protein food and they should be treated with the same standards of hygiene that are adopted for all raw meat, fish and poultry. All utensils must be thoroughly clean before use and hands should be washed before and after breaking eggs, particularly if cooked food is handled after raw eggs. Any unused beaten egg should be kept in a tightly covered container and placed in the refrigerator. It should be used within twenty-four hours. Egg whites can be frozen in a clean, airtight, rigid container. Remember to label the container with the number of whites which it contains. Once thawed, egg whites should always be used immediately.

DRIED FRUIT

Dried fruit includes raisins, sultanas, currants, dates, glacé cherries, candied peel and other fruits such as apricots, pears, peaches and apples. The smaller dried fruits, candied peel and cherries are those which are most commonly used when making cakes and biscuits. Most dried fruit is cleaned and seeded before it is packed and sold, but any stalks that may be left should be removed.

Raisins Raisins are dried grapes and the best are those obtained by drying the varieties of muscatel grape. These have to be mechanically seeded during processing. Alternatively, seedless grapes are dried. This avoids the necessity for seeding, but the quality of the raisins is not as good.

Sultanas These are dried, seedless green grapes and they are lighter in colour than raisins. They are slightly softer than raisins, and should be plump and sweet.

Currants These are smaller, darker and more shrivelled than raisins. They are dried, small black grapes which are produced mainly in Greece. Currants are used in large quantities for rich fruit cakes.

Dates Dried stoneless dates are sold ready for cooking, either in the form of a block which should be chopped before use or ready chopped and lightly coated in sugar. Both types are more suitable for cooking than the dessert dates which are boxed whole.

Figs Whole figs are dried. They should be chopped before use, although they are not as widely used as the smaller dried fruits.

Prunes There are two main types of dried prune available, either the whole dried fruit that must be washed and soaked overnight or for several hours before use or the stoned, ready-to-eat variety that is more convenient. Prunes are obtained by drying plums and they should be dark and shiny in appearance.

Cut Mixed Peel This is the mixed peel of citrus fruits, preserved by impregnating it with sugar. Lemon, orange and citron peel is usually included. Alternatively whole pieces of candied citrus peel can be purchased and individually chopped.

Glacé Cherries These are used in a wide variety of mixtures and they may be used as decoration. If they are very sticky, then they should be washed and thoroughly dried before use. The best way to do this is by placing the cherries in a sieve to wash them, then draining them well before drying them on absorbent kitchen paper. Before they are incorporated into many cake mixtures the cherries are dusted with a little of the measured flour.

Storing Dried Fruit Always keep dried fruit in clean, dry, airtight containers. They should be kept in a cool, dark cupboard that is quite dry.

NUTS

Nuts are used to flavour cakes and biscuits and to give texture to certain mixtures. They are also used for decorating cakes.

Almonds These can be purchased shelled with their skins on, blanched with skins removed, split, flaked or chopped. It is often a good idea to compare supermarket prices with those in wholefood shops.

To blanch almonds, place them in a saucepan with plenty of cold water and bring them just to the boil. Drain the nuts in a sieve and rinse them under a cold running tap, then pinch off their skins. Dry the blanched nuts on absorbent kitchen paper.

To split almonds, use a small, sharp, pointed kitchen knife and slide it into the side of the warm nuts.

To brown or roast almonds place them on a piece of foil on a baking sheet or in the grill pan and cook them under the grill, turning them frequently and taking care to prevent them from burning. Alternatively, they can be roasted by placing them on a baking sheet in a warm oven.

Ground almonds are used in cake and biscuit mixtures or to make marzipan and almond paste for covering and decorating cakes.

Walnuts These are not usually blanched before use in cake or biscuit mixtures. They are also used for decorating cakes. Walnuts are sold in halves or pieces, with pieces the most economical buy if the nuts are to be chopped.

Hazelnuts These can be bought with their skins on, skinned or chopped, and toasted. They are used to flavour cakes and biscuits or to coat the sides of gâteaux.

To remove the skins from hazelnuts, place them under the grill or in the oven, and roast them, turning frequently, until the skins can be rubbed off. To rub the skins off, place the nuts in a paper bag or in a cloth to avoid burning your fingers.

Hazelnuts can be ground in a food processor, coffee grinder (for small amounts), blender or in a rotary grater.

Peanuts Readily available shelled, either salted or unsalted, peanuts are most often used to make biscuits.

Pistachios Delicately flavoured nuts, tinged with green. They are often sold in their shells which are split open but not removed. They are expensive, so their use is limited.

Brazils, Pecans and Other Nuts A variety of other nuts are also used in cakes and biscuits. These are usually available ready shelled, particularly from wholefood shops.

Chopped Mixed Nuts These are an inexpensive alternative to chopped walnuts or hazelnuts but they can be dominated by the flavour of peanuts.

Desiccated Coconut This is finely shredded, dried coconut which is used in cakes and biscuits. It is also used to coat the outside of some baked items.

Long-thread Coconut Desiccated coconut which is very coarsely shredded to give long threads. Useful for decorating purposes but not usually incorporated into mixtures.

FLAVOURING INGREDIENTS

As well as the basic ingredients which go to make up the cake and biscuit mixtures, a wide variety of flavourings can be added. Here are notes on just a few of the most popular ingredients used for flavouring baked goods.

Vanilla A strong flavouring which comes from the seed pods of an orchid. The flavour develops during a period of maturation after the pods have been picked, by the action of enzymes naturally present. True vanilla essence is extracted from the black pods. Vanilla is expensive and the pods are usually sold individually or in pairs. As an alternative to real vanilla, a synthetically produced essence is readily available.

Vanilla is very strong and should be used sparingly. A vanilla pod can be placed in a jar of caster sugar to make vanilla sugar. The pod and sugar should be left to stand for at least three or four weeks. Shake the jar frequently to impart the flavour to the sugar.

Almond Essence Another strong flavouring which must be used with care. It is added to certain mixtures instead of the nuts. It can have a very synthetic flavour and must be used sparingly.

Ground Mixed Spice This mixture of spices is used to flavour cakes and biscuits. It usually consists of cinnamon, cloves, ginger and nutmeg.

Ground Ginger Another spice which is used to flavour both cakes and biscuits. It has a strong flavour and should be used according to recipe directions.

Ground Cinnamon A sweet spice which is used to flavour sweet mixtures. A little ground cinnamon can be mixed with caster sugar to make cinnamon sugar and this is used to dust doughnuts or biscuits.

Nutmeg This can be purchased ready ground or the whole nuts can be freshly grated on a small, tough grater as the spice is required. Freshly grated nutmeg has the best flavour.

Grated Fruit Rind The grated rind of oranges and lemons is often used to flavour cakes and biscuits. The fruit should be washed and dried before the rind is grated on a fine grater. When grating the rind avoid including any of the bitter pith which lies underneath.

CAKES

This section contains all the general background information that you will need for successful cake making, from the ins and outs of lining and greasing tins to a recipe collection that covers all the traditional and simple cakes plus a few exciting alternatives for special treats.

The chapters which follow offer plenty of ideas for plain cakes and favourite fruit cakes as well as more elaborate creations that will make any special occasion even more exciting. Traditional British cakes play a key role and they range from inexpensive Dripping Cake to dainty Iced Petits Fours. For times when you are feeling more adventurous there is a selection of the most famed of foreign cakes, or a small collection of tempting cheesecakes. Lastly, there is a chapter filled with small cakes.

Do remember to check the information in the previous section as it is relevant to cake making as well as to the preparation of biscuits. If you have any doubts about some of the basic techniques which are used in the recipes, read through the next few pages before embarking on any of the recipes.

BASIC TECHNIQUES AND METHODS OF MAKING CAKES

PREPARING TINS FOR BAKING

There is nothing quite as distressing as battling unsuccessfully to release a beautifully cooked cake in one piece from an ill-prepared tin. Difficulties with turning cakes out of tins can often be avoided if the tin is properly prepared in the first instance. Each recipe offers guidance on the size and shape of tin required and the method by which it should be prepared before the mixture is turned into it. Good cake tins are those to which the cooked mixture is not supposed to stick but this is little consolation when there is a fair chance that the tin you intend to use is quite likely to end up with the cake firmly stuck to it. So, if you have doubts about whether a particular tin is going to release the cake easily, do plan ahead and at least line the bottom of the tin. There are four main ways to prepare tins:

1 Bun tins, patty tins and baking sheets should be greased. In some instances the sheets should be dusted with flour after greasing.

2 For rubbed-in cakes each tin should be greased and the base should be lined. The lining paper should be greased before the mixture is placed in the tin.

3 For creamed mixtures it is best to line the base of each tin and in some cases, where the cake requires lengthy cooking, the sides of the tin should also be lined. The lining paper should be greased. The same preparation applies to cakes made by the melted method, for example gingerbread.

4 For whisked sponge cakes each tin should be greased and dusted with a little flour. If the tin is one to which the cake may stick on the base, then a circle of paper should be used to line the base of the tin. The floured sides of the tin provide a surface to which very light sponge mixtures may adhere as they rise during cooking.

Non-stick Tins Many non-stick tins do not have to be lined before they are used. The manufacturer's instructions should be followed carefully when preparing this type of tin.

FAT FOR GREASING

The most convenient fat for greasing is oil. A special 'oil well' gadget is designed to hold a small amount of oil with a suitable brush ready for greasing tins. Alternatively a few drops of oil can be tipped into the tin and brushed evenly over its surface. Lard or other white cooking fat is suitable for greasing tins but butter and margarine are not recommended. If butter or margarine is used it should be clarified first to remove all excess moisture and salt which it contains.

The purpose of greasing is obvious – to prevent the cake from sticking to the tin or to the lining paper. The process of lining tins is made easy if the tin itself is lightly greased first. The lining paper clings to the greased surface, allowing it to be pushed neatly up against the sides. Where the lining paper overlaps slightly, the under-piece should be lightly greased so that the top piece clings to it and stays in place.

CHOICE OF LINING PAPER

Greaseproof paper is the most common form of lining which is used when preparing tins. However non-stick baking parchment is available and this can be used instead. Follow the manufacturer's instructions when using this product as, in many cases, it does not require greasing before the cake mixture is placed on it. Heavy, re-usable non-stick baking paper is also available and this is particularly useful if you want to make a semi-permanent lining for a frequently used tin. The tin should of course be washed and the paper wiped clean between uses. Again the manufacturer's instructions should be followed for using this type of paper.

For making small cakes, paper cake cases can be used, either by standing them on a baking sheet or placing them in patty tins. If the cases are fairly flimsy, it is best to place them in tins for support. It is also possible to purchase large fluted paper cases that can be used to line full-sized cake tins. This is particularly useful if the cake is to be frozen once it is cooked.

For making rich fruit cakes, the tins are best lined with a double thickness of greaseproof paper. To protect the outside of the cake, near the sides and base of the tin, a thick piece of brown paper or newspaper can be tied securely around the outside of the tin, or a piece can be placed on a baking sheet underneath the tin. This is really only necessary when large cakes are baked for several hours and there may be a danger of the outside crust becoming dry.

LINING A SQUARE TIN

1 Place the tin flat on a single or double thickness of lining paper and draw all around the outside of the bottom. Cut out the shape as above, cutting slightly inside the pencil mark to allow for the thickness of the tin.

2 Measure a strip of paper for the sides of the tin as for lining a round tin. Make sure that there is enough to go all the way around the inside of the tin and that the strip is wide enough for a 2.5 cm/1 inch fold all around the bottom as well as to stand at least 2.5 cm/1 inch above the rim of the tin.

3 Lightly grease the tin and place one square of paper in the base if a double thickness is used; grease this lightly. Make a 2.5 cm/1 inch fold all along one side of the strip of paper.

4 Carefully lift the strip of paper into the sides of the tin. Have a pair of scissors ready to snip and fit the corners of the

paper into the tin. The overlap in the strip of paper should be positioned on one side of the tin, not at a corner.

5 Press the paper against the sides of the tin and into the first corner. Snip into the corner of the strip of paper sitting in the base of the tin.

6 Overlap the paper in the base of the tin in the first corner, to make a neat squared lining. Continue to press the paper smoothly against the side of the tin up to the next corner, then cut and fit the paper as before. Fit the paper into all four corners in this way.

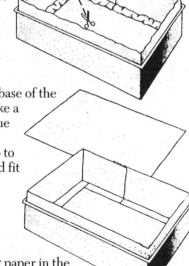

7 Place the square of lining paper in the base of the tin and brush all the inside evenly with a little oil.

LINING A ROUND TIN

1   Place the tin on a single or double piece of lining paper and draw around the outside edge of the bottom in pencil. Remove the tin and cut out the circle of paper, cutting slightly inside the drawn circle to allow for the thickness of the tin and to ensure that the paper will fit neatly inside the base of the tin.

2   Cut out a strip of paper which is long enough to go around the outside of the tin and overlap by 5 cm/2 inches. The paper should be at least 5 cm/2 inches wider than the depth of the tin, to allow for 2.5 cm/1 inch to sit neatly in the bottom of the tin and at least 2.5 cm/1 inch standing above the rim of the tin.

3   Make a 2.5 cm/1 inch fold all along one side of the strip of paper. Open out the fold and snip diagonally from the edge in as far as the foldline at 1-2.5 cm/½-1 inch intervals all along the length of the paper.

4   Very lightly grease the inside of the tin. If you are using a double thickness of paper, then place one circle in the base of the tin and grease it very lightly. If you are using a single thickness, then put the lining paper around the sides first. Carefully lower the strip of paper into the tin, placing the snipped folded edge downwards. The fold in the base of the strip should tuck neatly all around the inside of the bottom of the tin and the pieces of snipped paper should be overlapped. Place the circle of lining paper in the base of the tin.

5   Lightly grease the lining paper all over, making sure that it is pressed well into the shape of the tin.

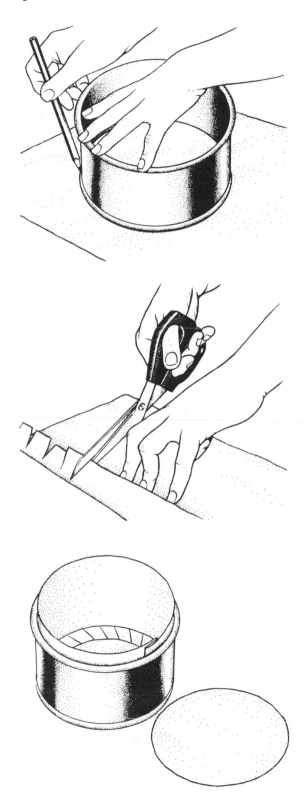

LINING A SWISS ROLL TIN

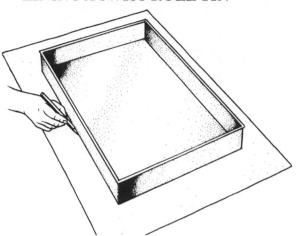

1 Stand the tin on a sheet of greaseproof paper and draw all around the outside of the bottom. Remove the tin.

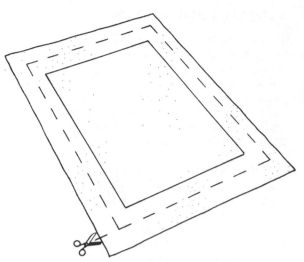

2 Cut out the shape, about 5 cm/2 inches outside of the drawn shape. This is to allow enough paper to line the sides of the tin and to stand about 2.5 cm/1 inch above the rim of the tin. The paper should not stand more than 2.5 cm/1 inch above the rim as this may impair the process of browning.

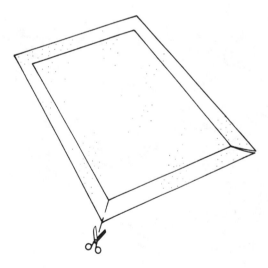

3 Cut from each outer corner of the paper into the corner of the drawn shape of the tin.

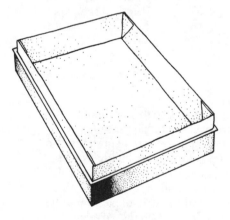

4 Lightly grease the inside of the tin. Turn the paper over so that the pencil mark is facing downwards, into the tin. Press the paper into the tin, overlapping it at the corners to make a neatly squared lining.

5 The paper will stay in place at the corners if it is greased between the overlap. Grease the lining paper evenly.

LINING A LOAF TIN

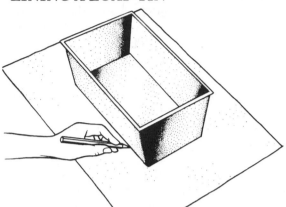

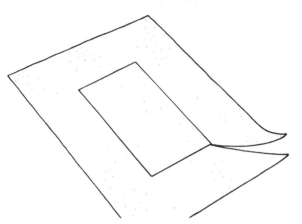

1   Cut a piece of paper large enough to cover the bottom of the tin, to come up both sides and the ends and to stand at least 2.5 cm/1 inch above the tin.

2   Stand the tin in the middle of the paper and draw all around the outside of the bottom.

3   Cut in from each outer corner of the piece of paper to the corner of the drawn shape.

4   Lightly grease the tin, then turn the paper over so that the pencil marks are downwards and lift the paper into the tin.

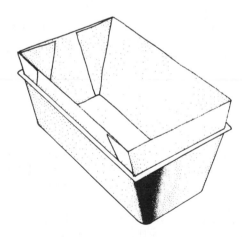

5   Press the paper neatly into the tin, overlapping the cut corners to make neat squares. Grease lightly between the overlap so that the paper clings together.

6   Grease the lining paper well.

BASE LINING TINS

If the recipe suggests that the base of the tin should be lined, then simply place the tin on a piece of paper, draw around the outside edge and cut out the shape. Lightly grease the base of the tin so that the paper will stay firmly in place. Place the piece of paper in the base of the tin, then grease the paper and the sides of the tin.

GREASING AND FLOURING TINS

Lightly grease the inside of the tin. Place a spoonful of flour in the tin. Hold the tin at an angle and turn it around and around, tapping the sides as you turn the tin, so that the flour evenly coats the inside. Tip out any excess flour.

BASIC METHODS OF MIXING CAKES

CREAMED METHOD

For this method, the fat and sugar are creamed together until they are very soft, pale in colour and light. If a brown sugar is used the mixture will not become very pale in colour but it should turn paler than it was when you started.

The fat should be warmed to room temperature if necessary so that it creams easily. Butter or margarine are the most common fats to use. Soft margarine can be creamed straight from the refrigerator.

When the creaming stage is complete the eggs are added. They should be beaten first so that they can be added gradually. The eggs should be lightly beaten in and a little of the measured flour sprinkled in if the mixture looks as though it may curdle.

When the eggs are incorporated the flour is folded in. It is important that this process is carried out correctly. A large metal spoon should be used and the mixture must not be beaten. The flour is folded in – it is sprinkled over the mixture and the spoon is used to lift the mixture and to cut the flour through it. Rather than stirring, a figure of eight motion is used. The aim is to incorporate the flour with the creamed ingredients without knocking out all the air that was beaten in during the first stage.

Dried fruit or other flavouring ingredients are folded in with the flour or immediately afterwards. Sometimes a little extra liquid is added to soften the mixture.

RUBBED-IN METHOD

The flour is sifted into a bowl and the fat is rubbed into it in the same way as for making shortcrust pastry.

For this method the fat should be chilled and all the other ingredients should be kept cool. When rubbing fat into flour it is important to use just the tips of the fingers.

Lift the mixture up and lightly rub it together, letting it fall back into the bowl. By lifting the mixture and rubbing it lightly you are incorporating air. This keeps it light.

Once the fat is incorporated the sugar and other dry ingredients are added and stirred in. The liquid is added last to bind the ingredients together.

WHISKED METHOD

The whisked method is used for making very light sponges. The eggs should be allowed to warm to room temperature. They are combined with the sugar in a bowl which is placed over a saucepan of barely simmering water. The water must not be boiling. An electric beater is best for this task but a rotary whisk can be used. It is hard work if an ordinary hand whisk of the balloon or spiral type is used and it can take a very long time with these simple utensils.

The eggs and sugar are whisked together until they are very thick, very pale and quite creamy. A common mistake with this method is to consider that the mixture is whisked sufficiently as soon as it is slightly thickened. The mixture should be thick enough to hold the trail of the whisk for at least 30 seconds. Once it is whisked sufficiently, remove the bowl from the pan of water and continue whisking for a further 5 minutes, until the mixture has cooled.

At this stage the other ingredients are folded in. Flour and a small amount of fat can be added. The fat is usually butter which is melted before it is dribbled slowly over the whisked mixture and folded in. The folding in process is vital to the success of whisked mixtures – a figure of eight motion should be used as for creamed mixtures and the whisked mixture should be gently lifted over the flour. On no account should the mixture be stirred or whisked as the air will be knocked out by the rapid movement. This type of cake relies on the air content to rise; if the air is knocked out the cake will not rise.

Simnel Cake (page 70)

Pineapple Upside-down Cake (page 71)

Battenburg Cake (page 78) and Swiss Roll (page 72)

Marble Cake (page 79) and St Clement's Cake (page 82)

MELTED METHOD

For this type of mixture the fat and sugar are melted together, usually with some form of flavouring. Treacle or syrup is often used, either in place of the sugar or with it.

Once all the fat is melted the mixture should be allowed to cool very slightly before the beaten eggs are added. Do not overheat the melted ingredients; use low heat and stir the mixture frequently. Any crystals of sugar on the sides of the saucepan may be brushed down into the mixture with a pastry brush.

Lastly, the dry ingredients are beaten in. The majority of melted mixtures should be quite soft when all the ingredients are mixed and some may have the consistency of a thick batter.

ONE-STAGE METHOD

This is a modern method of cake mixing, popularised by margarine manufacturers to promote soft margarine in the early days of its availability. As well as the development of soft margarine which requires less creaming than hard fats, the growth in the ownership of electric food mixers has also helped to make this method an easy alternative to the creaming method.

All the ingredients are placed in a bowl and they are beaten together until thoroughly combined, pale and creamy. A little extra raising agent is usually added to ensure a good rise and all the ingredients should be at room temperature, the best fat to use being soft margarine.

BAKING AND TURNING OUT CAKES

For good results it is important that the oven has an even heat distribution, that it heats correctly to the temperature selected and holds that temperature steadily. The oven should stand evenly; most cookers, whether built in or free standing, have adjustable feet to compensate for any uneven floors. If the oven is not level, the cake mixture will rise unevenly.

One of the most difficult areas of cake making is deciding exactly when the cake is cooked. Firstly, follow the timing given in the recipe as a guide, checking at the first suggested time.

Open the oven door carefully – if you can see that the cake still looks raw, then shut the door quickly. Do not bang doors and cause the oven to jerk as the cake is cooking.

The appearance of the cooked cake will vary slightly according to its type. Most cakes will be well risen, the exception being very rich fruit cakes which are not intended to rise during cooking. Sponge cakes should have risen to the top of the tin; about doubled in volume. The cake should be evenly browned, not too light and not too dark. The cake should have shrunk away from the sides of the tin very slightly and when pressed lightly it should feel springy on top and the cake should bounce back. If the surface feels at all wet and if the impression of a finger-print remains on top, then the sponge cake is not cooked.

Fruit cakes should not feel spongy, they should be firm and quite well browned. For deep cakes and fruit cakes the skewer test is a good way of determining whether the cake is cooked through.

The Skewer Test Take a clean metal skewer and insert it into the middle of the cake. Leave it for a few seconds, then take it out. If the cake is cooked the skewer should not have any mixture adhering to it. The skewer will be slightly greasy and there may be sticky marks on it, particularly if the cake contains a lot of fruit. However, there should not be crumbs or any wet mixture sticking to it. Instead of a skewer, the blade of a knife can be inserted into the middle of the cake.

Protecting the Top of a Cake Some cakes that require fairly long cooking may begin to look slightly too dark on top before the middle is cooked. This may be due to the type of mixture, in which case the recipe should warn you to check the cake during cooking, or it may be due to the oven. To prevent the surface of the cake from burning while the middle of the cake cooks through, a piece of foil should be placed loosely over the top of the cake, shiny side up. This will prevent the upper crust from burning.

RELEASING CAKES FROM TINS AND COOLING

It is important that the tin is well prepared because this stage can be disastrous if the cake is stuck to the base of the tin.

Some fruit cakes should be allowed to cool in the tin for a while before being turned out and the recipe will suggest this if necessary. If this is the case, then drape a clean tea-towel over the top of the tin to absorb steam and to prevent the cake from being exposed to dust or dirt.

To turn a cake out of a tin which is not fully lined, first slide a round-bladed knife gently around the inside of the tin, between it and the cake. Place a wire rack over the top of the tin and use an oven glove to hold both rack and tin firmly. Then invert the tin on to the rack and place it on the work surface. Lift the tin off the cake and remove any lining paper. To turn the cake back up the right way, place a second rack on it and invert it yet again.

If the tin has a loose bottom, then prepare some form of stand on which to place the cake in its tin, allowing the side to fall down, away from the cake. A suitable storage jar or large upturned basin is ideal. Carefully lower the side of the tin off the cake, then lift the cake and its base to a wire rack. Slide the cake from the base of the tin on to the rack and remove any lining paper. Alternatively, simply invert the cake and tin on to the rack as before and lift off the sides and base of the tin.

Certain cakes may require special treatment, for example Swiss roll. Light sponge cakes mark very easily and they can be turned on to a wire rack covered with a clean tea towel, or on to a piece of greaseproof paper which is sprinkled with caster sugar.

The cake should be allowed to cool completely before it is stored or wrapped, unless the recipe states otherwise.

STORING AND FREEZING

The keeping quality of cakes depends on the individual mixtures. Some cakes, particularly fruit cakes, improve with keeping. Light fruit cakes often taste better a few days after they are baked and very rich fruit cakes should be allowed to mature for at least a month in order to let all the individual flavours mingle.

Fatless sponge cakes do not keep well and they quickly become very dry. Ideally they should be eaten on the same day or at least the day after they are baked.

Victoria sandwich type cakes keep quite well in an airtight container and they can be stored for about a week, although the time depends on the flavouring ingredients and any filling, covering or decoration which is added. Cakes covered in soft icings do not keep as well as plain cakes.

Most cakes should be stored in an airtight container in a cool, dry place. Fruit cakes which are to be kept for long periods are best stored with the lining paper from cooking left on. The underside is usually pierced all over and sprinkled with a little brandy or rum, then the cake is wrapped in two or three layers of greaseproof paper. To introduce the liquor, the base lining paper should be peeled back and then replaced. The cake can be stored in a clean cardboard cake box or wrapped in foil. Foil must not be placed directly on the cake as it reacts with the fruit acids and may disintegrate in places, causing the surface of the cake to be dusted with foil particles. Rich cakes of this type should not be stored in plastic containers as they may sweat. It is important to keep a rich cake in a cool, dry place and to check it occasionally during storage.

Extra brandy or rum can be used to 'feed' the cake occasionally if it is stored for a long period but it is important not to overdo the liquor feeding as the cake can become soggy.

FREEZING CAKES

Most cakes that are not decorated freeze well. There is no point in freezing a rich fruit cake as it will improve on keeping as described above. Light fruit cakes can be frozen successfully; also cakes made by the creamed or melted methods. Fatless sponges, or those with little fat added, made by the whisked method freeze particularly well and they also thaw quickly at room temperature.

Packing Plain Cakes The cake should be allowed to cool completely before it is packed for freezing. When it is completely cold, pack the cake in a polythene bag, extracting all the air from the bag, and close it tightly. Label the cake with its type and date, then place it safely in the freezer, where it will not be crushed or damaged by other items.

Layers of cake should be separated by placing double thicknesses of greaseproof paper or special interleaving freezer film between them. The layers can then be packed together in one bag and frozen.

Undecorated cakes which are sandwiched together with a filling such as jam can be frozen as one plain cake, but it is best to freeze them unfilled, ready to be sandwiched together when thawed.

Freezing Decorated Cakes Cakes which are filled and covered with fresh cream, buttercream or frosting can be frozen successfully. Although the cake can be frozen with its filling and this type of icing, any decorations should not be added before freezing. Decorated cakes should not be frozen for long periods and it is best to keep them for just two to four weeks. It is sometimes useful to be able to make a decorated cake in advance of an occasion and freeze it. Cakes covered with royal icing, glacé icing or the softer moulding icings should not be frozen as the icing will not thaw successfully.

The technique to use when packing these cakes is to open freeze them. The decorated cake should be placed on freezer film or foil on a baking sheet and frozen uncovered until it is firm. Remember that the icing will not freeze hard and that it can be easily damaged during storage, particularly if there are any piped decorations. Once the cake is frozen it can be packed loosely in a polythene bag (it is best to support the cake on a piece of card first) or, better still, it can be placed in a large rigid container. Place a little crumpled absorbent kitchen paper around the side of the cake to prevent it from slipping against the sides of the container when moved.

The cake should be unpacked and transferred to a serving plate before being allowed to thaw in the refrigerator, preferably overnight or for several hours.

Packing Individual Slices It can be useful to have slices of cake in the freezer, to be removed one piece at a time as required. Either plain or decorated cakes can be packed in this way.

The cake should be cut into slices or wedges. A piece of interleaving film should be placed carefully between each slice and the cake re-shaped. Plain cakes can be packed as above or decorated cakes should be open frozen.

The required number of slices can be removed as they are wanted – this is particularly useful for lunch boxes or hasty family teas. A piece of plain cake can be packed still frozen in a lunch box first thing in the morning and it will have thawed in time for the midday break.

Freezing Small Cakes Small cakes cooked in paper cases can be packed neatly in rigid containers or polythene bags for freezing.

Tray cakes can be cut into squares or portions and frozen in rigid containers, or interleaved with freezer film and packed in bags. They can be removed and thawed a few at a time, as required.

HINTS FOR SUCCESSFUL CAKE MAKING

■ Check that all the ingredients and equipment are ready before you begin to mix the cake.

■ Weigh and measure correctly, and prepare the tins as suggested in the recipe.

■ Follow the recipe carefully, heating the oven when necessary.

■ For cakes made by the creamed method make sure that the fat is soft before beginning to beat it with the sugar – this makes the task much easier. Have the other ingredients at room temperature.

■ For the one-stage method all the ingredients should be thoroughly warmed to room temperature.

■ When making a cake by the melting method do not overheat the ingredients. Melt them over low heat until the fat is just melted. Do not let it become too hot. Leave the melted ingredients to cool slightly, if necessary, before adding any eggs.

■ Do not open the oven door when the cake is cooking until you think it is ready for checking. By opening the door in the early stages of cooking you can cause the cake to sink.

■ Test the cake to check if it is cooked before fully removing it from the oven. Use a pair of oven gloves and slide the shelf out slightly. Check the colour and texture of the cake, and use a skewer to test if the middle is cooked if necessary.

■ Allow the cake to stand for a few minutes in the tin and there is less chance of it breaking around the edges as it turns out. A rich cake should be allowed to cool in the tin until warm; a very rich cake is best left to cool completely in the tin.

SOME COMMON FAULTS AND THEIR LIKELY CAUSES

CAKE SUNK IN THE CENTRE

1 Too much raising agent used.

2 The fat and sugar were beaten for too long or the fat was too soft (almost runny when creamed).

3 The mixture was too soft before baking – this could be due to too little flour or too much liquid.

4 The oven door was opened too early or the cake removed from the oven before the mixture had time to set.

5 The cake was removed from the oven before it was fully cooked, in which case it would have sunk on cooling slightly.

CAKE RISEN TO A PEAK AND CRACKED ON TOP

1 Fat and sugar not creamed enough.

2 Oven too hot or uneven heat distribution in oven and cake cooked too near to the top of the oven, or in too hot an area of the oven.

3 The tin was too small for the amount of mixture.

UNEVENLY RISEN CAKE

1 The mixture was not levelled out before baking.

2 The oven was not prepared before the cake was put in – this does depend on the type of oven and the time it takes to heat up.

3 The cake was placed on a far corner or to one side of the shelf.

4 Too much raising agent used.

A VERY DRY CAKE

1 Not enough liquid added to the mixture.

2 The cake was baked for too long.

3 Far too much raising agent used.

THE CAKE HAS A COARSE, OPEN TEXTURE

1 If the mixture is a rubbed-in type, then the fat was not rubbed in enough. Alternatively the fat may have been of poor quality.

2 The fat and sugar were not creamed together for long enough.

3 The oven temperature was too high.

4 Too much raising agent used.

FRUIT SUNK TO THE BOTTOM OF THE CAKE

1 The mixture was too soft and would not support the fruit.

2 Cherries are the most common offender in this example. If the cherries are added to a light fruit cake they must be washed and dried first, then dusted with a little of the measured flour. If they are left coated in syrup this will cause them to sink. The dusting of flour helps them to adhere to the surrounding mixture and this prevents them from sinking.

THE CAKE HAS A SUGARY CRUST

1 Fat and sugar not creamed together long enough.

2 Too much sugar used.

3 The sugar was too coarse.

BASIC CAKES

The essential techniques that are used in the preparation of basic cakes apply equally to the most complicated gâteaux. Once these techniques are mastered, they can be applied to the array of elaborate cake-making ideas featured in later chapters.

PLAIN CAKE

fat for greasing
200 g/7 oz self-raising flour or 200 g/7 oz plain flour and 10 ml/2 tsp baking powder
1.25 ml/¼ tsp salt
75 g/3 oz margarine or blended white cooking fat, diced
75 g/3 oz sugar
2 small eggs
about 125 ml/4 fl oz milk

Line and grease a 15 cm/6 inch cake tin. Set the oven at 180°C/350°F/gas 4.

Mix the flour and salt together in a mixing bowl. Rub in the margarine or cooking fat until the mixture resembles fine bread-crumbs. Add the baking powder, if used, and the sugar.

In a bowl, beat the eggs with some of the milk and stir into the flour mixture. Add a little more milk if necessary to give a consistency which just drops off the end of a wooden spoon.

Spoon the mixture into the prepared cake tin and bake for 1-1½ hours or until cooked through. Cool on a wire rack.

MAKES ONE 15 CM/6 INCH CAKE

ONE-STAGE FRUIT CAKE

fat for greasing
225 g/8 oz self-raising flour
5 ml/1 tsp mixed spice (optional)
100 g/4 oz soft margarine
100 g/4 oz glacé cherries, chopped
100 g/4 oz currants
75 g/3 oz sultanas
25 g/1 oz cut mixed peel
100 g/4 oz soft light brown sugar
2 eggs
75 ml/3 fl oz milk

Line and grease an 18 cm/7 inch round cake tin. Set the oven at 180°C/350°F/gas 4. Mix the flour and spice, if used.

Put all the ingredients in a bowl, stir, then beat until smooth, allowing 2-3 minutes by hand or 1-1½ minutes with an electric mixer. Spoon the mixture into the prepared tin and bake for 2 hours. Cool on a wire rack.

MAKES ONE 18 CM/7 INCH CAKE

> **MRS BEETON'S TIP** The cherries will be easy to chop if you use a pair of kitchen scissors whose blades have been dipped in boiling water.

SMALL RICH CAKES

fat for greasing (optional)
100 g/4 oz self-raising flour
pinch of salt
100 g/4 oz butter or margarine
100 g/4 oz caster sugar
2 eggs, beaten

Grease 12-14 bun tins or support an equivalent number of paper cases in dry bun tins. Set the oven at 180°C/350°F/gas 4. Mix the flour and salt in a bowl.

In a mixing bowl, cream the butter or margarine with the sugar until light and fluffy. Beat in the eggs, then lightly stir in the flour and salt.

Divide the mixture evenly between the prepared paper cases or bun tins, and bake for 15-20 minutes until golden brown. Cool on a wire rack.

MAKES 12 TO 14

VARIATIONS

CHERRY CAKES Add 50 g/2 oz chopped glacé cherries with the flour.
CHOCOLATE CAKES Add 30 ml/ 2 tbsp cocoa with the flour and add 15 ml/ 1 tbsp milk.
COCONUT CAKES Add 50 g/2 oz desiccated coconut with the flour and 15-30 ml/ 1-2 tbsp milk with the eggs.
COFFEE CAKES Dissolve 10 ml/2 tsp instant coffee in 5 ml/1 tsp boiling water. Add with the eggs.
QUEEN CAKES Add 100 g/4 oz currants with the flour.

RICH CAKE

fat for greasing
200 g/7 oz plain flour
1.25 ml/¼ tsp salt
2.5 ml/½ tsp baking powder
150 g/5 oz butter or margarine
150 g/5 oz caster sugar
4 eggs, beaten
15 ml/1 tbsp milk (optional)

Line and grease a 15 cm/6 inch cake tin. Set the oven at 180°C/350°F/gas 4.

Sift the flour, salt and baking powder into a bowl. Place the butter or margarine in a mixing bowl and beat until very soft. Add the sugar and cream together until light and fluffy. Add the beaten eggs gradually, beating well after each addition. If the mixture shows signs of curdling, add a little flour.

Fold in the dry ingredients lightly but thoroughly, adding the milk if too stiff.

Spoon into the prepared tin, smooth the surface and make a hollow in the centre. Bake for 30 minutes, then reduce the oven temperature to 160°C/325°F/gas 3 and bake for 50 minutes more until firm to the touch. Cool on a wire rack.

MAKES ONE 15 CM/6 INCH CAKE

VARIATIONS

CORNFLOUR CAKE Use a mixture of equal parts cornflour and plain flour.
GROUND RICE CAKE Use a mixture of 150 g/5 oz plain flour and 50 g/2 oz ground rice.
LEMON OR ORANGE CAKE Add the grated rind of 2 lemons or oranges and use fruit juice instead of milk.

VICTORIA SANDWICH CAKE

The original Victoria Sandwich was oblong, filled with jam or marmalade and cut into fingers or sandwiches. Now, the basic mixture is used with many different flavourings and fillings and is served as a single, round cake. For a softer centred cake bake the mixture in a 20 cm/8 inch round cake tin, then split and fill. All loose crumbs must be brushed off before filling. Keep the filling fairly firm – if it is too moist, it will seep into the cake.

fat for greasing
150 g/5 oz butter or margarine
150 g/5 oz caster sugar
3 eggs, beaten
150 g/5 oz self-raising flour or plain flour
    and 5 ml/1 tsp baking powder
pinch of salt
raspberry or other jam for filling
caster sugar for dredging

Line and grease two 18 cm/7 inch sandwich tins. Set the oven at 180°C/350°F/gas 4.

In a mixing bowl cream the butter or margarine with the sugar until light and fluffy. Add the eggs gradually, beating well after each addition. Sift the flour, salt and baking powder, if used, into a bowl. Stir into the creamed mixture, lightly but thoroughly, until evenly mixed.

Divide between the tins and bake for 25-30 minutes. Cool on a wire rack, then sandwich together with jam. Sprinkle the top with caster sugar or spread with Glacé Icing (page 151).

MAKES ONE 18 CM/7 INCH CAKE

ONE-STAGE VICTORIA SANDWICH

fat for greasing
150 g/5 oz self-raising flour
pinch of salt
150 g/5 oz soft margarine
150 g/5 oz caster sugar
3 eggs

Line and grease two 18 cm/7 inch sandwich tins. Set the oven at 180°C/350°F/gas 4.

Put all the ingredients in a mixing bowl and stir. Beat until smooth, allowing 2-3 minutes by hand or 1-1½ minutes with an electric mixer.

Divide the mixture evenly between the tins and level each surface. Bake for 25–30 minutes. Cool on a wire rack, then fill and top as desired.

MAKES ONE 18 CM/7 INCH CAKE

🥣 **MRS BEETON'S TIP** A wholemeal Victoria sandwich cake can be made by substituting self-raising wholemeal flour for white flour. If self-raising wholemeal flour is not available, then use the plain type and add 10 ml/2 tsp of baking powder. Soften the mixture with 30 ml/2 tbsp of milk or orange juice after the flour is added. The resulting cake tends to have a closer, heavier texture.

FLAVOURINGS AND FILLINGS FOR VICTORIA SANDWICH CAKES

The basic mixture for Victoria Sandwich Cake can be adapted to make a variety of cakes. For example, sweet spices or citrus rinds can be added to the mixture. Alternatively, flavourings such as vanilla essence or almond essence can be added in small quantities to slightly alter the result.

There is a wide variety of commercial preserves and sweet spreads available and many of these are ideal for filling the sandwich cake. The following ideas can be used with the traditional recipe or the one-stage recipe.

CHOCOLATE SANDWICH CAKE Substitute 60 ml/4 tbsp of cocoa for an equal quantity of the flour. Sift the cocoa with the flour and continue as in the main recipe. Sandwich the cooled cakes together with chocolate spread and sift a little icing sugar over the top of the cake.

CINNAMON AND APPLE SAND-WICH CAKE Add 10 ml/2 tsp of ground cinnamon to the flour. Continue as in the main recipe. Peel, core and slice a large cooking apple, then cook it with a little sugar until it is reduced to a pulp. Press the pulp through a sieve, return it to the saucepan and add 10 ml/2 tsp of cornflour blended with 30 ml/2 tbsp of milk. Bring to the boil, stirring, and cook until thickened. Sweeten the purée to taste, then leave it to cool. Gradually fold in 50 ml/2 fl oz of whipped double cream, then use this apple cream to sandwich the cooled cakes together.

COFFEE SANDWICH CAKE Dissolve 30 ml/2 tbsp of instant coffe in 30 ml/2 tbsp boiling water and leave to cool. Fold this into the mixture last. Whip 150 ml/¼ pint double cream with 5 ml/1 tsp of instant coffee dissolved in 15 ml/1 tbsp of boiling water and 30 ml/2 tbsp of icing sugar. Sandwich the cooled cakes with this coffee cream.

GINGER SANDWICH CAKE The combination of ground ginger and lemon rind makes a delicious cake. Add the grated rind of 1 lemon to the fat and sugar. Sift 15 ml/1 tbsp of ground ginger with the flour. Prepare and bake the cake as in the main recipe. When cool, sandwich the layers with ginger marmalade.

HARLEQUIN SANDWICH CAKE Make the cake mixture as in the main recipe, then put half in one sandwich tin. Add pink food colouring to the second portion of mixture, making it a fairly strong colour. Put the second portion in the other sandwich tin and bake the cake. When cool, cut both cakes into rings: cut a 5 cm/2 inch circle from the middle of each cake, then cut a 10 cm/4 inch circle around it. Either use plain pastry cutters or cut out circles of paper and use a pointed knife to cut round them. You should have three rings of each cake. Carefully put the rings of cake together alternating the colours to make two layers. Sandwich the layers together with raspberry jam. Spread warmed raspberry jam over the top of the cake and sift icing sugar over it. Alternatively, fill the cake with whipped cream and swirl more whipped cream over the top. When slices are cut the pattern will show.

LEMON SANDWICH CAKE Add the grated rind of 1 large lemon to the fat and sugar. Continue as in the main recipe, then sandwich the cooled cakes together with lemon curd.

MOCHA SANDWICH CAKE Substitute 30 ml/2 tbsp of cocoa for an equal quantity of flour and sift it with the flour. Prepare the mixture as in the main recipe. Dissolve 10 ml/2 tsp of instant coffee in 15 ml/1 tbsp of boiling water and add it to the mixture. Sandwich the cooled cakes together with chocolate spread.

ORANGE SANDWICH CAKE Add the grated rind of 1 large orange to the fat and sugar, then continue as in the main recipe. Sandwich the cooled cakes together with orange marmalade.

SPONGE CAKE

fat for greasing
flour for dusting
3 eggs
75 g/3 oz caster sugar
75 g/3 oz plain flour
pinch of salt
pinch of baking powder

Grease an 18 cm/7 inch round cake tin or two 15 cm/6 inch sandwich tins. Dust with sifted flour, tapping out the excess. Set the oven at 180°C/350°F/gas 4.

Whisk the eggs and sugar together in a bowl over a saucepan of hot water, taking care that the base of the bowl does not touch the water. Continue whisking for 10-15 minutes until the mixture is thick and creamy. Remove the bowl from the pan. Whisk until cold.

Sift the flour, salt and baking powder into a bowl. Add to the creamed mixture, using a metal spoon. Do this lightly, so that the air incorporated during whisking is not lost. Pour the mixture into the prepared tins.

Bake a single 18 cm/7 inch cake for 40 minutes; two 15 cm/6 inch cakes for 25 minutes. Leave the sponge in the tins for a few minutes, then cool on a wire rack. Fill and top as desired.

MAKES ONE 18 CM/7 INCH CAKE OR TWO 15 CM/6 INCH LAYERS

MRS BEETON'S TIP If an electric mixer is used there is no need to place the bowl over hot water. Whisk at high speed for about 5 minutes until thick. Fold in the flour by hand.

GENOESE SPONGE OR PASTRY

For an 18 cm/7 inch square or 15 x 25 cm/6 x 10 inch oblong cake, use 75 g/3 oz flour, pinch of salt, 50 g/2 oz clarified butter or margarine, 3 eggs and 75 g/3 oz caster sugar.

fat for greasing
100 g/4 oz plain flour
2.5 ml/½ tsp salt
75 g/3 oz Clarified Butter (page 22) or
    margarine
4 eggs
100 g/4 oz caster sugar

Line and grease a 20 x 30 cm/8 x 12 inch Swiss roll tin. Set the oven at 180°C/350°F/gas 4.

Sift the flour and salt into a bowl and put in a warm place. Melt the clarified butter or margarine without letting it get hot.

Whisk the eggs lightly in a mixing bowl. Add the sugar and place the bowl over a saucepan of hot water. Whisk for 10-15 minutes until thick. Take care that the base of the bowl does not touch the water. Remove from the heat and continue whisking until at blood-heat. The melted butter should be at the same temperature.

Sift half the flour over the eggs, then pour in half the melted butter or margarine in a thin stream. Fold in gently. Repeat, using the remaining flour and fat. Spoon gently into the prepared tin and bake for 30-40 minutes. Cool on a wire rack.

MAKES ONE 20 x 30 CM/8 x 12 INCH CAKE

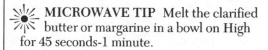 **MICROWAVE TIP** Melt the clarified butter or margarine in a bowl on High for 45 seconds-1 minute.

GINGERBREAD

fat for greasing
200 g/7 oz plain flour
1.25 ml/¼ tsp salt
10-15 ml/2-3 tsp ground ginger
2.5 ml/½ tsp bicarbonate of soda
75 g/3 oz lard
50 g/2 oz soft light brown sugar
50 g/2 oz golden syrup
50 g/2 oz black treacle
1 egg
milk (see method)

Line and grease a 15 cm/6 inch square tin. Set the oven at 160°C/325°F/gas 3.

Sift the flour, salt, ginger and bicarbonate of soda into a mixing bowl. Warm the lard, sugar, syrup and treacle in a saucepan until the fat has melted. Do not allow the mixture to become hot.

In a measuring jug, beat the egg lightly and add enough milk to make up to 125 ml/4 fl oz. Add the melted mixture to the dry ingredients with the beaten egg and milk mixture. Stir thoroughly; the mixture should run easily off the spoon.

Pour into the prepared tin and bake for 1¼-1½ hours until firm to the touch. Cool on a wire rack.

MAKES ONE 15 CM/6 INCH SQUARE CAKE

FLAVOURINGS AND FILLINGS FOR SPONGE CAKES

Both the Sponge Cake and the Genoese Sponge cake are light in texture, with a delicate flavour, and this should be reflected in the choice of flavouring ingredients or fillings that are added. Jams and other sweet preserves can be used to fill the cakes or whipped cream is ideal for this type of cake. Fresh fruit perfectly complements the lightness of these sponges.

The following suggestions can be used for both the recipes opposite.

CHOCOLATE CREAM SPONGE Make plain sponge cakes or substitute 15 ml/1 tbsp of cocoa for an equal quantity of flour, sifting it in with the flour to flavour the cakes. For the filling, melt 100 g/4 oz of milk chocolate with 50 g/2 oz of butter in a basin over hot water. Stir well and leave to cool but do not allow to set. Carefully fold in 150 ml/¼ pint of whipped double cream, then use this chocolate cream to sandwich the cakes together.

LEMON CREAM SPONGE Add the grated rind of 1 lemon to the eggs and sugar, then continue as in the main recipe. Whip 150 ml/¼ pint of double cream and fold in 60-90 ml/4-6 tbsp of lemon curd, to taste. Use this to sandwich the cakes together.

PEACHES AND CREAM CAKE Make the cakes as in the main recipe. Finely chop peeled and stoned fresh peaches or drained canned peaches and mix them with whipped cream or soft cheese. Sweeten with icing sugar and use this to sandwich the cakes together.

STRAWBERRY CREAM CAKE Make the cakes as in the main recipe and leave to cool. Hull and halve 225 g/8 oz of strawberries. Whip 150 ml/¼ pint of double cream with icing sugar to taste, then fold in the strawberries. Sandwich the cooled cakes together with the strawberry cream.

LARGE PLAIN CAKES

This chapter progresses from the basics of cake-making to offer a selection of recipes that are suitable for everyday baking, including a variety of gingerbreads. These cakes are not over-rich, they all keep well and they are ideal for a mid-week treat.

CHOCOLATE AND ALMOND LOAF

This tasty loaf needs no topping, but may be served with whipped cream for a special treat.

fat for greasing
200 g/7 oz plain flour
30 ml/2 tbsp cocoa
5 ml/1 tsp bicarbonate of soda
1.25 ml/¼ tsp salt
50 g/2 oz plain chocolate, broken into squares
100 g/4 oz butter or margarine
175 g/6 oz caster sugar
2 eggs, beaten
150 ml/5 fl oz soured cream or plain yogurt
30 ml/2 tbsp flaked almonds

Line and grease a 23 x 13 x 7.5 cm/9 x 5 x 3 inch loaf tin. Set the oven at 160°C/325°F/gas 3. Sift the flour, cocoa, bicarbonate of soda and salt into a bowl. Place the chocolate in a saucepan with 60 ml/4 tbsp water and melt over low heat, stirring once or twice.

In a mixing bowl cream the butter or margarine with the sugar until light. Add the beaten eggs gradually, beating well after each addition and adding a little of the flour mixture to prevent curdling.

Fold in the rest of the flour mixture, a third at a time, alternately with the soured cream or yogurt. Finally stir in the melted chocolate and the almonds.

Spoon into the prepared tin and bake for 50-60 minutes until cooked through and firm to the touch. Cool on a wire rack.

MAKES ONE 23 x 13 x 7.5 CM/9 x 5 x 3 INCH LOAF

> ☀ **MICROWAVE TIP** The chocolate may be melted in the microwave. Place it in a glass measuring jug with the water and heat on High for 1-2 minutes.

PLAIN CHOCOLATE LOAF

Serve this simple loaf sliced, with a chocolate and hazelnut spread for those who like to gild the lily.

fat for greasing
175 g/6 oz plain flour
50 g/2 oz cocoa
10 ml/2 tsp baking powder
2.5 ml/½ tsp bicarbonate of soda
1.25 ml/¼ tsp salt
150 g/5 oz sugar
2 eggs, beaten
75 g/3 oz butter or margarine, melted
250 ml/8 fl oz milk

Line and grease a 23 x 13 x 7.5 cm/9 x 5 x 3 inch loaf tin. Set the oven at 180°C/350°F/ gas 4. Sift the flour, cocoa, baking powder, bicarbonate of soda and salt into a mixing bowl. Stir in the sugar.

In a second bowl beat the eggs with the melted butter or margarine and milk. Pour the milk mixture into the dry ingredients and stir lightly but thoroughly.

Spoon into the prepared tin and bake for 40-50 minutes until cooked through and firm to the touch. Cool on a wire rack.

MAKES ONE 23 x 13 x 7.5 CM/9 x 5 x 3 INCH LOAF

A VARIETY OF CHOCOLATE LOAF CAKES

The recipe for Plain Chocolate Loaf can be used as a basis for making deliciously different chocolate cakes. Try some of these ideas, which include simple additional flavourings and clever ways of splitting and sandwiching the loaf cake.

CHOCOLATE LAYER LOAF The simplest way to enrich the loaf cake is to cut it horizontally into three layers and sandwich them together with chocolate and hazelnut spread. If you like, coat the top of the cake with melted chocolate softened with a knob of butter, and sprinkle toasted hazelnuts on top.

CHOCOLATE ORANGE SPLIT Add the grated rind of 1 orange to the dry ingredients, then continue as in the main recipe. Beat 225 g/8 oz curd cheese with enough orange juice to make it soft and creamy, then add icing sugar to taste. Stir in 50 g/2 oz of finely grated plain chocolate. Split the loaf vertically along its length into four slices. Sandwich the slices together with the cheese mixture and spread a thin layer over the top of the loaf. Sprinkle the top with extra grated chocolate.

CHOCOLATE WALNUT LOAF Add 100 g/4 oz of finely chopped walnuts to the dry ingredients, then continue as in the main recipe. Melt 50 g/2 oz of plain chocolate with 25 g/1 oz butter and stir in about 50 g/2 oz of chopped walnuts. Top the loaf with this nutty mixture.

CHOCOLATE BANANA LOAF Add 1 roughly chopped banana to the dry ingredients and continue as in the main recipe. Allow the loaf to cool, then spread individual slices with banana butter. To make the banana butter, cream 50 g/2 oz butter with a little icing sugar until very soft. Beat in 1 mashed banana and a little lemon juice.

MRS BEETON'S ALMOND CAKE

fat for greasing
100 g/4 oz butter or margarine
100 g/4 oz caster sugar
275 g/10 oz plain flour
10 ml/2 tsp baking powder
3 eggs
200 ml/7 fl oz milk
2.5 ml/½ tsp almond essence
50 g/2 oz flaked almonds

Line and grease a 15 cm/6 inch cake tin. Set the oven at 160°C/325°F/gas 3.

In a mixing bowl, cream the butter or margarine with the sugar until light and fluffy. Into another bowl, sift the flour and baking powder. In a measuring jug, beat the eggs with the milk.

Add the dry ingredients to the creamed mixture in 3 parts, alternately with the egg and milk mixture. Beat well after each addition. Lightly stir in the almond essence and the flaked almonds.

Spoon lightly into the prepared tin and bake for 1¼-1½ hours until cooked through and firm to the touch. Cool on a wire rack.

MAKES ONE 15 CM/6 INCH CAKE

MICROWAVE TIP If the butter or margarine is too hard to cream readily, soften it in the mixing bowl on High for 15-30 seconds.

WEEKEND WALNUT LOAF

Illustrated on page 17

fat for greasing
275 g/10 oz plain flour
50 g/2 oz cornflour
150 g/5 oz caster sugar
5 ml/1 tsp salt
50 g/2 oz walnuts, chopped
225 g/8 oz dates, pitted and chopped
30 ml/2 tbsp oil
1 large egg
10 ml/2 tsp bicarbonate of soda

Line and grease a 23 x 13 x 7.5 cm/9 x 5 x 3 inch loaf tin. Set the oven at 180°C/350°F/gas 4.

Sift the flour, cornflour, sugar and salt into a mixing bowl. Add the walnuts and dates. In a second bowl, whisk together the oil and egg. Add to the flour, fruit and nuts and mix well. Pour 250 ml/8 fl oz boiling water into a measuring jug, add the bicarbonate of soda and stir until dissolved. Add to the mixing bowl and mix well. Beat to a soft consistency.

Pour into the prepared loaf tin and bake for about 1 hour until cooked through and firm to the touch. Leave to cool slightly before inverting on a wire rack to cool completely.

MAKES ONE 23 x 13 x 7.5 CM/9 x 5 x 3 INCH LOAF

MRS BEETON'S TIP Use a light unflavoured oil, such as corn oil, for the best results. Never use olive oil; its flavour is too strong.

DATE AND WALNUT CAKE

fat for greasing
200 g/7 oz self-raising flour or 200 g/7 oz
    plain flour and 10 ml/2 tsp baking
    powder
pinch of grated nutmeg
75 g/3 oz margarine
75 g/3 oz dates, stoned and chopped
25 g/1 oz walnuts, chopped
75 g/3 oz soft light brown sugar
2 small eggs
about 125 ml/4fl oz milk

Line and grease a 15 cm/6 inch tin. Set the oven at 180°C/350°F/gas 4.

Mix the flour and nutmeg in a mixing bowl, and rub in the margarine until the mixture resembles fine breadcrumbs. Add the dates and walnuts with the sugar and baking powder, if used.

In a bowl, beat the eggs with the milk and stir into the dry ingredients. Mix well.

Spoon the mixture into the cake tin and bake for 1¼-1½ hours or until cooked through and firm to the touch. Cool on a wire rack.

MAKES ONE 15 CM/6 INCH CAKE

☀ **MICROWAVE TIP** Dried dates in a compact slab are often difficult to chop. Soften them by heating for 30-40 seconds on Defrost and the job will be made much easier.

BANANA AND WALNUT CAKE

fat for greasing
200 g/7 oz plain flour
1.25 ml/¼ tsp baking powder
3.75 ml/¾ tsp bicarbonate of soda
pinch of salt
100 g/4 oz butter
150 g/5 oz caster sugar
3 large bananas, mashed
2 eggs, beaten
45 ml/3 tbsp soured milk
50 g/2 oz walnuts, finely chopped

Line and grease either a 20 cm/8 inch ring tin, or two 23 cm/9 inch sandwich tins. Set the oven at 180°C/350°F/gas 4. Sift the flour, baking powder, bicarbonate of soda and salt into a bowl.

In a mixing bowl, cream the butter and sugar until light and creamy. Mix in the mashed banana at once, blending well. Add the eggs, one at a time, beating well after each addition. Add the dry ingredients, one-third at a time, alternately with the soured milk, beating well after each addition.

Stir in the walnuts and spoon into the prepared tin. Bake the ring cake for about 40 minutes; the sandwich cakes for about 30 minutes. Cool on a wire rack.

MAKES ONE 20 CM/8 INCH RING CAKE OR TWO 23 CM/9 INCH LAYERS

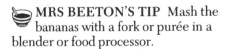 **MRS BEETON'S TIP** Mash the bananas with a fork or purée in a blender or food processor.

GOLDEN GINGERBREAD

fat for greasing
200 g/7 oz plain flour
1.25 ml/¼ tsp salt
10-15 ml/2-3 tsp ground ginger
2.5 ml/½ tsp bicarbonate of soda
grated rind of 1 orange
75 g/3 oz butter or margarine
50 g/2 oz golden granulated sugar
100 g/4 oz golden syrup
1 egg
milk (see method)

Line and grease a 15 cm/6 inch square tin. Set the oven at 160°C/325°F/gas 3.

Sift the flour, salt, ginger and bicarbonate of soda into a mixing bowl. Stir in the orange rind. Warm the butter or margarine with the sugar and syrup in a saucepan until the fat has melted but the mixture is not hot.

In a measuring jug, beat the egg lightly and add enough milk to make up to 125 ml/4 fl oz. Add the melted mixture to the dry ingredients with the beaten egg and milk mixture. Stir thoroughly; the mixture should run easily off the spoon.

Pour into the prepared tin and bake for 1¼-1½ hours until firm. Cool on a wire rack.

MAKES ONE 15 CM/6 INCH SQUARE CAKE

MRS BEETON'S TIP The easiest way to measure the ingredients for melting is to weigh the empty saucepan, then add the butter or margarine until the scale registers an additional 75 g/3 oz. Add the sugar to increase the weight by a further 50 g/2 oz, then, using a spoon dipped in boiling water, ladle in syrup until the scale registers a further 100 g/4 oz.

GINGERBREAD WITH PINEAPPLE

fat for greasing
200 g/7 oz plain flour
1.25 ml/¼ tsp salt
10-15 ml/2-3 tsp ground ginger
2.5 ml/½ tsp bicarbonate of soda
50 g/2 oz crystallised ginger, chopped
50 g/2 oz crystallised pineapple, chopped
75 g/3 oz butter or margarine
50 g/2 oz soft light brown sugar
50 g/2 oz golden syrup
50 g/2 oz black treacle
1 egg
milk (see method)

Line and grease a 15 cm/6 inch square tin. Set the oven at 160°C/325°F/gas 3.

Sift the flour, salt, ginger and bicarbonate of soda into a mixing bowl. Stir in the fruit. Warm the butter or margarine with the sugar, syrup and treacle in a saucepan until the fat has melted. Do not allow the mixture to become hot.

In a measuring jug, beat the egg lightly and add enough milk to make up to 125 ml/4 fl oz. Add the melted mixture to the dry ingredients with the beaten egg and milk mixture. Stir thoroughly; the mixture should run easily off the spoon.

Pour into the prepared tin and bake for 1¼-1½ hours until firm to the touch. Cool on a wire rack.

MAKES ONE 15 CM/6 INCH SQUARE CAKE

Dundee Cake (page 85)

Chicago Chocolate Cake (page 103) and Devil's Food Cake (page 96)

Swiss Carrot Cake (page 100)

Black Forest Gâteau (page 102)

NUT GINGERBREAD

fat for greasing
200 g/7 oz plain flour
1.25 ml/¼ tsp salt
10-15 ml/2-3 tsp ground ginger
10 ml/2 tsp ground cinnamon
2.5 ml/½ tsp bicarbonate of soda
50 g/2 oz chopped almonds or walnuts
75 g/3 oz butter or margarine
50 g/2 oz soft light brown sugar
100 g/4 oz golden syrup
1 egg
milk (see method)

Line and grease a 15 cm/6 inch square tin. Set the oven at 160°C/325°F/gas 3.

Sift the flour, salt, spices and bicarbonate of soda into a mixing bowl. Stir in the nuts. Warm the butter or margarine with the sugar and syrup in a saucepan until the fat has melted. Do not allow the mixture to become hot.

In a measuring jug, beat the egg lightly and add enough milk to make up to 125 ml/4 fl oz. Add the melted mixture to the dry ingredients with the beaten egg and milk mixture. Stir thoroughly; the mixture should run easily off the spoon.

Pour into the prepared tin and bake for 1¼-1½ hours until firm to the touch. Cool on a wire rack.

MAKES ONE 15 CM/6 INCH SQUARE CAKE

> ☀ **MICROWAVE TIP** To shell walnuts, place them in a glass bowl with 60 ml/4 tbsp water. Cover lightly and microwave on High for 1-2 minutes. Dry before removing the shells.

COUNTRY GINGERBREAD WITH CARAWAY SEEDS

fat for greasing
75 g/3 oz plain flour
1.25 ml/¼ tsp salt
15 ml/1 tbsp ground ginger
5 ml/1 tsp bicarbonate of soda
100 g/4 oz wholemeal flour
10 ml/2 tsp caraway seeds
75 g/3 oz soft light brown sugar
200 g/7 oz golden syrup
75 g/3 oz butter or margarine
1 egg
125 ml/4 fl oz milk

Line and grease a 20 cm/8 inch square tin. Set the oven at 160°C/325°F/gas 3. Sift the plain flour, salt, ginger and bicarbonate of soda into a mixing bowl. Add the wholemeal flour, caraway seeds and sugar.

Heat the syrup and butter or margarine gently in a saucepan until the fat has melted. In a bowl, beat the egg and milk together. Add the melted mixture to the dry ingredients with the egg and milk mixture and beat well. Spoon into the prepared tin and bake for 50 minutes or until cooked through and firm to the touch. Cool on a wire rack.

MAKES ONE 20 CM/8 INCH SQUARE CAKE

OATMEAL GINGERBREAD

fat for greasing
100 g/4 oz plain flour
1.25 ml/¼ tsp salt
15 ml/1 tbsp ground ginger
5 ml/1 tsp bicarbonate of soda
100 g/4 oz fine oatmeal
50 g/2 oz butter or margarine
50 g/2 oz soft light brown sugar
20 ml/4 tsp black treacle
1 egg
75 ml/5 tbsp milk or soured milk

Line and grease an 18 cm/7 inch square tin. Set the oven at 180°C/350°F/gas 4. Sift the flour, salt, ginger and bicarbonate of soda into a mixing bowl. Add the oatmeal.

Heat the butter or margarine with the sugar and treacle gently in a saucepan until the fat has melted.

In a bowl, beat the egg and milk together. Add the melted mixture to the dry ingredients with the beaten egg and milk mixture. Stir well. Pour into the prepared tin and bake for 1-1¼ hours until cooked through and firm to the touch. Cool on a wire rack.

MAKES ONE 18 CM/7 INCH SQUARE CAKE

★ **FREEZER TIP** Cut the cake into squares and wrap individually in foil before freezing for a ready supply of lunchbox or after-school treats.

RICH GINGERBREAD

fat for greasing
225 g/8 oz plain flour
1.25 ml/¼ tsp salt
10 ml/2 tsp ground ginger
2.5-5 ml/½-1 tsp ground cinnamon or
    grated nutmeg
5 ml/1 tsp bicarbonate of soda
100 g/4 oz butter
100 g/4 oz soft light brown sugar
100 g/4 oz golden syrup
1 egg
45 ml/3 tbsp plain yogurt
30 ml/2 tbsp ginger preserve

Line and grease a 23 cm/9 inch square tin. Set the oven at 160°C/325°F/gas 3.

Sift the flour, salt, spices and bicarbonate of soda into a mixing bowl. Heat the butter, sugar and syrup in a saucepan until the butter has melted.

In a bowl, beat the egg and yogurt together. Add to the dry ingredients, with the melted mixture, to give a soft, dropping consistency. Stir in the preserve.

Spoon into the prepared tin and bake for 50-60 minutes until cooked through and firm to the touch. Cool on a wire rack.

MAKES ONE 23 CM/9 INCH CAKE

MOIST GINGERBREAD

It is the grated carrot that gives this gingerbread its essential moistness. Do not be tempted to add more flour to the mixture – it is meant to have a batter-like consistency, and the results are excellent.

fat for greasing
200 g/7 oz plain flour
5 ml/1 tsp bicarbonate of soda
1.25 ml/¼ tsp salt
10 ml/2 tsp ground cinnamon
10 ml/2 tsp ground ginger
75 g/3 oz soft dark brown sugar
100 ml/3½ fl oz black treacle
100 ml/3½ fl oz golden syrup
150 g/5 oz butter or margarine
2 eggs, beaten
30 ml/2 tbsp ginger wine
1 medium carrot, grated

Line and grease a 20 cm/8 inch square tin. Set the oven at 180°C/350°F/gas 4.

Mix the flour, bicarbonate of soda, salt and spices in a mixing bowl. Add the sugar. Heat the treacle, syrup and butter or margarine gently in a saucepan until the fat has melted.

Stir the melted ingredients thoroughly into the dry ingredients, then beat in the eggs. Stir in the ginger wine and grated carrot.

Pour into the prepared tin and bake for 20 minutes, then reduce the oven temperature to 160°C/325°F/gas 3 for a further 25-30 minutes, until firm to the touch. Cool on a wire rack.

MAKES ONE 20 CM/8 INCH CAKE

TANGY CITRUS CAKE

fat for greasing
200 g/7 oz self-raising flour or 200 g/7 oz
    plain flour and 10ml/2 tsp baking
    powder
1.25 ml/¼ tsp salt
75 g/3 oz margarine
75 g/3 oz sugar
grated rind and juice of 1 lemon or orange
2 small eggs
30-60 ml/2-4 tbsp milk

Line and grease a 15 cm/6 inch cake tin. Set the oven at 180°C/350°F/gas 4.

Mix the flour and salt in a mixing bowl. Rub in the margarine until the mixture resembles fine breadcrumbs. Add the baking powder if used, sugar and grated citrus rind.

In a bowl, beat the eggs with 30 ml/2 tbsp of the milk and stir into the flour mixture. Gradually add the citrus juice, beating vigorously. If necessary, add the remaining milk to give a consistency which just drops off the end of a wooden spoon.

Spoon the mixture into the cake tin and bake for 1-1½ hours or until cooked through. Cool on a wire rack.

MAKES ONE 15 CM/6 INCH CAKE

APPLE AND GINGER CAKE

fat for greasing
175 g/6 oz plain flour
1.25 ml/¼ tsp salt
2.5 ml/½ tsp bicarbonate of soda
5 ml/1 tsp baking powder
5 ml/1 tsp ground ginger
100 g/4 oz crystallised ginger, chopped
100 g/4 oz butter or margarine
150 g/5 oz caster sugar
2 eggs, beaten
250 ml/8 fl oz sieved apple purée

Line and grease an 18 cm/7 inch square cake tin. Set the oven at 180°C/350°F/gas 4. Sift the flour, salt, bicarbonate of soda, baking powder and ginger into a bowl. Stir in the crystallised ginger and mix well. Set aside.

Place the butter or margarine in a mixing bowl and beat until very soft. Add the sugar and cream together until light and fluffy. Add the beaten eggs gradually, beating well after each addition. If the mixture shows signs of curdling, add a little of the flour mixture. Stir in the apple purée. Fold in the dry ingredients lightly but thoroughly. Spoon into the prepared tin, smooth the surface and make a hollow in the centre.

Bake for 30 minutes, then reduce the oven temperature to 160°C/325°F/gas 3 and bake for 15 minutes more until firm to the touch. Cool on a wire rack.

MAKES ONE 18 CM/7 INCH CAKE

YEAST CAKE

fat for greasing
50 g/2 oz butter
2 eggs
125 ml/4 fl oz milk
275 g/10 oz plain flour
100 g/4 oz soft light brown sugar
25 g/1 oz fresh yeast
150 g/5 oz currants
50 g/2 oz cut mixed peel

Line and grease a 15-18 cm/6-7 inch cake tin. Melt the butter in a saucepan and leave to cool. Add the eggs and milk and whisk until frothy. Combine the flour and sugar in a large bowl. In a cup, mix the yeast with a little warm water and leave to froth.

Make a hollow in the flour mixture and pour in the yeast. Add the butter and egg mixture, and mix well. Knead on a clean work surface to a smooth, soft dough, then return to the clean mixing bowl. Cover with a damp cloth, and place in a warm, draught-free place. Leave to rise for about 1½ hours or until the dough has doubled in bulk.

Add the dried fruit and peel, and knead until it is well distributed. Form the dough into a round and place in the prepared cake tin. Leave to rise for 30 minutes.

Set the oven at 200°C/400°F/gas 6. Bake the cake for 30 minutes, then reduce the oven temperature to 160°C/325°F/gas 3 and bake for a further 1 hour or until the cake sounds hollow when rapped on the base. Cool on a wire rack.

MAKES ONE 18 CM/7 INCH CAKE

> 🍲 **MRS BEETON'S TIP** Excessive heat kills yeast so take care that the water mixed with the yeast is merely at blood temperature.

FRUIT CAKES

A chapter filled with popular, light fruit cakes that are sure to be consumed with great pleasure by all the family. They are as versatile as they can be different; practical for enlivening a lunch box or perfect for Sunday tea.

BOILED FRUIT CAKE

fat for greasing
100 g/4 oz mixed dried fruit
50 g/2 oz margarine
25 g/1 oz soft light brown sugar
grated rind of 1 orange
200 g/7 oz plain flour
2.5 ml/½ tsp mixed spice
2.5 ml/½ tsp bicarbonate of soda

Line and grease a 15 cm/6 inch cake tin. Set the oven at 180°C/350°F/gas 4.

Combine the dried fruit, margarine, sugar and orange rind in a saucepan. Add 200 ml/7 fl oz water. Bring to the boil, reduce the heat and simmer for 5 minutes. Leave to cool until tepid.

Sift the flour, spice and bicarbonate of soda into the fruit mixture and mix well. Spoon into the prepared tin. Cover with greased paper or foil and bake for 1½-2 hours or until cooked through and firm to the touch. Cool on a wire rack.

MAKES ONE 15 CM/6 INCH CAKE

> MICROWAVE TIP Combine the dried fruit, margarine, sugar, water and orange rind in a mixing bowl. Cover lightly and microwave on High for 5 minutes, stirring twice. Leave to cool until tepid, then proceed as in the recipe above.

ONE-STAGE CHERRY CAKE

fat for greasing
225 g/8 oz glacé cherries
175 g/6 oz soft margarine
175 g/6 oz caster sugar
3 eggs
225 g/8 oz plain flour
12.5 ml/2½ tsp baking powder
50 g/2 oz ground almonds (optional)

Line and grease an 18 cm/7 inch round cake tin. Set the oven at 160°C/325°F/gas 3. Wash, dry and halve the cherries.

Put all the ingredients in a bowl and beat for 2-3 minutes until well mixed. Spoon the mixture into the prepared tin and bake for 1½-1¾ hours or until cooked through and firm to the touch. Cool on a wire rack.

MAKES ONE 18 CM/7 INCH CAKE.

> MRS BEETON'S TIP Instead of using plain flour, self-raising flour can be substituted and the quantity of baking powder reduced to 2.5 ml/½ tsp.

CHERRY CAKE

Illustrated on page 18

fat for greasing
200 g/7 oz plain flour
1.25 ml/¼ tsp salt
2.5 ml/½ tsp baking powder
100 g/4 oz glacé cherries, quartered
150 g/5 oz butter or margarine
150 g/5 oz caster sugar
4 eggs
15 ml/1 tbsp milk (optional)

Line and grease a 15 cm/6 inch cake tin. Set the oven at 180°C/350°F/gas 4. Sift the flour, salt and baking powder into a bowl. Add the cherries and mix well. Set aside.

Place the butter or margarine in a mixing bowl and beat until very soft. Add the sugar and cream together until light and fluffy. Add the beaten eggs gradually, beating well after each addition. If the mixture shows signs of curdling, add a little of the flour mixture.

Fold in the dry ingredients lightly but thoroughly, adding the milk if too stiff.

Spoon into the prepared tin, level the surface and make a hollow in the centre, Bake for 30 minutes, then reduce the oven temperature to 160°C/325°F/gas 3 and bake for 50 minutes more until cooked through and firm to the touch. Cool on a wire rack.

MAKES ONE 15 CM/6 INCH CAKE

MRS BEETON'S TIP When adding the cherries to the flour, be sure to mix them in thoroughly. If the cherries are coated in flour they will not sink to the bottom of the cake.

FESTIVAL FRUIT CAKE

fat for greasing
200 g/7 oz plain flour
1.25 ml/¼ tsp salt
2.5 ml/½ tsp baking powder
50 g/2 oz currants
50 g/2 oz sultanas
50 g/2 oz glacé cherries, chopped
50 g/2 oz cut mixed peel
150 g/5 oz butter or margarine
150 g/5 oz caster sugar
4 eggs
15 ml/1 tbsp milk (optional)

Line and grease an 18 cm/7 inch cake tin. Set the oven at 180°C/350°F/gas 4. Sift the flour, salt and baking powder into a bowl. Stir in the dried fruit and mixed peel and mix well. Set aside.

Place the butter or margarine in a mixing bowl and beat until very soft. Add the sugar and cream together until light and fluffy. Add the beaten eggs gradually, beating well after each addition. If the mixture shows signs of curdling, add a little of the flour mixture.

Fold in the dry ingredients lightly but thoroughly, adding the milk if too stiff.

Spoon into the prepared tin, smooth the surface and make a hollow in the centre. Bake for 30 minutes, then reduce the oven temperature to 160°C/325°F/gas 3 and bake for 40 minutes more until firm to the touch. Cool on a wire rack.

MAKES ONE 18 CM/7 INCH CAKE

COUNTESS SPICE CAKE

fat for greasing
100 g/4 oz plain flour
100 g/4 oz cornflour
2.5 ml/½ tsp ground ginger
3.75 ml/¾ tsp grated nutmeg
3.75 ml/¾ tsp ground cinnamon
1.25 ml/¼ tsp salt
75 g/3 oz margarine
10 ml/2 tsp baking powder
75 g/3 oz sugar
2 small eggs
about 125 ml/4 fl oz milk
50 g/2 oz currants
50 g/2 oz seedless raisins

Line and grease a 15 cm/6 inch cake tin. Set the oven at 180°C/350°F/gas 4.

Mix the flour, cornflour, spices and salt in a mixing bowl. Rub in the margarine until the mixture resembles fine breadcrumbs. Add the baking powder and the sugar.

In a bowl, beat the eggs with 50 ml/2 fl oz of the milk and stir into the flour mixture. Add more milk, if necessary, to give a consistency which just drops off the end of a wooden spoon. Stir in the currants and raisins.

Spoon the mixture into the prepared cake tin and bake for 1-1½ hours or until cooked through. Cool on a wire rack.

MAKES ONE 15 CM/6 INCH CAKE

MIXED FRUIT LOAF

Illustrated on page 18

fat for greasing
200 g/7 oz self-raising flour
pinch of salt
100 g/4 oz margarine
100 g/4 oz caster sugar
grated rind of 1 orange
225 g/8 oz mixed dried fruit, eg 25 g/1 oz
    glacé cherries, 25 g/1 oz cut mixed
    peel, 75 g/3 oz sultanas, 75 g/3 oz
    seedless raisins
1 egg
milk (see method)

Grease and line a 23 x 13 x 7.5 cm/9 x 5 x 3 inch loaf tin. Set the oven at 180°C/350°F/gas 4.

Mix the flour and salt in a mixing bowl and rub in the margarine until the mixture resembles fine breadcrumbs. Stir in the sugar and orange rind. Cut the cherries, if used, into 4-6 pieces each, depending on size, and add with the remaining fruit.

In a measuring jug, beat the egg lightly and add enough milk to make up to 125 ml/4 fl oz. Add to the flour mixture, stir in, then mix well. Spoon into the prepared tin and bake for about 1 hour or until firm to the touch. Cool on a wire rack.

MAKES ONE 23 x 13 x 7.5 CM/9 x 5 x 3 INCH LOAF

☀ **MICROWAVE TIP** The dried fruit may be cleaned and plumped in a single operation in the microwave. Place the fruit in a bowl with cold water to cover. Heat on High until the water boils, allow to stand until cool enough to handle, then drain the fruit, removing any stalks.

EVERYDAY BRAN CAKE

fat for greasing
175 g/6 oz self-raising flour
25 g/1 oz natural wheat bran
1.25 ml/¼ tsp salt
100 g/4 oz margarine
100 g/4 oz caster sugar or soft light brown
    sugar
150 g/5 oz mixed dried fruit (currants,
    sultanas, seedless raisins)
2 eggs
30 ml/2 tbsp milk

Line and grease a 15 cm/6 inch cake tin.
Set the oven at 180°C/350°F/gas 4.

Mix the flour, bran and salt in a mixing
bowl and rub in the margarine until the
mixture resembles fine breadcrumbs. Stir in
the sugar and fruit.

In a bowl, beat the eggs with the milk, add
to the dry ingredients and fruit and mix well.
Spoon into the prepared tin and bake for
about 1 hour or until cooked through. Cool
on a wire rack.

MAKES ONE 15 CM/6 INCH CAKE

HOLIDAY CAKE

fat for greasing
200 g/7 oz self-raising flour
1.25 ml/¼ tsp salt
1.25 ml/¼ tsp baking powder
75 g/3 oz margarine
75 g/3 oz sugar
100 g/4 oz currants
100 g/4 oz seedless raisins
1 large egg
100 ml/3½ fl oz milk

Line and grease a 15 cm/6 inch round cake
tin. Set the oven at 180°C/350°F/gas 4.

Sift the flour, salt and baking powder into
a mixing bowl. Rub in the margarine until
the mixture resembles fine breadcrumbs.
Stir in the sugar and dried fruit.

In a small bowl, beat the egg lightly and
add the milk. Stir into the dry ingredients
and fruit and beat to a soft consistency.
Spoon into the tin and bake for 1½ hours,
until cooked through. Cool on a wire rack.

MAKES ONE 15 CM/6 INCH CAKE

SPICED SULTANA CAKE

fat for greasing
200 g/7 oz self-raising flour
10 ml/2 tsp mixed spice
100 g/4 oz margarine
225 g/8 oz sultanas
100 g/4 oz soft light brown sugar
1 egg
milk (see method)

Line and grease a 15 cm/6 inch round cake
tin. Set the oven at 180°C/350°F/gas 4. Sift
the flour and spice. Rub in the margarine
until the mixture resembles fine breadcrumbs, then stir in the sultanas and sugar.

In a measuring jug, beat the egg lightly
and add enough milk to make up to 125 ml/4
fl oz. Add to the dry ingredients, stir, then
mix well. Spoon the mixture into the prepared tin and bake for about 1¼ hours or
until cooked through and firm to the touch.
Cool on a wire rack.

MAKES ONE 15 CM/6 INCH CAKE

☆ **FREEZING TIP** When the cake is
completely cold, wrap in foil, label and
freeze for up to 3 months.

LUNCH CAKE

It is always useful to have a cake ready to slice for lunchboxes. If making this with children in view you may wish to reduce the amount of spice.

fat for greasing
225 g/8 oz plain flour
1.25 ml/¼ tsp salt
10 ml/2 tsp mixed spice
2.5 ml/½ tsp ground cloves
5 ml/1 tsp ground cinnamon
5 ml/1 tsp cream of tartar
2.5 ml/½ tsp bicarbonate of soda
75 g/3 oz margarine
100 g/4 oz sugar
75 g/3 oz currants
50 g/2 oz seedless raisins
25 g/1 oz cut mixed peel
2 eggs
60 ml/2 fl oz milk

Line and grease a 15 cm/6 inch round cake tin. Set the oven at 180°C/350°F/gas 4.

Sift the flour, salt, spices, cream of tartar and bicarbonate of soda into a mixing bowl. Rub in the margarine until the mixture resembles fine breadcrumbs. Add the sugar, dried fruit and peel.

In a bowl beat the eggs lightly with the milk. Make a hollow in the dry ingredients and pour in the milk mixture. Stir, then beat lightly to a soft consistency. Spoon into the prepared tin and bake for 1¼ hours or until cooked through and firm to the touch. Cool on a wire rack.

MAKES ONE 15 CM/6 INCH CAKE

VINEGAR CAKE

fat for greasing
200 g/7 oz plain flour
1.25 ml/¼ tsp salt
75 g/3 oz margarine
75 g/3 oz soft dark brown sugar
50 g/2 oz currants
50 g/2 oz sultanas
25 g/1 oz cut mixed peel
175 ml/6 fl oz milk
5 ml/1 tsp bicarbonate of soda
15 ml/1 tbsp malt vinegar

Line and grease a 15 cm/6 inch round tin. Set the oven at 180°C/350°F/gas 4.

Mix the flour and salt in a mixing bowl and rub in the margarine until the mixture resembles fine breadcrumbs. Stir in the sugar, dried fruit and peel.

Warm half the milk in a small saucepan. Stir in the bicarbonate of soda until dissolved. Add this with the remaining milk and the vinegar to the dry ingredients and mix thoroughly.

Bake for 1 hour, then reduce the oven temperature to 160°C/325°F/gas 3 and bake for a further 30-40 minutes, or until cooked through and firm to the touch. Cool on a wire rack.

MAKES ONE 15 CM/6 INCH CAKE

SPECIAL CAKES

A special cake is an essential feature of any celebration, whether the occasion is a birthday tea, an informal gathering of friends or a grand wedding. Alongside seasonal cakes, this chapter includes exciting recipes that are just that bit different.

CHRISTMAS CAKE

fat for greasing
200 g/7 oz plain flour
1.25 ml/¼ tsp salt
5-10 ml/1-2 tsp mixed spice
200 g/7 oz butter
200 g/7 oz caster sugar
6 eggs, beaten
30-60 ml/2-4 tbsp brandy or sherry
100 g/4 oz glacé cherries, chopped
50 g/2 oz preserved ginger, chopped
50 g/2 oz walnuts, chopped
200 g/7 oz currants
200 g/7 oz sultanas
150 g/5 oz seedless raisins
75 g/3 oz cut mixed peel

COATING AND ICING
  Almond Paste (page 142)
  Royal Icing (page 156)

Line and grease a 20 cm/8 inch round cake tin. Use doubled greaseproof paper and tie a strip of brown paper around the outside. Set the oven at 160°C/325°F/gas 3.

Sift the flour, salt and spice into a bowl. In a mixing bowl, cream the butter and sugar together until light and fluffy. Gradually beat in the eggs and the brandy or sherry, adding a little flour if the mixture starts to curdle. Add the cherries, ginger and walnuts. Stir in the dried fruit, peel and flour mixture. Spoon into the prepared tin and make a slight hollow in the centre.

Bake for 45 minutes, then reduce the oven temperature to 150°C/300°F/gas 2 and bake for a further hour. Reduce the temperature still further to 140°C/275°F/gas 1, and continue cooking for 45 minutes-1 hour until cooked through and firm to the touch. Cool in the tin. Cover the cake with almond paste and decorate with royal icing.

MAKES ONE 20 CM/8 INCH CAKE

> **MRS BEETON'S TIP** The quickest way to complete the decoration on a Christmas cake is to apply the royal icing in rough peaks, then add bought decorations. For a change, why not bake the cake mixture in a shaped tin, for example in the shape of a star or a bell? Shaped tins can be hired from kitchen shops and cake decorating suppliers.
>
> To decide on the quantity of mixture which will fill the tin, pour water into the tin until it is full to the brim. Measure the quantity of water as you are pouring it into the tin. Do the same with a 20 cm/8 inch round tin. Compare the volumes and adjust the weight of ingredients accordingly.

SANTA CLAUS CAKE

Just the thing to leave out for Father Christmas when he delivers the presents. If you prefer cakes without lots of icing, then try one of the variations which follow this recipe.

fat for greasing
250 g/9 oz plain flour
5 ml/1 tsp instant coffee
5 ml/1 tsp mixed spice
2.5 ml/½ tsp ground ginger
200 g/7 oz butter
200 g/7 oz soft dark brown sugar
4 eggs
5 ml/1 tsp black treacle
5 ml/1 tsp vanilla essence
10 ml/2 tsp rum or lemon juice
grated rind of 1 lemon
25 g/1 oz blanched almonds, chopped
25 g/1 oz glacé cherries, quartered
200 g/7 oz currants
200 g/7 oz sultanas
200 g/7 oz seedless raisins
25 g/1 oz cut mixed peel

COATING AND ICING
  Almond Paste (page 142)
  Royal Icing (page 156)

Line and grease a 20 cm/8 inch round cake tin. Use doubled greaseproof paper and tie a strip of brown paper around the outside of the tin. Set the oven at 160°C/325°F/gas 3.

Sift the flour, instant coffee, mixed spice and ginger into a bowl. In a mixing bowl, cream the butter and sugar together until soft and fluffy. Beat in the eggs gradually. Using a spoon dipped in boiling water, add the treacle then stir in the essence, rum or lemon juice, and the lemon rind.

Stir the almonds and cherries into the flour with the remaining dried fruit, then stir both flour and fruit into the creamed mixture.

Spoon into the prepared tin and make a slight hollow in the centre.

Bake for 1 hour, then reduce the oven temperature to 150°C/300°F/gas 2 and bake for a further 1½-2 hours until cooked through and firm to the touch. Cool in the tin. Cover with almond paste and decorate with royal icing.

MAKES ONE 20 CM/8 INCH CAKE

MRS BEETON'S TIP If you find the almond paste and royal icing on top of traditional Christmas cake all too rich, then why not add an attractive topping of fruit or nuts before or after the cake is baked?

To make a splendid nut topping, shell fresh brazils, walnuts or pecans, almonds and hazelnuts. Blanch walnuts or almonds to remove their skins and lightly toast hazelnuts before rubbing off their skins. Arrange the whole nuts in circles to cover the top of the cake completely. The topping can be glazed with warmed and sieved apricot jam before it is served.

Alternatively, add an attractive topping of glacé fruits to the cooled cake. Brush a little apricot jam on the cake, then arrange halved glacé cherries, pieces of glacé pineapple, sliced crystallised ginger and roughly chopped angelica on top. Tie a festive red ribbon around the cake to complete the decoration.

*T*WELFTH NIGHT CAKE

The tradition of the Twelfth Night Cake goes back to the days of the early Christian Church and beyond. In the Middle Ages, whoever found the bean in his cake became the 'Lord of Misrule' or 'King' for the festivities of Twelfth Night, with the finder of the pea as his 'Queen'. Finding the bean was thought to bring luck. The tradition survived until near the end of the nineteenth century.

fat for greasing
150 g/5 oz margarine
75 g/3 oz soft dark brown sugar
3 eggs
300 g/11 oz plain flour
60 ml/4 tbsp milk
5 ml/1 tsp bicarbonate of soda
30 ml/2 tbsp golden syrup
2.5 ml/½ tsp mixed spice
2.5 ml/½ tsp ground cinnamon
pinch of salt
50 g/2 oz currants
100 g/4 oz sultanas
100 g/4 oz cut mixed peel
1 dried bean (see above)
1 large dried whole pea (see above)

Line and grease a 15 cm/6 inch round cake tin. Set the oven at 180°C/350°F/gas 4.

In a mixing bowl, cream the margarine and sugar until light and fluffy. Beat in the eggs, one at a time, adding a little flour with each. Warm the milk, add the bicarbonate of soda and stir until dissolved. Add the syrup.

Mix the spices and salt with the remaining flour in a bowl. Add this to the creamed mixture alternately with the flavoured milk. Lightly stir in the dried fruit and peel. Spoon half the cake mixture into the prepared tin, lay the bean and pea in the centre, then cover with the rest of the cake mixture. Bake for about 2 hours. Cool on a wire rack.

MAKES ONE 15 CM/6 INCH CAKE

*S*IMNEL CAKE

Illustrated on page 35

fat for greasing
200 g/7 oz plain flour
2.5 ml/½ tsp baking powder
1.25 ml/¼ tsp salt
150 g/5 oz butter
150 g/5 oz caster sugar
4 eggs
100 g/4 oz glacé cherries, halved
150 g/5 oz currants
150 g/5 oz sultanas
100 g/4 oz seedless raisins
50 g/2 oz cut mixed peel
50 g/2 oz ground almonds
grated rind of 1 lemon

DECORATION
Double quantity Almond Paste (page 142) or 450 g/1 lb marzipan
30 ml/2 tbsp smooth apricot jam (see method)
1 egg, beaten
White Glacé Icing (page 151) using 50 g/ 2 oz icing sugar
Easter decorations

Line and grease an 18 cm/7 inch cake tin. Set the oven at 180°C/350°F/gas 4.

Sift the flour, baking powder and salt into a bowl. In a mixing bowl, cream the butter and sugar together well and beat in the eggs, adding a little of the flour mixture if necessary. Fold the flour mixture, cherries, dried fruit, peel and ground almonds into the creamed mixture. Add the lemon rind and mix well.

Spoon half the mixture into the prepared tin. Cut off one third of the almond paste and roll it to a pancake about 1 cm/½ inch thick and slightly smaller than the circumference of the tin. Place it gently on top of the cake mixture and spoon the remaining cake mixture on top.

Bake for 1 hour, then reduce the oven temperature to 160°C/325°F/gas 3 and bake for 1½ hours more. Cool in the tin, then turn out on a wire rack.

Warm, then sieve the apricot jam. When the cake is cold, divide the remaining almond paste in half. Roll one half to a round slightly narrower than the circumference of the cake. Brush the top of the cake with apricot jam and press the almond paste lightly on to it. Trim the edge neatly.

Make 11 small balls with the remaining paste and place them around the edge of the cake. Brush the balls with the beaten egg and brown under the grill. Pour the glacé icing into the centre of the cake and decorate with chickens and Easter eggs.

MAKES ONE 18 CM/7 INCH CAKE

*P*INEAPPLE UPSIDE-DOWN CAKE

Illustrated on page 36

Serve this delicious cake with cream as a dessert, or cold for afternoon tea.

1 (227 g/8 oz) can pineapple rings
100 g/4 oz butter
275 g/10 oz soft dark brown sugar
8 maraschino or glacé cherries
450 g/1 lb self-raising flour
5 ml/1 tsp ground cinnamon
5 ml/1 tsp ground nutmeg
2 eggs
250 ml/8 fl oz milk

Drain the pineapple rings, reserving the syrup. Melt 50 g/2 oz of the butter in a 20 cm/8 inch square baking tin. Add 100 g/4 oz of the sugar and 15 ml/1 tbsp pineapple syrup and mix well. Arrange the pineapple rings in an even pattern on the base of the tin, and place a cherry in the centre of each ring. Set the oven at 180°C/350°F/gas 4.

Sift the flour, cinnamon and nutmeg into a mixing bowl. In a second bowl, beat the eggs with the remaining brown sugar. Melt the remaining butter in a saucepan and add to the eggs and sugar with the milk; stir into the spiced flour and mix well.

Pour this mixture carefully over the fruit in the baking tin without disturbing it. Bake for 45-50 minutes. Remove the tin from the oven and at once turn upside-down on to a plate; allow the caramel to run over the cake before removing the baking tin.

MAKES ONE 20 CM/8 INCH CAKE

VARIATIONS

APRICOT UPSIDE-DOWN CAKE
Substitute canned apricot halves for the pineapple, placing them rounded-side down in the tin. Arrange the cherries between the apricots.
PLUM UPSIDE-DOWN CAKE
Arrange halved and stoned fresh plums in the bottom of the tin instead of pineapple. Use orange juice instead of the pineapple syrup and place the plums cut side down. Omit the cherries.
PEAR UPSIDE-DOWN PUDDING
Use canned pears instead of the pineapple. If you like, substitute ground ginger for the nutmeg.

SWISS ROLL

Illustrated on page 37

fat for greasing
3 eggs
75 g/3 oz caster sugar
75 g/3 oz plain flour
2.5 ml/½ tsp baking powder
pinch of salt
about 60 ml/4 tbsp jam for filling
caster sugar for dusting

Line and grease a 20 x 30 cm/8 x 12 inch Swiss roll tin. Set the oven at 220°C/425°F/gas 7.

Combine the eggs and sugar in a heatproof bowl. Set the bowl over a pan of hot water, taking care that the bottom of the bowl does not touch the water. Whisk for 10-15 minutes until thick and creamy, then remove from the pan and continue whisking until the mixture is cold.

Sift the flour, baking powder and salt into a bowl, then lightly fold into the egg mixture. Pour into the prepared tin and bake for 10 minutes. Meanwhile warm the jam in a small saucepan.

When the cake is cooked, turn it on to a large sheet of greaseproof paper dusted with caster sugar. Peel off the lining paper. Trim off any crisp edges. Spread the cake with the warmed jam and roll up tightly from one long side. Dredge with caster sugar and place on a wire rack, with the join underneath, to cool.

MAKES ONE 30 CM/12 INCH SWISS ROLL

A VARIETY OF ROLLED CAKES

The classic Swiss Roll is quick and easy to make once you have mastered the technique of rolling the hot cake. The basic recipe for the light, rolled sponge can be used as a base for making cakes that are just that little bit different.

The following variations suggest combinations of flavouring ingredients, fillings and coatings.

CHOCOLATE ICE ROLL Make the Chocolate Roll following the recipe on the right. Leave the rolled cake to cool completely. Using a shallow spoon, scoop flat portions of ice cream and place them on a baking sheet lined with cling film. Replace them in the freezer so that they are firmly frozen. Just before the cake is to be served, unroll it and fill with the ice cream, pressing it down lightly with a palette knife. Quickly re-roll the cake and sprinkle with icing sugar. Serve at once, with whipped cream.

CHOCOLATE RUM ROLL Make this luscious, rich, rolled cake for special occasions. Prepare the Chocolate Roll, following the recipe on the right, and allow it to cool. Soak 50 g/2 oz of seedless raisins in 60 ml/4 tbsp of rum for 30 minutes. Drain the raisins and add the rum to 150 ml/¼ pint of double cream. Add 15 ml/1 tbsp of icing sugar to the cream and lightly whip it. Fold in the raisins and 30 ml/2 tbsp of chopped Maraschino cherries. Spread this cream over the unrolled cake and re-roll.

EASTER ALMOND ROLL Make the Swiss Roll following the recipe on the left. Leave to cool completely. Roll out 350 g/12 oz marzipan or almond paste into an oblong the same width as the length of the roll, and long enough to wrap around the roll. Brush the outside of the Swiss Roll with warmed apricot jam and place it on the rolled out marzipan or almond paste. Wrap the paste around the roll, trimming off excess and making sure that the join is underneath. Decorate the top of the roll with miniature chocolate Easter eggs.

GINGER CREAM ROLL Make the plain Swiss Roll following the recipe on the left. Place a sheet of greaseproof paper in the hot roll instead of adding the jam, then leave it to cool completely. Whip 300 ml/½ pint of double cream with 45 ml/3 tbsp of ginger wine. Mix 30 ml/2 tbsp of finely chopped crystallised ginger into half the cream and spread this over the unrolled cake, then re-roll it. Cover the outside with a thin layer of the remaining cream and pipe rosettes of cream along the top. Decorate the roll with crystallised ginger.

RASPBERRY MERINGUE ROLL Make a plain Swiss Roll as left, rolling it up with sheet of greaseproof paper instead of spreading it with jam. Whip 150 ml/¼ pint of double cream with 30 ml/2 tbsp of icing sugar, then fold in 175 g/6 oz of raspberries. Spread this over the unrolled cake and roll it up again.

Whisk 2 egg whites until stiff, then whisk in 100 g/4 oz caster sugar. Continue whisking until the mixture is smooth, stiff and glossy. Swirl or pipe this meringue all over the roll. Brown the meringue under a moderately hot grill. Decorate with a few raspberries.

ST CLEMENT'S ROLL Make a Swiss Roll as left, adding the grated rind of 1 orange to the eggs and sugar. Instead of jam, use lemon curd to fill the cake.

WALNUT AND ORANGE ROLL Make a Swiss Roll following the recipe on the left and adding the grated rind of 1 orange to the eggs and sugar. Roll the cake with a sheet of greasproof paper instead of adding the jam, then leave it to cool.

Finely chop 100 g/4 oz of fresh walnuts. Beat 15-30 ml/1-2 tbsp of honey, to taste, into 100 g/4 oz of soft cheese. Stir in the nuts and spread this mixture over the cake before re-rolling it.

CHOCOLATE ROLL

fat for greasing
3 eggs
75 g/3 oz caster sugar
65 g/2½ oz plain flour
30 ml/2 tbsp cocoa
2.5 ml/½ tsp baking powder
pinch of salt
Chocolate Buttercream (pages 144-145)
    for filling
caster sugar for dusting

Line and grease a 20 x 30 cm/8 x 12 inch Swiss roll tin. Set the oven at 220°C/425°F/ gas 7.

Combine the eggs and sugar in a heat-proof bowl. Set the bowl over a pan of hot water, taking care that the bottom of the bowl does not touch the water. Whisk for 10-15 minutes until thick and creamy, then remove from the pan and continue whisking until the mixture is cold.

Sift the flour, cocoa, baking powder and salt into a bowl, then lightly fold into the egg mixture. Pour into the prepared tin and bake for 10 minutes.

When the cake is cooked, turn it on to a large sheet of greaseproof paper dusted with caster sugar. Peel off the lining paper. Trim off any crisp edges. Place a second piece of greaseproof paper on top of the cake and roll up tightly from one long side, with the paper inside. Cool completely on a wire rack.

When cold, unroll carefully, spread with the buttercream and roll up again. Dust with caster sugar.

MAKES ONE 30 CM/12 INCH SWISS ROLL

ALMOND MACAROON CAKE

fat for greasing
150 g/5 oz self-raising flour
pinch of salt
150 g/5 oz butter or margarine
150 g/5 oz caster sugar
3 eggs
100 g/4 oz ground almonds
grated rind of 1 lemon
25 g/1 oz blanched split almonds to
    decorate

MACAROON
1 egg white
50 g/2 oz ground almonds
75 g/3 oz caster sugar
5 ml/1 tsp ground rice
few drops almond essence

Line and grease a 15 cm/6 inch loose-bottomed cake tin. Set the oven at 180°C/350°F/gas 4. Start by making the macaroon mixture: whisk the egg white in a bowl until frothy, then add the rest of the ingredients, beating well.

Make the cake mixture. Mix the flour and salt in a bowl. In a mixing bowl, cream the butter or margarine and sugar. Add the eggs, one at a time with a spoonful of flour. Stir in, then beat well. Fold in the rest of the flour, the ground almonds, and the lemon rind.

Spread a 2 cm/¾ inch layer of the cake mixture on the base of the prepared tin. Divide the macaroon mixture into 2 equal portions; put half in the centre of the cake mixture. Add the rest of the mixture and spread the rest of the macaroon mixture on top. Cover with the blanched split almonds.

Bake for 1¼ hours, covering the top with greaseproof paper as soon as it is pale brown. Cool on a wire rack.

MAKES ONE 15 CM/6 INCH CAKE

GRANDMOTHER'S CAKE

200 g/7 oz mixed dried fruit
60 ml/4 tbsp milk or brandy
fat for greasing
100 g/4 oz butter or margarine
100 g/4 oz soft light brown sugar
30 ml/2 tbsp golden syrup
150 g/5 oz plain flour
2.5 ml/½ tsp salt
5 ml/1 tsp baking powder
5 ml/1 tsp mixed spice
75 g/3 oz glacé cherries
50 g/2 oz mixed peel or coarse-cut
    marmalade
milk (see method)
3 eggs, beaten

Soak the dried fruit in a bowl with the milk or brandy for 2 hours before making the cake.

Line and grease a 15 cm/6 inch cake tin. Set the oven at 180°C/350°F/gas 4. In a large mixing bowl, cream the butter or margarine with the sugar until light and fluffy. Beat in the syrup.

In a second bowl, sift the flour, salt, baking powder and spice. Mix 25-50 g/1-2 oz of the flour mixture with the plumped-up dried fruit, cherries and mixed peel, if used.

Stir the beaten eggs and the flour mixture alternately into the creamed mixture, beating well between each addition. Lightly fold in the floured fruit mixture with the marmalade, if used. Stir in just enough milk to make a soft dropping consistency.

Spoon the mixture into the prepared tin and bake for 25 minutes, then reduce the oven temperature to 150°C/300°F/gas 2 and bake for a further 2-2½ hours. Cool on a wire rack, then coat with almond paste and decorate with royal icing, if liked.

MAKES ONE 15 CM/6 INCH CAKE

Coffee Gâteau (page 106)

Apricot Gâteau (page 107)

*P*INEAPPLE BIRTHDAY CAKE

Glacé pineapple adds a delicious, fruity tang to this special cake which is also flavoured with walnut pieces. If you like, use walnut halves and pieces of glacé pineapple to decorate the top of the cake.

150 g/5 oz sultanas
200 g/7 oz currants
100 g/4 oz glacé cherries
100 g/4 oz glacé pineapple
100 g/4 oz walnut pieces
100 g/4 oz cut mixed peel
50 g/2 oz ground almonds
grated rind of 1 lemon
15 ml/1 tbsp brandy
fat for greasing
200 g/7 oz butter
200 g/7 oz soft light brown sugar
250 g/9 oz self-raising flour
pinch of salt
4 eggs, beaten
2.5 ml/½ tsp almond essence
2.5 ml/½ tsp vanilla essence
30 ml/2 tbsp black treacle or golden syrup

COATING AND ICING
Almond Paste (page 140)
Royal Icing (page 156)
Glacé Icing (page 151) (optional)

Combine the sultanas and currants in a large bowl. Cut the cherries into 4-6 pieces each, depending on size, and add to the dried fruit. Chop the pineapple, and add to the bowl with the walnuts, peel, ground almonds and lemon rind. Add the brandy and stir well; cover and leave while preparing the rest of the mixture.

Line and grease a 23 cm/9 inch round cake tin. Set the oven at 180°C/350°F/gas 4. In a mixing bowl cream the butter and sugar until soft and pale.

Sift the flour and salt into a second bowl. Add the eggs to the creamed mixture a little at a time, adding a little flour each time. Stir in, then beat well. Beat in the essences, treacle or syrup, and a little more flour. Lastly, stir in the remaining flour, with the fruit and nuts.

Spoon into the prepared tin and bake for 1 hour, then reduce the oven temperature to 140°C/275°F/gas 1 and continue cooking for 1¾-2 hours until firm. When the cake is sufficiently brown on top, cover it with greaseproof paper. Cool on a wire rack.

Coat the cake with almond paste and decorate with royal icing; or ice only with glacé icing.

MAKES ONE 23 CM/9 INCH CAKE

BATTENBURG CAKE

Illustrated on page 37

fat for greasing
100 g/4 oz self-raising flour
pinch of salt
100 g/4 oz butter or margarine
100 g/4 oz caster sugar
2 eggs
pink food colouring
Apricot Glaze (page 140)
200 g/7 oz Almond Paste (page 142)

Line and grease a 23 x 18 cm/9 x 7 inch Battenburg tin, which has a metal divider down the centre; or use a 23 x 18 cm/9 x 7 inch tin and cut double greaseproof paper to separate the mixture into 2 parts. Set the oven at 190°C/375°F/gas 5. Mix the flour and salt in a bowl.

In a mixing bowl, cream the butter or margarine and sugar together until light and fluffy. Add the eggs, one at a time with a little flour. Stir in, then beat well. Stir in the remaining flour lightly but thoroughly.

Place half the mixture in one half of the tin. Tint the remaining mixture pink, and place it in the other half of the tin. Smooth both mixtures away from the centre towards the outside of the tin.

Bake for 25-30 minutes. Leave the cakes in the tin for a few minutes, then transfer them to a wire rack and peel off the paper. Leave to cool completely.

To finish the Battenburg, cut each slab of cake lengthways into 3 strips. Trim off any crisp edges and rounded surfaces so that all 6 strips are neat and of the same size. Arrange 3 strips with 1 pink strip in the middle. Where the cakes touch, brush with the glaze and press together lightly. Make up the other layer in the same way, using 2 pink with 1 plain strip in the middle. Brush glaze over the top of the base layer and place the second layer on top.

Roll out the almond paste thinly into a rectangle the same length as the strips and wide enough to wrap around them. Brush it with glaze and place the cake in the centre. Wrap the paste around the cake and press the edges together lightly. Turn so that the join is underneath; trim the ends. Mark the top of the paste with the back of a knife to make a criss-cross pattern.

MAKES ONE 23 x 18 CM/9 x 7 INCH CAKE

☀ **MICROWAVE TIP** Almond paste that has hardened will become soft and malleable again if heated in the microwave for a few seconds on High.

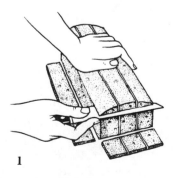

1

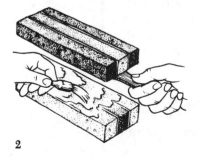

2

3

MARBLE CAKE

Illustrated on page 38

fat for greasing
175 g/6 oz butter or margarine
175 g/6 oz caster sugar
3 eggs, beaten
few drops of vanilla essence
225 g/8 oz self-raising flour
pinch of salt
30 ml/2 tbsp milk
30 ml/2 tbsp strong black coffee
50 g/2 oz chocolate, broken into chunks
Chocolate Buttercream (pages 144-145)
15 ml/1 tbsp grated chocolate

Line and grease a 20 cm/8 inch round cake tin. Set the oven at 180°C/350°F/gas 4.

In a mixing bowl cream the butter or margarine with the sugar until light and fluffy. Add the eggs gradually, beating well after each addition. Stir in the vanilla.

Sift the flour and salt into a bowl. Stir into the creamed mixture, lightly but thoroughly, until evenly mixed. Place half the mixture in a second bowl and beat in the milk.

Combine the coffee and chocolate in a bowl set over a saucepan of simmering water. Heat gently until the chocolate melts. Stir thoroughly, then add to the cake mixture in the mixing bowl, beating well.

Put alternate spoonfuls of plain and chocolate mixture into the prepared cake tin. Bake for 45 minutes-1 hour, until firm to the touch. Cool on a wire rack. Top with the buttercream and grated chocolate.

MAKES ONE 20 CM/8 INCH CAKE

VARIATION

THREE-TONE MARBLE CAKE This is popular with children. Divide the cake mixture into 3 equal parts, leaving one plain, flavouring one with chocolate and tinting the third pink with food colouring. Combine and bake as suggested left.

CHOCOLATE LAYER CAKE

fat for greasing
150 g/5 oz butter or margarine
150 g/5 oz caster sugar
3 eggs, beaten
few drops of vanilla essence
100 g/4 oz self-raising flour or plain flour
    and 5 ml/1 tsp baking powder
25 g/1 oz cocoa
pinch of salt
Chocolate Buttercream (pages 144-145)
    for filling
caster sugar for dredging

Line and grease two 18 cm/7 inch sandwich tins. Set the oven at 180°C/350°F/gas 4.

In a mixing bowl cream the butter or margarine with the sugar until light and fluffy. Add the eggs gradually, beating well after each addition. Stir in the vanilla essence.

Sift the flour, cocoa, salt and baking powder, if used, into a bowl. Stir into the creamed mixture, lightly but thoroughly, until evenly mixed.

Divide between the tins and bake for 25-30 minutes. Cool on a wire rack, then sandwich together with the buttercream. Sprinkle the top with caster sugar.

MAKES ONE 18 CM/7 INCH CAKE

> **MRS BEETON'S TIP** Always use eggs at room temperature. Eggs that have been kept in the refrigerator may be brought to the correct temperature by placing in warm water for a few minutes.

COFFEE CREAM CAKE

fat for greasing
15 ml/1 tbsp instant coffee
150 g/5 oz butter or margarine
150 g/5 oz caster sugar
3 eggs, beaten
150 g/5 oz self-raising flour or plain flour
    and 5 ml/1 tsp baking powder
pinch of salt

FILLING AND TOPPING
    150 ml/5 fl oz whipping cream
    15 ml/1 tbsp caster sugar
    Coffee Buttercream (pages 144-145)

Line and grease two 18 cm/7 inch sandwich tins. Set the oven at 180°C/350°F/gas 4. In a cup, mix the instant coffee with 10ml/ 2 tsp boiling water. Set aside.

In a mixing bowl, cream the butter or margarine with the sugar until light and fluffy. Add the eggs gradually, beating well after each addition.

Sift the flour, salt and baking powder, if used, into a bowl. Stir into the creamed mixture, lightly but thoroughly, until evenly mixed. Stir in the coffee mixture, mixing well. Divide between the tins and bake for 25-30 minutes. Cool on a wire rack.

Place the cream in a bowl and whip until it holds its shape. Add the caster sugar and whip until thick. Use to sandwich the cake layers together. Top with the buttercream.

MAKES ONE 18 CM/7 INCH CAKE

MRS BEETON'S TIP Spread the top layer of the cake with the buttercream before assembling the cake. This is much easier than first filling the cake with the cream and then trying to ice the top without causing the centre to ooze out!

HAZELNUT CAKE

fat for greasing
75 g/3 oz self-raising flour
2.5 ml/½ tsp salt
75 g/3 oz butter or margarine
75 g/3 oz caster sugar
15 ml/1 tbsp strong black coffee
1 egg, separated, plus 1 egg white
75 g/3 oz hazelnuts, skinned and ground

FILLING
    Coffee Buttercream (pages 144-145)

ICING
    Chocolate Glacé Icing (page 151)

Line and grease a 15 cm/6 inch cake tin. Set the oven at 180°C/350°F/gas 4. Sift the flour and salt into a bowl. In a mixing bowl, cream the butter or margarine and sugar until light and fluffy. Beat the coffee and egg yolk into the creamed mixture. Stir in the ground hazelnuts with the flour mixture.

In a clean, dry bowl, whisk both egg whites until stiff, and fold into the mixture. Spoon into the prepared tin and bake for 45 minutes.

When cool, split the cake in half horizontally, brushing off excess crumbs. Sandwich together with coffee buttercream and cover with chocolate glacé icing.

MAKES ONE 15 CM/6 INCH CAKE

CRUMBLED WALNUT LAYER

fat for greasing
150 g/5 oz butter or margarine
150 g/5 oz caster sugar
3 eggs, beaten
150 g/5 oz self-raising flour or plain flour
    and 5 ml/1 tsp baking powder
pinch of salt

COATING AND FILLING
Coffee Buttercream (pages 144-145)
30 ml/2 tbsp lightly browned fine cake
    crumbs
30 ml/2 tbsp finely chopped walnuts

TOPPING
Glacé Icing (page 151), using 100 g/4 oz
    icing sugar
8 walnut halves

Line and grease a 20 cm/8 inch cake tin. Set the oven at 180°C/350°F/gas 4.

In a mixing bowl cream the butter or margarine with the sugar until light and fluffy. Add the eggs gradually, beating well after each addition.

Sift the flour, salt and baking powder if used, into a bowl. Stir into the creamed mixture, lightly but thoroughly, until evenly mixed.

Spoon into the prepared tin and bake for 40 minutes. Cool on a wire rack. When quite cold, carefully split the cake in half horizontally, brushing all loose crumbs off the cut sides.

Using about one third of the buttercream, sandwich the layers together. Mix the cake crumbs and chopped walnuts together and spread on a sheet of greaseproof paper. Coat the sides of the cake with the remaining buttercream and roll in the crumb and nut coating, pressing it into place.

Surround the cake with a paper band, then pour the glacé icing on to the centre of the top of the cake, smoothing it over to cover. Press the walnuts into the icing on the rim of the cake to decorate. Leave to set.

MAKES ONE 20 CM/8 INCH CAKE

VARIATION

FEATHER-ICED LAYER CAKE If preferred, fill the cake and coat the sides with white buttercream (see page 144), using 50 g/2 oz butter. Roll the sides of the cake in 60 ml/4 tbsp browned cake crumbs and decorate the top with Feather Icing (see page 193), using Glacé Icing (see page 151) made from 150 g/5 oz icing sugar tinted with the food colouring of your choice.

ST CLEMENT'S CAKE

Illustrated on page 38

fat for greasing
150 g/5 oz butter or margarine
150 g/5 oz caster sugar
grated rind of 1 orange or lemon
3 eggs, beaten
150 g/5 oz self-raising flour or plain flour
    and 5 ml/1 tsp baking powder
pinch of salt
Orange or Lemon Buttercream (page 144)
    for filling
caster sugar for dredging

Line and grease two 18 cm/7 inch sandwich tins. Set the oven at 180°C/350°F/gas 4.

In a mixing bowl cream the butter or margarine with the sugar until light and fluffy. Stir in the grated citrus rind. Add the eggs gradually, beating well after each addition.

Sift the flour, salt and baking powder, if used, into a bowl. Stir into the creamed mixture, lightly but thoroughly, until evenly mixed.

Divide between the tins and bake for 25-30 minutes. Cool on a wire rack, then sandwich together with the buttercream. Sprinkle the top with caster sugar or spread with Orange or Lemon Glacé Icing (see page 151).

MAKES ONE 18 CM/7 INCH CAKE

THREE TIERED WEDDING CAKE

If possible, prepare the three tiers together, using a very large bowl. Cream the butter and sugar, and mix in the other ingredients by hand. Few ovens are large enough to bake all the tiers simultaneously; leave the cake(s) awaiting baking in a cool place overnight if necessary.

Make the cakes at least two months before covering and icing them with almond paste and royal icing. For instructions on icing and decorating the cakes, see pages 242 and 247.

When cool, the outside of each tier may be pricked with a skewer and sprinkled with brandy.

To store, wrap in clean greaseproof paper and a clean tea-towel, and keep in a cool, dry place.

If the top tier of a wedding cake is to be kept for some time, fresh almond paste and royal icing should be applied when it is used.

SMALL TIER
    fat for greasing
    100 g/4 oz currants
    100 g/4 oz sultanas
    100 g/4 oz seedless raisins
    50 g/2 oz glacé cherries, chopped
    25 g/1 oz blanched whole almonds,
        chopped
    25 g/1 oz cut mixed peel
    grated rind of 1 small orange
    30 ml/2 tbsp brandy
    100 g/4 oz plain flour
    1.25 ml/¼ tsp salt
    2.5 ml/½ tsp mixed spice
    1.25 ml/¼ tsp grated nutmeg
    100 g/4 oz butter
    100 g/4 oz soft dark brown sugar
    2 large eggs, beaten
    15 ml/1 tbsp treacle
    25 g/1 oz ground almonds

Line and grease a 15 cm/6 inch round or 13 cm/5 inch square cake tin. Use doubled greaseproof paper and tie a strip of doubled brown paper around the outside of the tin. Set the oven at 140°C/275°F/gas 1.

Place the dried fruit in a bowl, removing any stalks. Add the cherries, almonds, peel, orange rind and brandy and stir well. Cover and put to one side while preparing the rest of the cake mixture.

Sift the flour, salt and spices into a large bowl. In a large mixing bowl, cream the butter and sugar until pale and fluffy. Add the beaten eggs, a quarter at a time, with a little of the flour, beating thoroughly after each addition.

Using a spoon dipped in boiling water, add the treacle. Add the rest of the flour, the ground almonds and the fruit in brandy, and stir until evenly mixed. Spoon the mixture into the prepared tin and make a slight hollow in the centre. Bake for 2¾-3 hours, until firm to the touch. Cover with ungreased greaseproof paper after 1½ hours to prevent overbrowning. Cool in the tin. Leave for 24 hours before turning out.

MIDDLE TIER
  225 g/8 oz currants
  200 g/7 oz sultanas
  200 g/7 oz seedless raisins
  100 g/4 oz glacé cherries
  50 g/2 oz blanched whole almonds
  50 g/2 oz cut mixed peel
  grated rind of 1 large orange
  45 ml/3 tbsp brandy
  200 g/7 oz plain flour
  2.5 ml/½ tsp salt
  5 ml/1 tsp mixed spice
  5 ml/1 tsp grated nutmeg
  30 ml/2 tbsp treacle
  200 g/7 oz butter
  200 g/7 oz soft dark brown sugar
  4 large eggs
  50 g/2 oz ground almonds

Make as for the small tier. Bake in a prepared 20 cm/8 inch round tin or 18 cm/ 7 inch square tin, in an oven preheated to 140°C/275°F/gas 1 for 4-4½ hours. Cover the

top with ungreased greaseproof paper when the cake is sufficiently brown. Cool as for the small tier.

LARGE TIER
  575 g/1¼ lb currants
  450 g/1 lb sultanas
  450 g/1 lb seedless raisins
  225 g/8 oz glacé cherries
  100 g/4 oz blanched whole almonds
  100 g/4 oz cut mixed peel
  grated rind of 2 large oranges
  125 ml/4 fl oz brandy
  450 g/1 lb plain flour
  5 ml/1 tsp salt
  10 ml/2 tsp mixed spice
  10 ml/2 tsp grated nutmeg
  75 ml/5 tbsp treacle
  450 g/1 lb butter
  450 g/1 lb soft dark brown sugar
  10 large eggs
  100 g/4 oz ground almonds

Line and grease a 28 cm/11 inch round or 25 cm/10 inch square cake tin. Use doubled greaseproof paper and tie at least three bands of brown paper around the outside of the tin. Make the cake as for the small tier. Bake in an oven preheated to 140°C/275°F/ gas 1 for about 5½ hours. After 2 hours cover the top with doubled greaseproof paper, and gently give the tin a quarter turn. Turn again after each 30 minutes to avoid overbrowning. Cool as for the small tier.

MAKES ONE THREE-TIER CAKE

TRADITIONAL BRITISH CAKES

This chapter is a celebration of traditional British cake-making, with recipes that are both seasonal and regional, ranging from simple Rock Cakes, Classic Madeira Cake and Dundee Cake to fancy Iced Petits Fours and Black Bun.

BLACK BUN

A rich cake, encased in pastry, from the Highlands of Scotland, served either on Twelfth Night (traditionally) or at Hogmanay to celebrate the new year.

400 g/14 oz plain flour
100 g/4 oz blanched whole almonds,
    roughly chopped
700 g/1½ lb muscatel raisins, seeded
700 g/1½ lb currants
100 g/4 oz cut mixed peel
200 g/7 oz caster sugar
30 ml/2 tbsp ground ginger
30 ml/2 tbsp ground cinnamon
30 ml/2 tbsp mixed spice
2.5 ml/½ tsp freshly ground black pepper
10 ml/2 tsp bicarbonate of soda
5 ml/1 tsp cream of tartar
250 ml/8 fl oz milk
15 ml/1 tbsp brandy

PASTRY
    450 g/1 lb plain flour
    225 g/8 oz butter
    5 ml/1 tsp baking powder
    flour for rolling out
    beaten egg for glazing

Sift the flour into a large bowl. Add the almonds, dried fruit, peel, sugar and spices and mix well. Stir in the bicarbonate of soda and the cream of tartar, then moisten with the milk and brandy. Set the oven at 200°C/400°F/gas 6.

Make the pastry. Put the flour into a mixing bowl. Rub in the butter until the mixture resembles fine breadcrumbs, then add the baking powder. Stir in enough water (about 125 ml/4 fl oz) to form a stiff dough. Leave the dough to rest for a few minutes then roll out on a lightly floured surface to a thickness of about 5 mm/¼ inch. Using three-quarters of the pastry, line a 23 cm/9 inch round cake tin (about 10 cm/4 inches deep), leaving a border around the edges for overlap. Roll out the remaining pastry for the lid.

Fill the pastry-lined tin with the cake mixture, and turn the edges of the pastry over it. Moisten the edges with water, put on the lid and seal. Decorate the pastry with any trimmings, prick with a fork all over the top and brush with egg.

Bake for 1 hour then reduce the oven temperature to 160°C/325°F/gas 3, cover the top of the bun loosely with paper or foil and continue baking for 2 hours more.

Leave the bun to cool in the tin for 20 minutes; then remove it from the tin and cool completely. Keep for 1 month in an airtight tin before using.

MAKES ONE 23 CM/9 INCH CAKE

CLASSIC MADEIRA CAKE

Illustrated on page 17

fat for greasing
150 g/5 oz butter or margarine
150 g/5 oz caster sugar
4 eggs, beaten
200 g/7 oz plain flour
10 ml/2 tsp baking powder
pinch of salt
grated rind of 1 lemon
caster sugar for dredging
1 thin slice candied or glacé citron peel

Line and grease a 15 cm/6 inch round cake tin. Set the oven at 180°C/350°F/gas 4.

In a mixing bowl, cream the butter or margarine with the sugar until light and fluffy. Gradually add the eggs, beating well after each addition. Sift the flour, baking powder and salt together into a second bowl, then fold into the creamed mixture. Stir in the lemon rind and mix well. Spoon into the prepared tin. Dredge the top with caster sugar.

Bake for 20 minutes, then lay the slice of peel on top. Bake for a further 45-50 minutes or until cooked through and firm to the touch. Cool on a wire rack.

MAKES ONE 15 CM/6 INCH CAKE

☕ **MRS BEETON'S TIP** If you do not have a sugar dredger, place a small amount of sugar in a tea strainer and pass it over the top of the cake.

DUNDEE CAKE

Illustrated on page 55

fat for greasing
200 g/7 oz plain flour
2.5 ml/½ tsp baking powder
1.25 ml/¼ tsp salt
150 g/5 oz butter
150 g/5 oz caster sugar
4 eggs, beaten
100 g/4 oz glacé cherries, quartered
150 g/5 oz currants
150 g/5 oz sultanas
100 g/4 oz seedless raisins
50 g/2 oz cut mixed peel
50 g/2 oz ground almonds
grated rind of 1 lemon
50 g/2 oz blanched split almonds

Line and grease an 18 cm/7 inch round cake tin. Set the oven at 180°C/350°F/gas 4. Sift the flour, baking powder and salt into a bowl. In a mixing bowl, cream the butter and sugar together well, and beat in the eggs. Fold the flour mixture, cherries, dried fruit, peel and ground almonds into the creamed mixture. Add the lemon rind and mix well.

Spoon into the prepared tin and make a slight hollow in the centre. Bake for 20 minutes, by which time the hollow should have filled in. Arrange the split almonds on top.

Return the cake to the oven, bake for a further 40-50 minutes, then reduce the temperature to 160°C/325°F/gas 3 and bake for another hour. Cool on a wire rack.

MAKES ONE 18 CM/7 INCH CAKE

WESTMORLAND PARKIN

This makes a dense, dark parkin with excellent keeping qualities.

fat for greasing
200 g/7 oz butter or clarified dripping
  (page 23)
450 g/1 lb black treacle
450 g/1 lb fine oatmeal
200 g/7 oz plain flour
5 ml/1 tsp ground ginger
2.5 ml/½ tsp salt
10 ml/2 tsp baking powder
200 g/7 oz demerara sugar
100 ml/3½ fl oz milk
5 ml/1 tsp bicarbonate of soda

Line and grease two 20 cm/8 inch square tins. Set the oven at 160°C/325°F/gas 3.

Heat the butter or dripping and treacle gently in a saucepan, stirring until the fat has melted. Mix all the dry ingredients, except the bicarbonate of soda, in a mixing bowl and make a well in the centre.

In a saucepan over low heat warm the milk to hand-hot. Stir in the bicarbonate of soda until dissolved. Pour into the dry ingredients and mix well. Stir in the melted butter and treacle.

Spoon the mixture into the prepared tins and bake for about 1¼ hours or until cooked through and firm to the touch. Cool in the tins, then cut into squares.

MAKES TWO 20 CM/8 INCH CAKES (ABOUT 32 SQUARES)

MRS BEETON'S TIP A lighter cake may be made by substituting honey for half the treacle.

OLD ENGLISH CIDER CAKE

fat for greasing
225 g/8 oz plain flour
7.5 ml/1½ tsp grated nutmeg
1.25 ml/¼ tsp ground cinnamon
5 ml/1 tsp baking powder
pinch of salt
100 g/4 oz butter or margarine
100 g/4 oz caster sugar
2 eggs
125 ml/4 fl oz dry still cider

Line and lightly grease a shallow 20 cm/ 8 inch square cake tin. Set the oven at 180°C/350°F/gas 4.

Sift the flour into a bowl with the spices, baking powder and salt. Cream the butter or margarine with the sugar until light and fluffy, then beat in the eggs. Beat half the flour mixture into the creamed mixture. Beat in half the cider. Repeat, using the remaining flour and cider.

Spoon the mixture into the prepared tin and bake for 50-55 minutes until the cake is cooked through and firm to the touch. Cool on a wire rack.

MAKES ONE 20 CM/8 INCH CAKE

MRS BEETON'S TIP A nutmeg grater is an invaluable accessory, but is difficult to clean. A child's toothbrush, kept specifically for the purpose, is ideal.

PATTERDALE PEPPER CAKE

Store this traditional British cake for at least a week before cutting.

fat for greasing
450 g/1 lb self-raising flour
15 ml/1 tbsp ground ginger
1.25 ml/¼ tsp ground cloves
2.5 ml/½ tsp freshly ground black pepper
100 g/4 oz butter
200 g/7 oz caster sugar
100 g/4 oz seedless raisins
100 g/4 oz currants
25 g/1 oz cut mixed peel
200 g/7 oz golden syrup, warmed
2 large eggs, lightly beaten
125 ml/4 fl oz skimmed milk

Line and grease a deep 18 cm/7 inch square cake tin or a somewhat shallower 20 cm/8 inch tin.

Set the oven at 160°C/325°F/gas 3. Sift the flour, spices and black pepper into a mixing bowl. Rub in the butter until the mixture resembles fine breadcrumbs. Stir in the sugar, and add the fruit and peel. Make a well in the flour mixture, pour in the syrup, eggs and milk, and beat lightly.

Spoon the mixture into the prepared tin and bake for 2½ hours or until cooked through and firm to the touch. Cool on a wire rack.

MAKES ONE 18 CM/7 INCH CAKE

☀ **MICROWAVE TIP** Warming the syrup will make it easier to measure. If you are using syrup in a glass jar, remove the lid and heat the jar on High for 1 minute. Do not attempt this if the syrup is in a tin.

BOODLES CAKE

fat for greasing
200 g/7 oz self-raising flour or 200 g/7 oz plain flour and 10 ml/2 tsp baking powder
2.5 ml/½ tsp mixed spice
75 g/3 oz margarine
75-100 g/3-4 oz sugar
75 g/3 oz sultanas
75 g/3 oz seedless raisins
50 g/2 oz currants
2 small eggs
about 125 ml/4 fl oz milk

Line and grease a 15 cm/6 inch cake tin. Set the oven at 180°C/350°F/gas 4.

Mix the flour and spice in a mixing bowl and rub in the margarine until the mixture resembles fine breadcrumbs. Add the sugar, dried fruit and baking powder, if used.

In a bowl, beat the eggs with the milk and add to the dry ingredients and fruit. Stir well.

Spoon the mixture into the prepared tin and bake for 45 minutes, then reduce the oven temperature to 160°C/325°F/gas 3 and bake for a further 30 minutes until cooked through and firm to the touch. Cool on a wire rack.

MAKES ONE 15 CM/6 INCH CAKE

DRIPPING CAKE

Perhaps not the healthiest cake, but certainly economical.

fat for greasing
200 g/7 oz self-raising flour
pinch of salt
1.25 ml/¼ tsp mixed spice
100 g/4 oz clarified beef dripping (page 23)
75 g/3 oz sugar
75 g/3 oz seedless raisins
50 g/2 oz currants
1 egg
100 ml/3½ fl oz milk

Line and grease a 15 cm/6 inch round cake tin. Set the oven at 180°C/350°F/gas 4.

Mix the flour, salt and spice in a mixing bowl. Rub in the dripping until the mixture resembles breadcrumbs. Add the sugar and dried fruit.

In a bowl, beat the egg with the milk and add to the dry ingredients. Stir well, then beat until smooth. Spoon into the prepared tin and bake for 1 hour 10 minutes or until cooked through and firm to the touch. Cover the top with greaseproof paper after 1 hour if the cake is already brown enough.

MAKES ONE 15 CM/6 INCH CAKE

MRS BEETON'S TIP Use clarified dripping (see page 23) which does not have too strong a flavour. If it has been kept in the refrigerator, allow it to come to room temperature.

SHEARING CAKE

In Welsh this simple cake is known as 'Cacen Gneifio' and traditionally it was prepared to serve with tea for all the farm workers who gathered to help on days when the sheep were sheared and dipped.

butter for greasing
400 g/14 oz plain flour
pinch of salt
10 ml/2 tsp baking powder
200 g/7 oz butter
225 g/8 oz soft light brown sugar
grated rind of ½ lemon
20 ml/4 tsp caraway seeds
5 ml/1 tsp grated nutmeg or to taste
2 eggs
200 ml/7 fl oz milk

Line and grease a 20 cm/8 inch round cake tin. Set the oven at 180°C/350°F/gas 4.

Sift the flour, salt and baking powder into a mixing bowl. Rub in the butter until the mixture resembles breadcrumbs, then stir in the sugar, lemon rind and spices. In a second bowl, beat the eggs lightly with the milk, then stir gradually into the dry ingredients.

Spoon the mixture into the prepared tin and bake for 1½ hours or until cooked through and firm to the touch, covering the surface with a piece of greased paper or foil if it browns too quickly. Cool for 10 minutes in the tin, then invert on a wire rack to cool completely.

MAKES ONE 20 CM/8 INCH CAKE

★ **FREEZING TIP** Wrap in foil or freeze in a sealed polythene bag. Thaw the cake, still wrapped, for 3-4 hours at room temperature.

SEED CAKE

fat for greasing
200 g/7 oz plain flour
1.25 ml/¼ tsp salt
2.5 ml/½ tsp baking powder
15 ml/1 tbsp caraway seeds
150 g/5 oz butter or margarine
150 g/5 oz caster sugar
4 eggs, beaten
15 ml/1 tbsp milk (optional)

Line and grease a 15 cm/6 inch cake tin. Set the oven at 180°C/350°F/gas 4. Sift the flour, salt and baking powder into a bowl. Stir in the caraway seeds and mix well. Set aside.

Place the butter or margarine in a mixing bowl and beat until very soft. Add the sugar and cream together until light and fluffy. Add the beaten eggs gradually, beating well after each addition. If the mixture shows signs of curdling, add a little of the flour mixture.

Fold in the dry ingredients lightly but thoroughly, adding the milk if too stiff.

Spoon into the prepared tin, smooth the surface and make a hollow in the centre. Bake for 30 minutes, then reduce the oven temperature to 160°C/325°F/gas 3 and bake for 50 minutes more until firm to the touch. Cool on a wire rack.

MAKES ONE 15 CM/6 INCH CAKE

GUY FAWKES GINGERBREAD

Make this gingerbread at least a week before eating and store in an airtight tin. It is best eaten sliced and spread with butter. An excellent treat for November 5th!

fat for greasing
200 g/7 oz plain flour
1.25 ml/¼ tsp salt
15 ml/1 tsp ground ginger
50 g/2 oz soft light brown sugar
50 g/2 oz butter or margarine
100 g/4 oz black treacle
75 ml/5 tbsp milk
5 ml/1 tsp bicarbonate of soda
1 egg, beaten

Line and grease an 18 cm/7 inch square tin or a 23 x 13 x 7.5 cm/9 x 5 x 3 inch loaf tin. Set the oven at 180°C/350°F/gas 4.

Sift the flour, salt and ginger into a mixing bowl. Add the sugar. Heat the butter or margarine, treacle, and most of the milk gently in a saucepan until the fat has melted.

In a second saucepan, warm the remaining milk and stir in the bicarbonate of soda until dissolved. Pour the melted mixture into the dry ingredients. Add the beaten egg with the milk and soda mixture and beat well.

Pour into the prepared tin and bake for 20 minutes. Reduce the oven temperature to 150°C/300°F/gas 2 and bake for a further 30-40 minutes until cooked through and firm to the touch.

MAKES ONE 18 CM/7 INCH SQUARE CAKE OR ONE 23 x 13 x 7.5 CM/9 x 5 x 3 INCH LOAF

*I*CED PETITS FOURS

fat for greasing
75 g/3 oz plain flour
2.5 ml/½ tsp salt
50 g/2 oz Clarified Butter (page 22) or
    margarine
3 eggs
75 g/3 oz caster sugar

FILLING
    jam, lemon curd or Buttercream (page
        144), using 50 g/2 oz butter

ICING AND DECORATION
    Glacé Icing (page 151)
    food colouring
    crystallised violets
    silver balls
    glacé fruits
    angelica
    chopped nuts

Line and grease a 15 x 25 cm/6 x 10 inch rectangular cake tin. Set the oven at 180°C/350°F/gas 4.

Sift the flour and salt into a bowl and put in a warm place. Melt the clarified butter or margarine without letting it get hot. Put to one side.

Whisk the eggs lightly in a mixing bowl. Add the sugar and place the bowl over a saucepan of hot water. Whisk for 10-15 minutes until thick. Take care that the bottom of the bowl does not touch the water. Remove from the heat and continue whisking until at blood-heat. The melted butter should be at the same temperature.

Sift half the flour over the eggs, then pour in half the melted butter or margarine in a thin stream. Fold in gently. Repeat, using the remaining flour and fat. Spoon gently into the prepared tin and bake for 30-40 minutes. Cool on a wire rack.

Cut the cold cake in half horizontally, spread with the chosen filling and sandwich together again. Cut the cake into small rounds, triangles or squares and place on a wire rack set over a large dish. Brush off any loose crumbs.

Make up the icing to a coating consistency which will flow easily. Tint part of it with food colouring, if wished. Using a small spoon, coat the top and sides of the cakes with the icing or, if preferred, pour it over the cakes, making sure that the sides are coated evenly all over. Place the decorations on top and leave to set. The cakes may be served in paper cases, if liked

MAKES 18 TO 24

> **MRS BEETON'S TIP** For perfect petits fours it is important that all loose crumbs are brushed away so that they do not spoil the appearance of the icing. The cake is easier to cut, and produces fewer crumbs, if it is chilled in the freezer for about an hour. It should be firm but not thoroughly frozen. Use a very sharp, serrated knife to cut the cakes cleanly and chill them again briefly before coating them with the icing. Any cake trimmings can be used to make trifle, or frozen for later use.

CHOCOLATE PETITS FOURS

These tempting little chocolate cakes should be served with plain sponge petits fours if a mixture of the little fancies are being offered.

Chocolate Roll (page 73)
Almond Paste (page 142), using 450 g/1 lb
   almonds
30 ml/2 tbsp cocoa
60 ml/4 tbsp apricot jam

ICING AND DECORATION
   225 g/8 oz plain chocolate
   15 ml/1 tbsp brandy or rum
   30 ml/2 tbsp sunflower oil
   walnut halves
   crystallised ginger, sliced
   blanched almonds
   50 g/2 oz white chocolate

Prepare and bake the cake following the recipe instructions, then leave it to cool in the tin. Do not roll it up.

The almond paste is flavoured by kneading the cocoa into it until it is evenly combined. Roll out the chocolate almond paste to a rectangle large enough to cover the top of the cake.

Warm and sieve the apricot jam, then spread it over the cake. Lift the almond paste over the cake and gently press it in place. Trim the edges. Use plain biscuit cutters to cut out the petits fours, making them round, oval or diamond shaped.

For the icing, break the plain chocolate into a basin and stand it over a saucepan of hot, not boiling water. Stir occasionally until all the chocolate has completely melted. Remove the basin from over the water and gradually add the rum and oil, stirring until the chocolate is smooth and shiny. Leave to cool slightly.

Place a wire rack over a baking sheet lined with cling film. Stand the petits fours on the rack and coat them with the chocolate icing. Any icing which falls through on to the film can be saved and warmed. Leave the petits fours until half set.

Decorate half the iced petits fours with walnut halves, slices of crystallised ginger or blanched almonds. Set these decorated cakes aside to set completely.

Melt the white chocolate in a basin over hot water. Place it in a greaseproof paper icing bag and cut off just the tip. Pipe lines of white chocolate across the remaining undecorated petits fours. Leave to dry completely. If you like, place the petits fours in chocolate-coloured paper cases.

MAKES 35 TO 40

> **MRS BEETON'S TIP** Instead of the icings given in these petits fours recipes, pouring fondant icing can be used to give excellent results. Chocolate cake should be covered with plain almond paste if it is to be coated in an icing which is not flavoured with chocolate; this ensures that the dark cake does not show through.

MISS MUFFET CHEESECAKE

You don't need the whey for this traditional treat, but the curds are essential. Make them 24 hours before you intend to bake the cheesecake.

Pastry Base (page 113), using 100 g/4 oz
    plain flour
flour for rolling out

FILLING
500 ml/18 fl oz milk
15 ml/1 tbsp rennet essence
50 g/2 oz butter, melted
1 egg, beaten
25 g/1 oz self-raising flour
2.5 ml/½ tsp baking powder
pinch of salt
75 g/3 oz sugar
25 g/1 oz currants
grated nutmeg

First make the curds for the filling. Pour the milk into a saucepan and heat to blood heat (about 37°C/98.6°F). Transfer the milk to a bowl and stir in the rennet. Leave to stand at room temperature for 1 hour.

Line a sieve or colander with a thin scalded damp cloth and stand it over a bowl or shallow dish. Spoon the curds carefully into the cloth. Bring the corners of the cloth together, tie securely with string and hang above the bowl for 18 hours. By this time all the whey will have run out and the curds will be firm. You should have about 75 g/3 oz.

Roll out the pastry on a lightly floured surface and use it to line an 18 cm/7 inch flan ring. Set the oven at 190°C/375°F/gas 5.

Transfer the curds to a bowl and break them down with a fork. If they are very firm, rub them through a sieve. Add the melted butter, beaten egg, flour, baking powder, salt, sugar, currants and a little grated nutmeg and mix thoroughly. Spoon the mixture into the flan case. Bake for 25-30 minutes until the pastry is lightly browned and the filling set. Serve warm or cold.

SERVES 4 TO 6

ROCK CAKES

fat for greasing
200 g/7 oz self-raising flour
1.25 ml/¼ tsp salt
1.25 ml/¼ tsp grated nutmeg
75 g/3 oz margarine
75 g/3 oz sugar
75 g/3 oz mixed dried fruit (currants,
    sultanas, mixed peel, glacé cherries)
1 egg
milk (see method)

Thoroughly grease 2 baking sheets. Set the oven at 200°C/400°F/gas 6.

Sift the flour and salt into a mixing bowl. Add the nutmeg. Rub in the margarine until the mixture resembles fine breadcrumbs. Stir in the sugar and dried fruit.

Put the egg into a measuring jug and add enough milk to make up to 125 ml/4 fl oz. Add the liquid to the dry ingredients and mix with a fork to a sticky stiff mixture that will support the fork.

Divide the mixture into 12-14 portions. Form into rocky heaps on the prepared baking sheets, allowing about 2 cm/¾ inch between each for spreading. Bake for 15-20 minutes or until each bun is firm to the touch on the base. Cool on a wire rack.

MAKES 12 TO 14

Strawberry Meringue Torte (page 108)

Lemon Cheesecake (page 114) and Curd Cheesecake (page 110)

CAKES FROM AROUND THE WORLD

The art of cake-making is one that varies from country to country, according to the ingredients available, the climate and the temperament of the people. Here you will find just a few examples of the types of cake that are typical of other countries.

BÛCHE DE NOËL

A traditional French Yule Log to be served at Christmas time. The light sponge mixture is flavoured with rum, and chestnut buttercream is used for the filling and decoration.

SPONGE
    butter for greasing
    100 g/4 oz icing sugar
    3 eggs
    20 ml/4 tsp rum
    65 g/2½ oz self-raising flour
    icing sugar for dusting
    marrons glacés to decorate

FILLING
    2 (440 g/15½ oz) cans unsweetened
        chestnut purée
    275 g/10 oz softened butter
    100 g/4 oz caster sugar
    30 ml/2 tbsp rum

Line and grease a 33 x 25 cm/13 x 10 inch Swiss roll tin. Set the oven at 220°C/425°F/gas 7.

Warm a mixing bowl with hot water, then dry it. Sift in the icing sugar, and break in the eggs. Whisk vigorously for 5-10 minutes until the mixture is very light and fluffy. Add the rum while beating. When the mixture resembles meringue, fold in the flour gently. Pour the mixture into the prepared tin and bake for 7 minutes. Meanwhile, prepare a sheet of greaseproof paper 40 x 30 cm/16 x 12 inches in size and dust it with icing sugar.

Remove the sponge from the oven, loosen the sides from the tin if necessary, and turn it on to the greaseproof paper. Peel off the lining paper. Trim the edges of the sponge if crisp. Starting at one of the long sides, roll it up tightly with the greaseproof paper into a Swiss roll shape. Cool completely.

Meanwhile, prepare the chestnut buttercream for the filling. Turn the purée into a bowl, beat in the softened butter; then add the sugar and rum.

When the sponge is cold, unroll it carefully. Minor blemishes and cracks do not matter since they will be covered with buttercream. Cover the surface of the sponge with just over half the buttercream, laying it on thickly at the further edge. Roll the sponge up again, then place it on a sheet of greaseproof paper, with the join underneath. Cover the roll with the remaining buttercream, either using a knife or an icing bag fitted with a ribbon nozzle, imitating the knots and grain of wood. Chill before serving surrounded by marrons glacés.

SERVES 6 TO 8

DEVIL'S FOOD CAKE

Illustrated on page 56

fat for greasing
plain flour for dusting
100 g/4 oz butter
350 g/12 oz sugar
5 ml/1 tsp vanilla essence
3 eggs, separated
250 g/9 oz plain flour
50 g/2 oz cocoa
7.5 ml/1½ tsp bicarbonate of soda
5 ml/1 tsp salt

FILLING AND DECORATION
American Frosting (see page 152)

Grease and lightly flour three 20 cm/8 inch sandwich tins. Set the oven at 180°C/350°F/gas 4.

Cream the butter with 225 g/8 oz of the sugar until light, then add the vanilla essence. Add the egg yolks, one at a time alternately with 250 ml/8 fl oz cold water, beating well after each addition. Beat in the flour, cocoa, bicarbonate of soda and salt.

Whisk the egg whites to soft peaks, add the remaining sugar and continue whisking until stiff peaks form. Fold the egg whites into the creamed mixture.

Gently pour one-third of the cake mixture into each prepared sandwich tin. Bake for 30-35 minutes, until the cakes are firm. When cold, fill and cover with American Frosting.

MAKES ONE 20 CM/8 INCH LAYER CAKE

☆ **FREEZING TIP** Open freeze the cake until solid, then wrap in cling film and place in a polythene bag. Seal, label and freeze for up to 3 months.

ANGEL FOOD CAKE

flour for dusting
100 g/4 oz plain flour
275 g/10 oz caster sugar
12 egg whites (measuring 300 ml/½ pint)
7.5 ml/1½ tsp cream of tartar
1.25 ml/¼ tsp salt
5 ml/1 tsp vanilla essence
1.25 ml/¼ tsp almond essence

DECORATION
Quick American Frosting (page 153) or
Maraschino Glaze (page 141)

Sift the plain flour and 150 g/5 oz of the sugar 6 times. In a spotlessly clean bowl, whisk the egg whites with the cream of tartar, salt, vanilla and almond essence until they form soft peaks. Add the remaining sugar, 30 ml/2 tbsp at a time, whisking well; continue whisking until the whites form stiff peaks.

Sift about a quarter of the flour mixture over the egg whites; fold in. Repeat the sifting and folding in 3 more times.

Spoon the cake mixture into an ungreased 25 cm/10 inch ring tin dusted with flour and bake for 35-40 minutes, or until the cake is pale gold on top, and springs back when lightly pressed with the finger. Cool in the tin.

Decorate with American Frosting or Maraschino Glaze.

MAKES ONE 25 CM/10 INCH CAKE

🥣 **MRS BEETON'S TIP** Angel food cake is very delicate so do not cool it on a wire rack or it will mark. The traditional way to cool the cake in the tin is to invert the tin over the neck of a bottle. When the cake is completely cool, loosen it with a spatula and remove from the tin.

SACHER TORTE

This most famous of all Austrian cakes is often served as a dessert, with sweetened whipped cream.

fat for greasing
flour for dredging
125 g/4½ oz butter
125 g/4½ oz sugar
125 g/4½ oz plain chocolate
6 eggs, separated
125 g/4½ oz self-raising flour
about 50 g/2 oz apricot jam

FILLING
25 g/1 oz icing sugar
50 g/2 oz plain chocolate, grated
40 g/1½ oz softened unsalted butter

ICING
175 g/6 oz plain chocolate, grated
150 g/5 oz lump sugar
25 g/1 oz unsalted butter

Line and grease an 18 cm/7 inch loose-bottomed cake tin. Dust with flour, shaking out the excess. Set the oven at 190°C/375°F/gas 5.

In a mixing bowl, cream the butter and sugar until light and fluffy. Melt the chocolate in a bowl over a saucepan of hot water, cool slightly, then stir it into the creamed mixture. Beat in the egg yolks, one by one, until thoroughly mixed.

Sift the flour into a second bowl and in a third, whisk the egg whites to firm peaks. Fold the stiffly beaten whites into the mixture alternately with the flour, using either a metal spoon or an electric mixer on the lowest speed. Pour the mixture into the prepared tin. Set on a baking sheet. Make a slight hollow in the centre of the cake to ensure even rising.

Bake for about 1½ hours. If the cake begins to overbrown after 1 hour, lower the oven temperature to 160°C/325°F/gas 3 and continue baking until the cake is fully cooked and a skewer inserted in the centre comes out clean. Leave the cake in the tin for a few minutes, then remove from the tin and place on a wire rack to cool completely at room temperature.

Make the filling when the cake is cold. Sift the icing sugar. Melt the chocolate in a bowl over a saucepan of hot water. In another bowl cream the icing sugar and butter together. Add the melted chocolate and beat until very smooth and fully blended.

Split the cold cake in half, dusting off the crumbs, and spread the filling over the cut surfaces. Sandwich the coated halves together. Warm the apricot jam until liquid, and spread it very thinly over the top and sides of the cake.

Make the icing. Melt the chocolate in a bowl over a pan of hot water. Keep it soft over the hot water while preparing the syrup. Put the sugar in a heavy-bottomed saucepan with 175ml/6 fl oz water. Bring to the boil, and boil until the mixture forms a thread (see page 145). Gradually stir this into the melted chocolate, and beat until the icing coats a wooden spoon thickly, and can be drawn up to a point. Do not overbeat or the mixture will lose its gloss. Stir in the butter. Spread the icing quickly and smoothly over the cake.

MAKES ONE 18 CM/7 INCH CAKE

 MRS BEETON'S TIP Use a knife dipped in hot water to spread the icing.

LINZERTORTE

This cake improves in flavour if kept for two to three days before being served.

100 g/4 oz butter
75 g/3 oz caster sugar
1 egg yolk
1.25 ml/¼ tsp almond essence
grated rind of 1 small lemon
juice of ½ lemon
100 g/4 oz plain flour
5 ml/1 tsp ground cinnamon
50 g/2 oz ground almonds
flour for rolling out
200 g/7 oz raspberry jam
15 ml/1 tsp icing sugar

In a mixing bowl, cream the butter and sugar until pale and fluffy. Beat in the egg yolk, almond essence, lemon rind and juice. Add the flour, cinnamon and ground almonds, and mix to a smooth dough. Wrap in foil and leave in a cool place for 1 hour. Set the oven at 160°C/325°F/gas 3.

Roll out the dough on a lightly floured surface and use three-quarters of it to line an 18 cm/7 inch flan ring set on a baking sheet. Spread the jam over the dough base. Roll out the remaining dough into a rectangle 18 cm/7 inches long, and cut into strips about 5 mm/¼ inch wide. Arrange the strips in a lattice on top of the jam. Bake for about 1 hour, until golden-brown. Leave to cool, then remove from the flan ring and dredge with icing sugar. Serve cold with whipped cream, if liked.

SERVES 5 TO 6

★ **FREEZING TIP** Open freeze, then wrap in foil or seal in a polythene bag. Thaw for 3-4 hours at room temperature.

HASELNUSSTORTE

fat for greasing
flour for dusting
200 g/7 oz hazelnuts
5 eggs, separated
150 g/5 oz caster sugar
grated rind of ½ lemon

FILLING
250 ml/8 fl oz double cream
few drops of vanilla essence

DECORATION
whole hazelnuts
grated chocolate

Grease and flour two 23 cm/9 inch springform or loose-bottomed cake tins. Set the oven at 180°C/350°F/gas 4, then roast the hazelnuts on a baking sheet for 10 minutes, until the skins split. Rub the nuts in a cloth to remove the skins. Grind coarsely.

In a mixing bowl, beat the egg yolks and sugar together until light and creamy, and mix in the nuts and lemon rind. In a second bowl, whisk the egg whites until stiff but not dry. Fold them gently and quickly into the nut mixture. Spoon into the prepared tins, levelling the surfaces.

Bake for 1 hour or until a warmed skewer pushed into the centre of each cake comes out dry, and the sides of each cake start to shrink slightly from the edges. Cool the cakes on wire racks for a few minutes, then remove from the tins and cool completely.

Make the filling: in a bowl, whip the cream with the vanilla essence until stiff. When the cake layers are cold, sandwich them together with some of the cream, and cover the top with the remainder. Decorate with a few whole hazelnuts and chocolate.

SERVES 10 TO 12

LEKACH

fat for greasing
flour for dusting
150 g/5 oz caster sugar
2 eggs
30 ml/2 tbsp corn oil
200 g/7 oz honey or golden syrup
300 g/11 oz plain flour
5 ml/1 tsp baking powder
5 ml/1 tsp ground ginger
5 ml/1 tsp bicarbonate of soda
2.5 ml/½ tsp mixed spice
100 g/4 oz blanched halved almonds

Line and grease a 25 cm/10 inch square shallow tin. Dust with flour, shaking out excess. Set the oven at 180°C/350°F/gas 4. In a mixing bowl, beat the sugar and eggs together well. Add the oil and honey or syrup, and mix thoroughly.

Sift the flour into a bowl with all the other dry ingredients. Add alternately with 150 ml/¼ pint warm water to the honey mixture. Stir in the almonds.

Pour into the prepared tin and bake for 1 hour or until a skewer inserted into the cake comes out clean. Cool on a wire rack.

MAKES ONE 25 CM/10 INCH SQUARE CAKE

DANISH ALMOND CAKE

fat for greasing
100 g/4 oz butter
20 ml/4 tsp top of the milk
4 eggs
275 g/10 oz caster sugar
200 g/7 oz plain flour
10 ml/2 tsp baking powder

TOPPING
50 g/2 oz blanched almonds, chopped
75 g/3 oz unsalted butter
75 g/3 oz caster sugar
15 ml/1 tbsp single cream
15 ml/1 tbsp plain flour

Line and grease a 20 cm/8 inch loose-bottomed tin. Set the oven at 200°C/400°F/gas 6. Melt the butter in a saucepan, remove from the heat and stir in the milk. Leave to cool.

In a bowl, whisk the eggs with the sugar until light and foamy. Stir in the flour and baking powder alternately with the melted butter mixture. Pour into the prepared tin and bake for 35 minutes.

Meanwhile make the topping. Mix all the ingredients in a saucepan and bring to the boil. Pour over the cake while still hot (see Mrs Beeton's Tip).

Return the cake to the oven and bake for 10 minutes more. Cool in the tin for 10 minutes, then carefully remove and continue cooling on a wire rack.

MAKES ONE 20 CM/8 INCH CAKE

 MRS BEETON'S TIP Before topping the partially-cooked cake, check that it can bear the additional weight by placing a tablespoon on top of it.

APPLESAUCE CAKE

fat for greasing
400 g/14 oz cooking apples
15 ml/1 tbsp butter
75 g/3 oz sugar
200 g/7 oz self-raising flour
1.25 ml/¼ tsp salt
1.25 ml/¼ tsp ground cinnamon
2.5 ml/½ tsp ground cloves
2.5 ml/½ tsp grated nutmeg
100 g/4 oz margarine
200 g/7 oz caster sugar
1 egg
100 g/4 oz seedless raisins
100 g/4 oz currants

ICING
Lemon Glacé Icing (page 151)

Line and grease a 15 cm/6 inch square cake tin. Set the oven at 180°C/350°F/gas 4.

Peel and core the apples and slice them thinly. In a heavy-bottomed saucepan, melt the butter and add the apples, sugar and 30ml/2 tbsp water. Cook gently until soft and fluffy, then beat well. Measure out 250 ml/8 fl oz of the sauce.

Sift the flour, salt and spices into a bowl. Cream the margarine with the sugar in a mixing bowl until light and fluffy. Beat in the egg, then the apple sauce. Fold in the flour mixture and the dried fruit.

Bake for 40 minutes, then reduce the oven temperature to 160°C/325°F/gas 3 and bake for a further 20-30 minutes. Cool on a wire rack. When cold, top the cake with lemon glacé icing.

MAKES ONE 15 CM/6 INCH CAKE

SWISS CARROT CAKE

Illustrated on page 57

This dessert or party cake depends for its success of equal proportions of the main ingredients, so weigh the carrots after grating.

fat or oil for greasing
5 eggs, separated
275 g/10 oz caster sugar
grated rind of ½ lemon
275 g/10 oz ground almonds
275 g/10 oz grated carrot
2.5 ml/½ tsp ground cinnamon
pinch of ground cloves
45 ml/3 tbsp plain flour and 5 ml/1 tsp
    baking powder or 45 ml/3 tbsp self-
    raising flour
pinch of salt
15 ml/1 tbsp rum, kirsch or lemon juice
Apricot Glaze (page 140)

ICING
150 g/5 oz icing sugar
15 ml/1 tbsp egg white
20 ml/4 tsp kirsch or lemon juice

Grease a shallow 25 cm/10 inch cake tin or pie dish. Set the oven at 190°C/375°F/gas 5. Place the egg yolks in a mixing bowl, beat lightly, then add the sugar and beat together until pale and creamy. Stir in the lemon rind and almonds and beat well. Add the grated carrot and stir.

In a bowl, mix the spices, flour and salt and stir into the carrot mixture. Add the rum, kirsch or lemon juice.

In a clean dry bowl, whisk the egg whites until stiff but not dry. Stir 30 ml/2 tbsp into the carrot mixture, to lighten it, then fold in the rest lightly with a metal spoon. Turn the mixture into the prepared cake tin or pie dish and bake for 1-1½ hours or until a thin hot skewer inserted in the centre comes out clean. Cool for a few minutes, then transfer to a wire rack set over a plate.

Warm the apricot glaze in a small saucepan and spread it on the warm cake. Make the icing by combining the icing sugar, egg white and kirsch or lemon juice in a small bowl and mixing well. The mixture should be fairly stiff. Transfer it to an icing bag fitted with a small plain nozzle and pipe a pattern of concentric rings on to the cake. Leave to cool before serving.

MAKES ONE 25 CM/10 INCH CAKE

☀ **MICROWAVE TIP** If preferred, the apricot glaze may be warmed in the microwave oven for 1-1½ minutes on High.

KOEKSISTERS

These plaited doughnuts come from South Africa, where they are a popular treat. It is important that the syrup be very cold and the koeksisters very hot when dipped.

225 g/8 oz plain flour
pinch of salt
10 ml/2 tsp baking powder
50 g/2 oz butter
1 egg
105 ml/7 tbsp milk
oil for deep frying
flour for rolling out

SYRUP
225 g/8 oz sugar
stick of cinnamon or 1.25 ml/¼ tsp ground
ginger

Start by making the syrup. Combine all the ingredients in a heavy-bottomed saucepan. Add 125 ml//4 fl oz water and heat gently, stirring, until the sugar has dissolved. Bring to the boil, and boil for 2 minutes without stirring. Divide between 2 bowls, chilling both.

To make the koeksisters, sift the flour, salt and baking powder into a mixing bowl. Rub in the butter until the mixture resembles breadcrumbs. Beat the egg with the milk in a measuring jug. Make a well in the centre of the flour and pour in the egg and milk mixture. Gradually work in the flour to form a soft dough.

Heat the oil to 180-190°C/350-375°F or until a cube of bread added to the oil browns in 30 seconds. Roll out the dough on a lightly floured surface to a thickness of 5 mm/¼ inch. Cut into strips, each measuring 7.5 x 4 cm/3 x 1½ inches. Cut each strip into three lengthways and plait them together. Dampen the ends and press firmly to prevent the plaits from unravelling.

Drop 3-4 koeksisters at a time into the hot oil. Cook until golden-brown underneath, then turn them over with a slotted spoon and cook for 1 minute on the second side. Lift them out with a slotted spoon and transfer them immediately to the chilled syrup (see Mrs Beeton's Tip). Lift out the koeksisters and drain on a wire rack set over a plate to catch the excess syrup. Return the bowl of syrup to the refrigerator to chill again. Use the bowls of syrup alternately, so that the bowl in use is as cold as possible.

MAKES 8 TO 12

 MRS BEETON'S TIP Use a skewer to turn the koeksisters in the chilled syrup.

BLACK FOREST GATEAU

Illustrated on page 58

fat for greasing
150 g/5 oz butter or margarine
150 g/5 oz caster sugar
3 eggs, beaten
few drops of vanilla essence
100 g/4 oz self-raising flour or plain flour
    and 5 ml/1 tsp baking powder
25 g/1 oz cocoa
pinch of salt

FILLING AND TOPPING
    250 ml/8 fl oz double cream
    125 ml/4 fl oz single cream
    1 (540 g/18 oz) can Morello cherries
    kirsch (see method)
    25 g/1 oz plain chocolate, grated

Line and grease a 20 cm/8 inch cake tin. Set the oven at 180°C/350°F/gas 4.

In a mixing bowl, cream the butter or margarine with the sugar until light and fluffy. Add the eggs gradually, beating well after each addition. Stir in the vanilla.

Sift the flour, cocoa, salt and baking powder, if used, into a bowl. Stir into the creamed mixture, lightly but thoroughly, until evenly mixed.

Spoon into the prepared tin and bake for 40 minutes. Cool on a wire rack. When quite cold, carefully cut the cake into three layers, brushing all loose crumbs off the cut sides.

Make the filling. Combine the creams in a bowl and whip until stiff. Place half the whipped cream in another bowl.

Drain the cherries, reserving the juice. Set aside 11 whole cherries and halve and stone the remainder. Gently fold the halved cherries into one of the bowls of cream. Set aside. Strain the reserved cherry juice into a jug and add kirsch to taste.

Prick the cake layers and sprinkle with the cherry juice and kirsch until well saturated. Sandwich the layers together with the whipped cream and cherries. When assembled, cover with the remaining plain cream and use the whole cherries to decorate the top. Sprinkle with the grated chocolate.

SERVES 10 TO 12

PASSOVER SPONGE CAKE

fat for greasing
3 eggs, separated
100 g/4 oz caster sugar
grated rind and juice of ½ lemon
15 ml/1 tbsp corn oil
50 g/2 oz fine matzo meal
50 g/2 oz potato flour
pinch of salt
icing sugar for dusting (optional)

Line and grease a 25 cm/10 inch round cake tin. Set the oven at 190°C/375°F/gas 5.

In a mixing bowl, whisk the egg yolks and sugar together until thick and pale. Add the lemon rind and juice, the oil and 15 ml/1 tbsp water. Beat well. Gently fold in the matzo meal and potato flour.

Combine the salt and the egg whites in a clean, dry bowl, whisk until stiff, then fold into the mixture. Pour into the prepared tin.

Bake for 30-35 minutes. Cool on a wire rack. When cold, dust with icing sugar, if liked.

MAKES ONE 25 CM/10 INCH CAKE

CHICAGO CHOCOLATE CAKE

Illustrated on page 56

fat for greasing
flour for dusting
200 g/7 oz plain flour
300 g/11 oz caster sugar
50 g/2 oz cocoa
10 ml/2 tsp bicarbonate of soda
2.5-5 ml/½-1 tsp salt
100 g/4 oz soft margarine
200 ml/7 fl oz milk
2 eggs
5 ml/1 tsp vanilla essence

FILLING
Chocolate Buttercream (page 144-145)
Chocolate Slivers (page 235)

Line and grease two 20 cm/8 inch sandwich tins or a 33 x 23 x 5 cm/13 x 9 x 2 inch tin. Dust the lining paper with flour mixed with a little cocoa to prevent any white flour residue on the baked cake, shaking out the excess. Set the oven at 180°C/350°F/gas 4.

Sift all the dry ingredients into a mixing bowl. Add the margarine and 175 ml/6 fl oz of the milk. Stir, then beat well until smooth, allowing 2 minutes by hand or 1-1½ minutes with an electric mixer. Add the remaining milk, the eggs and essence, and beat for 1 more minute.

Spoon into the prepared tin or tins and bake for 35-40 minutes if using 2 tins, or 40-45 minutes if using a single oblong tin. When done, the cakes should be firm to the touch. Leave to cool until firm before turning out on to a wire rack to cool completely.

When cold, split the oblong cake into 2 layers crossways, brushing off excess crumbs. Sandwich together with just under half the buttercream. Sandwich the layer cake in the same way. Swirl the rest of the buttercream on top of the cake and sprinkle with chocolate slivers.

MAKES ONE 20 CM/8 INCH ROUND CAKE OR ONE TRIANGULAR CAKE

AMERICAN WALNUT CAKE

fat for greasing
200 g/7 oz self-raising flour
1.25 ml/¼ tsp salt
75 g/3 oz walnuts, chopped
150 g/5 oz butter or margarine
150 g/5 oz caster sugar
3 eggs
15 ml/1 tbsp milk

FILLING AND TOPPING
Buttercream (page 144) adding 50 g/
    2 oz chopped walnuts
American Frosting (page 152)

Line and grease an 18 cm/7 inch round cake tin. Set the oven at 180°C/350°F/gas 4. Mix the flour and salt in a bowl and stir in the walnuts.

In a mixing bowl, cream the butter or margarine with the sugar until light and fluffy. Beat in the eggs gradually, then stir in the flour and nuts, and finally the milk.

Spoon into the prepared tin and bake for 1¼-1½ hours, until cooked through and firm to the touch. Cool on a wire rack. When quite cold, split the cake into three layers. Brush off the excess crumbs, then sandwich the layers together with the walnut buttercream. Cover with American frosting.

MAKES ONE 18 CM/7 INCH CAKE

*I*TALIAN CANDIED FRUIT GATEAU

Make this marvellous gâteau 24 hours before serving to allow the flavours to develop.

CAKE
> 75 g/3 oz butter or margarine
> 75 g/3 oz caster sugar
> 2 small eggs, beaten
> 75 g/3 oz self-raising flour
> pinch of salt

FILLING AND COATING
> 150 ml/5 fl oz double cream
> 75 g/3 oz caster sugar
> 225 g/8 oz ricotta cheese, sieved
> thinly grated rind and juice of 1 lemon
> 75 ml/5 tbsp orange liqueur
> 50 g/2 oz glacé cherries, chopped
> 50 g/2 oz cut mixed peel, chopped
> 50 g/2 oz angelica, chopped
> 50 g/2 oz crystallised ginger, chopped
> 50 g/2 oz glacé pineapple slices, chopped
> 50 g/2 oz bitter-sweet dessert chocolate, grated

ICING
> 100 g/4 oz plain chocolate
> 100 g/4 oz icing sugar
> 100 g/4 oz butter
> 20 ml/4 tsp rum

First make the cake. Line and grease an 18 cm/7 inch cake tin. Set the oven at 180°C/350°F/gas 4. In a mixing bowl, cream the butter or margarine with the sugar until light and fluffy. Add the eggs gradually, beating well after each addition. Sift the flour and salt into a bowl. Stir into the creamed mixture, lightly but thoroughly, until evenly mixed. Spoon into the prepared tin and bake for 30-40 minutes until cooked through. Cool on a wire rack.

Meanwhile put the double cream in a bowl and chill in the coldest part of the refrigerator for 2 hours.

Whip the chilled cream to soft peaks, adding 30 ml/2 tbsp of the caster sugar. Spoon half the whipped cream into a second bowl and set aside for decoration. To the remaining whipped cream add the sieved cheese, the lemon rind and juice, and the liqueur. Beat until very smooth and light. Add the chopped fruits, the grated chocolate and the remaining caster sugar.

Split the cake in half, brushing off excess crumbs. Fill it with about half of the cream mixture, then use the remaining mixture to coat the sides smoothly. Chill while making the icing.

Combine all the icing ingredients in the top of a double saucepan set over simmering water. Heat until both the chocolate and the butter have melted, then remove from the heat and beat until smooth. Cool until tepid, then spread over the top of the sponge. When firm, decorate with the reserved whipped cream. Chill overnight before serving.

SERVES 6

PAVLOVA

Make the pavlova shell on the day when it is to be eaten, as it does not store well. Fill it just before serving.

3 egg whites
150 g/5 oz caster sugar
2.5 ml/½ tsp vinegar
2.5 ml/½ tsp vanilla essence
10 ml/2 tsp cornflour

FILLING
250 ml/8 fl oz double cream
caster sugar (see method)
2 peaches, skinned and sliced
glacé cherries and angelica to decorate

Line a baking sheet with greaseproof paper or non-stick baking parchment. Draw a 20 cm/8 inch circle on the paper and very lightly grease the greaseproof paper, if used. Set the oven at 150°C/300°F/gas 2.

In a large bowl, whisk the egg whites until very stiff. Continue whisking, gradually adding the sugar until the mixture stands in stiff peaks. Beat in the vinegar, vanilla and cornflour.

Spread the meringue over the circle, piling it up at the edges to form a rim, or pipe the circle and rim from a piping bag fitted with a large star nozzle.

Bake for about 1 hour or until the pavlova is crisp on the outside and has the texture of marshmallow inside. It should be pale coffee in colour. When cool, carefully remove the paper and put the pavlova on a large plate.

Make the filling by whipping the cream in a bowl with caster sugar to taste. Add the sliced peaches and pile into the pavlova shell. Decorate with glacé cherries and angelica and serve as soon as possible.

SERVES 4 TO 6

VARIATIONS

FRUIT AND LIQUEUR Add 15-30 ml/1-2 tbsp liqueur to the cream when whipping it. Stir in the fruit of your choice (pineapple, apricots, grapes, kiwi fruit, strawberries or raspberries). Pile into the pavlova case.

BANANAS AND BRANDY Thinly slice 4 bananas into a bowl. Add 30 ml/2 tbsp brandy and chill for 1 hour, turning the fruit from time to time. In a second bowl, lightly whip 250 ml/8 fl oz double cream. Fold in the bananas and brandy and add 100 g/4 oz halved, stoned, fresh or maraschino cherries. Pile into the pavlova case and sprinkle generously with grated chocolate and nuts.

LIGHT RASPBERRY AND ALMOND Instead of using double cream as the base for the filling, why not try fromage frais as a light alternative? You will need 450 g/1 lb of fromage frais. Before stirring it, drain off any thin liquid on the surface. Sweeten the fromage frais to taste with honey, then fold in 225 g/8 oz of raspberries and spoon into the pavlova case. Sprinkle lightly toasted flaked almonds over the filling.

SOFT CHEESE AND STRAWBERRY Another alternative to a double cream filling is one based on low-fat soft cheese, for example curd cheese. You will need 225 g/8 oz of curd cheese. Beat it with icing sugar to taste, then work in enough thoroughly mashed strawberries to make a soft, creamy mixture. Add about 175 g/6 oz of halved strawberries, then pile the mixture into the pavlova case.

GATEAUX AND CHEESECAKES

From light sponge-based gâteaux to luscious meringues, this chapter introduces a selection of irresistible bakes and cheesecakes that may be served for dessert or as the centrepiece for a celebration tea.

COFFEE GATEAU

Illustrated on page 75

fat for greasing
20 ml/4 tsp instant coffee
150 g/5 oz butter
150 g/5 oz caster sugar
3 eggs, beaten
150 g/5 oz self-raising flour

BUTTERCREAM
30 ml/2 tbsp instant coffee
150 g/5 oz butter
450 g/1 lb icing sugar

DECORATION
50-75 g/2-3 oz walnuts, chopped
10-12 walnuts, halved

Line and grease two 20 cm/8 inch sandwich tins. Set the oven at 160°C/325°F/gas 3. In a cup, mix the instant coffee with 20 ml/4 tsp boiling water. Set aside to cool.

In a mixing bowl cream the butter with the sugar until light and fluffy. Beat in the cooled coffee. Add the eggs gradually, beating well after each addition and adding a little of the flour, if necessary, to prevent curdling.

Sift the flour and fold it into the creamed mixture, using a metal spoon. Divide between the tins and bake for 35-40 minutes or until well risen, firm and golden brown.

Leave in the tins for 2-3 minutes, then cool on a wire rack.

Make the buttercream. In a cup, mix the instant coffee with 30 ml/2 tbsp boiling water and leave to cool. Cream the butter with half the icing sugar in a bowl. Beat in the cooled coffee, then add the rest of the icing sugar. Beat to a creamy mixture.

Using about a quarter of the buttercream, sandwich the cake layers together. Spread about half the remaining buttercream on the sides of the cake, then roll in the chopped walnuts. Spread most of the remaining buttercream on top of the cake and mark with a fork in a wavy design. Spoon any remaining buttercream into an icing bag fitted with a small star nozzle and pipe 10-12 rosettes on top of the cake. Decorate with walnut halves.

SERVES 8 TO 12

MRS BEETON'S TIP Fresh coffee essence gives the very best flavour to cakes, icings and fillings or other coffee recipes, such as ice cream. Make very strong black coffee by filtering hot water through ground coffee. Allow the coffee to cool, then pour spoonfuls of it into an ice cube tray and freeze. Pack the frozen essence in a double polythene bag and seal tightly. Remove individual cubes as they are required.

APRICOT GATEAU

Illustrated on page 76

This dessert cake looks elaborate, but is actually very easy to make.

fat for greasing
75 g/3 oz plain flour
pinch of salt
50 g/2 oz Clarified Butter (page 22) or
    margarine
3 eggs
75 g/3 oz caster sugar

FILLING AND TOPPING
30 ml/2 tbsp sherry
22-24 sponge fingers
1 (540 g/18 oz) can unsweetened apricot
    halves in natural juice
1 (142 g/5 oz) packet lemon jelly
30 ml/2 tbsp smooth apricot jam
600 ml/1 pint double cream
25 g/1 oz caster sugar
angelica (see method)

Line and grease a 15 cm/6 inch round cake tin. Set the oven at 180°C/350°F/gas 4.

Sift the flour and salt into a bowl and put in a warm place. Melt the clarified butter or margarine in a saucepan without letting it get hot. Set aside.

Whisk the eggs lightly in a mixing bowl. Add the sugar and place the bowl over a saucepan of hot water. Whisk for 10-15 minutes until thick. Take care that the bottom of the bowl does not touch the water. Remove from the heat and continue whisking until at blood-heat. The melted butter should be at the same temperature.

Sift half the flour over the eggs, then pour in half the melted butter or margarine in a thin stream. Fold in gently. Repeat, using the remaining flour and fat. Spoon gently into the prepared tin and bake for 30-40 minutes. Cool on a wire rack.

To assemble the gateau, place the sponge on a serving plate and sprinkle the sherry over. Trim the sponge fingers to a length of about 7.5 cm/3 inches. The base of each sponge finger should be level, so that it will stand straight. Drain the apricots, reserving 125 ml/4 fl oz juice in a small saucepan.

Heat the reserved apricot juice, add the lemon jelly and stir until dissolved. Pour into a shallow bowl and leave to cool but not set. Add the jam to the saucepan and heat it.

Brush the sugar-free side of each trimmed sponge finger with the apricot jam to a depth of 2.5 cm/1 inch. Dip one long side of each finger into the liquid jelly and attach to the sponge cake. The sponge fingers should touch each other, with the jam-coated sides facing inwards and the jelly sealing each to its neighbour. They should extend above the cake to form a shell. When all the sponge fingers are in place, tie a 2 cm/¾ inch wide ribbon around the finished cake, if liked, to hold the fingers in position. Place in a cool place until set.

Reserve 6 apricot halves for decoration and chop the rest. Put the cream in a bowl and whip until just stiff; stir in the sugar. Reserve 45 ml/3 tbsp of the cream. Stir the chopped apricots and the rest of the liquid jelly into the remaining cream. Place in the refrigerator until on the point of setting, then spoon on top of the sponge cake, filling the cavity formed by the wall of sponge fingers.

Return the gateau to the refrigerator for 1 hour until set. Top with the reserved cream and arrange the reserved apricot halves on top. Decorate with angelica. Chill until ready to serve.

SERVES 8 TO 10

HAZELNUT MERINGUE GATEAU

75 g/3 oz hazelnuts
3 egg whites
150 g/5 oz caster sugar
2-3 drops vinegar
2-3 drops vanilla essence

FILLING AND TOPPING
125 ml/4 fl oz double cream
5-10 ml/1-2 tsp caster sugar

Reserve a few hazelnuts for decorating the gâteau. Bake the rest in a preheated 180°C/350°F/gas 4 oven for 10 minutes. Rub off the skins. Chop the nuts very finely. Set aside. Do not turn off the oven.

Line 2 baking sheets with greaseproof paper or non-stick baking parchment. Draw a 15 cm/6 inch circle on each and very lightly oil the greaseproof paper, if used.

Combine the egg whites and caster sugar in a heatproof bowl. Set over a saucepan of gently simmering water and whisk until the mixture is very thick. Add the vinegar, vanilla essence and chopped nuts.

Spread the meringue inside the marked circles or place it in a piping bag fitted with a 1 cm/½ inch plain nozzle. Starting from the middle of one circle, pipe round and round to form a coiled, flat round 15 cm/6 inches in diameter. Repeat on the other sheet. Bake for 35-40 minutes, until crisp and lightly browned. Cool.

Whip the cream in a bowl until it stands in stiff peaks, then stir in caster sugar to taste. Place one of the meringue rounds on a serving plate and spread with most of the cream. Put the second meringue round on top and decorate with the rest of the cream and the reserved hazelnuts.

SERVES 4 TO 6

STRAWBERRY MERINGUE TORTE

Illustrated on page 93

Serve as soon as possible after assembling the torte or the meringue will soften. Do not refrigerate.

4 egg whites
pinch of salt
100 g/4 oz granulated sugar
100 g/4 oz caster sugar

FILLING
450 g/1 lb fresh strawberries, hulled
juice of 1 lemon
30 ml/2 tbsp caster sugar
125 ml/4 fl oz double cream or whipped cream flavoured with brandy or kirsch (page 161)

Line a baking sheet with greaseproof paper or non-stick baking parchment. Draw a 15 cm/6 inch circle on the paper and very lightly oil the greaseproof paper if used. Set the oven at 110°C/225°F/gas ¼.

Combine the egg whites, salt and sugars in a heatproof bowl. Set over a saucepan of gently simmering water and whisk until the meringue mixture is very thick and holds its shape.

Spread some of the meringue all over the circle to form the base of the meringue case. Put the rest of the mixture into a piping bag fitted with a large star nozzle. Pipe three quarters of the mixture around the edge of the ring to make a 5 cm/2 inch rim or border. Use the remaining mixture to pipe small meringue shapes on the paper around the case.

Bake the case for 3-4 hours; the small shells for 1½-2 hours. Leave to cool.

Make the filling. Put the strawberries in a bowl and sprinkle with lemon juice and caster sugar. Chill in the refrigerator until the meringue case is cool. Reserve a few choice berries for decoration. Halve and drain the rest and put them into the meringue case. In a bowl, whip the cream lightly and cover the fruit, or simply spoon the liqueur-flavoured cream over. Decorate with the small meringues and reserved strawberries. Serve at once.

SERVES 4

MRS BEETON'S TIP If preferred, use a spoon to make the rim of the meringue shell. The effect will not be as sophisticated, but the torte will taste just as good.

RASPBERRY VACHERIN

Make the most of the soft fruits of summer with this delectable dessert.

3 egg whites
pinch of salt
150 g/5 oz caster sugar
275 g/10 oz fresh raspberries
250 ml/8 fl oz double cream
5 ml/1 tsp caster sugar
kirsch
angelica leaves to decorate

Line 2 baking sheets with greaseproof paper or non-stick baking parchment. Draw a 15 cm/6 inch circle on each and very lightly oil the greaseproof paper, if used. Set the oven at 110°C/225°F/gas ¼.

Combine the egg whites, salt and caster sugar in a heatproof bowl. Set over a saucepan of gently simmering water and whisk until the meringue mixture is very thick and holds its shape. Spoon into a piping bag fitted with a 1 cm/½ inch plain nozzle. Starting from the middle of one circle, pipe round and round to form a coiled, flat round 15 cm/6 inches in diameter. Pipe a similar round on the other sheet. Use any remaining mixture to pipe small meringue shells. Bake for 1-1½ hours, then leave to cool.

Meanwhile make the filling. Pick over the raspberries, and leave on a plate for 30 minutes. Clean and pat dry. Reserve a few choice berries for decoration. Pour the double cream into a bowl and whip until thick and standing in firm peaks, then stir in the caster sugar and kirsch to taste.

Place one of the meringue rounds on a serving plate, spread with some of the cream, and arrange half the raspberries on top in a flat layer. Put the second meringue on top of the raspberries, arrange the rest of the raspberries in the centre, and pipe rosettes or a decorative edge of cream around the berries. Decorate the sides of the vacherin with the small meringues and angelica leaves. Serve cut in wedges like a cake, using a flat cake slice to lift the meringue on to individual plates.

SERVES 4

MRS BEETON'S TIP When filling the vacherin do not make the cream layer too thick or the vacherin will be difficult and messy to eat and serve.

CURD CHEESECAKE

Illustrated on page 94

fat for greasing
75 g/3 oz curd cheese
2 eggs, separated
50 g/2 oz butter, melted
grated rind and juice of ½ lemon
50 g/2 oz ground almonds
50 g/2 oz caster sugar
30 ml/2 tbsp self-raising flour

DECORATION
75 ml/3 fl oz double cream, whipped
6 blanched almonds

Grease and line an 18 cm/7 inch sandwich tin. Set the oven at 220°C/425°F/gas 7. In a mixing bowl, mash the curd cheese. Stir in the egg yolks, melted butter, lemon rind and juice, ground almonds and caster sugar.

In a clean dry bowl, whisk the egg whites until stiff.

Sift the flour into the curd cheese mixture, and fold in. Fold in the whites. Spoon the mixture into the prepared tin and bake for 10 minutes; then lower the oven temperature to 180°C/350°F/gas 4 and cook for about 15 minutes until the cake is dry in the centre when tested with a skewer. If the top begins to overbrown, cover loosely with foil or greaseproof paper. Cool in the tin.

Turn the cheesecake out and mark the top into portions with a knife. Decorate with whipped cream and blanched almonds.

SERVES 6

COFFEE CHEESECAKE

BASE
50 g/2 oz butter or margarine
50 g/2 oz caster sugar
1 egg
50 g/2 oz self-raising flour
2.5 ml/½ tsp baking powder

FILLING
75 g/3 oz butter
100 g/4 oz caster sugar
30 ml/2 tbsp instant coffee
15 ml/1 tbsp orange juice
30 ml/2 tbsp brandy
1 egg
50 g/2 oz plain flour
75 g/3 oz sultanas
450 g/1 lb full-fat soft cheese
250 ml/8 fl oz double cream

Combine all the ingredients for the base in a bowl and beat until smooth. Spread the mixture over the base of a deep loose-bottomed 20 cm/8 inch cake tin. Set the oven at 160°C/325°F/gas 3.

Make the filling. In a mixing bowl, cream the butter and sugar until light and fluffy. Put the coffee in a cup. Add 15 ml/1 tbsp boiling water and stir until dissolved. Add the orange juice and leave to cool. Beat into the creamed mixture with the brandy and egg. Fold in the flour and sultanas.

In a separate bowl, beat the cheese until smooth. Gradually beat in the cream. Fold the cheese mixture carefully into the butter mixture and pour into the prepared tin.

Bake for 1¼-1½ hours or until firm. Cool in the tin. Carefully remove the sides of the tin and transfer the cheesecake to a plate. Serve cold.

SERVES 10 TO 12

English Madeleines (page 119) and Butterfly Cakes (page 118)

Mocha Fingers (page 124) and Corkers (page 121)

CHEDDAR CHEESECAKE

A traditional British-style cheesecake; the sweetened Cheddar cheese mixture is baked in a pastry flan case. The filling can be enriched by adding a few raisins or sultanas that have been soaked in fresh orange juice until plump, then drained. Serve with lightly whipped double cream or luxurious clotted cream.

BASE
    175 g/6 oz plain flour
    75 g/3 oz margarine
    1 egg yolk
    15-30 ml/1-2 tbsp water
    flour for rolling out

FILLING
    1 egg, separated, plus 1 egg white
    grated rind and juice of 1 lemon
    75 ml/5 tbsp plain yogurt
    25 g/1 oz self-raising flour
    75 g/3 oz caster sugar
    150 g/5 oz Cheddar cheese, grated

Set the oven at 200°C/400°F/gas 6. To make the pastry base, sift the flour into a bowl, then rub in the margarine until the mixture resembles fine breadcrumbs. Add the egg yolk and enough water to mix the ingredients into a short pastry. Press the pastry together gently with your fingertips.

Roll out the pastry on a lightly floured surface and use to line a 20 cm/8 inch flan ring or dish. Line the pastry with greaseproof paper and fill with baking beans. Bake 'blind' for 10 minutes, then remove the paper and beans. Return to the oven for 5 minutes, then cool completely. Reduce the oven temperature to 160°C/325°F/gas 3.

In a bowl, combine the egg yolk, lemon rind and juice, yogurt, flour and sugar. Mix well, then fold in the grated cheese.

Combine both egg whites in a clean, dry bowl and whisk until stiff. Stir 15 ml/1 tbsp of the whisked egg white into the cheese mixture to lighten it, then lightly fold in the remaining egg white.

Spoon gently into the cool flan case and bake for 35-45 minutes or until firm in the centre and lightly browned. Serve cold.

SERVES 6 TO 8

MRS BEETON'S TIP For a savoury Cheddar Cheesecake, simple omit the sugar from the filling and add salt and pepper to taste. Garnish with gherkin fans.

LEMON CHEESECAKE

Illustrated on page 94

BASE
    100 g/4 oz digestive biscuits
    50 g/2 oz butter
    25 g/1 oz caster sugar

FILLING
    200 g/7 oz full-fat soft cheese
    75 g/3 oz caster sugar
    2 eggs, separated
    125 ml/4 fl oz soured cream
    15 g/½ oz gelatine
    grated rind and juice of 1 lemon

DECORATION
    whipped cream
    crystallised lemon slices

Make the base. Place the biscuits between two sheets of greaseproof paper (or in a paper bag) and crush finely with a rolling pin. Alternatively, crumb the biscuits in a food processor.

Melt the butter in a small saucepan and mix in the crumbs and sugar. Press the mixture on to the base of a loose-bottomed 15 cm/6 inch cake tin. Put in a cool place until the cheesecake has set.

Make the filling. In a mixing bowl, beat the cheese and sugar together. Add the egg yolks and beat well. Stir in the soured cream.

Place 45 ml/3 tbsp water in a small basin and sprinkle the gelatine on to the liquid. Stand the basin over a saucepan of hot water and stir the gelatine until it has dissolved completely. Stir the lemon rind, juice and dissolved gelatine into the cheese mixture.

In a clean, dry bowl whisk the egg whites until stiff and fold carefully into the mixture. Pour into the prepared tin and chill for 45 minutes-1 hour until firm. When quite cold,

remove from the tin and decorate with whipped cream and crystallised lemon slices.

SERVES 4 TO 6

VARIATIONS

LIME CHEESECAKE Fresh limes are readily available in good supermarkets and they can be used to make a delicious cheesecake. Substitute the rind and juice of 2 limes for the lemon in the main recipe.

PINEAPPLE CHEESECAKE Pour 1 (376 g/13 oz) can of crushed pineapple into a sieve and leave to drain over a basin. Squeeze as much juice as possible out of the fruit, then mix the pineapple into the soft cheese and sugar. Dissolve the gelatine in the strained juice and omit the water.

STRAWBERRY CHEESECAKE A very simple, fresh fruit topping turns cheesecake into a spectacular summer speciality. Top the cheesecake with halved strawberries, over-lapping them in concentric circles out from the middle of the cheesecake. Warm 30 ml/2 tbsp of redcurrant jelly in a basin over hot water and stir in 15 ml/1 tbsp of port wine. Leave to cool slightly, then brush this glaze over the strawberries.

☀ **MICROWAVE TIP** Dissolve the gelatine in the microwave if preferred. Stir it into the water in a small bowl, let stand until spongy, then cook on High for 30-45 seconds.

RASPBERRY YOGURT CHEESECAKE

BASE
   fat for greasing
   50 g/2 oz butter
   50 g/2 oz caster sugar
   15 ml/1 tbsp golden syrup
   25 g/1 oz walnuts, chopped
   50 g/2 oz crisp rice cereal

FILLING
   15 ml/1 tbsp gelatine
   300 g/11 oz cottage cheese
   125 ml/4 fl oz raspberry flavoured yogurt
   15 ml/1 tbsp lemon juice
   3 eggs, separated
   225 g/8 oz caster sugar
   250 ml/8 fl oz double cream
   1 (175 g/6 oz) can raspberries

GLAZE (optional)
   syrup from canned raspberries
   10 ml/2 tsp arrowroot
   few drops of red food colouring

Grease a 20 cm/8 inch loose-bottomed cake tin. Melt the butter, sugar and syrup together in a saucepan. Add the walnuts and crisp rice cereal. Stir well and press the mixture on to the base of a prepared cake tin. Chill for 10 minutes.

Make the filling. Place 45 ml/3 tbsp water in a small basin and sprinkle the gelatine on to the liquid. Stand the basin over a saucepan of hot water and stir the gelatine until it has dissolved completely .

Sieve the cottage cheese into a bowl, add the yogurt and lemon juice and beat until smooth. Combine the egg yolks and 150 g/5 oz of the sugar in a saucepan and cook over low heat, stirring all the time, until the mixture thickens. Remove from the heat and pour into a mixing bowl. Add the dissolved gelatine, mix well, then allow to cool until the mixture is beginning to thicken.

Stir the yogurt and cheese mixture into the cooled gelatine mixture. In a clean dry bowl, whisk the egg whites until stiff, then gradually whisk in the remaining sugar. In a separate bowl, whip the cream until it just holds its shape. Fold the cream into the mixing bowl, then fold in the egg whites. Pour carefully into the prepared tin. Chill the mixture for at least 4 hours.

If leaving the cake unglazed, remove from the tin, discard the syrup from the can of raspberries and arrange the fruit on top. Chill before serving. If glazing the cake, make up the can syrup to 125 ml/4 fl oz with water and blend it into the arrowroot in a small saucepan. Bring to the boil, stirring all the time, then reduce the heat and simmer for 2-3 minutes until the sauce thickens and clears. Add a few drops of red food colouring. Arrange the fruit on top of the cake and coat with the glaze. Chill in the refrigerator before serving.

SERVES 8 TO 10

VARIATIONS

Use the same quantity of canned or frozen peaches, strawberries, blackcurrants, apricots or black cherries with the appropriate yogurt and food colouring.

SMALL CAKES

From Basic Buns and tray bakes to Mocha Fingers and Mayfair Cakes, this section illustrates that small cakes can be simple or special. Whether you intend to batch bake for the freezer or prepare a treat for tea, small cakes are quick to make and simple to serve.

*B*ASIC BUNS

These small buns may be baked in paper cases or greased patty tins if preferred, in which case the consistency should be softer than when the buns are put on a baking sheet. The mixture should drop off the spoon with a slight shake, so increase the milk to about 125 ml/4 fl oz. If baked in patty tins, the mixture will make 14 to 16 buns.

fat for greasing
200 g/7 oz self-raising flour
1.25 ml/¼ tsp salt
75 g/3 oz margarine
75 g/3 oz sugar
1 egg
milk (see method)
Glacé Icing (page 151) to decorate
    (optional)

Thoroughly grease 2 baking sheets. Set the oven at 200°C/400°F/gas 6.

Sift the flour and salt into a mixing bowl. Rub in the margarine until the mixture resembles fine breadcrumbs. Stir in the sugar. Put the egg into a measuring jug and add enough milk to make up to 125 ml/4 fl oz. Add the liquid to the dry ingredients and mix with a fork to a sticky stiff mixture that will support the fork.

Divide the mixture into 12-14 portions. Form into rocky heaps on the prepared baking sheets, allowing about 2 cm/¾ inch between each for spreading. Bake for 15-20 minutes or until each bun is firm to the touch

on the base. Cool on a wire rack, then coat with icing, if liked.

MAKES 12 TO 14

VARIATIONS

CHOCOLATE BUNS Add 50 g/2 oz cocoa to the flour and 5 ml/1 tsp vanilla essence with the milk.
CHOCOLATE CHIP BUNS Add 100 g/4 oz of cooking chocolate chips with the sugar.
COCONUT BUNS Add 75 g/3 oz desiccated coconut with the flour and an extra 10 ml/2 tsp milk.
FRUIT BUNS Add 75 g/3 oz mixed dried fruit with the sugar.
SEED BUNS Add 15 ml/1 tbsp caraway seeds with the sugar.
SPICE BUNS Add 5 ml/1 tsp mixed spice or 2.5 ml/½ tsp ground cinnamon and 2.5 ml/½ tsp grated nutmeg with the flour.
WALNUT ORANGE BUNS Add the grated rind of 1 orange to the flour. Stir in 100 g/4 oz finely chopped walnuts with the sugar.

 MRS BEETON'S TIP Plain flour may be used for the buns, but add 10 ml/2 tsp baking powder with the sugar.

RASPBERRY BUNS

fat for greasing
200 g/7 oz self-raising flour
1.25 ml/¼ tsp salt
75 g/3 oz margarine
75 g/3 oz sugar
1 egg
milk (see method)
60-75 ml/4-5 tbsp raspberry jam
beaten egg for brushing
caster sugar for sprinkling

Thoroughly grease 2 baking sheets. Set the oven at 200°C/400°F/gas 6.

Sift the flour and salt into a mixing bowl. Rub in the margarine until the mixture resembles fine breadcrumbs. Stir in the sugar. Put the egg into a measuring jug and add enough milk to make up to 125 ml/4 fl oz. Add the liquid to the dry ingredients and mix with a fork to a sticky stiff mixture that will support the fork.

Divide the mixture into 12-14 portions. Form into 12-14 balls with lightly floured hands. Make a deep dent in the centre of each and drop 5 ml/1 tsp raspberry jam inside. Close the bun mixture over the jam. Brush with egg and sprinkle with sugar, then arrange on the prepared sheets, allowing about 2 cm/¾ inch between each for spreading. Bake for 15-20 minutes or until each bun is firm to the touch on the base. Cool on a wire rack.

MAKES 12 TO 14

GINGER BUNS

fat for greasing (optional)
150 g/5 oz self-raising flour
pinch of salt
5 ml/1 tsp ground ginger
1.25 ml/¼ tsp ground cinnamon
75 g/3 oz butter or margarine
50 g/2 oz soft light brown sugar
25 g/1 oz blanched almonds, chopped
1 egg
20 ml/4 tsp black treacle
20 ml/4 tsp golden syrup
30 ml/2 tbsp milk

Grease 18-20 bun tins or arrange an equivalent number of paper cake cases on baking sheets. Set the oven at 190°C/375°F/gas 5.

Sift the flour, salt and spices into a mixing bowl. Rub in the butter or margarine until the mixture resembles fine breadcrumbs. Stir in the sugar and almonds.

Put the egg into a measuring jug and add the treacle, syrup and milk. Mix well. Add the liquid to the dry ingredients and beat until smooth.

Divide the mixture between the prepared bun tins or paper cases. Bake for 15-20 minutes or until well risen and cooked through. Cool on a wire rack.

MAKES 18 TO 20

> ☀ **MICROWAVE TIP** The jug in which the egg, treacle, syrup and milk were mixed will be easy to clean if filled with water and heated in the microwave on High for 2-3 minutes. Take care when pouring the water away; it will be very hot. The steam generated in the microwave oven will have the added effect of loosening any grease on the walls, so give the cabinet a quick wipe at the same time.

HONEY BUNS

fat for greasing (optional)
200 g/7 oz self-raising flour
pinch of salt
75 g/3 oz butter or margarine
25 g/1 oz caster sugar
1 egg
30 ml/2 tbsp clear honey
30 ml/2 tbsp milk

Grease 18-20 bun tins or arrange an equivalent number of paper cake cases on baking sheets. Set the oven at 190°C/375°F/gas 5.

Sift the flour and salt into a mixing bowl. Rub in the butter or margarine until the mixture resembles fine breadcrumbs. Stir in the sugar.

Put the egg into a measuring jug and add the honey and milk. Mix well. Add the liquid to the dry ingredients and beat until smooth.

Divide the mixture between the prepared bun tins or paper cases. Bake for 15-20 minutes or until well risen and cooked through. Cool on a wire rack.

MAKES 18 TO 20

BUTTERFLY CAKES

Illustrated on page 111

fat for greasing
100 g/4 oz self-raising flour
pinch of salt
100 g/4 oz butter or margarine
100 g/4 oz caster sugar
2 eggs, beaten

DECORATION
150 ml/5 fl oz double cream
5 ml/1 tsp caster sugar
1.25 ml/¼ tsp vanilla essence
icing sugar for dusting

Grease 12-14 bun tins. Set the oven at 180°C/350°F/gas 4. Mix the flour and salt in a bowl.

In a mixing bowl, cream the butter or margarine with the sugar until light and fluffy. Beat in the eggs, then lightly stir in the flour and salt. Divide the mixture evenly between the prepared bun tins, and bake for 15-20 minutes until golden brown. Cool on a wire rack.

In a bowl, whip the cream with the caster sugar and vanilla essence until stiff. Transfer to a piping bag fitted with a large star nozzle.

When the cakes are cold, cut a round off

the top of each. Cut each round in half to create two 'butterfly wings'. Pipe a star of cream on each cake, then add the 'wings', placing them cut side down, and slightly apart. Dust with icing sugar.

MAKES 12 TO 14

ENGLISH MADELEINES

Illustrated on page 111

fat for greasing
100 g/4 oz self-raising flour
pinch of salt
100 g/4 oz butter or margarine
100 g/4 oz caster sugar
2 eggs, beaten

DECORATION
45 ml/3 tbsp smooth apricot jam
25 g/1 oz desiccated coconut
glacé cherries, halved
20 angelica leaves

Thoroughly grease 10 dariole moulds. Set the oven at 180°C/350°F/gas 4. Mix the flour and salt in a bowl.

In a mixing bowl cream the butter or margarine with the sugar until light and fluffy. Beat in the eggs, then lightly stir in the flour and salt. Divide the mixture evenly between the prepared moulds and bake for 15-20 minutes until golden brown. Cool on a wire rack.

Trim off the rounded ends of the cakes, if necessary, and stand upright. Warm the jam in a small saucepan, then brush the cakes all over. Toss in coconut. Decorate the top of each with a glacé cherry or angelica leaves or both.

MAKES 10

CHOCOLATE MOTHS

fat for greasing
100 g/4 oz self-raising flour
pinch of salt
30 ml/2 tbsp cocoa
100 g/4 oz butter or margarine
100 g/4 oz caster sugar
2 eggs, beaten
15 ml/1 tbsp milk

DECORATION
Buttercream (page 144), using 50 g/2 oz butter
chocolate vermicelli

Grease 12-14 bun tins. Set the oven at 180°C/350°F/gas 4. Mix the flour, salt and cocoa in a bowl.

In a mixing bowl, cream the butter or margarine with the sugar until light and fluffy. Beat in the eggs and milk, then lightly stir in the flour mixture. Divide the mixture evenly between the prepared bun tins, and bake for 15-20 minutes until golden brown. Cool on a wire rack.

Make the buttercream and place it in an icing bag fitted with a large star nozzle.

When the cakes are cold, cut a round off the top of each. Cut each round in half to create 2 'moth wings'. Pipe a star of buttercream on each cake, then add the 'wings', placing them cut side down, and slightly apart. Sprinkle with chocolate vermicelli.

MAKES 12 TO 14

APRICOT BASKETS

fat for greasing
100 g/4 oz self-raising flour
pinch of salt
100 g/4 oz butter or margarine
100 g/4 oz caster sugar
2 eggs, beaten

DECORATION
1 (425 g/15 oz) can apricot halves in syrup
¼ (142 g/5 oz) packet lemon jelly cubes
1 (15 cm/6 inch) stick angelica
150 ml/5 fl oz double cream
5 ml/1 tsp caster sugar

Grease 12-14 bun tins. Set the oven at 180°C/350°F/gas 4. Mix the flour and salt in a bowl.

In a mixing bowl, cream the butter or margarine with the sugar until light and fluffy. Beat in the eggs, then lightly stir in the flour and salt. Divide the mixture evenly between the prepared bun tins, and bake for 15-20 minutes until golden brown. Cool on a wire rack.

While the cakes are cooling, drain the apricots, reserving 125 ml/4 fl oz of the syrup in a small saucepan. Bring the syrup to the boil, then add the jelly cubes and stir until dissolved. Set aside to cool.

Soften the angelica (see Mrs Beeton's Tip), then cut it into 12-14 strips 5 mm/ ¼ inch wide. In a bowl, whip the cream with the sugar until stiff.

When the cakes are cold and the jelly is just on the point of setting, place half an apricot, rounded side uppermost, on the top of each cake. Coat each apricot with jelly. Using a piping bag fitted with a small star nozzle, pipe stars of cream around the apricots. Arch the strips of angelica over the cakes to form handles, pushing them in to the sides of the cakes.

MAKES 12 TO 14

MRS BEETON'S TIP Soften the angelica by placing it in a bowl of very hot water for 3-4 minutes. Pat dry on absorbent kitchen paper.

CORKERS

Illustrated on page 112

fat for greasing
100 g/4 oz self-raising flour
pinch of salt
100 g/4 oz butter or margarine
100 g/4 oz caster sugar
2 eggs, beaten

DECORATION
Apricot Glaze (page 140)
15 g/½ oz pistachio nuts, blanched and
　chopped
150 ml/5 fl oz double cream
icing sugar for dusting

Grease 12-14 bun tins. Set the oven at
180°C/350°F/gas 4. Mix the flour and salt in a
bowl.

In a mixing bowl, cream the butter or
margarine with the sugar until light and
fluffy. Beat in the eggs, then lightly stir in the
flour and salt. Divide the mixture evenly
between the prepared bun tins, and bake for
15-20 minutes until golden brown. Cool on a
wire rack.

When the cakes are cold, remove a small
cylindrical section about 1-2 cm/½-⅓ inch
deep from the centre of each cake, using an
apple corer or small cutter. Have both the
apricot glaze and the chopped nuts ready.

Dip the top of each cake cork in glaze then
in nuts. Spoon the rest of the glaze into the
hollows in each cake.

In a bowl, whip the cream until stiff. Using
a piping bag fitted with a star nozzle, pipe a
cream star on top of the glaze in each cake
hollow. Return the corks, pressing them
down lightly, then dust with icing sugar.

MAKES 12 TO 14

BROWNIES

*Brownies should be moist and chewy. Do not
overbake them.*

fat for greasing
150 g/5 oz margarine
150 g/5 oz caster sugar
2 eggs
50 g/2 oz plain flour
30 ml/2 tbsp cocoa
100 g/4 oz walnuts, chopped

Line and grease a shallow 15 cm/6 inch
square tin. Set the oven at 180°C/350°F/
gas 4.

Cream the margarine and sugar in a
mixing bowl until light and fluffy. Beat in the
eggs. Sift the flour and cocoa into a second
bowl, then fold in. Add half the chopped
walnuts to the mixture.

Spread the mixture evenly in the prepared
tin and bake for 10 minutes; then sprinkle
the rest of the walnuts all over the surface.
Bake for 15 minutes more. Cool in the tin.
When cold, cut into squares.

MAKES ABOUT 9

VARIATION

CAROB BROWNIES Follow the recipe
above but substitute 45 ml/3 tbsp carob
powder for the cocoa.

BUTTERSCOTCH BROWNIES

Rich, gooey and delightfully chewy, these are bound to prove popular.

fat for greasing
75 g/3 oz butter
175 g/6 oz soft light brown sugar
1 egg, beaten
5 ml/1 tsp vanilla essence
75 g/3 oz plain flour
5 ml/1 tsp baking powder
1.25 ml/¼ tsp salt
50 g/2 oz dates, chopped
50 g/2 oz blanched almonds, chopped

Line and grease an 18 cm/7 inch square tin. Set the oven at 160°C/325°F/gas 3.

Combine the butter and sugar in a large heavy-bottomed saucepan and heat gently until all the sugar has dissolved, stirring occasionally. Remove from the heat, cool slightly, then blend in the egg and vanilla essence.

Sift the flour, baking powder and salt into a bowl. Add the dates and mix to coat in flour. Stir the flour mixture into the saucepan with the almonds and mix well.

Spoon the mixture into the prepared tin and bake for 20-30 minutes. Cool in the tin. When cold, cut into squares.

MAKES 20

CHOCOLATE SPICE SQUARES

The combination of chocolate and cinnamon makes these delicious tray-bake cakes just that bit different. If you want to make them extra special, top them with melted chocolate.

fat for greasing
225 g/8 oz margarine
225 g/8 oz soft light brown sugar
4 eggs
225 g/8 oz self-raising flour
30 ml/2 tbsp cocoa
10 ml/2 tsp cinnamon

Base-line and grease a roasting tin, measuring about 25 x 30 cm/10 x 12 inches. Set the oven at 180°C/350°F/gas 4.

Cream the margarine and sugar together until soft and light. Beat in the eggs. Sift the flour with the cocoa and the cinnamon, then fold these dry ingredients into the mixture.

Turn the mixture into the prepared tin and smooth it out evenly. Bake for about 1 hour, until the mixture is evenly risen and firm to the touch. Leave to cool in the tin for 15 minutes, then cut the cake into 5 cm/2 inch squares and transfer them to a wire rack to cool completely.

MAKES 35

☆ **FREEZING TIP** The squares of cake freeze very well and individual portions can be removed as required – ideal for lunch boxes. Pack the pieces of cake in a large rigid container leaving a very small space between each square. Alternatively, open freeze the squares on a baking sheet lined with cling film. When solid, stack the squares in polythene bags and seal.

A VARIETY OF TRAY BAKES

By baking a large quantity of cake mixture in a roasting tin or large baking tin, then cutting it into squares, you can make a good batch of individual cakes very speedily. It is a good idea to set aside a roasting tin specifically for baking cakes. Use the mixture for the Chocolate Spice Squares as a base and try some of the ideas given here.

FRUIT 'N' NUT SQUARES Omit the cocoa from the mixture. Instead, fold in 225 g/8 oz of chopped nuts – walnuts, hazelnuts or mixed nuts – and 100 g/4 oz of mixed dried fruit.

ALMOND SQUARES Omit the cocoa from the Chocolate Spice Squares. Add a few drops of almond essence to the fat and sugar. Fold in 225 g/8 oz of ground almonds with the flour. Sprinkle 100 g/4 oz of flaked almonds over the mixture once it is smoothed in the tin.

COCONUT SQUARES The chocolate can be omitted if liked, or it can be left in the mixture as its flavour is complementary to the coconut. Add 225 g/8 oz of desiccated coconut after the flour is folded in. Soften the mixture with 60 ml/4 tbsp of milk or orange juice. The cooked squares can be spread with apricot or raspberry jam and sprinkled with desiccated or long-thread coconut.

MARBLED SQUARES Prepare the mixture, omitting the cocoa. Divide it into two portions and flavour one half with cocoa. Add a little grated orange rind and juice to the second portion. Drop small spoonfuls of the mixture into the prepared tin and drag the point of a knife through just once. Do not over-swirl the two flavours or they will blend into one during cooking. Top the cooled cakes with melted chocolate.

MARMALADE SQUARES Make up the cake mixture, creaming 60 ml/4 tbsp of marmalade with the fat and sugar and omitting the cocoa. Glaze the tops of the cakes with warmed marmalade.

CRUMBLY APPLE SQUARES

fat for greasing
150 ml/¼ pint apple purée
1 Cox's Orange Pippin apple, peeled, cored and chopped
100 g/4 oz butter or margarine
100 g/4 oz sugar
1 egg
175 g/6 oz self-raising flour

TOPPING
50 g/2 oz plain flour
25 g/1 oz butter or margarine
30 ml/2 tbsp caster sugar
100 g/4 oz walnuts, chopped
1.25 ml/¼ tsp ground cloves
5 ml/1 tsp cinnamon

Line and grease an 18 cm/7 inch shallow, square tin, allowing the paper to stand above the rim of the tin by 2.5 cm/1 inch. Set the oven at 180°C/350°F/gas 4.

Make sure that the apple purée is very smooth and absolutely cold, then stir in the chopped apple. Cream the butter or margarine and sugar until pale and very soft. Beat in the egg and the apple purée. Fold in the flour. Transfer the mixture to the prepared tin, spreading it out evenly.

For the crumble topping, sift the flour into a bowl and rub in the butter or margarine until the mixture resembles fine breadcrumbs. Stir in the sugar, nuts and spices, then sprinkle this crumble lightly over the top of the cake mixture. Bake for 50-60 minutes, until the cake is evenly risen and the topping crisp and brown.

Allow to cool in the tin for 15 minutes, then cut into squares and transfer to a wire rack to cool completely. Store in an airtight container.

MAKES 16

MOCHA FINGERS

Illustrated on page 112

fat for greasing
75 g/3 oz plain flour
2.5 ml/½ tsp salt
50 g/2 oz Clarified Butter (page 22) or
    margarine
3 eggs
75 g/3 oz caster sugar

DECORATION
    Coffee Buttercream (pages 144-145)
        using 50 g/2 oz butter
    50 g/2 oz toasted almond flakes
    icing sugar for dredging

Line and grease a 15 x 25 cm/6 x 10 inch rectangular cake tin. Set the oven at 180°C/350°F/gas 4.

Sift the flour and salt into a bowl and put in a warm place. Melt the clarified butter or margarine without letting it get hot.

Whisk the eggs lightly in a mixing bowl. Add the sugar and place the bowl over a saucepan of hot water. Whisk for 10-15 minutes until thick. Take care that the bottom of the bowl does not touch the water. Remove from the heat and continue whisking until at blood-heat. The melted butter should be at the same temperature.

Sift half the flour over the eggs, then pour in half the melted butter or margarine in a thin stream. Fold in gently. Repeat, using the remaining flour and fat. Spoon gently into the tin and bake for 30-40 minutes. Cool.

Spread the top of the cold sponge with the buttercream. Cover with the toasted almonds and dredge with icing sugar. Cut into 20 2.5 cm/1 inch fingers.

MAKES 20

MAYFAIR CAKES

fat for greasing
100 g/4 oz plain flour
2.5 ml/½ tsp salt
75 g/3 oz Clarified Butter (page 22) or
    margarine
4 eggs
100 g/4 oz caster sugar

DECORATION
    300 ml/½ pint double cream
    10 ml/2 tsp caster sugar
    chocolate vermicelli

Line and grease a 20 x 30 cm/8 x 12 inch Swiss roll tin. Set the oven at 180°C/350°F/gas 4.

Sift the flour and salt into a bowl and put in a warm place. Melt the clarified butter or margarine without letting it get hot. Put to one side.

Whisk the eggs lightly in a mixing bowl. Add the sugar and place the bowl over a saucepan of hot water. Whisk for 10-15 minutes until thick. Take care that the bottom of the bowl does not touch the water. Remove from the heat. Continue whisking until the mixture is at blood-heat. The melted butter or margarine should be at the same temperature.

Sift half the flour over the eggs, then pour in half the melted butter or margarine in a thin stream. Fold in gently. Repeat, using the remaining flour and fat. Spoon gently into the prepared tin and bake for 30-40 minutes. Cool on a wire rack.

Cut the cold sponge into about eighteen 4 cm/1½ inch rounds. In a bowl, whip the cream with the sugar until fairly stiff. Use most of the cream to spread over the top and sides of each cake. Coat with chocolate vermicelli, spreading it lightly with a round-bladed knife. Using a piping bag fitted with a large rose nozzle, pipe the remaining cream on to each cake in a star.

MAKES 18

SWISS SHORTCAKES

150 g/5 oz butter
50 g/2 oz caster sugar
150 g/5 oz plain flour
few drops of vanilla essence

DECORATION
  glacé cherries
  angelica, cut into diamonds
  smooth red jam

Place 16 paper cases in dry bun tins. Set the oven at 180°C/350°F/gas 4.

In a mixing bowl, cream the butter and sugar until light and fluffy. Work in the flour and vanilla essence, then spoon the mixture into a piping bag fitted with a large star nozzle. Pipe the mixture in whorls into the prepared paper cases.

Bake for 15-20 minutes. Cool on a wire rack. Decorate the shortcakes with glacé cherries and angelica diamonds kept in place with a tiny dab of jam.

MAKES 16

🥣 MRS BEETON'S TIP Make mini-shortcakes for a child's birthday party. Fit a small star nozzle on the piping bag and pipe the mixture into paper sweet cases instead of cupcake cases. Bake for about 10 minutes.

WHOLEMEAL ALMOND SHORTCAKES

fat for greasing
75 g/3 oz butter
40 g/1½ oz soft dark brown sugar
100 g/4 oz wholemeal flour
1.25 ml/¼ tsp salt
25 g/1 oz ground almonds

Grease a 15 cm/6 inch sandwich tin. Set the oven at 160°C/325°F/gas 3.

Cream the butter and sugar in a mixing bowl until light and fluffy. Mix the flour and salt in a second bowl, then add to the creamed mixture with the ground almonds, working the mixture with the hands until the dough is smooth. Press into the prepared sandwich tin and bake for 50 minutes. Cut into 8 wedges while still warm. Cool in the sandwich tin.

MAKES 8

COCONUT PYRAMIDS

fat for greasing
2 eggs, separated
150 g/5 oz caster sugar
150 g/5 oz desiccated coconut

Grease a baking sheet and cover with rice paper. Set the oven at 140°C/275°F/gas 1. In a clean dry bowl, whisk the egg whites until stiff, then fold in the sugar and coconut, using a metal spoon. Divide the mixture into 12 portions and place in heaps on the rice paper. Using a fork, form into pyramid shapes. Bake for 45 minutes-1 hour until pale brown in colour. Cool on the baking sheet.

MAKES 12

MUSHROOM CAKES

fat for greasing
100 g/4 oz self-raising flour
pinch of salt
100 g/4 oz butter or margarine
100 g/4 oz caster sugar
2 eggs, beaten

DECORATION
  Apricot Glaze (page 140)
  Almond Paste (page 142), using 75 g/3 oz
    almonds
  icing sugar and ground cinnamon for
    dusting
  Buttercream (page 144) using 50 g/2 oz
    butter

Grease 12-14 bun tins. Set the oven at 180°C/350°F/gas 4. Mix the flour and salt.

In a mixing bowl, cream the butter or margarine with the sugar until light and fluffy. Beat in the eggs, then lightly stir in the flour and salt. Divide the mixture evenly between the prepared bun tins, and bake for 15-20 minutes until golden brown. Cool.

Brush the sides and tops of the cold cakes with apricot glaze. Roll out the almond paste thinly and cut rounds to cover the top and sides of the cakes; press into position.

Mix the icing sugar and cinnamon together and place on a sheet of greaseproof paper. Holding each cake near its base, roll it in the cinnamon sugar.

Put the buttercream in an icing bag fitted with a small star nozzle and pipe threads on the surface of each cake, radiating from the centre to the edge, to represent gills. Use the almond paste trimmings to make tiny stalks and place one of these in the centre of each cake, making a small hole with a skewer.

MAKES 12 TO 14

CAULIFLOWERS

fat for greasing
100 g/4 oz plain flour
2.5 ml/½ tsp salt
75 g/3 oz Clarified Butter (page 22) or
    margarine
4 eggs
100 g/4 oz caster sugar

DECORATION
  green food colouring
  Almond Paste (page 142) using 200 g/7 oz
    almonds
  Apricot Glaze (page 140)
  150 ml/5 fl oz double cream
  5 ml/1 tsp caster sugar

Line and grease a 20 x 30 cm/8 x 12 inch Swiss roll tin. Set the oven at 180°C/350°F/gas 4.

Sift the flour and salt into a bowl and put in a warm place. Melt the clarified butter or margarine without letting it get hot.

Whisk the eggs lightly in a mixing bowl. Add the sugar and place the bowl over a saucepan of hot water. Whisk for 10-15 minutes until thick. Take care that the bottom of the bowl does not touch the water. Remove from the heat and continue whisking until at blood-heat. The melted butter should be at the same temperature.

Sift half the flour over the eggs, then pour in half the melted butter or margarine in a thin stream. Fold in gently. Repeat, using the remaining flour and fat. Spoon gently into the prepared tin and bake for 30-40 minutes. Cool on a wire rack.

Cut the cold sponge into about eighteen 4 cm/1½ inch rounds. Work a few drops of green food colouring into the almond paste, roll it out thinly and cut out five 4 cm/1½ inch rounds for each cake.

Brush the sides of each cake with apricot glaze. Press the circles of almond paste round the sides of each cake, overlapping them slightly. Bend the centre top of each piece outwards to represent cauliflower leaves. In a bowl, whip the cream with the sugar until stiff. Using a piping bag fitted with a small star nozzle, pipe tiny rosettes of cream on top of each cake to represent the cauliflower florettes.

MAKES 18

CINNAMON DOUGHNUTS

150 g/5 oz self-raising flour
2.5 ml/½ tsp salt
2.5 ml/½ tsp ground cinnamon
50 g/2 oz margarine
25 g/1 oz sugar
1 egg, beaten
15-30 ml/1-2 tbsp milk
flour for rolling out
oil for deep frying
caster sugar and ground cinnamon for
    dusting

Mix the flour, salt and cinnamon together in a mixing bowl. Rub in the margarine until the mixture resembles fine breadcrumbs. Stir in the sugar. Add the beaten egg with the milk and mix to a soft, scone-like dough.

Roll out the dough to a thickness of about 1cm/½ inch on a floured board. Cut into rounds with a 5 cm/2 inch cutter, then remove the centres with an apple corer. Gather the trimmings together, roll out again and cut more rounds.

Heat the fat (see recipe right) and fry the doughnuts, turning once with a slotted spoon when brown on the underside. Drain on kitchen paper and while still hot, toss in caster sugar flavoured with cinnamon.

MAKES 8 TO 10

RING DOUGHNUTS

200 g/7 oz plain flour
1.25 ml/¼ tsp salt
pinch of ground cinnamon or nutmeg
7.5 ml/1½ tsp baking powder
40 g/1½ oz butter or margarine
45 ml/3 tbsp sugar
1 egg, lightly beaten
about 60 ml/4 tbsp milk
flour for rolling out
oil for deep frying
caster sugar for dusting

Sift the flour, salt, spice and baking powder into a mixing bowl. Rub in the butter or margarine until the mixture resembles breadcrumbs. Stir in the sugar. Make a well in the centre of the dry ingredients and add the egg. Gradually work it into the dry ingredients, adding enough milk to make a soft dough.

Roll out the dough to a thickness of 1 cm/½ inch on a floured board. Heat the oil to 180-190°C/350-375°F or until a cube of bread added to the oil browns in 30 seconds. Cut the dough into rings using a 6 cm/2½ inch and a 2 cm/¾ inch cutter. Re-roll and re-cut the trimmings.

Fry 1 or 2 doughnuts in the hot oil until light brown underneath; then carefully turn with a slotted spoon and cook the second side. Lift the doughnuts out and drain well on absorbent kitchen paper.

Put some caster sugar in a large paper bag and add the doughnuts while still hot. Toss them gently until coated. Transfer to absorbent paper dusted with sugar. Continue until all the doughnuts are fried. Bring the oil back to temperature between each batch.

MAKES ABOUT 12

CAKE DECORATING

The art of creating beautifully decorated cakes is now at everyone's fingertips – the only essential qualification is enthusiasm. As with many other culinary skills, cake decorating has been simplified over the past decade with the introduction of labour-saving ingredients, icings and utensils. You certainly do not have to be a professional to achieve excellent results.

Perhaps the greatest revolution has been in the availability of sugar paste and moulding icings. This has produced a new style of decoration. The icing is simply rolled out and smoothed over the cake to give a softer line than was possible with royal icing. Sugar paste sets hard enough to decorate, it may also be moulded into shapes and flowers so that mastery of the icing bag is no longer a prerequisite for cake decorating.

Having tasted success the easy way, the enthusiast may advance to royal icing, run-outs, Garrett frills, collars and flowers. The pages that follow are packed with information, instructions and ideas for everything from basic cakes decorated with buttercream to the more advanced decorations for the ultimate wedding cake.

Three-tiered Wedding Cake (page 248)

Single-tier Wedding Cake (page 248)

INGREDIENTS AND EQUIPMENT

The correct choice of ingredients and equipment lays the foundation for success when decorating cakes. Here you will find a wealth of useful information, from a list of simple, shop-bought cake decorations to the details of specialist equipment.

Like all crafts, cake decorating employs traditional tools and time-honoured methods, but today these exist in tandem with new products, ready-made to ease the burden on the busy cook. These commercial products do not necessarily demean the craft; indeed they frequently enable us to develop it further and increase our skills. This chapter lists, and briefly discusses, the main ingredients and items of equipment which are used for decorating cakes.

INGREDIENTS

ALMOND PASTE

Almond paste is believed to have originated in the Middle East and is made from ground almonds, eggs and sugar. It is used to cover rich fruit cakes to prevent the crumbs from discolouring the icing. It also provides a smooth, flat surface for the icing. Almond paste may also be moulded to make cake decorations. Home-made almond paste is usually made with a mixture of caster and icing sugar and has a slightly grainy texture.

APRICOT GLAZE

Apricot glaze is a smooth, clear syrup made from boiled, sieved apricot jam and is used as a glaze or brushed over fruit cakes before covering with almond paste. Any jam or marmalade of similar colour may be used.

BUTTER

Fresh butter gives a good flavour to buttercreams but it may need to be softened before use. Alternatively, use one of the butterfats mixed with vegetable oil for easy spreading. Whenever possible use unsalted butter for making icings.

CHOCOLATE

Dark plain, milk and white chocolate have a variety of uses in cake decorating. They may be used to make icings and coverings as well as decorations. Chocolate and chocolate work is discussed in detail in the section beginning on page 234.

CORNFLOUR

Cornflour is used as a dusting powder when modelling with sugar paste.

EGGS

Ensure that eggs are fresh and from a reputable source as they are used raw in cake decorating. Eggs should be stored in their container in the refrigerator. Before use they should be thoroughly washed and dried with absorbent kitchen paper. Separate eggs carefully and place the whites in a clean, greasefree bowl. Remove the stringy parts from the white and ensure that no yolk is present. Use whites for icing and yolks for rich buttercream and confectioners' custard.

EGG SUBSTITUTES

Dried egg white, albumen powder and albumen substitute are available from specialist cake decorating shops or sold under brand names in supermarkets. If stored in an airtight container in a cool, dry place dried egg white has a long shelf life. It is therefore a valuable storecupboard ingredient and eliminates the problem of what to do with the egg yolks. If used correctly, it gives excellent results in icings. It is either made up to a liquid or sifted dry with the icing sugar. Follow the package instructions.

FOOD COLOURINGS

Colourings are available as pastes, liquids or powders. Paste colours are strong and are recommended for sugar paste as they will not alter the consistency. Use the weaker liquid colours for royal icing, glacé icing and fondant. Use either with buttercreams. Powder colours tend to be a little messy. Except for gold and silver all colours are edible but will vary as to derivation. Pure natural colours tend to lack clarity but are sold in a limited range as are tartrazine-free colours. Read the labels for more information.

Compounds are also available. They are concentrated liquids that combine colouring and flavouring. Compounds should always be used sparingly.

FRESH CREAM

Not long ago, the choice of creams was limited to single or double, depending upon the butterfat content. Today, supermarkets offer a wide range of creams, including half fat cream, whipping cream, pre-whipped and aerosol creams, long life or frozen cream and 'alternative' creams which include a percentage of vegetable fats.

Cream should be kept in a cool place or refrigerator until ready to use. Check the 'sell' or 'use by' date, especially in warm weather. Use as a filling for cakes and gâteaux.

GLYCERINE

This is a thick, sweet, colourless liquid that helps to keep icing soft. It is available from chemists.

GROUND ALMONDS

Usually a mixture of bitter and sweet almonds. Use when as fresh as possible and store in a well-sealed container in a cool, dark place or in the refrigerator.

ICING SUGAR

Icing sugar is the basis for most icings, although granulated and caster sugar are both used in frostings. Icing sugar is usually sold in 500 g/1 lb packets but it is more economical to buy the 3 kg/6.6 lb bags from supermarkets. Store the sugar in a cool, dry place, re-sealing the bag after use. Alternatively, keep it in a large screw-topped jar. Most brands of icing sugar contain a moisture-absorbing substance to prevent the formation of lumps but for professional results when making royal icing always sift the sugar two or three times.

INSTANT ROYAL ICING

This commercial product is available from grocers and supermarkets. It is sold in 500 g/1 lb packets. Dried egg white and corn starch have been mixed with icing sugar and only water needs to be added. It is simple to use and makes very good royal icing. Good when only small amounts are required.

LIQUID GLUCOSE

Sometimes called glucose syrup, this is a clear tasteless syrup available from chemists and specialist shops. It is used to make sugar paste pliable. When measuring, warm the syrup first or use a hot, metal spoon and scrape away any excess underneath the spoon to ensure accurate measuring. Glucose syrup has a limited shelf life.

MARZIPAN

Marzipan usually refers to a commercial product made with confectioners' sugar and liquid glucose. It is smoother and more pliable than almond paste and inexpensive brands are often coloured bright yellow. Use only white almond paste or marzipan under white icing.

PETAL PASTE

Petal paste is available in powder or paste form from specialist shops. It is used on its own for modelling flowers or may be added to sugar paste for decorations that need to set hard and strong. Store in a cool place (not a refrigerator). It has a limited shelf life.

PIPING GEL

A clear colourless flavourless jelly (usually coloured and flavoured for gâteaux), piping gel is mixed in very small quantities with royal icing for fine brushwork to prevent the icing from drying out too quickly. It is available from specialist shops.

PURE ALCOHOL

This usually means brandy, but other spirits may be used to brush over cakes or to stick sugar paste decorations on to dry icing. Cooled, boiled water may be used instead.

SUGAR PASTE

Also known as decorating icing or mallow paste, or sometimes referred to as fondant icing, this is used in the same way as almond paste. It may be rolled out to cover both fruit and sponge cakes and may also be moulded to make decorations. It is easy to use and gives a soft finish, both in texture and appearance. It may be home-made or is available by the 450 g/1 lb or in 5 kg/11 lb packs from specialist shops and some bakers. A ready-to-roll icing is available under a trade name from supermarkets and grocers. Sold in 227 g/8 oz packets, it is sweeter and softer in texture than sugar paste and should be kneaded with a little sifted icing sugar to a manageable consistency before use. Always keep sugar paste well wrapped to prevent it drying out.

DECORATIONS

All decorations on a cake should be edible unless they are large enough to be lifted off easily before cutting the cake; for example bride and groom, horseshoes, candles and holders, novelty characters. Small, inedible decorations could be harmful if swallowed.

SIMPLE DECORATIONS TO BUY

These may be readily purchased from grocers, supermarkets and sweet shops. A specialist cake-decorating shop will have a wider selection, especially as regards sugar flowers and other piped items. Avoid using strongly coloured decorations, as the colour tends to ooze when damp.

- angelica
- candy orange and lemon slices
- chocolate buttons (brown and white), chocolate chips, chocolate coffee beans, chocolate vermicelli, chocolate eggs, chocolate flakes and chocolate wafer mints
- coconut (shredded or desiccated)
- crystallised flowers and fruits
- crystallised pineapple
- crystallised violets and rose leaves
- dragees (silver and coloured shiny sugared balls)
- glacé cherries (red, green and yellow)
- jellies and jelly beans
- liquorice sweets, laces and comfits
- marshmallows
- pastilles
- piped sugar flowers
- sugar-coated chocolate beans
- sugar-coated cumin and mimosa balls
- sugar drops
- sugar strands
- sugared almonds
- strawberry and chocolate crunch

SIMPLE DECORATIONS TO MAKE

Instructions for making these will be found in the chapters that follow.

- chocolate, grated, piped, scrolled, leaves, used for dipping nuts, fruits and marzipan
- desiccated coconut, toasted or coloured
- marzipan – moulded into fruits, vegetables, leaves, characters
- nuts, toasted, halved, slivered, chopped, chocolate dipped, praline
- royal icing, piped into flowers, birds and various designs, also run-outs
- sugar, frosted flowers and leaves; coloured sugar
- sugar paste, moulded into shapes, characters or flowers; rolled out and cut into motifs and badges

EQUIPMENT

Having the right equipment can make all the difference to successful cake decorating, but the vast array of implements and utensils available in specialist shops can be bewildering. This chapter lists some of the more useful items.

It is important to keep cake decorating equipment away from general use, as all utensils must be clean and grease-free. Egg whites will not whisk up successfully if there is a trace of grease on bowl or whisk, and a sieve used previously for soup will flavour and colour the icing accordingly!

Ensure that all equipment is thoroughly rinsed and dried after use and stored in bags or containers away from dust, grease and kitchen steam. A fisherman's plastic tool box makes an excellent keeper for all the smaller items, such as paint brushes and nozzles.

BEATERS

Food mixers may be used for albumen-based icings but care should be taken that whisks are clean. Do not use a food processor. For whipping cream, use a small wire balloon whisk or, for large quantities, a hand-held electric whisk.

BOARD

An 18 × 25 cm/7 × 10 inch laminex board used with a laminex rolling pin will ensure paper-thin paste without sticking. Avoid cutting the surface with sharp knives and do not use for any other purpose.

BOWLS

When making icings or frostings, use un-cracked china or glass bowls. Metal bowls tend to discolour the icing and plastic ones are easily scratched. For whipping cream, use a large glass, china or aluminium bowl. Avoid plastic, as it is difficult to clean and may taint the cream.

CRIMPERS

Several designs are available for pressing designs into soft sugar paste. Similar effects may be achieved with a fork, potato peeler or butter curler.

ICING BAGS AND NOZZLES

For professional results, throw away the icing gun and use paper icing bags and good quality nozzles. **Paper icing bags** are available in various sizes from specialist shops or may be home-made (see page 138). **Nylon icing bags** should be used with savoy nozzles for piping buttercream. Wash and rinse well before drying thoroughly.

Choose good quality, smooth, seamless nozzles. Metal nozzles are better than plastic ones, since they give sharper definition. Always wash and dry each nozzle well after use and avoid distorting the pattern end. Do not buy any nozzles with ridges or collars that prevent them sitting neatly in the icing bag.

Each nozzle has a special function and is available in several sizes. Beginners are advised to select the medium sizes. The finer nozzles are for professional work and the large ones require considerable control of the icing. For some applications, left-handed nozzles are available. The table on page 139 shows how the various nozzles are best used. Please note, however, that because manufacturers differ in the number codes they allocate to nozzles, only writing nozzles may be identified by numbers.

MARZIPAN SPACERS

These are useful devices to ensure even rolling of marzipan or sugar paste. A good idea for those cooks who find it difficult to apply even pressure when rolling out.

MODELLER

This is similar to a potter's tool. It is usually double ended for smoothing, gouging out or marking a pattern.

PAINT BRUSHES

Use fine, good quality sable brushes that will not lose their hairs. Use with powder or liquid food colouring for brush embroidery, writing and fine art work. Wash and dry brushes carefully, making sure that all hairs are lying flat.

PALETTE KNIVES

A 10 cm/4 inch blade is ideal for icing the sides of cakes, while a larger 15 cm/6 inch blade is used for spreading icing over the top.

PAPERS

Greaseproof paper is available in rolls or sheets in various qualities. It is used for wrapping cakes, lining cake tins, making small icing bags and tracing patterns.

Non-stick baking parchment (silicone paper) is sold in rolls under various trade names. It is used in much the same way as greaseproof paper, but because it is stronger it is particularly suitable for making large icing bags. It may also be used for run-outs, piping flowers etc. It will not stick to adhesive tape and must be secured with pins.

Waxed paper is more expensive than either greaseproof or silicone. Available in rolls or sheets, it is excellent for large run-outs and when icing flowers, but is not suitable where heat is required. When using it for run-outs, choose the sheet form, as it is essential that the paper be flat and uncreased. It will not stick to adhesive tape – use pins instead.

PASTRY BRUSHES

Keep a wide, flat pastry brush for brushing away dry cake crumbs, and a second brush for applying glaze.

RIBBON INSERTION TOOL

Used for cutting slits in the icing when threading ribbon, this is a useful tool for anyone who regularly ices celebration cakes.

ROLLING PIN

A long, non-stick laminex rolling pin is best for rolling out large quantities of sugar paste, but these are expensive. Alternatively, use a china or new wooden rolling pin or wooden dowel. The latter must be dusted frequently with cornflour to prevent sticking. A 23 cm/9 inch laminex rolling pin is necessary for rolling sugar paste very thinly when making flowers or a frill.

RULER OR STRAIGHT EDGE

This is a stainless steel rigid rule for flat icing the top of a cake. A rigid, well-scrubbed wooden ruler may be used instead.

SCISSORS

A small pair of sharp pointed scissors will prove useful.

SCRAPER

Used for smoothing the icing on the sides of cakes. Buy a firm plastic or stainless steel scraper; avoid any that bend easily. Some have a serrated side for a decorative finish.

SIEVE

Buy a fine nylon mesh sieve, kept solely for sifting icing sugar. A metal sieve may taint or discolour the icing.

TURNTABLE

A turntable is invaluable for flat icing a round cake. Choose one that is well balanced and will not slide across the table. Turntables may be made from plastic, injection-moulded nylon or aluminium. Prices vary considerably. Buy the best quality that you can afford if your use will justify the cost.

WOODEN SPOONS

Buy new spoons in various sizes. A small batter paddle with a hole in the centre is useful when making royal icing.

USEFUL EXTRAS

Cutters Sets of sharp straight-edged and fluted cutters. Alternatively, cut around upturned saucers, lids, cups, etc.

Dummy Polystyrene artificial 'cake' in various sizes and shapes used to practise icing techniques. It is a good idea to secure the dummy to a heavy base with glue and/or nails through the base.

Flower nail Used for piping flowers. Alternatively, make your own by using a cork on the end of a short knitting needle or wooden meat skewer.

Glass-headed stainless steel pins For securing ribbon or marking positions.

Tweezers Useful for placing small decorations into position.

Wooden cocktail sticks For piping roses (see page 230) and Garrett frill.

Wooden meat skewer Use blunt end rounded off when working with sugar paste.

FINISHING TOUCHES

BOARDS

Use deep drum boards for all fruit cakes and large gâteaux. The thinner boards are for lighter sponges and plaques. The boards are available in various shapes and sizes and should be at least 5 cm/2 inches larger than the cake. A 'universal' board may be used for either round or square cakes. The boards are covered in silver, gold or Christmas paper and only a specialist shop will stock the whole range. A limited supply of traditional round or square boards is available in most stationers, bakers and suppliers of artists' materials.

BOARD EDGES

Gilt or silver paper ribbon may be purchased to place around the edge of drum boards to give a professional finish.

ICING PENS

These resemble fine felt-tip pens and are used for direct art work on hard icing. They are particularly useful for adding details such as eyes.

PILLARS

Plastic or plaster pillars are used to separate the tiers of a cake. Available in white, gold or silver finish.

RIBBONS

Although most haberdashers will offer a range of ribbons you will probably find a greater selection at a specialist cake-decorating shop. Double-faced satin ribbon is sold in a variety of colours and widths ranging from 1.5 mm to 2.5 cm (1/16 – 1 inch) and wider. Single-faced ribbon may also be used. When matching ribbon to icing, remember that the icing tends to dry to a darker shade. Iron the ribbon, if necessary, before use and leave to cool before measuring and attaching to the cake.

SEQUIN RIBBON

These shiny sequinned bands make ideal substitutes for ribbon on gold, silver and ruby wedding aniversary cakes. Available from haberdashers.

SPARKLE OR LUSTRE

Fine coloured reflective powder which may be lightly dusted on to brush embroidery or flowers to add an effect. 'Sparkle' has larger reflective particles than 'Lustre'.

MAKING A PAPER ICING BAG

Use greaseproof paper, non-stick baking parchment (silicone paper) or waxed paper.

1 Cut a 20 cm/8 inch square piece of paper and cut it in half diagonally.

2 Position paper as shown in diagram and hold 'B' flat on to the table with your left hand. Take hold of 'A' in your right hand.

3 Fold 'A' round towards you until it meets 'B' to form a cone.

4 Hold 'A' and 'B' firmly in position with your right hand, positioning fingers on top and thumb underneath. Take hold of 'C' in your left hand.

5 Lift the cone off the table and wrap 'C' around the cone to meet 'B' at the back.

6 Points A, B and C should now be together.

7 Fold down points to secure the bag.

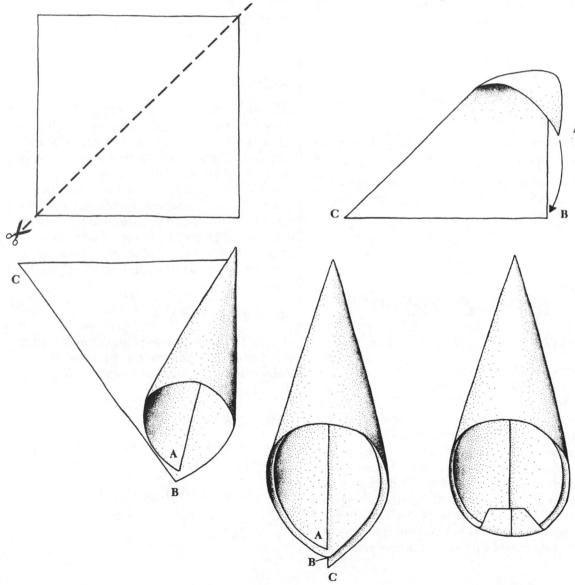

NOZZLES AND THEIR USES

NOZZLE	USE
'Writer" Plain Sizes 00, 0, 1, 2, 3. (Select 0 and 1 for general use)	Writing, straight lines, line work, dots, beads, outline work, scribbles, lace and embroidery work
Shell	Edging cakes at base or around the top. Scrolls
Star Available as 5, 6, 7, 8, 9, 11 and 12 points	Stars or simpler 'shell' effect for piping around the edge and base of the cake
Ribbon	Basket weave
Petal	Piping flowers such as small roses
Leaf	Leaves or petals
Savoy Preferably metal with fine star 'teeth'	Piping buttercreams and softer icings

'Writer' Plain   Shell

Star   Ribbon   Petal

Leaf   Savoy

CAKE COVERINGS AND FILLINGS

Even a simple cake can be made extra special by adding a little icing, a golden glaze or a nutty topping. This chapter includes recipes to complement formal cakes as well as plain ones. In addition, a quick-reference chart provides a useful guide to selecting the right icing for the type of cake.

GLAZES AND COATINGS

Glazes are used to give a shiny coating to food. Pastry, cakes and biscuits may be glazed with egg white, egg wash, sugar syrup or warmed jam such as apricot glaze, and then covered with crumbs, ground nuts, coconut, marzipan, almond paste or praline. Fruit flans or tartlets are often coated with a sweet liquid thickened with arrowroot.

APRICOT GLAZE

Brush this glaze over a cake before applying the marzipan. Any yellow jam or marmalade may be used.

225 g/8 oz apricot jam

Warm the jam with 30 ml/2 tbsp water in a small saucepan over a low heat until the jam has melted. Sieve the mixture and return the glaze to the clean saucepan. Bring slowly to the boil. Allow to cool slightly before use.

SUFFICIENT TO COAT THE TOP AND SIDES OF ONE 20 CM/8 INCH CAKE

> ☀ MICROWAVE TIP Melt the jam with the water in a bowl on High. Sieve into a small basin and heat the syrup on High. Cool slightly before use.

CHOCOLATE GLAZE

A little oil gives this icing sugar glaze its shine. It may be poured over chocolate cakes or it can be used to coat plain sponge cakes or Victoria Sandwich Cake (page 46) to provide a contrast in flavour. Store any leftover glaze in an airtight container in the refrigerator.

100 g/4 oz plain chocolate, broken into small pieces
5 ml/1 tsp vegetable oil
25 g/1 oz caster sugar

Combine the chocolate, oil and caster sugar in a heatproof bowl. Stir in 45 ml/3 tbsp boiling water. Place the bowl over hot water and stir gently until the chocolate has melted. Remove from the heat and cool slightly before pouring the chocolate glaze over the cake.

SUFFICIENT TO COVER TOP AND SIDES OF ONE 18 CM/7 INCH CAKE

> ☀ MICROWAVE TIP Melt all the ingredients in a small bowl on Medium for 2-3 minutes.

MARASCHINO GLAZE

Unlike the apricot glaze, this one is based upon icing sugar, with milk and butter added to enhance the shiny effect.

30 ml/2 tbsp softened butter
175 g/6 oz icing sugar
30-45 ml/2-3 tbsp milk
5-10 ml/1-2 tsp maraschino liqueur or
    syrup from maraschino cherries
1-2 drops red food colouring (optional)

Put the butter into a bowl. Using a wooden spoon, gradually work in the icing sugar until thoroughly mixed. Bring the milk to the boil in a small saucepan and stir it into the mixture, with the liqueur or syrup. Add a couple of drops of colouring, if liked, to tint the icing a pale pink. The glaze should be thick enough to spread lightly, yet be able to trickle over the edge of a cake and drip down the sides.

SUFFICIENT TO COVER ONE 25 CM/10 INCH RING CAKE OR 24 SMALL CAKES

MRS BEETON'S TIP An icing sugar glaze of this kind may be used on top of an icing of a different colour and flavour. Maraschino glaze looks particularly good on chocolate icing.

GLAZE FOR SWEET FLANS

This slightly thickened glaze is useful for coating fresh or canned fruit as a decoration for light gâteaux. It can also be used with fresh fruit to top a plain cheesecake.

5 ml/1 tsp arrowroot
150 ml/¼ pint fruit syrup from canned or
    bottled fruit or 150 ml/¼ pint water
    and 25 g/1 oz sugar
1-3 drops food colouring
lemon juice

In a bowl, mix the arrowroot to a paste with a little of the cold fruit syrup or water. Pour the remaining syrup into a saucepan and bring to the boil. If using water, add the sugar and bring to the boil, stirring constantly until all the sugar has dissolved. Pour on to the arrowroot mixture, stir well, then return to the saucepan. Bring to the boil, stirring constantly. Add the appropriate food colouring, then stir in lemon juice to taste. Use at once.

SUFFICIENT TO GLAZE ONE 18 CM/7 INCH FRUIT FLAN OR 12-16 TARTLETS

MICROWAVE TIP Mix the arrowroot with a little of the syrup in a medium bowl. Add the remaining syrup and cook on High for 1 minute. Stir, then cook for 1 minute more or until the glaze clears. Add food colouring and lemon juice as above.

ALMOND PASTE AND MARZIPAN

Either almond paste or marzipan may be used to cover a Battenburg cake, to fill a simnel cake or as a base for royal icing on a Christmas or wedding cake. Both almond paste and marzipan provide a flat, even surface over which icing will flow in a smooth glossy sheet, and as a bonus, will prevent crumbs from the cake spoiling the appearance of the icing. Marzipan resembles almond paste, but is smoother and more malleable. It is easier to use than almond paste when making moulded decorations or petits fours. For use and quantities required for individual cakes see opposite.

MARZIPAN

1 egg
1 egg white
200 g/7 oz icing sugar, sifted
200 g/7 oz ground almonds
5 ml/1 tsp lemon juice
few drops of almond essence

Whisk the egg, egg white and icing sugar in a heatproof bowl over hot water until thick and creamy. Add the ground almonds with the lemon juice and almond essence and mix well. Work in more lemon juice, if necessary. When cool enough to handle, knead lightly until smooth. Use as for almond paste, or for making moulded decorations (see page 218).

MAKES ABOUT 400 G/14 OZ

ALMOND PASTE

This recipe makes a pale, creamy yellow coloured paste that can be used to cover and decorate cakes, as well as for a base coat before applying icing.

225 g/8 oz ground almonds
100 g/4 oz caster sugar
100 g/4 oz icing sugar
5 ml/1 tsp lemon juice
few drops of almond essence
1 egg, beaten

Using a coarse sieve, sift the almonds, caster sugar and icing sugar into a mixing bowl. Add the lemon juice, almond essence and sufficient egg to bind the ingredients together. Knead lightly with the fingertips until smooth.

Wrap in cling film and overwrap in foil or a plastic bag to prevent the paste drying out. Store in a cool place until required.

MAKES ABOUT 450 G/1 LB

> MRS BEETON'S TIP Don't knead the paste too much: this can draw the oils from the almonds and make the paste greasy. It will then be unsuitable as a base for icing.

COOKED ALMOND PASTE

This makes a smoother and more malleable paste than the uncooked mixture. Use it for moulding decorations and for covering wedding cakes.

450 g/1 lb granulated sugar
1.25 ml/¼ tsp cream of tartar
300 g/11 oz ground almonds
2 egg whites
5 ml/1 tsp almond essence
50 g/2 oz icing sugar

Place the sugar with 150 ml/¼ pint water in a saucepan over moderate heat. Stir occasionally until all the sugar has melted, then bring the syrup to the boil.

In a cup, dissolve the cream of tartar in 5 ml/1 tsp water and stir it into the syrup. Boil, without stirring, until the syrup registers 115°C/240°F on a sugar thermometer, the soft ball stage (see Mrs Beeton's Tip).

Remove the pan from the heat and immediately stir in the ground almonds followed by the unbeaten egg whites and almond essence. Return the pan to a low heat and cook, stirring constantly, for 2 minutes. Set the pan aside until the mixture is cool enough to handle.

Sift the icing sugar on to a clean work surface, place the marzipan in the centre and knead with the fingertips until the sugar is absorbed. If the marzipan is sticky, leave to cool for longer and then add a little more icing sugar, if necessary. Cover lightly until cold, then wrap and store in a cool place, as for almond paste.

MAKES 900 G/2 LB

> **MRS BEETON'S TIP** If you do not have a sugar thermometer, drop about 2.5 ml/½ tsp syrup into a bowl of iced water. If you can mould the syrup between your fingers to make a soft ball, the syrup is ready.

ALMOND PASTE/MARZIPAN

Quick guide to quantities required to cover fruit cakes

Round	Quantity	Square	Quantity
15 cm/6 inches	350 g/12 oz	15 cm/6 inches	500 g/18 oz
18 cm/7 inches	500 g/18 oz	18 cm/7 inches	575 g/1¼ lb
20 cm/8 inches	575 g/1¼ lb	20 cm/8 inches	800 g/1¾ lb
23 cm/9 inches	800 g/1¾ lb	23 cm/9 inches	900 g/2 lb
25 cm/10 inches	900 g/2 lb	25 cm/10 inches	1 kg/2¼ lb
28 cm/11 inches	1 kg/2¼ lb	28 cm/11 inches	1.1 kg/2½ lb
30 cm/12 inches	1.25 kg/2½ lb	30 cm/12 inches	1.4 kg/3 lb

BUTTER ICINGS AND FUDGE ICINGS

These are soft icings made with butter and icing sugar which may be used for filling or covering lighter cakes and gâteaux. On drying, an outer crust forms but the icing remains soft underneath. The iced cake should be stored away from heat or direct sunlight.

Use unsalted butter if possible and flavour the icing as required. Soften the butter before using or try using a butter mixture that spreads easily even when chilled – these usually contain vegetable oil and therefore little or no extra liquid will be required when mixing the icing.

When adding food colouring to butter-based icings, do not expect clear colours. Avoid adding blue, as the yellow in the butter will turn it green!

All these icings may be spread with a palette knife or piped using a savoy nozzle.

★ **FREEZER TIP** Buttercream can be frozen successfully, unless the recipe contains egg, in which case it may curdle. When piping with buttercream it is necessary to make slightly more than required; however any leftovers can be frozen for future use as a filling for cakes. The prepared buttercream can be flavoured before or after freezing. Pack the buttercream in a rigid container, then leave it to thaw in the refrigerator or in a cool place and beat it thoroughly before use.

RICH BUTTERCREAM

This buttercream is enriched by the addition of an egg yolk. Use only very fresh eggs and make sure that all utensils used to prepare the buttercream are perfectly clean.

1 egg yolk
200 g/7 oz icing sugar, sifted
100 g/4 oz butter, softened
flavouring

Beat the egg yolk in a mixing bowl, adding the sugar gradually until the mixture is smooth. Beat in the butter, a little at a time with the flavouring.

SUFFICIENT TO FILL AND TOP A 20 CM/8 INCH CAKE

BUTTERCREAM

100 g/4 oz butter, softened
15 ml/1 tbsp milk or fruit juice
225 g/8 oz icing sugar, sifted

In a mixing bowl, cream the butter with the milk or juice and gradually work in the icing sugar. Beat the icing until light and fluffy. Alternatively, work all the ingredients in a food processor, removing the plunger for the final mixing to allow air to enter the buttercream mixture.

SUFFICIENT TO FILL AND TOP A 20 CM/8 INCH CAKE

FLUFFY BUTTERCREAM

2 egg whites
200 g/7 oz icing sugar, sifted
100 g/4 oz butter, softened
flavouring

Whisk the egg whites in a large bowl until stiff. Add the icing sugar, a third at a time, whisking between each addition until the mixture forms peaks.

In a mixing bowl, cream the butter until light and fluffy. Gradually fold in the meringue mixture. Flavour as required.

SUFFICIENT TO FILL AND TOP A 20 CM/8 INCH CAKE

VARIATIONS

These flavourings may be used with any of the buttercreams.

CHOCOLATE BUTTERCREAM Grate 50 g/2 oz block plain chocolate. Place it in a basin over hot water with 15 ml/1 tbsp milk, stir until dissolved, then cool. Use instead of the liquid in the plain buttercream.

COFFEE BUTTERCREAM Dissolve 5 ml/1 tsp instant coffee in 15 ml/1 tbsp hot water. Cool before use. Use instead of the milk or fruit juice in the plain buttercream.

LEMON OR ORANGE BUTTERCREAM Use 15 ml/1 tbsp juice and a little grated rind.

VANILLA BUTTERCREAM Add 2.5 ml/½ tsp vanilla essence with the milk.

WALNUT BUTTERCREAM Add 25 g/1 oz chopped walnuts.

FRENCH BUTTER ICING

This resembles a frosting, in that the sugar is boiled and added as a syrup to the other ingredients. The high percentage of butter, however, assures it of a place in this section.

50 g/2 oz granulated sugar
1 egg yolk
150 g/5 oz butter, cut into small pieces

Mix the sugar with 125 ml/4 fl oz water in a small heavy saucepan. Stirring occasionally, heat gently until all the sugar has dissolved. Increase the heat and boil, without stirring, until the syrup registers 105°C/220°F on a sugar thermometer, the thread stage (see Mrs Beeton's Tip).

Place the egg yolk in a bowl, whisk lightly, then gradually whisk in the syrup. Continue whisking until cool, then add the butter, a little at a time, whisking constantly.

SUFFICIENT TO COAT THE TOP AND SIDES OF A 20 CM/8 INCH CAKE

VARIATION

CHOCOLATE FRENCH BUTTER ICING Break up 100 g/4 oz plain dark chocolate and stir into the warm syrup mixture until melted. Beat until smooth and glossy.

MRS BEETON'S TIP If you do not have a sugar thermometer, test the syrup by dipping a spoon in the syrup and then pressing another spoon on to the back of it and pulling away. If a thread forms, the syrup is ready.

CHOCOLATE FUDGE ICING

100 g/4 oz plain chocolate, broken into
  pieces
50 g/2 oz butter, cut up
1 egg, beaten
175 g/6 oz icing sugar, sifted

Combine the chocolate and butter in a heatproof bowl. Set over hot water until the chocolate has melted. Beat in the egg, then remove the bowl from the heat and stir in half the icing sugar. Beat in the remaining sugar and continue beating until the icing is smooth and cold. Use immediately.

SUFFICIENT TO FILL AND TOP A 20 CM/8 INCH CAKE

VARIATIONS

CHOCOLATE WALNUT FUDGE ICING Add 50 g/2 oz of finely chopped walnuts to the icing just before spreading it on the cake.

CHOCOLATE RUM FUDGE ICING Add 30 ml/2 tbsp of rum to the icing with the egg and continue as in the main recipe.

CHOCOLATE ORANGE FUDGE ICING Add the grated rind of 1 orange to the chocolate and butter. Continue as in the main recipe. This icing is excellent on Victoria Sandwich Cake which has the grated rind of 1 orange added to the mixture.

☀ **MICROWAVE TIP** Melt the chocolate with the butter in a small bowl on Medium for 1-2 minutes.

DARK FUDGE ICING

75 g/3 oz butter
75 g/3 oz soft dark brown sugar
30 ml/2 tbsp milk
225 g/8 oz icing sugar, sifted

Combine the butter, brown sugar and milk in a saucepan. Place over moderate heat, stirring occasionally until the sugar has melted. Remove the pan from the heat, add the icing sugar and beat until cool. Use immediately.

SUFFICIENT TO COAT THE TOP AND SIDES OF A 20 CM/8 INCH CAKE

VARIATIONS

DARK HONEY FUDGE ICING Use 15 ml/1 tbsp of honey instead of 25 g/1 oz of the sugar in the main recipe.

COFFEE FUDGE ICING Add 5 ml/1 tsp of instant coffee to the butter, sugar and milk mixture. Continue as in the recipe.

DARK NUT FUDGE ICING Stir in 30 ml/2 tbsp of smooth peanut butter before adding the icing sugar. This icing can be used to sandwich plain biscuits in pairs or it can be used as a topping for chocolate brownies or small plain cakes.

DARK GINGER FUDGE ICING Add a pinch of ground ginger to the butter, sugar and milk mixture. Beat in 30 ml/2 tbsp of finely chopped preserved stem ginger or crystallised ginger. This icing makes an unusual topping for gingerbread.

☀ **MICROWAVE TIP** Melt the butter and sugar in a bowl with the milk on Medium for 1-2 minutes.

Girl's Christening Cake (page 249)

Boy's Christening Cake (page 250)

Silver or Golden Anniversary Cake (page 250)

Ruby Anniversary Cake (page 251) decorated with moulded roses with moulded carnations nearby

GLACÉ ICING

Glacé icing is mainly used as a covering for small cakes, sponge cakes or other light cakes. It is quick and easy to make and therefore ideal for simple, informal cakes. It gives a smooth, slightly crisp coating that complements piped buttercream edges. This icing can also be used to coat plain biscuits. Basically a mixture of icing sugar and warm water, it may also contain flavourings and colourings or extra ingredients as in the Chocolate Glacé Icing on page 151.

There is also a recipe for a Glacé Fondant (overleaf) which is based on the same ingredients as glacé icing but it is heated and enriched with a little butter to give a very glossy result. It should not be confused with Traditional Fondant which is a more formal icing.

The consistency of the icing is all important; it should be stiff enough to coat the back of a wooden spoon thickly, otherwise it will run off the surface of the cake and drip down the sides.

Glacé icing should be used immediately. If left to stand, even for a short while, the surface should be covered completely with damp greaseproof paper or cling film. Any crystallised icing on the surface should be scraped off before use. Because the icing sets so quickly, any additional decorations must be put on as soon as the cake is iced, or the surface will crack

The choice of decorations to use with glacé icing is important. Do not use decorations liable to melt, run or be damaged by damp. Crystallised flower petals, chocolate decorations and small sweets which will shed colour should not be used.

GLACÉ ICING

This simple, basic icing is quickly prepared and is ideal for topping a plain sponge cake or a batch of small cakes. Make the icing just before it is to be used and keep any extra decorations to the minimum.

100 g/4 oz icing sugar, sifted
food colouring, optional

Place the icing sugar in a bowl. Using a wooden spoon gradually stir in sufficient warm water (about 15 ml/1 tbsp) to create icing whose consistency will thickly coat the back of the spoon. Take care not to add too much liquid or the icing will be too runny. At first the icing will seem quite stiff, but it slackens rapidly as the icing sugar absorbs the water. Stir in 1-2 drops of food colouring, if required.

SUFFICIENT TO COVER THE TOP OF ONE 18 CM/7 INCH CAKE

VARIATIONS

LEMON OR ORANGE GLACÉ ICING Use 15 ml/1 tbsp strained lemon or orange juice instead of the water.

COFFEE GLACÉ ICING Dissolve 5 ml/1 tsp instant coffee in 15 ml/1 tbsp warm water and add instead of the water in the main recipe.

LIQUEUR-FLAVOURED GLACÉ ICING Replace half the water with the liqueur of your choice.

CHOCOLATE GLACÉ ICING

An icing that contains dessert chocolate and/or butter will thicken and set more readily than one which merely contains a liquid.

50 g/2 oz plain chocolate, broken into
    small pieces
knob of butter
100 g/4 oz icing sugar, sifted

Combine the chocolate and butter in a heatproof bowl. Add 15 ml/1 tbsp water. Place the bowl over hot water. When the chocolate has melted, stir the mixture, gradually adding the sugar. Add a little more water, if necessary, to give a smooth coating consistency. Use at once.

SUFFICIENT TO COAT THE TOP OF ONE 18 CM/7 INCH CAKE

☀ **MICROWAVE TIP** Melt the chocolate, butter and water in a bowl on Medium for 1-2 minutes.

GLACÉ FONDANT

225 g/8 oz icing sugar, sifted
2.5 ml/½ tsp lemon juice
knob of butter

Combine the icing sugar and lemon juice in a small saucepan and mix well. Add the butter and cook over a low heat, stirring with a wooden spoon, until the butter has melted and the icing is well blended. Immediately pour over the cake.

SUFFICIENT TO COVER THE TOP OF A 20 CM/8 INCH CAKE

FROSTINGS

Frosting is usually spread thickly all over a cake, covering the sides as well as the top. When set, it is crisper than glacé icing, because the sugar is heated or boiled when making it. It should have a soft, spreading consistency when applied. Have the cake ready before starting to make the frosting.

AMERICAN FROSTING

225 g/8 oz granulated sugar
pinch of cream of tartar
1 egg white
2.5 ml/½ tsp vanilla essence or a few drops
    lemon juice

Combine the sugar and cream of tartar in a small saucepan. Add 60 ml/4 tbsp water. Place over a low heat, stirring occasionally until the sugar has melted. Heat, without stirring until the syrup registers 115°C/240°F, the soft ball stage, on a sugar thermometer (see Mrs Beeton's Tip, page 143). Remove from the heat.

In a large grease-free bowl, whisk the egg white until stiff. Pour on the syrup in a thin stream, whisking continuously. Add the flavouring and continue to whisk until the frosting is thick and glossy and stands in peaks when the whisk is lifted.

Quickly spread over the cake. As the frosting cools, it may be swirled with a knife and lifted to form peaks.

SUFFICIENT TO COVER THE TOP AND SIDES OF ONE 18 CM/7 INCH CAKE

🥣 **MRS BEETON'S TIP** Make sure that both bowl and whisk are free from grease, otherwise the frosting will not whisk up well.

QUICK AMERICAN FROSTING

175 g/6 oz caster sugar
1 egg white
pinch of cream of tartar
pinch of salt

Heat a mixing bowl over a large saucepan of simmering water. Remove the bowl and place all the ingredients in it. Add 30 ml/2 tbsp water and whisk with a rotary or electric whisk until the ingredients are well mixed.

Remove the saucepan of simmering water from the heat, place the bowl over the water, and whisk until the frosting forms soft peaks. Use immediately.

SUFFICIENT TO COVER THE TOP AND SIDES OF ONE 18 CM/7 INCH CAKE

CARAMEL FROSTING

350 g/12 oz soft light brown sugar
1.25 ml/¼ tsp cream of tartar
2 egg whites
pinch of salt
5 ml/1 tsp vanilla essence

Heat a mixing bowl over a large saucepan of boiling water. Remove the bowl and add all the ingredients except the vanilla essence. Add 150 ml/¼ pint water and whisk with a rotary or electric whisk until well mixed.

Place the bowl over the water and continue to whisk until the frosting forms soft peaks. Remove the bowl from the water, add the essence and whisk the frosting for about 2 minutes more, until it reaches a spreading consistency. Use immediately.

SUFFICIENT TO FILL, TOP AND COVER THE SIDES OF ONE 18 CM/7 INCH CAKE

WHIPPED CREAM FROSTING

The addition of gelatine not only makes the cream more stable but also increases the volume.

10 ml/2 tsp gelatine
rind and juice of ½ lemon
pinch of salt
30 ml/2 tbsp icing sugar
250 ml/8 fl oz double cream

Place 30 ml/2 tbsp tepid water in a bowl and sprinkle the gelatine into the water. Stand the bowl over a saucepan of hot water and stir until the gelatine has dissolved completely.

Combine the lemon rind and juice, salt and icing sugar in a blender. Add 30 ml/2 tbsp of the cream, with the gelatine mixture. Process for 1 minute. Alternatively, whisk hard for 3 minutes.

Pour the mixture into a bowl and chill until it has the consistency of unbeaten egg white.

Whip the remaining cream until it forms soft peaks and fold it carefully into the gelatine mixture. Chill.

SUFFICIENT TO FILL AND TOP ONE 20 CM/ 8 INCH CAKE

TRADITIONAL FONDANT

Not to be confused with moulding icings or sugar paste icing. Traditional fondant is poured over the cake. It sets to a dry, shiny finish that remains soft inside. It is widely used by commercial confectioners for petits fours. Some specialist shops sell fondant icing in powdered form. This is a boon because small quantities may be made up by adding water or stock syrup. To make up and use fondant icing see page 194. You will need a sugar thermometer to make fondant.

450 g/1 lb caster or lump sugar
20 ml/4 tsp liquid glucose

Put the sugar in a heavy-bottomed saucepan which is absolutely free from grease. Add 150 ml/¼ pint water and heat gently until the sugar has completely dissolved. Stir very occasionally and use a wet pastry brush to wipe away any crystals that form on the sides of the pan. When the sugar has dissolved add the liquid glucose and boil to 115°C/240°F, the soft ball stage (see Mrs Beeton's Tip, page 143), without stirring. Keep the sides of the pan clean by brushing with the wet brush when necessary. Remove from the heat and allow the bubbles in the mixture to subside.

Pour the mixture slowly into the middle of a wetted marble slab and allow to cool a little. Work the sides to the middle with a sugar scraper or palette knife to make a smaller mass.

With a wooden spatula in one hand and the scraper in the other, make a figure of eight with the spatula, keeping the mixture together with the scraper. Work until the mass is completely white.

Break off small amounts and knead well, then knead all the small pieces together to form a ball.

Store in a screw-topped jar, or wrap closely in several layers of polythene. When required, dilute with stock syrup (below).

MAKES ABOUT 450 G/1 LB FONDANT

MRS BEETON'S TIP To give the fondant a hint of flavour use vanilla sugar instead of ordinary caster sugar or lump sugar. Vanilla sugar is made by placing a vanilla pod in a jar of caster sugar. The sugar should be left for a few weeks, shaking the jar occasionally, until it has absorbed the flavour of the vanilla.

STOCK SYRUP

Use this syrup when diluting fondant. It may also be kneaded into commercially made almond paste to make the paste more pliable.

150 g/5 oz granulated sugar

Put the sugar in a saucepan and add 150 ml/¼ pint water. Heat, stirring occasionally, until the sugar has dissolved, then boil without stirring for 3 minutes. Use a spoon to remove any scum that rises to the surface.

Allow the syrup to cool, then strain into a jar and cover with a lid. If not required immediately, store in a cool place (not the refrigerator) for up to 2 months.

QUICK FONDANT

30 ml/2 tbsp liquid glucose
225 g/8 oz icing sugar, sifted
food colouring (optional)

Mix the liquid glucose with 30 ml/2 tbsp boiling water in a large bowl. Beat in the icing sugar gradually, adding a few drops of food colouring, if desired.

Place the bowl over a pan of hot water to warm the icing before using for coating. Add a few drops of water if the icing becomes too thick.

SUFFICIENT TO COVER THE TOP AND SIDES OF ONE 18 CM/7 INCH CAKE

MICROWAVE TIP Put the glucose in a bowl with 60 ml/4 tbsp cold water. Heat on Medium for 30 seconds and add the icing sugar and food colouring as above.

SYRUP-BASED FONDANT

45 ml/3 tbsp warm Sugar Syrup (recipe follows)
275 g/10 oz icing sugar, sifted
food colouring, optional

Place the sugar syrup in a bowl and beat in sufficient icing sugar to coat the back of the spoon. Add a few drops of food colouring, if desired. Use at once or allow to cool, knead well and store as for fondant.

SUFFICIENT TO COVER THE TOP AND SIDES OF ONE 23 CM/9 INCH CAKE

SUGAR SYRUP

An essential part of Syrup-based Fondant icing, this may also be added to chocolate when piping. Flavoured with liqueur or fruit juices it is ideal for moistening cakes. It will keep for up to two months without refrigeration.

225 g/8 oz granulated sugar
1.25 ml/¼ tsp cream of tartar

Place the sugar with 15 ml/1 tbsp water in a small, heavy-bottomed saucepan over low heat and stir occasionally until the sugar has melted. Increase the heat and bring to the boil.

In a cup, dissolve the cream of tartar in 5 ml/1 tsp water, add to the saucepan and continue to boil the syrup, without stirring, until it registers 105°C/220°F on a sugar thermometer, the thread stage (see Mrs Beeton's Tip, page 145).

Remove the syrup from the heat, cool, strain and store in a screw-topped jar.

MAKES 125 ML/4 FL OZ

MRS BEETON'S TIP Always heat a sugar thermometer in hot water before putting it into the boiling syrup. To register the correct temperature, the thermometer must not touch the base of the pan. After use rest the thermometer on a saucer until it is cool enough to be washed in hot soapy water.

ROYAL ICING

Royal Icing is used for special celebration cakes, especially for wedding cakes, because the icing has sufficient strength when it sets hard to hold the tiers. The icing cannot be applied directly to the cake because it would drag the crumbs and discolour badly, so rich fruit cakes are usually covered with a layer of almond paste or marzipan before the royal icing is applied.

Traditionalists believe that royal icing can only be made successfully with egg whites and hard beating, but dried egg white or albumen powder is fast gaining in popularity because the icing can be made in a food mixer or with an electric whisk. Whichever method you choose, the secret of successful royal icing work, be it flat icing or piping, depends upon making the icing to the correct consistency. This is discussed further on the opposite page.

ROYAL ICING

Quick guide to quantities of Royal Icing required to cover cakes (sufficient for 3 coats)

ROUND	ROYAL ICING
15 cm/6 inch	575 g/1¼ lb
18 cm/7 inch	675 g/1½ lb
20 cm/8 inch	800 g/1¾ lb
23 cm/9 inch	900 g/2 lb
25 cm/10 inch	1 kg/2¼ lb
28 cm/11 inch	1.25 kg/2¾ lb
30 cm/12 inch	1.4 kg/3 lb

SQUARE	ROYAL ICING
15 cm/6 inch	675 g/1½ lb
18 cm/7 inch	800 g/1¾ lb
20 cm/8 inch	900 g/2 lb
23 cm/9 inch	1 kg/2¼ lb
25 cm/10 inch	1.25 kg/2¾ lb
28 cm/11 inch	1.4 kg/3 lb
30 cm/12 inch	1.5 kg/3¼ lb

ROYAL ICING (USING EGG WHITE)

It is vital to ensure that the bowl is clean and free from grease. Use a wooden spoon kept solely for the purpose and do not be tempted to skimp on the beating – insufficient beating will produce an off-white icing with a heavy, sticky texture.

2 egg whites
450 g/1 lb icing sugar, sifted

Place the egg whites in a bowl and break them up with a fork. Gradually beat in about two-thirds of the icing sugar with a wooden spoon, and continue beating for about 15 minutes until the icing is pure white and forms soft peaks. Add the remaining icing sugar, if necessary, to attain this texture. Cover the bowl with cling film and place a dampened tea towel on top. Place the bowl inside a plastic bag if storing overnight or for longer.

Before use, lightly beat the icing to burst any air bubbles that have risen to the surface. Adjust the consistency for flat icing or piping.

SUFFICIENT TO COAT THE TOP AND SIDES OF A 20 CM/8 INCH CAKE

> **MRS BEETON'S TIP** If the icing is to be used for a single cake, glycerine may be added to prevent it from becoming too brittle when dry. Add 2.5 ml/½ tsp glycerine during the final beating. Do not, however, use glycerine for a tiered cake where the icing must be hard in order to hold the tiers.

ROYAL ICING (USING DRIED EGG WHITE)

15 ml/1 tbsp dried egg white (albumen powder)
450 g/1 lb icing sugar

Place 60 ml/4 tbsp warm water in a bowl. Add the dried egg white, mix thoroughly and leave for 10-15 minutes. Whisk with a fork and strain the mixture into a mixing bowl.

Gradually beat in about two-thirds of the icing sugar and continue beating for 5 minutes in a food mixer or with a hand-held electric whisk until the icing is pure white, light and stands in soft peaks. Add extra icing sugar, if necessary.

Cover and use as for the royal icing (using egg white) except that fewer air bubbles will be present.

VARIATION

ALBUMEN SUBSTITUTE May be used in place of albumen powder. Sift it into the bowl. Beat for 5 minutes as above.

> **MRS BEETON'S TIP** Be careful not to beat the icing for too long or it may break when piped.

QUICK GUIDE TO CONSISTENCY OF ROYAL ICING FOR DIFFERENT APPLICATIONS

Once the required consistency has been achieved, cover the icing with a damp cloth, even during use.

CONSISTENCY	DESCRIPTION	USE
Thin Icing	Just finds its own level when gently tapped	Run-outs and flooding
Soft Peak (1)	Forms a soft peak when the spoon is lifted out but readily falls over	Embroidery work. Very fine 00 writing nozzles
Soft Peak (2)	Forms a soft peak but only tip bends over	Flat icing
Medium Peak	Firmer peak that holds its shape	Most piping except patterns using the larger nozzles
Firm Peak	Stiffer peak but still soft enough to push through a nozzle without excessive pressure	Petals for flowers, large shell and similar nozzles

MOULDING ICINGS

SUGAR PASTE

Since the introduction of this versatile and easy-to-use icing from the humid regions of Australia and South Africa, where royal icing does not dry well, cake decorating in this country has been revolutionised. Sugar paste, also known as decorating icing or mallow paste, resembles commercially made marzipan in its properties, texture and application (although not in colour or flavour). Sometimes it is referred to as fondant icing but it must not be confused with a traditional, pouring fondant. It is rolled out and moulded over the cake. In many cases this makes a base layer of marzipan unnecessary. It is, therefore, widely used on sponge cakes and because it can be easily coloured, makes wonderful novelty cakes.

There are several recipes for sugar paste: try them all and find the one which suits you best.

If well wrapped in polythene the icing will keep for several weeks in a cupboard. Do not store it in the refrigerator as it would lose its elasticity and become difficult to work.

Sugar paste is malleable and may be moulded into shapes and petals for flowers. When worked into very thin pieces, it will dry hard and brittle and can be used for plaques and Garrett frills. For more information, see Moulded Decorations (page 218).

As a general rule, it is best not to freeze a whole cake covered in this icing, especially if different colours have been used. This is because the icing becomes wet and the colours may run into each other. If only a small area of the cake has paste icing, as in a novelty cake covered in buttercream with moulded icing features, the cake can be frozen. When required, it must be taken out of the freezer, all wrappings removed and left at room temperature for 4-5 hours to allow the icing to dry off.

SUGAR PASTE

Quick guide to quantities required to cover cakes

ROUND	SUGAR PASTE
15 cm/6 inch	450 g/1 lb
18 cm/7 inch	575 g/1¼ lb
20 cm/8 inch	675 g/1½ lb
23 cm/9 inch	800 g/1¾ lb
25 cm/10 inch	900 g/2 lb
28 cm/11 inch	1 kg/2¼ lb
30 cm/12 inch	1.1 kg/2½ lb

SQUARE	SUGAR PASTE
15 cm/6 inch	575 g/1¼ lb
18 cm/7 inch	675 g/1½ lb
20 cm/8 inch	800 g/1¾ lb
23 cm/9 inch	900 g/2 lb
25 cm/10 inch	1 kg/2¼ lb
28 cm/11 inch	1.1 kg/2½ lb
30 cm/12 inch	1.4 kg/3 lb

SUGAR PASTE

675 g/1½ lb icing sugar, sifted
2 medium egg whites
30 ml/2 tbsp warmed liquid glucose
5 ml/1 tsp glycerine

Place the icing sugar in a clean, greasefree bowl. Add the remaining ingredients and work together with either a clean wooden spoon or the fingertips. Place the rough mixture on a clean surface dusted with icing sugar and knead hard for several minutes until smooth, pliable and not sticky, adding a little extra icing sugar if necessary. Wrap the sugar paste in polythene and leave to rest for 24 hours before using.

SUFFICIENT TO COVER THE TOP AND SIDES OF A 20 CM/8 INCH CAKE

GELATINE-BASED SUGAR PASTE

The gelatine replaces the egg white in this recipe and helps to keep the icing malleable. Be careful to measure the ingredients accurately. This paste is ideal for covering cakes and for making cut-out decorations, but it is not firm enough for making moulded decorations.

10 ml/2 tsp gelatine
5 ml/1 tsp glycerine
15 ml/1 tbsp warmed liquid glucose
about 450 g/1 lb icing sugar, sifted

Dissolve the gelatine in 20 ml/4 tsp warm water (see Mrs Beeton's Tip). Add the glycerine and liquid glucose.

Place the icing sugar in a large bowl, pour over the gelatine mixture and work the mixture together with a clean wooden spoon or the fingertips, adding a little extra icing sugar if necessary, Knead the paste until smooth. Use warm or wrap well and store.

SUFFICIENT TO COVER THE TOP AND SIDES OF A 15 CM/6 INCH CAKE

MRS BEETON'S TIP To dissolve the gelatine, sprinkle the powder over the warm water in a small bowl. Stand the bowl over a saucepan of hot water and stir until the gelatine has dissolved completely.

MICROWAVE TIP For easy measuring, the liquid glucose may be softened for a few seconds on Defrost. Be careful not to make it too hot.

MOULDING PASTE

This icing can be readily made from storecupboard ingredients but it is not as malleable as the sugar pastes and needs to be worked more quickly. The colour of the fat determines the colour of the finished paste.

25 g/1 oz butter
15 ml/1 tbsp lemon juice
350 g/12 oz icing sugar, sifted

Combine the butter and lemon juice in a small saucepan with 15 ml/1 tbsp water. Place over a low heat until the butter has melted.

Add 100 g/4 oz of the icing sugar, mix well and stir for 2 minutes or until the mixture begins to boil. Do not overcook. Immediately remove the pan from the heat and stir in 100 g/4 oz of the remaining icing sugar. Place the mixture in a clean bowl and beat with a wooden spoon, gradually adding extra icing sugar until it forms a soft dough.

Place the dough on a clean surface lightly dusted with icing sugar and knead until smooth and cool. Use immediately or cover until cold, then wrap in polythene.

SUFFICIENT TO COVER THE TOP OF A 20 CM/8 INCH CAKE

VARIATION

WHITE MOULDING PASTE Use a white fat but add a few extra drops of lemon juice, or rose water or almond essence to flavour.

MRS BEETON'S TIP If the paste becomes too dry to handle when stored, sprinkle with a little cooled, boiled water and re-seal bag. Leave for several hours to soften.

FILLINGS

If an icing or frosting makes an immediate impact, a filling is a taste of the unexpected. A good filling should complement a cake or gâteau, either enhancing an existing flavour or providing an interesting contrast without being overwhelming. This section of the book introduces lots of new ideas alongside old favourites like jam, lemon curd, fresh cream and fruit purées. When using fruit, make sure that the filling is not too wet, or the cake will become soggy.

Most of the buttercreams listed in an earlier section may be used as fillings, and more recipes will be found in the sections on Healthier Alternatives and Custards.

Use the fillings for large and small cakes, tray bakes and gâteaux. Multi-layered, and filled and topped with soft icing or cream, a gâteau is usually eaten with a fork or spoon, often as a dessert. A cake generally has a firmer filling, and may be held in the hand to be eaten.

RUM AND WALNUT FILLING

Use this as a filling for spice cakes or Applesauce Cake (page 100).

50 g/2 oz butter
75 g/3 oz soft light brown sugar
15 ml/1 tbsp rum
50 g/2 oz walnuts, chopped

Cream the butter and sugar together in a mixing bowl until soft. Gradually add the rum and beat well until the icing is light and fluffy. Fold in the walnuts.

SUFFICIENT FOR A SINGLE LAYER IN ONE 18 CM/7 INCH CAKE

COCONUT FILLING

This crunchy filling is suitable for Victoria Sandwich Cake (page 46) or for slightly heavier cakes similar to Classic Madeira Cake (page 85). It can also be used as an unusual topping for small cakes.

50 g/2 oz icing sugar, sifted
1 egg yolk
15 ml/1 tbsp lemon juice
25 g/1 oz desiccated coconut

Place the icing sugar, egg yolk and lemon juice in a small bowl and mix to a smooth paste. Place the bowl over a saucepan of hot water over a low heat and cook the mixture for 5-7 minutes, stirring constantly, until the mixture thickly coats the back of the wooden spoon. Remove the bowl from the heat and stir in the coconut. Leave to cool and thicken before use.

SUFFICIENT FOR A SINGLE LAYER IN ONE 18 CM/7 INCH CAKE

VARIATION

Toast the desiccated coconut under a grill or replace with ground toasted nuts.

🥄 **MRS BEETON'S TIP** These full-flavoured, nutty fillings go very well with cakes that are slightly more dense in texture or those that are well flavoured, for example chocolate cakes. Lighter fillings with a smooth texture are more suitable for airy, fatless sponge cakes.

CREAM FILLINGS

Fresh cream is still a prime favourite as a filling for gâteaux and afternoon tea cakes. Double cream has the best flavour and may be whipped and piped in much the same way as royal icing. Once whipped, it may be frozen on the decorated gâteaux and will not lose its shape when thawed. To reduce the risk of over-whipping, which might cause the cream to separate in hot weather, add 15 ml/ 1 tbsp milk to each 150 ml/¼ pint cream or replace up to one-third of the double cream with single cream. There is no need to add sugar to whipped cream.

TO WHIP THE CREAM

Choose a cool area of the kitchen in which to work and chill the bowl and whisk before use, by placing them in the refrigerator or freezer for a few minutes. A small wire balloon whisk is the best utensil, but for large quantities a hand-held electric whisk may be used with care.

Stand the bowl on a wet cloth or a non-slip surface, add the cream and tip the bowl. While whipping, incorporate as much air as possible. If using an electric whisk, start on high and reduce speed to low as the cream begins to thicken. Be very careful not to overwhip. Stop whipping as soon as the cream will stand in soft peaks and has doubled in volume.

The cream will continue to thicken slightly on standing and when piped, so stop whipping just before you think the cream is ready. It should be smooth and shiny in appearance. Overwhipped cream will 'frill' at the edges when piped.

For best results, use the whipped cream immediately, or cover and store in the refrigerator until required, giving it a gentle stir before use.

If the finished gâteau is to stand in a warm room for any length of time, whip in 5 ml/1 tsp gelatine, dissolved in 10 ml/2 tsp warm water and cooled. See also Whipped Cream Frosting (page 153).

FLAVOURINGS

Add any flavouring to cream when it has been whipped to soft peaks. Lemon or orange juice, liqueur or sherry may be used and should be added gradually during the final whipping. Once the cream has been whipped, finely chopped nuts, glacé fruits or grated citrus rind may be added.

REDUCING THE FAT CONTENT

For a low-fat whipped cream, replace up to one third with low or full-fat plain yogurt. This will not only make the cream less rich, but will prevent overwhipping and keep the cream smooth and shiny.

FREEZING

Cakes decorated with cream should be frozen and stored in a large domed plastic box. Alternatively, open freeze and then cocoon carefully in a dome of foil. Label well to avoid other items being inadvertently placed on top.

To thaw, remove the wrappings and thaw the cakes in a cool place, refrigerator or microwave (following the manufacturer's directions).

Small quantities of leftover cream may be whipped with a little caster sugar and piped in small stars on non-stick baking parchment for freezing. They may then be lifted off and placed, still frozen, on desserts and gâteaux for instant decoration.

CUSTARD FILLINGS

Confectioners' Custard, sometimes called Crème Patissière, makes an excellent filling for cakes. Thickened with eggs, flour or cornflour the custard sets to a thick cream when cold. Mock Cream is a simple filling based on milk thickened with cornflour and enriched with butter, while Quick Diplomat Cream is richer still, with double cream used as its base.

Unless using a double saucepan, it is easier to make these custards with yolks rather than whole eggs as the whites cook more quickly and lumps of cooked egg white may spoil the texture.

Vanilla sugar may be used instead of caster sugar in the recipes that follow. The vanilla pod or essence should then be omitted.

To prevent the formation of a skin on the cooked custard, press a dampened piece of greaseproof paper lightly on the surface. Do not use plasticised cling film for this purpose when the custard is hot.

> **MRS BEETON'S TIP** These light fillings, thickened with eggs, go very well with light sponge cakes and gâteaux that are filled or decorated with fresh fruit. They can also be used to decorate cheesecakes. This type of filling should not be frozen as it tends to curdle.

CONFECTIONERS' CUSTARD

300 ml/½ pint milk
1 vanilla pod or a few drops of vanilla essence
2 egg yolks
50 g/2 oz caster sugar
25 g/1 oz plain flour

Place the milk and vanilla pod, if used, in a small saucepan and bring to the boil over low heat. Remove from the heat and leave to one side, adding the vanilla essence, if used.

Whisk the egg yolks with the sugar in a bowl until thick and creamy, then add the flour. Remove the vanilla pod and very gradually add the milk to the egg mixture, beating constantly until all has been incorporated. Pour the mixture back into the saucepan and stir over a low heat for 1-2 minutes to cook the flour. The custard should thickly coat the back of the wooden spoon and be smooth and shiny.

Pour the custard into a clean bowl, cover and leave to cool. Beat well then cover again and chill until required.

MAKES ABOUT 300 ML/½ PINT

VARIATIONS

CHOCOLATE CUSTARD Stir 25 g/1 oz grated chocolate into the custard while still hot.

CRÈME ST HONORE Whisk 2 egg whites with 10 ml/2 tsp of caster sugar until stiff. Fold into cold custard. Use for choux pastry or as an alternative cream for gâteaux.

CRÈME FRANGIPANE Omit the vanilla flavouring. Add 40 g/1½ oz finely chopped butter to final cooking. When cold, fold in 75 g/3 oz crushed almond macaroons or 50 g/2 oz ground almonds and a few drops of almond essence.

CONFECTIONERS' CUSTARD WITH BRANDY

25 g/1 oz cornflour
360 ml/½ pint milk
3 egg yolks
40 g/1½ oz caster sugar
2.5 ml/½ tsp brandy, rum or liqueur

In a bowl mix the cornflour with a little milk, then beat in the egg yolks and sugar. Heat the remaining milk in a saucepan until tepid and pour slowly on to the cornflour mixture, stirring constantly. Pour the mixture back into the saucepan and stir over a low heat, without boiling, until the custard thickens and thickly coats the back of the wooden spoon. Remove from the heat, stir in the brandy, rum or liqueur and pour into a clean bowl. Cover and cool, then beat well. Cover again and chill until required.

MAKES ABOUT 300 ML/½ PINT

MOCK CREAM

10 ml/2 tsp cornflour
150 ml/¼ pint milk
50 g/2 oz butter, softened
50 g/2 oz icing or caster sugar
few drops of vanilla or almond essence

Mix the cornflour with a little milk in a small saucepan. Gradually stir in the remaining milk and cook over a low heat, stirring constantly until the mixture thickens. Cover and leave until tepid.

Cream the butter and sugar together in a bowl until light and fluffy. Gradually add the custard mixture to the butter, beating well between each addition. Beat in the essence, cover and chill.

SUFFICIENT FOR 2 LAYERS IN ONE 18 CM/ 7 INCH CAKE

QUICK DIPLOMAT CREAM

15 ml/1 tbsp custard powder
10 ml/2 tsp caster sugar
150 ml/¼ pint milk
150 ml/¼ pint double cream
few drops of vanilla essence

Mix the custard powder and sugar with a little milk in a small saucepan. Gradually stir in the remaining milk and stir over a low heat for 1 minute until thick. Transfer the mixture to a bowl, cover and leave to cool. Beat well then cover again and chill.

In a clean bowl, whisk the cream with the vanilla essence until thick. Beat the custard until smooth and lightly fold in the cream until well blended. Chill until required.

MAKES ABOUT 300 ML/½ PINT

VARIATIONS

ORANGE OR LEMON Fold in 5 ml/1 tsp finely grated orange or lemon rind.
CHOCOLATE Stir 50 g/2 oz grated chocolate into the hot custard.
LIQUEUR Replace the essence with brandy or liqueur.

TOPPINGS

These simple toppings may be prepared in advance and used to quickly decorate and finish a cake or gâteau. Most toppings can be stored in a screw-topped jar or in a cardboard box for several months. For a comprehensive list of shop-bought toppings and decorations see page 134.

COCONUT

Coconut has an interesting texture and makes a good topping on plain cakes. Choose good-quality desiccated coconut with large strands and use plain or colour as follows: Place about 50 g/2 oz coconut in a screw top jar, leaving at least 2.5 cm/1 inch space at the top. Add a few drops of food colouring (liquid colours are best), screw on the lid and shake the jar vigorously for a few minutes until the coconut is evenly coloured. Use the same day or spread the coconut out on a piece of greaseproof paper and leave in a warm place to dry before storing in a dry screw-topped jar.

Toasted coconut is prepared in the same way as Toasted Nuts (method follows).

COLOURED SUGAR CRYSTALS

Use either granulated sugar or roughly crushed sugar lumps and colour and dry in the same way as the coloured coconut above.

TOASTED NUTS

Whole flaked or chopped nuts may be lightly toasted to improve both colour and flavour. Almonds and hazelnuts are the most commonly used varieties.

To toast nuts, remove the rack from the grill pan and line the pan with a piece of foil. Spread the nuts over the foil. Heat the grill and toast the nuts under a medium heat, stirring occasionally until evenly browned. This will only take a few seconds. Lift out the foil carefully and leave the nuts to cool. This method may also be used to remove the skins from hazelnuts. Roast them under the grill, then rub the skins off while the nuts are still hot.

Toasted nuts are best used on the same day; alternatively, store when cold in a screw-topped jar for a few days.

PRALINE

This is a fine powder of crushed nuts and caramel used to flavour creams and fillings. Crushed roughly, it may be used as a cake decoration.

oil for greasing
50 g/2 oz caster sugar
50 g/2 oz almonds, toasted

Brush a baking sheet with oil. Place the sugar and nuts in a small, heavy-bottomed saucepan and heat slowly until the sugar melts, stirring occasionally. Continue cooking until the sugar turns from pale golden in colour to deep golden. Quickly pour the caramel on to the prepared baking sheet and leave until cold.

Crush the caramel to a fine powder with a rolling pin or pestle and mortar. Alternatively, break it up roughly and crush in a blender. Store the powder in a dry screw-topped jar for up to 3 months.

MAKES ABOUT 100 G/4 OZ

FROSTED FLOWERS AND LEAVES

Suitable flowers include freshly picked small, thin-petalled flowers such as primroses, sweet peas, violets and fruit blossom. Check that the selected flower is not poisonous if eaten. Suitable leaves include rose leaves, mint, sage and French parsley.

Prepare the flowers by gently shaking them upside down. Spread them out on absorbent kitchen paper. Leave for about 20 minutes to ensure any insects have crawled out. To prepare the leaves, gently swish through cold water. Shake dry and spread the leaves out on absorbent kitchen paper to dry. Frost at least three times as many flowers or leaves as you may require as they are very fragile.

1 egg white
caster sugar

In a bowl, lightly beat the egg white with 5 ml/1 tsp water until the egg is no longer stringy but not frothy. Using a fine paint brush, paint a thin layer of egg wash over and under the petals or leaves, being careful not to miss any part. Sprinkle them lightly all over with sugar until evenly coated. Spread the frosted flowers out on greaseproof paper or non-stick baking parchment.

Leave them to dry in an airy place away from direct sunlight until dry and hard. They can be easily removed from the paper.

Store the frosted flowers and leaves between sheets of tissue paper in a small cardboard box for up to several weeks. Check them occasionally and discard any that have crumpled.

SUGARED STRANDS

The thin coloured rind of most citrus fruits may be crystallised in thin strands to sprinkle over cakes and tarts. Lemon and orange are the fruits most frequently used.

1 orange or lemon
50 g/2 oz granulated sugar

Scrub the fruit with a small brush under running water. Using a potato peeler, shave off the peel in long, thin strips. With a small sharp knife, cut the peel into long, very fine strands. Place the strands in a small saucepan with 125 ml/4 fl oz water. Simmer for 2 minutes until the peel is tender. Remove strands with a slotted spoon and drain on absorbent kitchen paper.

Stir the sugar into the water and simmer over a low heat until melted. Increase the heat and boil rapidly, without stirring, until the syrup is reduced by half. Return the peel to the pan and cook, uncovered, until well glazed. Remove the peel with a slotted spoon and leave to cool on non-stick baking parchment. When cold, store the sugared strands in a box between leaves of waxed paper or non-stick baking parchment.

☀ MICROWAVE TIP The whole process may be done in the microwave using a suitable small bowl. Timings will be approximately the same but take care that the sugar does not brown too much. Check every 10 seconds once the syrup is boiling.

GRILLED TOPPINGS

These toppings are used on plain and light fruit cakes instead of icing and are spread over while the cake is still warm.

GOLDEN NUT TOPPING

50 g/2 oz butter, softened
100 g/4 oz soft light brown sugar
45 ml/3 tbsp single cream
100 g/4 oz chopped mixed nuts

Cream the butter and sugar together in a bowl, then beat in the cream and fold in the mixed nuts.

Spread the topping over the cake while it is cooling. Place the cake under a preheated low grill. Heat for 2-3 minutes until the topping is bubbling and light golden in colour. Leave the cake to cool before cutting.

SUFFICIENT TO COVER TWO 15 CM/6 INCH SQUARE CAKES

VARIATION

WALNUT TOPPING Use 100 g/4 oz chopped walnuts instead of mixed nuts.

GOLDEN COCONUT TOPPING

50 g/2 oz butter, softened
100 g/4 oz soft light brown sugar
75 g/3 oz desiccated coconut
45 ml/3 tbsp single cream

Combine the butter, sugar and coconut in a bowl and work ingredients together until well blended. Stir in the cream and spread the topping over the warm cake. Place the cake under a preheated low grill for 3-4 minutes until the topping is golden brown in colour. Leave to cool before cutting.

SUFFICIENT TO COVER TWO 15 CM/6 INCH SQUARE CAKES

VARIATION

ORANGE COCONUT TOPPING Use granulated sugar and orange juice instead of the brown sugar and cream.

> MRS BEETON'S TIP Take great care when browning coconut under the grill, either on its own or in a topping. Do not have the grill too hot and watch the topping closely as it browns quickly and it may become scorched if it is left to cook unattended.

Twenty-first Birthday Cake (page 251)

Musical Notes Birthday Cake (page 252)

Brush Embroidery Cakes (page 252)

Easter Cakes (page 253)

HEALTHIER ALTERNATIVES

Whether you are counting the calories or courting healthier eating habits, you may wish to use less sugar and fat in your recipes.

Sugar not only provides sweetness but also bulk, so this should be replaced with fruit, ground nuts or low-fat cream cheese. Butter may be replaced with vegetable oil-based spreads or low-fat cream cheese. Use plenty of natural flavourings or add a few drops of liqueur, and the results will be just as tasty as when conventionally made.

APRICOT SPREAD

8 apricot halves, canned in natural juice, drained
175 g/6 oz low-fat cream cheese
few drops of lemon juice

Purée or sieve the apricots. In a bowl, cream the cheese and lemon juice together and gradually beat in the apricot purée. Alternatively, place all ingredients in a blender or a food processor and work until the mixture is light and creamy. Chill the spread before use.

SUFFICIENT TO FILL A 20 CM/8 INCH CAKE

MRS BEETON'S TIP Fresh apricots or dried apricots may be substituted for canned. Soak dried apricots overnight and simmer in soaking liquor for 5-10 minutes.

APPLE AND BLACKCURRANT SPREAD

This is a thick fruit purée which may replace jam in a recipe. Because of its low sugar content, it will not keep for more than a week.

225 g/8 oz cooking apples, peeled and chopped
175 g/6 oz blackcurrants, topped and tailed
150 ml/¼ pint unsweetened apple juice
30 ml/2 tbsp apple concentrate
grated rind and juice of 1 orange

Combine the apples, blackcurrants and apple juice in a small saucepan. Cover and cook over a low heat until the fruit is soft, stirring occasionally.

Add the apple concentrate, orange rind and juice and simmer, uncovered, until the mixture is thick and pulpy. Stir occasionally to prevent the mixture from burning on the base. The purée is ready when the base of the saucepan can be seen as the mixture is stirred. Place the purée in a clean container, cover and when cold refrigerate for up to 1 week.

SUFFICIENT FOR TWO LAYERS IN ONE 18 CM/7 INCH CAKE

CITRUS CHEESE ICING

100 g/4 oz low-fat cream cheese
75 g/3 oz icing sugar, sifted
10 ml/2 tsp finely grated lemon or orange rind
30 ml/2 tbsp lemon or orange juice

Place cheese and sugar in a bowl and blend them together. Add rind and juice and beat all the ingredients together until light.

SUFFICIENT TO FILL A 20 CM/8 INCH CAKE

QUICK GUIDE TO USING COVERINGS, FILLINGS AND TOPPINGS WITH PLAIN CAKES

The following chart offers a quick-reference guide to using the recipes in this chapter with the cakes from the first section of the book. The cakes are grouped according to their type in the headings across the top of the chart and a variety of recipes for each type can be found in the chapters on cake making. The following are a few examples.

Small Cakes These include Small Rich Cakes (page 45), Basic Buns (page 116), Honey Buns (page 118) and Brownies (page 121).

Victoria Sandwich Cake This can be made by the traditional method or a one-stage cake can be prepared (page 46).

Sponge Cakes Either Sponge Cake (page 48), Genoese Sponge Cake or Pastry (page 48) or Swiss Roll (page 72).

Madeira Cake As well as this traditional, plain cake (page 85), other cakes with similar textures include Mrs Beeton's Almond Cake

	Small Cakes	Victoria Sandwich Cake	Sponge Cakes	Madeira Cake	Chocolate Cakes	Light Fruit Cakes	Rich Fruit Cakes	Cheese-cakes
GLAZES AND COATINGS								
Apricot Glaze	■	■		■		■	■	■
Chocolate Glaze	■	■	■		■			
Maraschino Glaze		■	■					■
Glaze for Sweet Flans			■					■
ALMOND PASTE AND MARZIPAN								
Marzipan				■		■	■	
Almond Paste				■		■	■	
Cooked Almond Paste				■		■	■	
BUTTER ICINGS AND FUDGE ICINGS								
Buttercream	■	■		■	■			
Rich Buttercream	■	■	■	■	■			
Fluffy Buttercream		■	■		■			
French Butter Icing		■	■		■			
Chocolate Fudge Icing	■				■			
Dark Fudge Icing	■	■			■			
GLACÉ ICINGS								
Glacé Icing	■	■	■	■	■			
Chocolate Glacé Icing					■			
Glacé Fondant	■	■	■	■				
FROSTINGS								
American Frosting		■	■	■	■			
Quick American Frosting		■	■	■	■			
Caramel Frosting		■	■	■	■			
Whipped Cream Frosting		■	■	■	■			
FONDANTS								
Traditional Fondant	■		■	■	■		■	
Quick Fondant	■		■	■	■		■	
Syrup-based Fondant	■		■	■	■		■	

(page 52), Banana and Walnut Cake (page 53) or Apple and Ginger Cake (page 62). The flavoured cakes are usually covered with a light icing, such as glacé icing, rather than a more formal moulding icing.

Chocolate Cakes The filling and icing on any of the chocolate cakes can be varied. Plain Chocolate Loaf (page 50) or Chocolate and Almond Loaf (page 51) can be split and filled or coated in icing. Instead of icings, glazes can be used with toppings. Devil's Food Cake (page 96) or Marble Cake (page 79) can be varied by using alternative toppings to those suggested in the recipes.

Light Fruit Cakes One-stage Fruit Cake (page 44), Countess Spice Cake (page 65), Everyday Bran Cake (page 66) or Holiday Cake (page 66) can all be glazed, iced or topped.

Rich Fruit Cakes The chart on page 241 gives quantities for making rich fruit cakes of different sizes. A comprehensive recipe for a Three Tier Wedding Cake is included on page 82.

Cheesecakes The Lemon Cheesecake (page 114) can be glazed and a topping can be added. The chart indicates alternatives to whipped cream for decoration.

	Small Cakes	Victoria Sandwich Cake	Sponge Cakes	Madeira Cake	Chocolate Cakes	Light Fruit Cakes	Rich Fruit Cakes	Cheese-cakes
ROYAL ICING								
Using egg white or dried egg white						■	■	
MOULDING ICINGS								
Sugar Paste	■	■		■		■	■	
Gelatine-based Sugar Paste	■	■		■		■	■	
Moulding Paste	■	■		■		■	■	
FILLINGS								
Rum and Walnut Filling		■	■		■			
Coconut Filling	■	■		■	■			
Cream Fillings		■	■		■			■
Custard Fillings		■	■		■			■
Confectioners' Custard		■	■					■
Confectioners' Custard with Brandy		■	■		■			■
Mock Cream		■	■		■			
Quick Diplomat Cream		■	■		■			■
TOPPINGS								
Toasted Nuts	■	■	■	■	■	■		■
Praline			■	■	■			■
Coconut	■	■		■				
Coloured Sugar Crystals				■		■		
Frosted Flowers and Leaves				■			■	
Sugar Strands	■	■	■					
GRILLED TOPPINGS								
Golden Nut Topping		■		■		■		
Golden Coconut Topping		■		■		■		
HEALTHIER ALTERNATIVES								
Citrus Cheese Icing	■	■	■		■			
Apricot Spread		■	■					
Apple and Blackcurrant Spread		■	■					

BASIC FILLING AND COVERING TECHNIQUES

Before progressing to piping designs of intricate detail, master the basic techniques in this chapter. From applying the first coat of glaze to achieving a perfect finish on a flat-iced cake, all the advice you need to ensure success is included here.

As with most skills, there are several ways of achieving the desired result; this is particularly true of cake decorating. In this chapter, the basic methods of filling and covering cakes are explained, using various recipes from the previous chapter. This first process of coating or covering forms the base for any decoration, simple or elaborate. Occasionally, an alternative method is given and it is a good idea to experiment with different methods to find out which suits you best.

The quality of the cake is important in determining the finished appearance. For example, the flatter the top of the cake, the better will be the final result. Make sure that you use the correct sized cake tin for the quantity of cake mixture, as peaked cakes are usually the result of using too small a tin for the mixture. Try to avoid slicing the top off a fruit cake; if this is not possible, never invert the cut side on to a cake board as this tends to draw the moisture out of the cake.

Before you begin to decorate a cake, make sure that you have all the equipment to hand and, if possible, choose a time when you are least likely to be disturbed until you have finished. Some icings set or stiffen quickly, so they need to be used efficiently without even a short break. The cake should be placed on a plate, board or wire rack, depending on the type of icing used. Use a dry pastry brush to brush away all loose crumbs which may spoil the icing.

A turntable is useful if you are coating the side of a round cake with icing. Alternatively, stand the cake on its board on a biscuit tin or upturned cake tin to raise the height of the cake and to make it easier to rotate. All the equipment must be scrupulously clean and the work surface must also be absolutely clean, dry and free of any specks of dust if the icing or cake covering is rolled out.

FILLING AND COVERING CAKES WITH APRICOT GLAZE

Apricot glaze can be used to sandwich cake layers together or it can be applied as a decorative coating. A variety of toppings can be sprinkled on to the glaze to complete the decoration. For example, try toasted, chopped or flaked nuts, toasted or coloured desiccated coconut, grated or flaked chocolate, finely chopped glacé fruits, chocolate vermicelli or praline. Before you begin, make sure that you have the following items prepared and close by ready to be used:

Apricot Glaze (page 140)
dry pastry brush
palette knife
the prepared topping (if used)
greaseproof paper or non-stick baking parchment
a plate or board for the completed cake

If not freshly prepared, re-heat the glaze with an additional 5 ml/1 tsp of water and bring it to the boil. Then leave it to cool a little but use it while still warm. Brush any loose crumbs from the top and sides of the cake. If you are adding a topping, have it prepared and spread it in a thick layer on a piece of greaseproof paper.

TO COAT THE SIDES OF THE CAKE

Quickly brush the glaze around the sides of the cake, making sure they are evenly coated. If using topping, place one hand on the top of the cake and the other under it, then lightly roll the cake in the topping until the sides are evenly covered. Press the cake down very lightly to coat the glaze thinly in topping. If too much topping is taken up at first, then the covering will be uneven and some areas will be sticky with glaze. Place the cake on a plate or board.

TO COVER THE TOP OF THE CAKE

Lightly brush the glaze over the top of the cake and sprinkle it liberally with topping. Lay a piece of clean greaseproof paper on top and press it down lightly to ensure that the coating sticks. Remove the paper.

FILLING AND TOPPING CAKES WITH BUTTERCREAM

Have the following items prepared and at hand before you begin:

the prepared cake
large serrated knife
Buttercream (page 144)
palette knife
plate or board for the completed cake

CUTTING THE CAKE INTO LAYERS

Place the cake on a flat surface and use a large serrated knife to slice horizontally through the cake, about 5 cm/2 inches in towards the centre. Slowly rotate the cake as you cut, then continue rotating and slicing the cake until it is sliced right through into two equal layers. Lift off the top layer and place it on a flat surface, top side uppermost.

TO FILL AND TOP THE CAKE

The buttercream should be of soft spreading consistency. If it was made in advance beat it to soften the mixture, adding a few drops of milk or fruit juice if necessary. Alternatively, the buttercream may be softened by warming in the microwave for 5 seconds on Defrost. Stiff icing is difficult to spread and it will drag the surface of the cake.

Use about one-third of the buttercream to sandwich the cake layers. Using a palette knife, lightly spread the buttercream evenly over the base layer of the cake, to within 5 mm/¼ inch of the edge. Carefully position the second cake layer on top. Spread the remaining buttercream on top of the cake in the same way. Finish the cake by smoothing the buttercream with the palette knife, then marking it with a fork or serrated scraper.

TO COAT THE SIDES OF THE CAKE

If the sides of the cake are covered with buttercream, divide the quantity of buttercream into four. Use one quarter for the filling, two quarters to cover the sides of the cake and the remaining quarter for the top. Spread the buttercream around the cake. The sides can be lightly rolled in a dry topping as when filling and covering with apricot glaze (see left).

If the top of the cake is to be covered in Glacé Icing (page 151), spread the buttercream up into a small ridge around the top edge of the cake to stop the icing spilling over the side.

COATING CAKES WITH GLACÉ ICING

This simple icing is not firm enough for piping or rolling. It is poured over the cake and allowed to set before any decoration is added. Glacé icing is usually only used on the top of a cake. When it dries, it is brittle and it tends to craze, especially if you move the cake before the icing is quite dry. The consistency of the icing should be similar to thick cream that will just flow to find its own level. It must not be so thin that it runs off the cake. Do not make the icing until you are ready to use it. There are two ways of coating the top of a cake with glacé icing.

Method 1 This method is used if the sides of the cake are coated with buttercream or a glaze and topping. The sides of the cake must be decorated first, taking care to extend the covering up along the top edge to form a small, even ridge.

Make up the glacé icing and pour it in a slow, steady stream starting at the centre of the cake and working in a circular movement towards the edge. The icing should find its own level but small areas may have to be teased towards the edge using the pointed end of a knife. Leave the icing to set, undisturbed, for several hours.

Method 2 If the sides of the cake are not covered, cut out a band of double-thick non-stick baking parchment to fit round the cake and extend about 1 cm/½ inch above the top edge. Place the collar in position so that it fits the cake tightly and secure it in place with a paper clip.

Make the icing and pour it on to the top of the cake as in Method 1. When the icing is dry, use a hot, dry knife to slice between the icing and the paper collar as you peel away the paper.

COATING CAKES WITH FROSTINGS OR FUDGE ICINGS

Most frostings have to be spread quickly over the cake as soon as they have been made or they will set in the bowl. It is, therefore, important to have the cake ready to ice before you begin. As they are spread on the cake, frostings and fudge icings begin to set, so it is not possible to pipe with them. Hot water is used to heat a palette knife for spreading the icing but the knife must be dried before use. It is essential to have everything organised before you begin to make the icing, so that it can be used immediately:

cake, ready-filled if required
plate or board
dry pastry brush
small palette knife
small quantity of hot water for heating the palette knife
any decorations or toppings
ingredients for frosting or fudge icing

Place the cake on a flat plate or board. Alternatively, rest it on an upturned plate so that when the icing has set, the cake can be transferred easily to its serving plate without the icing being touched and spoilt. Brush away any loose cake crumbs. Place the palette knife in the hot water. Make the icing, following the chosen recipe, and cover the cake immediately, using either of the methods that follow. Add any decorations to the cake before the icing sets.

FOR A SOFT FINISH

Pour all the icing on top of the cake and work quickly using the *dry*, hot knife. Draw the icing over the cake and down the sides, working in small circular movements from the centre outwards. Using a clean, hot knife, swirl the icing into peaks as it begins to set.

FOR A STIFFER ICING

First cover the sides of the cake. Spread about two-thirds of the icing round the sides, using the *dry*, hot knife and working quickly in small circular movements. Draw the icing up towards the top of the cake.

Spoon the remaining icing on the top of the cake and work quickly to draw the blobs of icing together to make an even coating. Use a clean, hot knife to quickly swirl the icing into soft peaks.

COVERING CAKES WITH TRADITIONAL FONDANT

Traditional fondant may be used as a cake covering when warmed and diluted with stock syrup. When dry it gives a smooth, shiny finish. It is most frequently used to coat small, fancy cakes such as petits fours. Fruit cakes must have a base coating of marzipan or almond paste before a coating of traditional fondant is applied. On a larger cake, it is essential that the surface is uncut and level, or the icing will flow away from the centre. Turn the cake upside down if necessary. Before you start, check through the following list, making sure that everything is ready:

Traditional Fondant (page 154)
basin
saucepan of hot water
wooden spoon
Stock Syrup (page 154) or boiled water
food colouring, if used
the prepared cake, or cakes
wire rack
baking sheet lined with non-stick baking
    parchment
dry pastry brush
Apricot Glaze (page 140)
small palette knife
small pointed knife

PREPARING THE FONDANT

Place the fondant in the basin over the saucepan of hot water and stir it occasionally until it has melted. Dilute the fondant to the consistency of thick cream by adding a little stock syrup or water. Add a few drops of food colouring at this stage, if used.

PREPARING THE CAKE

Place the cake on a wire rack and stand it over the lined baking sheet. Brush the cake with a dry brush to remove excess crumbs. Prepare the apricot glaze and brush it lightly over the cake. A small ball of marzipan may be placed in the centre of each cake when making petits fours.

COATING WITH FONDANT

When the fondant is ready, spoon it carefully over the cake and let it run down the sides to coat the cake completely. Use the pointed end of the knife to tease small areas of icing into place, if necessary, to ensure that the cake is evenly coated. Any fondant that drips through the rack can be collected and re-used, providing it is free from crumbs and glaze. Stir the fondant occasionally to prevent a skin from forming. Leave the fondant to set, then neaten the base of the cake by trimming away excess icing.

SWIRLED FONDANT

Alternatively, the icing can be applied more thickly and swirled with a knife as it sets.

COVERING CAKES WITH ALMOND PASTE OR MARZIPAN

Fruit cakes must be covered with almond paste or marzipan before they are coated with royal icing or covered with rolled-out icings or traditional fondant. The almond paste provides a flat surface for the icing and it also prevents the fruit in the cake from discolouring the icing. The cake covered with almond paste should be left in a dry place for at least a week, and up to two weeks for a wedding cake, before the icing is added. Lay a piece of greaseproof paper loosely over the top of the cake to protect it from dust. Never put the almond-paste-coated cake in an airtight tin or the paste will go mouldy.

For a professional finish, the surface must be as flat as possible. Even the flattest cake will need a little building up at the edge but if the cake is too domed, the almond paste will have to be very thick to compensate. When working, it is important to keep all crumbs away from the almond paste. Any that find their way on to the surface of the paste may discolour the icing. Assemble all the equipment and ingredients before you begin to work with the almond paste, and make sure that the work surface is scrupulously clean and dry. You will need:

the prepared cake or cakes
non-stick baking parchment
scissors
cake board
dry pastry brush
Apricot Glaze (page 140) or pure alcohol
Almond Paste (page 142) or Marzipan (page 142)
sifted icing sugar for dusting surface
rolling pin
sharp knife
small palette knife
string
small spirit level (optional)
spacers (optional)

TO COVER THE TOP OF THE CAKE

There are two methods that can be used for covering the top of the cake with almond paste or marzipan. Method 2 is suitable for small and medium-sized cakes, but you may find method 1 easier when covering larger cakes, for example, the bottom tier of a large wedding cake.

Method 1 Cut a piece of parchment to fit the top of the cake exactly. To do this either measure the cake accurately or stand the cake on a piece of parchment and draw round it, then transfer the pattern to a clean

Method 1

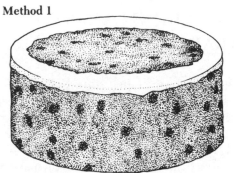

1 Press small rolls of paste around the edge of the cake to ensure the top is level.

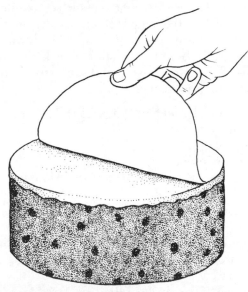

2 Invert the paper pattern and the paste on top of the cake, press lightly, then peel away the paper.

piece of parchment. Remember that if you draw round the tin in which the cake was cooked, you will need to cut slightly within the line to compensate for the thickness of the tin. Lightly dust the paper pattern with icing sugar.

Place the cake in the centre of the cake board and brush away all loose crumbs. Lightly glaze the top of the cake, around the outer edge only, with apricot glaze or alcohol.

Knead small pieces of almond paste and shape them into thin sausages. Place these all round the top outer edge of the cake. Holding the side firmly, with one hand extended to the height of the cake, press and mould the paste towards the centre of the cake to level the top. Lay a sheet of parchment on the top of the cake and roll it lightly with a rolling pin (do not use the paper pattern for this). Remove the parchment and brush the top of the cake with more glaze or alcohol.

Knead one-third of the remaining almond paste lightly into a ball and press it out on the centre of the paper pattern. Lightly dust the rolling pin with icing sugar and roll out the almond paste evenly, rotating the paper until the paste is even in thickness and the same size as the paper. If you have spacers, then use them to make sure that the paste is rolled out evenly. Trim the edges if necessary.

Lift up the paper pattern and the paste, then invert the paste on to the cake, positioning it carefully. Lightly press to stick the almond paste, then peel off the paper.

Method 2 Lightly dust the work surface with icing sugar and brush the top of the cake with apricot glaze or alcohol.

Lightly knead about one third of the paste and roll it out evenly, using spacers if available, to 2.5 cm/1 inch larger than the top of the cake. Invert the cake, glazed side downwards, on to the paste.

Using the palette knife, carefully work round the edge of the cake, pushing and easing the paste under the cake to fill the

Method 2

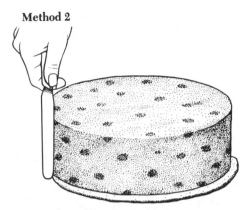

Invert the cake on to the paste, then use a palette knife to ease the edges of the paste around the cake to make a level top.

gap. This ensures that the paste will be level.

Trim off any excess paste where necessary, then carefully turn the cake over, making sure that the almond paste is not left behind on the work surface. Centre the cake, paste-side uppermost, on the cake board.

TO COVER THE SIDES OF THE CAKE

Two alternative methods are given and they can be used with either almond paste or marzipan for all shapes of cake. Method 1 is the best to use for very large cakes.

Method 1 Measure the height of the cake accurately with a piece of string. Measure the circumference with string and add on 1 cm/ ½ inch to compensate for the thickness of the almond paste. From a sheet of parchment, cut a paper pattern that measures twice the height and half the circumference of the cake. Lightly dust the pattern with icing sugar. Brush the sides of the cake to remove all crumbs.

Lightly knead the remaining almond paste and shape it into a flat sausage the same length as the pattern. Place the paste down the middle of the paper pattern. Flatten the roll, then roll it out evenly across the width to fit the pattern exactly. Trim the edges, if necessary. With the sharp knife, cut the strip of paste in half along its length to make two equal strips, then following the same cutting line made by the knife, cut the paper in half with scissors.

Small Round Cakes Brush the side of the cake with apricot glaze or alcohol. Hold the top and bottom of the cake between the palms of your hands and position the side of the cake carefully on one piece of paste, then roll the cake along its length. Repeat with the second piece. Place the cake in the middle of the cake board, carefully peel off the paper and smooth the joins with a palette knife.

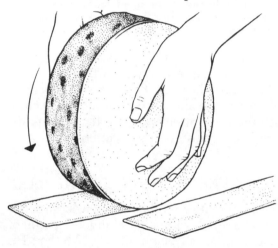

Large Round Cakes Position the cake in the middle of the cake board and brush apricot glaze or alcohol around the side. Lift up one strip of paste on the paper and place it in position around the cake. Repeat with the second piece. Carefully remove the paper and smooth the joins. Smooth around the cake with your hands to press the almond paste securely on to the cake.

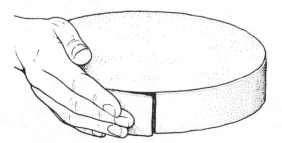

Square Cakes Attach the almond paste to a square cake as for the large round cake. It is easier if you to avoid having the joins on the corners. Mould the corners neatly once the paste is in position and when the joins have been smoothed. For very large square cakes, divide each length of paste into two for easier handling.

Method 2 Position the cake in the centre of the board. Measure the height and circumference of the cake, then lightly brush the cake with apricot glaze or alcohol.

Dust the work surface with icing sugar, then lightly knead the remaining almond paste and roll it into a long, plump sausage. Flatten the paste and roll it into a strip that measures the same height as the cake, and the same length as the circumference of the cake. Trim the edges of the paste and roll it up loosely. Place one end of the roll on the cake and unroll the paste, pressing it firmly on to the side of the cake. Smooth the join together with a palette knife.

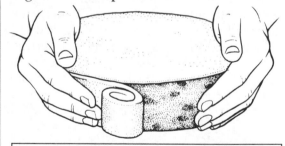

MRS BEETON'S TIP It is worth spending time on covering the cake smoothly with almond paste as it is difficult to compensate for unevenness when coating with icing. Check the level of your work surface with a spirit level before you begin – you may be surprised how much a surface can slope. Check the level of the cake when the top has been covered with paste and smooth out any uneven areas with a rolling pin, if necessary. There is no need to stick a fruit cake on to the cake board as the weight of mixture and finished icing will be sufficient to keep it in place.

COVERING CAKES WITH SUGAR PASTE AND MOULDING ICINGS

Rolled out icing can be applied directly on to a light cake. Fruit cakes should be covered with a layer of almond paste before the icing is placed on top, otherwise the icing will quickly discolour. If you dislike almond paste, try placing two layers of sugar paste over the cake, allowing the first layer to dry well before adding the second. This is not suitable for a wedding cake or any cake that is intended to be kept but for most other occasions you might get away with it.

Make sure that all your equipment is clean and free from grease. It is also a good idea to wear a large, clean apron, as small flecks of fluff from your clothing can easily fall on to the icing. Scrub the work surface and dry it thoroughly. Remove any rings from your fingers, as these would mark the icing when smoothing the surface on the cake. If you have long fingernails, take care not to mark the icing with them as you work. Impressions on the icing are difficult to eradicate.

Do not use cornflour for rolling out sugar paste that is to be placed directly on the cake as the starch will ferment. Use finely sifted icing sugar to lightly dust the work surface and the rolling pin. Cornflour can be used on the icing which is not directly in contact with a moist cake, for example to buff the top surface, for moulding flowers or making other decorations. Knead the paste lightly, using just the fingertips and use only a fine dusting of sugar. If you knead the paste too vigorously air pockets will be trapped and the surface will be uneven.

Choose a cool time of day to work and avoid using artificial light. Hairline cracks may not be seen until the morning when it will be too late to remove them. Similarly, colouring should be added to the paste in daylight. Remember, colours dry a shade or two darker.

TO COLOUR SUGAR PASTE

Remove a piece of paste about the size of a large walnut from the weighed-out quantity. Add a little paste colour to this small ball of icing and knead it in well. The ball will probably be several shades darker than required. Break off small pieces of the coloured paste and knead them lightly but thoroughly into the white paste, adding extra pieces of colour as required.

If you are matching the colour of the icing to a fabric or similar, break off a small piece, press it out thinly and leave it to dry for a few hours before checking the colour. Carefully wrap the remaining pieces of paste separately until required. When the required depth of colour has been obtained, break off a small piece and wrap it up well, keeping it, and any of the remaining deeply coloured ball, in case extra icing has to be coloured.

WORKING WITH SUGAR PASTE

Assemble all the ingredients and utensils before you begin to work on the cake:

cake, on a cake board
dry pastry brush
Apricot Glaze (page 140), alcohol or Butter-
    cream (page 144)
sifted icing sugar
rolling pin
spacers (optional)
knife
cornflour for buffing the icing

Measure the surface of the cake to be covered, including the depth of the side. Brush away all loose crumbs from the cake. If the cake is covered in almond paste, lightly coat it with apricot glaze or alcohol. Spread a thin layer of buttercream over a sponge or similar cake which is not covered in almond paste. Clean the board.

Lightly dust the work surface with icing sugar, then lightly knead the paste with the fingertips until it is smooth. Shape the ball of paste into the final shape required; for example shape a ball for a round cake, a box for a square cake or a sausage shape for a long thin strip of cake.

Lightly dust the rolling pin with icing sugar and roll out the paste evenly, using spacers, if available. The rolled out paste should be no thicker than 5 mm/¼ inch and it should be about 2.5 cm/1 inch shorter than required, as the icing will stretch and drop when it is hung over the edge of a cake. For example, if the cake to be covered is 20 cm/8 inches in diameter and 5 cm/2 inches deep, the paste should be rolled to a diameter of 28 cm/11 inches.

TO COVER A ROUND CAKE

Carefully slide the rolling pin under the paste, lift it up and position it accurately over the cake. With clean, dry hands, lightly dusted in cornflour, work the icing with the palm of your hand in a circular movement from the centre of the cake towards the edge. The icing will drop down the side and should

be lightly pressed and smoothed around the cake. Always work in a light, circular movement and avoid marking the icing with your fingernails. Trim the paste at the base of the cake, if necessary. You will probably find that you need to wash your hands again at this stage. Ensure they are well dried, dust them very lightly with cornflour and quickly but lightly buff up the surface of the cake with the palm of one hand. Using both hands, one either side of the cake, buff up the side with small circular movements, rotating the cake as necessary.

TO MAKE A SHARPER TOP EDGE FOR PIPING

Do this before the final buffing. Using both hands, one to extend the icing on the side of the cake upwards slightly and the other to smooth the paste on the top of the cake, mould a sharp edge. This step is only necessary if you intend adding a piped edge around the cake.

TO COVER A SQUARE CAKE

Follow the instructions for covering a round cake but pay attention to the corners immediately you have laid the rolled out icing over the cake. Lift the icing and work it away from the corner, not towards it. Gently ease the paste back along the sides of the cake until it is smooth. You must do this at once, otherwise thick pleats form on the corners of the cake. Continue smoothing the icing as for the round cake, trimming the edges neatly and moulding sharp edges and corners.

Leave the cake to dry out at room temperature for at least 24 hours before adding any decoration, longer if possible. Cover the top with a piece of greaseproof paper when the surface is dry to protect it from dust.

TIERED CAKES

If you are decorating a tiered cake, follow the instructions on page 242 for setting on the pillars at this stage.

COATING CAKES WITH ROYAL ICING

This icing sets harder than any other icing and it is traditionally used for wedding cakes because it can support the weight of the tiers. Glycerine should not be added when the icing is used for tiered cakes because it softens the icing. Royal icing made with albumen or albumen substitutes tends to set harder than icing made with fresh egg white. Royal icing gives sharper edges and corners than the moulding icing or softer icings. This is better for piping a border or for adding an edging as decoration.

Royal icing can only be applied to firm cakes that are covered with almond paste or marzipan and have a firm, flat surface on which to apply icing. Make sure the almond paste or marzipan is completely dry before applying the icing. When working on a single cake, or one layer or a tiered-cake allow a minimum of 3 days to ice the cakes plus one week for the icing to dry. Allow 2 weeks or more for the icing on a tiered cake to dry.

WORKING WITH ROYAL ICING

For a good finish, three coats of royal icing should be applied; the final coat gives no thickness but makes a smooth, fine surface. Make up the full quantity of icing for all the cakes to be covered and mix the icing to a soft-peak consistency. Leave the icing to stand, covered, for 3-4 hours to dispel air bubbles.

After applying the first coat, carefully scrape the remaining icing into a clean bowl taking care that no particles of dried icing from the sides of the bowl are included. Cover the icing with a damp cloth and wrap the whole bowl in a polythene bag. The next day the icing will be a little slacker; give it a quick beat before applying it to the cake. Store the icing as before. Again, the icing will be slightly slacker for the next application.

Do not thicken the icing to the original consistency as thinner coats give a smoother finish.

It is important not to allow even one dried particle of icing to mix with the soft icing as this, when dragged across the cake, will leave a trail. If you do have particles of dried icing in the soft icing, then press it through a very fine, clean, nylon sieve. Keep the icing covered at all times with a clean, damp cloth.

Before starting, check that the work surface is level. When icing the top of the cake, the correct height is one at which you can stand with your arm bent at the elbow and your lower arm parallel to the cake.

Stand with your feet slightly apart, with one foot in front of the other. When you begin levelling the cake, start with the pressure on your front foot and gradually transfer this to the other foot as you draw the ruler across the top of the cake towards you. You will find that this enables you to complete the action with even pressure, and in one continuous movement.

Practise this position before you begin to ice the cake. Wear a large, clean apron as small flecks of fluff, hairs or specks of dust easily find their way from clothes on to the icing. If possible, ice the cake in daylight and choose a time when you are unlikely to be disturbed. Stand the cake board on a damp cloth or rubber mat to prevent it from slipping. Assemble all the equipment and ingredients that you will need before you begin to ice the cake:

marzipanned cake on board
Royal Icing (page 156), mixed to soft-peak
　　consistency
large palette knife
small palette knife
clean damp cloth
ruler
scraper
small sharp knife (not serrated)
turntable (for a round cake)
glass-headed stainless steel pin

TO FLAT ICE THE TOP OF A ROUND OR SQUARE CAKE

Lightly beat the icing and place about half in the centre of the cake. Using the large palette knife, work the icing backwards and forwards, spreading it across the cake to cover the almond paste or marzipan. Pay particular attention to the edges and corners. Use the palette knife flat on the cake and press quite hard to break any air bubbles in the icing as you work. There is no need to use a hot knife unless your icing is too stiff. Never use a wet knife as the water will make the icing brittle.

Hold the ruler with both hands and position it at the back of the cake at an angle of 45 degrees. Ensure that the ruler is parallel to the cake at both ends. Position your feet correctly and with a firm, quick movement, draw the ruler across the cake towards you. Lift the ruler off sharply and

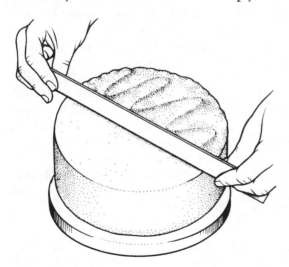

scrape the excess icing into the bowl; then cover the bowl of icing again.

If necessary, give the cake a quarter turn and repeat the process with a clean ruler. Using the sharp knife, scrape away the excess icing from the edge of the cake to give a clean sharp edge; discard this trimmed icing – do not return it to the bowl. Use a pin to prick any air bubbles that are visible on the surface of the icing. Leave the cake to dry for 4–5 hours or more before icing the sides.

> **MRS BEETON'S TIP** Be confident and quick with the ruler. A slow, hesitant movement will result in a ridged effect in the icing.

TO ICE THE SIDE OF THE CAKE

Round Cake Place the cake on the turntable positioning it on a damp cloth, if necessary, to ensure that the board does not slip. Using the small palette knife, spread the icing evenly around the cake, making sure that you draw it up to the top edge. Position your left hand as far round the back of the turntable as possible so that it can be fully turned in one movement. Hold the scraper in the right hand parallel to the side of the cake and at an angle of 45 degrees. Rotate the turntable at an even speed, keeping regular pressure on the scraper until just before you reach the point at which you started, when you should slightly ease the pressure, then sharply pull away the scraper. Make sure that you move the turntable, not the scraper. Repeat a second time, if necessary, with a clean scraper, then trim off excess icing at the top edge, holding the blade parallel to the top of

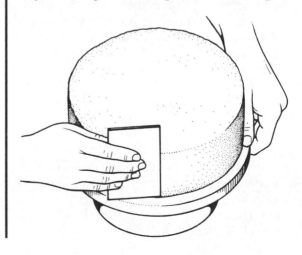

the cake. Using a pin, immediately prick any air bubbles that appear in the icing.

Square Cake Ice two opposite sides at a time, leaving them to dry for 4-6 hours before icing the remaining two sides.

Spread the icing on the side, paying particular attention to the top edge and corners. Hold the scraper parallel to the cake at an angle of 45 degrees and start at the back

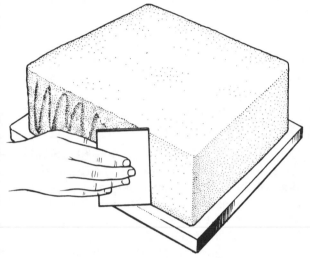

of the cake, drawing the scraper with a firm, even pressure towards you. Repeat a second time, if necessary, with a clean scraper, then scrape off the excess icing on the top edge and at the corners. Repeat this process on the opposite side.

SECOND OR THIRD COATS

Leave the first layer of icing to dry for 24 hours in a dry, cool place before adding a second layer. The same techniques should be used for each application of icing.

> **MRS BEETON'S TIP** Royal icing will not dry in a damp atmosphere. If the room is too hot, the almond paste or marzipan may sweat and discolour the icing.

TIPS FOR SUCCESS WITH ROYAL ICING

■ Make sure that all equipment is spotlessly clean before you begin as any tiny particles of dust or dirt will spoil the icing.

■ Always thoroughly sift the icing sugar before making the icing.

■ Make sure that the icing is well beaten and free of lumps before applying it to the cake.

■ Check the consistency of the icing before use, making sure that it is neither too soft or too stiff for spreading or piping.

■ Keep the icing sealed in an airtight container to prevent it drying out when it is not being used.

■ Avoid getting any particles of dry icing into the container of soft icing.

■ Leave layers of icing to dry thoroughly before adding another coating to the cake.

SIMPLE CAKE DECORATING TECHNIQUES

Presentation is always important when serving food, sweet or savoury, to give pleasure as well as to whet the appetite. In this chapter you will find lots of clever ideas and simple designs for decorated cakes. They are all fairly quick to complete and they do not demand years of experience or highly developed skills to ensure success. The finished decorations are all attractive and tasteful – ideal for anyone who is in the early stages of learning the fulfilling craft of cake decorating.

DECORATING CAKES WITH APRICOT GLAZE OR JAM

Apricot Glaze (page 140) or warmed and sieved jam can be used as a base for adding finishing touches to light sponge cakes. There are a few quick and easy ideas.

DOILY DESIGN

Coat the sides of the cake in glaze and roll in chopped nuts, desiccated or long-thread coconut, or grated chocolate. Lay a paper doily on top of the cake (or fold a circle of paper and cut out a series of shapes to make your own pattern). Place a little icing sugar in a small sieve and gently sift it over the doily on the cake, moving the sieve all over the cake to make an even layer of sugar. Using

both hands, carefully lift the doily straight upwards off the cake.

ALMOND PASTE AND APRICOT GLAZE DECORATION

Roll out a piece of almond paste to fit around the sides of the cake (page 180). Brush the sides of the cake with apricot glaze and press the almond paste into position. Cut a circle of paper to fit the top of the cake, fold it in half and roll out a piece of almond paste to fit the semi-circle, then cut the paste into four equal wedges.

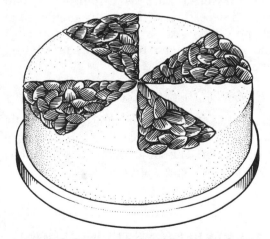

Spread the top of the cake with glaze and place the wedges of almond paste on top leaving alternate gaps of glaze. Sprinkle the wedges of glaze with toasted flaked almonds if you like.

Harvest Cake (page 253) decorated with marzipan fruits with marzipan vegetables nearby

Bell Cake (page 254)

DECORATING WITH PIPED BUTTERCREAM OR WHIPPED CREAM

Keep your hands as cool as possible when piping with buttercream or whipped fresh cream. Warm hands holding the piping bag can cause the cream to melt or become runny because of the butterfat content. Keep the kitchen cool and only fill the icing or piping bag one third full; start again with a fresh bag if the icing or cream does begin to melt. Chill the icing and cream before you start; alternatively, spoon the cream or icing into the icing bag and put the bag in the refrigerator for 10 minutes before using it.

If you want to cover a large area, for example, when decorating novelty cakes, use a large piping bag fitted with a savoy star nozzle (page 139). Avoid using a nylon bag, if possible, as these tend to make the icing or cream sweat. Do not hold the bag in the palms of your hands but squeeze it from the top. If you do need to support the bag, use only the fingers of your other hand and place them near the nozzle. If you are piping over a small area of the cake, for example around the base or the sides, use a double thickness paper icing bag (page 138) with a large nozzle.

Because buttercream and whipped cream are soft, the amount of pressure used will determine the size of the decoration. Use only light pressure, otherwise the stars will be too thick and you may run out of icing or cream before you have finished. It is best to have extra buttercream or whipped cream. If you are piping small areas have about one third more than you need; allow two thirds extra when piping over large areas of cake.

DECORATING WITH BUTTERCREAM

Unless otherwise stated, these designs may be used on any shape of cake.

FORK PATTERNS

Spread the sides of the cake with buttercream and roll them in chopped nuts, desiccated coconut or grated chocolate. Cover the top of the cake with buttercream; use a palette knife to smooth it over, then use a fork to mark a decorative pattern.

STRIPED-TOP CAKE

Roll out almond paste to fit the sides of the cake (page 180). Brush the sides with glaze (page 174) and press on the almond paste. Spread the top of the cake thinly with buttercream. Divide the remaining buttercream in half, colour each portion differently with food colouring and place them in separate icing bags fitted with star nozzles. Pipe lines of one colour across the top of the cake, leaving room for another line of icing

between each row. Pipe lines of the contrasting colour between the first rows of piping.

SCRAPER DESIGN

Cover the top of the cake with buttercream; smooth it over. Spread buttercream around the sides of the cake. Mark a comb pattern

round the side, using the serrated edge of a scraper. Hold the scraper at an angle of 45 degrees and rotate the cake. If you have not got a turntable place the cake on a small biscuit tin or similar so that it is easier to rotate the cake. Use a fork or scalded, new hair comb if you do not have a scraper.

Put the remaining buttercream in a large icing bag fitted with a savoy star nozzle and pipe six or eight large swirls on the top of the cake. Alternatively, use two teaspoons to shape neat blobs of buttercream on the cake. Top each swirl with a nut, a piece of glacé cherry or a small sweet.

MUSHROOM CAKE

This is a clever idea for a round cake. Roll out a strip of almond paste to fit the side of the cake plus 1 cm/½ inch wider (page 180). Spread chocolate or pink buttercream thickly over the top of the cake and thinly around the side. Using a fork, mark the icing on the top of the cake from the edge, towards the

centre to represent the 'gills' of a mushroom. Press the almond paste on to the side of the cake and fold the top edge neatly, and loosely, down over the buttercream. Mould a small piece of almond paste to represent a stalk and dip the end in drinking chocolate powder. Position the stalk, brown end uppermost, in the centre of the cake.

For a child's birthday cake, cut out small

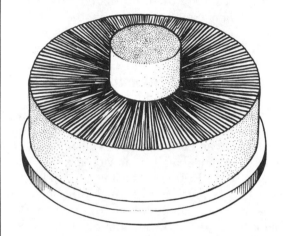

circles of red almond paste and stick them on to the side with a little jam or buttercream.

This design also works well with small cakes (page 126).

TWO-COLOUR STAR CAKE

Spread the side of a round cake thinly with buttercream and roll it in grated chocolate or chocolate vermicelli. Spread the top of the cake thinly with buttercream.

Divide the remaining buttercream between two basins and colour them as you wish; for example add melted chocolate or brown colouring to one portion and yellow to the second, or colour one portion pink and the second portion green. Place one portion in an icing bag fitted with a large star nozzle and pipe a circle of stars in the centre of the

cake. Pipe two rows of stars in the same colour round the edge of the cake. Put the second portion of buttercream in a clean bag fitted with the same size nozzle. Pipe stars to fill in the top of the cake and pipe a row of stars round the lower edge of the cake. This simple decoration can be adapted to suit a square cake by piping a square of stars in the centre, then piping the edge and filling in.

PIPED STAR DESIGN

Another idea for decorating a round cake. Spread buttercream thinly over the surface and use a palette knife to smooth it over.

Spread the sides with buttercream and draw a fork from the base upwards all round to mark a pattern in the cream on the side.

Place the remaining cream in a bag fitted with a large star nozzle and gently pipe small stars on the top of the cake to divide it into six or eight segments. Pipe a row of stars around the edge of the cake. If you like, sprinkle different, small decorations into each segment, for example hundreds and thousands, chocolate vermicelli, sprinkles or chopped nuts.

SIMPLE BIRTHDAY CAKE

Spread buttercream evenly over the top and sides of the cake and use a fork or the serrated edge of a scraper to mark a vertical pattern up the sides. Clean the scraper or fork and mark a pattern across the top of the cake. Place the remaining buttercream in a bag fitted with a large star nozzle and pipe stars around the top and bottom edges of the

cake. Place buttercream in a contrasting colour, in an icing bag fitted with a plain nozzle and write 'Happy Birthday' on top of the cake. Alternatively, bought decorations can be put on top of the cake instead of writing.

SIMPLE DESIGNS USING WHIPPED CREAM

Whipped fresh cream can be used in the same way as buttercream but take care not to over-handle the piping bag and always work in a cool place. Unless otherwise stated, these designs may be used on any shape of cake.

CHOCOLATE SCROLL CAKE

Spread cream thinly over the top of the cake and thickly around the side. Comb the side using a scraper with a serrated edge held at an angle of 45 degrees to the cake. Rotate the cake, either using a turntable or by placing the cake on a small cake tin which makes it easier to turn. Use a fork if you do not have a scraper. Cover the top of the cake with a generous pile of chocolate scrolls (page 238).

SKEWER PATTERN

Spread cream over the top and sides of the cake and use a palette knife to smooth the top as neatly as possible. Spread cocoa powder or instant coffee powder over a piece of paper and lay a long, plain metal skewer in it. Press the skewer across the cake to mark diagonals. Wash, dry and re-dip the skewer as necessary. Press chocolate curls (page 238) or chocolate finger biscuits around the side of the cake. An excellent design for square cakes.

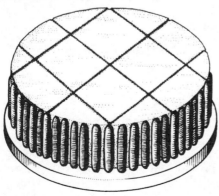

GLACÉ FRUITS AND CREAM

Spread the top of the cake thinly with cream. Spread cream thickly on the sides and use a fork or serrated scraper to mark a vertical

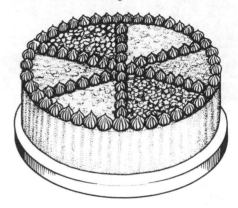

pattern in the cream. Pipe small stars of cream around the top edge and across the cake to divide it into six equal segments. Fill each segment with mixed finely chopped glacé fruits. This design works best on a round cake, but a square cake could be divided into blocks and filled in the same way.

CHOCOLATE ALMOND CAKE

Spread cream around the sides of the cake and roll it in toasted flaked almonds. Spread

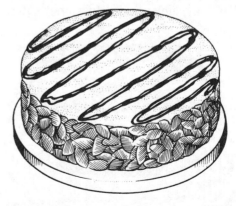

cream over the top of the cake and use a palette knife to smooth it over. Drizzle melted chocolate over the top (page 236).

SIMPLE DECORATIONS USING GLACÉ ICING

FEATHER ICING

This is an attractive technique using coloured glacé icing. The colours and basic design can be varied but first follow the instructions for the basic method. Remember that the icing and decoration must be completed before the icing sets. Melted chocolate can be used instead of an icing in a contrasting colour (page 236).

Make the icing and brush any crumbs off the cake. Place 30 ml/2 tbsp of the icing in a small basin and add a few drops of food colouring to contrast with the main colour. Place the coloured icing in a paper icing bag (page 138). You do not need a nozzle.

Feather Icing

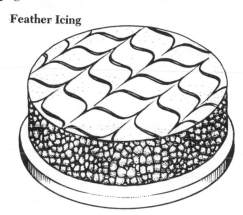

Fan Feather Icing

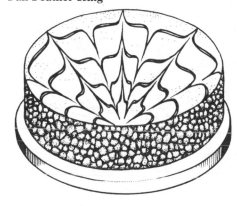

Use the main batch of icing to cover the top of the cake (page 176). Snip a small corner off the icing bag and immediately pipe lines of coloured icing across the cake about 1 cm/½ inch apart. Using a skewer or the point of a knife, draw lines across the piped coloured icing at 1 cm/½ inch intervals. Draw the skewer alternately in opposite directions. The coloured icing will sink into the main icing and it will drag into an attractive pattern as the skewer is drawn through it, creating the feathered effect.

Circular Feather Icing

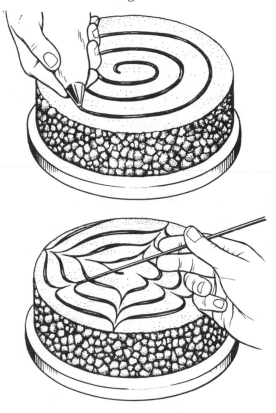

CIRCULAR FEATHER ICING

Instead of piping lines across a round cake, pipe circles at even distances out from the centre. Alternatively the circles can be piped to radiate out from one side like a fan (this works well on square cakes). Drag the icing with the skewer to create the feather effect.

SIMPLE DECORATIONS USING FONDANT

Traditional fondant thinned with stock syrup is too soft to use for elaborate piping or for swirling but it may be used as a pouring icing and can also be drizzled thinly over cakes for simple decorative effect. When decorating large cakes, the fondant should be poured over the top after the sides have been coated in another covering, for example apricot glaze and chopped nuts. Coat the sides of the cake in the chosen glaze and topping. Pour most of the fondant over the top of the cake and keep the extra warm. When the fondant on the cake is almost set, add a few drops of colouring to the warm fondant and place 30 ml/2 tbsp of it in a small, paper icing bag (page 138). Snip off just the point to make a very small hole and quickly drizzle the coloured fondant backwards and forwards across the top of the cake.

FEATHERED FONDANT

A feathered effect can be made by piping on the icing when the base coat is still wet and following the instructions for feathering glacé icing (page 193).

PLAIN FONDANT TOPPING

Coat the sides of the cake with a strip of almond paste (page 180) and pour fondant over the top of the cake. When the fondant has set, pipe small stars of whipped cream or buttercream around the edge.

FONDANT-COATED CAKE

Cover the top and sides of the cake in fondant (page 177). Piped chocolate motifs (page 236) can be added as simple decoration around the top of the cake. For a birthday cake use numerals denoting the age of the person as the shape for the chocolate motifs.

DECORATING CAKES WITH ALMOND PASTE OR MARZIPAN

Either almond paste or marzipan may be used as the main ingredient for cake decorations. Paste or marzipan may be coloured or moulded. Unless otherwise stated, the designs that follow may be used on any shape of cake.

TO COLOUR ALMOND PASTE OR MARZIPAN

Use a paste food colouring to avoid making the mixture sticky. Lightly knead the colour into the almond paste or marzipan on a work surface dusted with icing sugar. Take care not to overhandle it or it will become oily.

PLAITED-BASE CAKE

Cover the top and sides of the cake with almond paste or marzipan (page 178). Use a modelling tool or fork to press a design around the top edge of the cake. Place a plait of almond paste or marzipan around the base

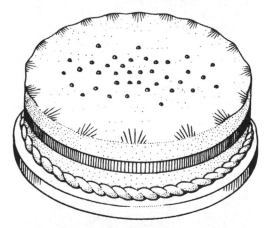

of the cake (see sugar paste ropes, twists and plaits, page 196). Sprinkle coloured sugar balls over the top of the cake and gently press them into the paste with a palette knife.

RIBBON WEAVE DESIGN

Cover the sides of the cake with roughly chopped nuts or toasted flaked almonds. Brush the top of the cake generously with apricot glaze.

Roll out almond paste or marzipan thickly and cut it into 1 cm/½ inch wide strips. Arrange two strips in a cross shape on top of the cake. Lay two more strips on the cake, one above and one below the first strip, leaving about 1 cm/½ inch between the strips.

Place two strips in the opposite direction, interweaving them with the previous two strips. Continue adding strips of paste, interweaving them until the surface of the

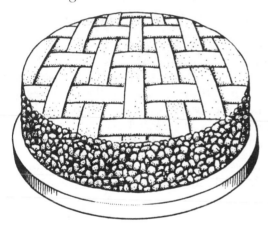

cake is completely covered. Trim the ends of the strips all round the edge of the cake. A colourful design can be achieved by using different coloured strips.

CRYSTAL FRUIT TOPPING

Roll out a strip of almond paste or marzipan to fit the sides of the cake. Use a modelling tool, fork or potato peeler to press out a pattern evenly over the paste. Brush the sides of the cake with apricot glaze and place the strip of almond paste in position.

Brush the top of the cake with apricot glaze, then cover it with a mixture of roughly chopped coloured glacé fruits, such as

yellow, green and red cherries, mixed peel and crystallised ginger. Roll small balls of almond paste or marzipan and place them around the top edge of the cake.

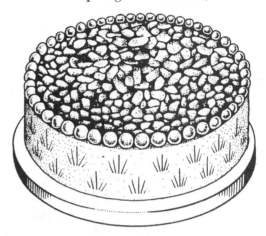

POINSETTIA CAKE

Cover the top and sides of the cake with almond paste or marzipan coloured pale green. Using red-coloured almond paste or marzipan, cut out small oval petal shapes for the sides and larger ones for the top of the cake. Use a little apricot glaze to stick the

small petals in a border round the base of the cake. Overlap the large petals on the top to form a flower, again keeping them in place with a little apricot glaze. Cut a tiny circle of red almond paste to neaten the centre of the flower and place it in position.

SIMPLE DECORATIONS USING SUGAR PASTE

This is a wonderfully versatile icing which can be used to smooth-ice a cake or it can be moulded into simple decorations such as ropes, figures, plaques and flowers. It is also an invaluable ingredient for making novelty cakes. Here are some simple ideas; more complicated moulding techniques are explained later.

COVERING THE CAKE BOARD

Although cake boards are attractive, sometimes the soft line of a cake covered with sugar paste is enhanced if the icing extends to the edge of the board. The board can be covered in one operation when covering the cake but it is easier and neater to apply the icing to the board separately. The sugar paste should be rolled out and smoothed with a little cornflour. The measurements given are for a board which is 5 cm/2 inches larger than the cake. When the icing is completely dry, neaten the board by placing a strip of board edging or ribbon around it.

TO COVER A ROUND BOARD

Measure the circumference of the cake with string and divide the result by two if the cake is a small one, or by three or four if the cake is large. Centre the cake on the board.

Roll out pieces of sugar paste to the required lengths and make them 3 cm/1¼ inches wide. Place one strip on the cake board, butting one edge neatly up to the base of the cake. Gently ease the paste around the curve. Repeat with the remaining strip or strips, butting the joins together neatly, then smoothing them out with a palette knife. Trim off the excess paste at the edge of the board.

TO COVER A SQUARE BOARD

Place the square cake on the board. Roll out a strip of paste 3 cm/1¼ inches wide and the same length as one side of the board. Place the strip on the board, butting one edge neatly against the cake. Repeat with the remaining sides, loosely overlapping the paste at the corners.

Using a sharp knife, cut firmly and neatly diagonally from each corner of the cake to the corner of the board. Remove excess paste by gently lifting up the corners. Smooth the join with a palette knife or make it a feature by piping small stars or dots along it. Trim off excess paste at the edges of the board.

ROPES, TWISTS AND PLAITS

These are quick, simple edges which can be used to neaten the base of any cake; regardless of shape. They can be applied at the same time as covering the cake or later, when the paste has dried, in which case a little alcohol or cooled boiled water should be used to stick the edging to the cake.

Rope Measure the circumference of the cake and divide the total into two or four depending on the size of the cake. Small cakes can be edged with one piece of paste.

Lightly dust the work surface and your hands with cornflour and mould about 25 g/1 oz of sugar paste into a fat sausage. Place both hands over the middle of the roll, with your index fingers side by side. Using the pressure from the base of the fingers, especially the index fingers, begin rolling the paste backwards and forwards and at the same time gradually move your hands away from each other until a long, evenly thick rope is formed. The rope should be at least the required length plus 5 cm/2 inches and about 5 mm/¼ inch thick.

Twist Roll two ropes and loosely twist them together.

Twist

Plait

Plait Roll three ropes slightly thinner than 5 mm/¼ inch and loosely plait them together.

TO FIX THE EDGE ON TO THE CAKE

Lay the piece of rope around the base of the cake, taking care not to stretch it. Press it lightly on to the cake, brushing it first as you work with a little alcohol or boiled water, if necessary. Leave 2.5 cm/1 inch loose at each end. Fix any remaining pieces in place. Join the ropes by loosely twisting them together in a decorative manner; loose ends can be draped on the board or trimmed.

COLOURED EDGES

Colour the rope a contrasting colour to the main sugar paste. The twists and plaits can be made in two or more different colours.

> ☕ **MRS BEETON'S TIP** Before fixing the ropes on to the cake, decide which is be the front so that the joins can be positioned either at the side or at the back and front.

CUT OUT SHAPES

Cut out sugar paste shapes are a simple and effective means of decorating cakes coated in sugar paste. They stick well on both dried and freshly rolled paste.

Colour the sugar paste as required and use the reverse side of a laminex board as a surface for rolling, if possible. Alternatively, dust a clean, dry, smooth work surface with a little cornflour. Use a small, clean, smooth rolling pin.

Using cutters Roll out the paste evenly to about the same thickness as short crust pastry. Stamp out shapes sharply and peel away excess paste. Slide a palette knife under the paste shape and lift it on to its position on the cake. With fingertips lightly dusted with cornflour, smooth the shape on to the cake using a small, circular movement.

Using a template Draw the required shape and cut it out in thin, white card. Roll out the sugar paste and lightly dust the surface with cornflour. Lay the template on the paste and cut around it with a small pointed knife. Take care not to press too heavily on the template or it may stick to the icing. Remove the template and peel away the excess paste. Lift the shape and smooth it on to the cake as above.

USING MODELLING TOOLS

Modelling tools, available from cake decorating suppliers, can only be used on sugar paste or similar icings when still soft, so mark the pattern in the icing as soon as you have covered the cake smoothly. A variety of tools are available to create different designs. Simply press the selected tool firmly into the sugar paste, then draw it up sharply to make a neat indentation. If the tool tends to stick to the icing, lightly dust it with cornflour.

Specialist marking tools are not essential for creating patterns. With a little imagination forks, vegetable peelers, spoon handles, pointed knives and other similar objects may also be used to create attractive patterns.

PATTERNS MADE WITH CRIMPERS

Crimpers are used to press designs around the edge of the soft paste. Several different designs are available. You do need to practise the technique on a thick piece of sugar paste if you are a novice at this type of decorating. Mistakes made directly on the cake are difficult to erase. If you do make a mistake, smooth over the icing with your fingertips, working in a circular movement.

To regulate the space between the crimpers, place an elastic band about 2.5 cm/1 inch from the open end so that the ends are fixed about 5 mm/¼ inch apart. Dip the ends of the crimpers in icing sugar or cornflour during use to prevent them sticking to the paste. Before starting, use a pin to prick a line around the cake to ensure that you mark the pattern in a straight line.

Press the crimpers into the icing, then gently pinch them together until the paste between the crimpers is 3 mm/⅛ inch thick. Re-open the crimpers to the fixed gap of 5 mm/¼ inch before lifting them away. It is very important to release the pressure and open the crimpers slightly *before* lifting them away or the paste may lift away with them.

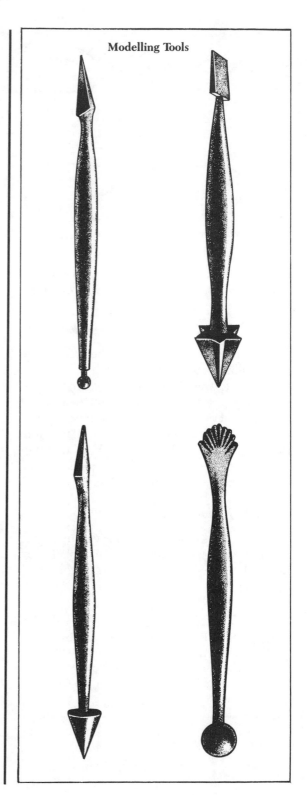

Modelling Tools

INSERTING RIBBON INTO SUGAR PASTE

The aim when attaching ribbon to a cake by this method is to give the impression that the ribbon is woven into the icing. The ribbon must be attached as soon as the cake is covered with sugar paste and while the icing is still soft. Take care not to mark the soft icing with your knuckles or fingernails as you work. If you wait until the icing has set, the ribbon will not readily stick into the slots.

Choose a narrow, satin ribbon which contrasts with the colour of the main icing. Ribbon which is a few shades darker looks best; remember that the sugar paste will be slightly darker when it is dry. Buy sufficient ribbon to go around the cake at least one and a quarter times. Cut the ribbon into 2 cm/¾ inch lengths and place these on a clean saucer.

Before you begin, cut a strip of clean greaseproof paper that equals the height of the cake and extends beyond the circumference by at least 5 cm/2 inches. Measure up from the bottom of the paper to the position where the ribbon is to be inserted and make pencil marks at 1 cm/½ inch intervals along the length of the paper. Assemble all equipment and ingredients before you start to cover the cake with paste:

cake on its board
Sugar Paste (page 158)
cornflour for buffing
ribbon pieces
ribbon insertion tool or a metal nail file
2 glass-headed pins
paper pattern

Cover the marzipanned cake with sugar paste (for quantities, see Chart, page 158) and buff the surface (page 182). Position the cake on a cake tin and sit down so that the cake is at eye level.

Lightly dust the paper pattern with cornflour and place it around the cake securing it in place with a pin at the back.

Prick out the position of the ribbon design on to the cake, then carefully remove the pattern. Smooth over any other marks which you may have made on the cake.

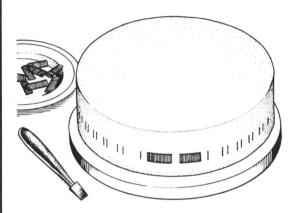

Cut vertical slits the same width as the ribbon around the cake at the marked 1 cm/½ inch intervals. Do this with a special ribbon insertion tool or the rounded, blunt end of a sterilised metal nail file. Be careful not to cut too deeply, or you will pierce right through to the almond paste or marzipan.

Start at the back of the cake and use the tool or file to press one end of a piece of cut ribbon into a slit. Leaving a small loop, insert the other end into the next slit. Leave a 1 cm/½ inch gap and insert the next piece of ribbon into the following slit. Continue around the cake.

The slits can be decorated with small piped beads or embroidery (pages 203 and 207). Small narrow strips of ribbon can be used in the same way to highlight a pattern made with crimpers.

MRS BEETON'S TIP Instead of cutting all the slits around the cake at the same time you may prefer to cut each slit as you insert the ribbon, at least for the first few lengths, so that you are sure that the spacing is correct for the cake.

SIMPLE DESIGNS USING SUGAR PASTE

These simple designs (see diagrams) are suitable for round or square cakes. Any home-made or shop-bought moulding icing can be used instead of sugar paste.

MODELLING TOOL DESIGN

Cover the top and the sides of the cake with sugar paste and mark a pattern around the top edge with a modelling tool. Place a single

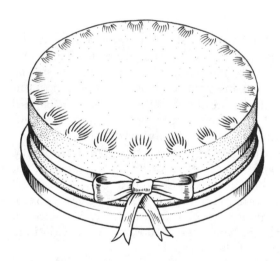

rope of sugar paste around the base of the cake and finish with a band of ribbon tied in a large bow.

CRIMPER DESIGN

Cover the top and the sides of the cake with sugar paste and use crimpers to mark a pattern around the top edge. Place a twisted rope of sugar paste around the base of the cake and a band of ribbon above. Add a bought greetings plaque or other decoration

to the top of the cake. Alternatively, cut out an appropriate numeral from rolled-out sugar paste in a contrasting colour.

BALLOON CAKE

Cover the top and the sides of the cake with sugar paste. Cover the board with paste. Cut

a template of a teddy bear, then cut out the shape in coloured sugar paste and position it on the cake. Cut balloons from paste in contrasting colours and position them around the cake. When the sugar paste is dry, use coloured icing pens to draw the string from the balloons to the teddy. Finish the cake by tying a narrow ribbon around its base.

SIMPLE SILK FLOWER CAKE

Cover the top and the sides of the cake with tinted sugar paste. Place a plaited rope of paste, tinted a slightly deeper colour, around the base of the cake. Decorate the cake with a small spray of silk flowers.

NIGHT SKY CAKE

Cover the side of the cake with apricot glaze and dark chocolate vermicelli. Cover the top

of the cake with sugar paste coloured midnight blue. Trim the edges neatly. Cut out small stars and a moon from yellow sugar paste and place them in position on the top of the cake.

SIMPLE TECHNIQUES FOR ROYAL ICING

Royal icing does not have to be smoothed over the cake to give a flat finish. It can be swirled and peaked to give a snow scene effect or it can be combed to create various designs.

PEAKED ICING

The icing should be of soft-peak consistency (page 157), so that the tip of the peak just falls. Spread the icing thickly over the cake. Using a small palette knife, press it firmly into the icing and quickly draw it towards you by about 2 cm/¾ inch before pulling it sharply away from the icing and flicking it towards the back of the cake to form a soft swirly peak of icing. Move the cake around making random peaks all over the surface.

COMBED ICING

A turntable is useful for this method of neatening the sides of the cake. Alternatively, place the cake on a cake tin to raise its height to a comfortable level.

Spread the icing over the sides of the cake making sure it comes well up to the top edge. Use a scraper with a serrated edge. Position your left hand as far around the cake as possible to hold the turntable or board. Hold the scraper in the right hand at an angle of 45 degrees to the side of the cake. Rotate the cake as the scraper sweeps over the icing in one movement. Release the pressure on the scraper slightly just as you reach the place where you started and quickly pull it away. The point where you pull off the scraper will be the back of the cake. You may have to repeat the process to get a good finish.

PIPING TECHNIQUE AND MORE COMPLICATED DECORATIVE DESIGNS

Develop your cake-decorating skills by following the instructions in this chapter. Lace work, embroidery, run-outs and basket weave icing are all included along with ideas for piping plain or star patterns. Extension work and the knack of making a Garrett frill complete the guidance for the confident cake decorator.

PIPING WITH ROYAL ICING

Fine piping is a skill which is developed with practice; and it calls for a steady hand as well as an artistic approach. Equally important is the quality of the actual icing – if its consistency is wrong, you will never achieve good results. Icing which is too stiff will break the icing bag; if the icing is too slack the design will not hold its shape on the cake.

THE CORRECT CONSISTENCY

The consistency required depends on the type of design which is being piped and the size of the nozzle.

It is better to beat the icing by hand for piping otherwise there may be too many air bubbles in it which might cause the piping to break. Make the icing on the day you intend to use it, otherwise it tends to become heavy. Do leave the icing to stand for a few hours to dispel any air bubbles. Always keep the icing well covered and do not let any particles of dried icing get into the fresh icing. Even the tiniest particles can block a fine nozzle.

THE ICING BAG

Make several paper icing bags (page 138) before you begin, and store them one inside the other. When required, snip off the end of one of the bags and insert the nozzle – put a little icing in the nozzle to weight it if you have difficulty in inserting it. The amount to snip off the bag depends on the nozzle. A writing nozzle needs a small hole of about 5 mm/¼ inch but some larger nozzles, such as petals or shells will need a larger hole. The nozzle should not protrude more than half-way out of the bag, otherwise the paper may split.

Use a teaspoon to fill the icing bag. Fold the top of the icing bag down and hold it between the thumb and forefinger. These fingers will guide the bag, the remaining fingers will provide the pressure. If you are piping without a nozzle, fill the bag before snipping off the point.

PIPING PRACTICE

Choose medium-sized nozzles and practise piping on a tray or work surface until you can regulate the amount of pressure required. Small designs are piped with the minimum of pressure; more pressure is necessary when piping larger designs such as shell or scroll work. It is best to start with a plain writing nozzle size 0 or 1.

CORRECT POSITION

It is important to position the icing bag correctly. For piping on top of the cake it is best to stand up, especially for work where the nozzle is held at an angle of 90 degrees to the cake, for example, when piping stars and beads. When piping on the sides of the cake, sit down and raise the cake on a turntable or cake tin so that it is at eye level.

DESIGNS WITH THE PLAIN WRITING NOZZLE

DOTS OR BEADS

These should resemble small round balls; they must not end in a peak. Place the point of the nozzle on the surface and hold the bag at an angle of 90 degrees to the cake. Start pressing out a little icing – the more you press out, the bigger the dot will be. Do not lift the nozzle away until you have stopped squeezing out the icing otherwise the dot will have a peak.

Small beads can be used to outline or fill in a shape; they can also form part of embroidery work (page 207). Larger beads can be used to edge the top of the cake and the base of the cake can be finished with very large beads. It is important that all the dots are of uniform size.

STRAIGHT LINES

Hold the bag at an angle of 45 degrees to the surface of the cake and support it, if necessary, with the left hand, placed near the nozzle. Place the nozzle on the surface, start squeezing, then raise the nozzle off the surface. Keep squeezing and at the same time slowly move the nozzle towards you so that a thread of icing is formed. Do not pull too quickly or the icing will break; similarly, if you stop squeezing, the icing will break.

Hold the thread of icing about 2.5 cm/1 inch above the surface and let it fall gently into the required position. If you hold the nozzle too near the cake, the line will be crooked. Finish the line by lowering the nozzle and easing off the pressure. Touch the nozzle on to the surface, then quickly lift it off to make a neat end.

PIPING WITH COLOURED ICINGS

First pipe the design in white, then when it is dry, pipe another line directly on top of it in the coloured icing. This will prevent the colour bleeding on to the main surface, especially if a dark colour, such as red, is used.

TRELLIS OR LATTICE WORK

Pipe straight lines parallel to each other then pipe more parallel lines at right angles or aslant. It is important to keep each set of lines parallel.

Dots and Straight Lines

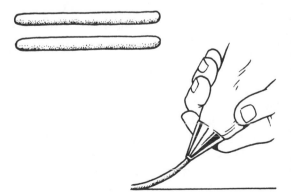

Trellis or Lattice Work

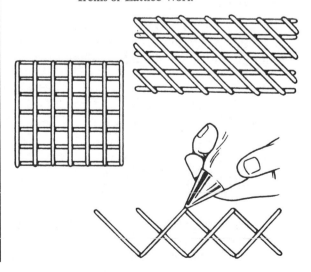

DOUBLE TRELLIS OR LATTICE

Repeat the pattern by piping over the lines of the first set of trellis, in the same order in which they were first piped. Care must be taken when finishing off each line and it is best to extend it just beyond the base trellis and down on to the cake. The trellis can be neatened by piping small beads round the edges.

RAISED LATTICE WORK

This is piped over a shape, such as an upturned bun tin, boat-shaped tartlet mould, or deep-bowled spoon. Lightly grease the mould with lard first. Allow the piping to dry

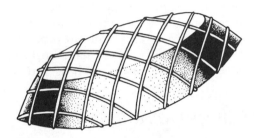

well before carefully lifting it off and arranging it on the cake. Neaten the edges with small piped beads.

FILIGREE, CORNELLI WORK OR SCRIBBLING

Use a no 0 or 1 nozzle; the smaller nozzle gives the most delicate design. The consistency of the icing should be slightly softer

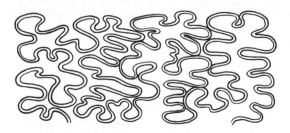

than for straight lines as it should look as though it is part of the flat icing on the cake.

Hold the bag in one hand only and place the nozzle at an angle of 45 degrees to the surface. Start squeezing and moving the bag at random backwards and forwards within a given area, just lifting the nozzle above the surface and occasionally letting it touch the surface. The line should remain unbroken.

When using this technique to fill in an area between a design and the outer edge of a cake, start piping at the edge of the cake and return to the edge before breaking off to rest.

> 🥣 **MRS BEETON'S TIP** If the top edge of the cake is to be neatened with a shell border, finish the filigree about 3 mm/⅛ inch short of the edge. Alternatively, while the icing is still soft, trim the edge with a sharp knife so that there is a flat surface on which to pipe the shell edge.

WRITING

Use a no 1 or 2 nozzle. Writing is better piped freehand than to a pattern. Practise on a tray first so that you know how much space each letter will take.

After the initial letter, pipe lower case letters as these flow more easily and can be piped in a smooth continuous line. Do not attempt to pipe the letters as you would write them, otherwise you will find that you pipe over some lines twice. Form each letter separately, starting at the top and ending with the loop to join it to the next letter. Be careful when removing the nozzle from the letter that you stop squeezing before you lift up the nozzle, otherwise small peaks will make the writing untidy.

Use the same technique as for straight lines but lay the thread of icing down in the curves of the letters. Pipe in white icing, or icing that is the same colour as the surface of the cake. When the piping is dry, pipe over it a second layer of coloured icing if liked, to raise the letters and make them stand out.

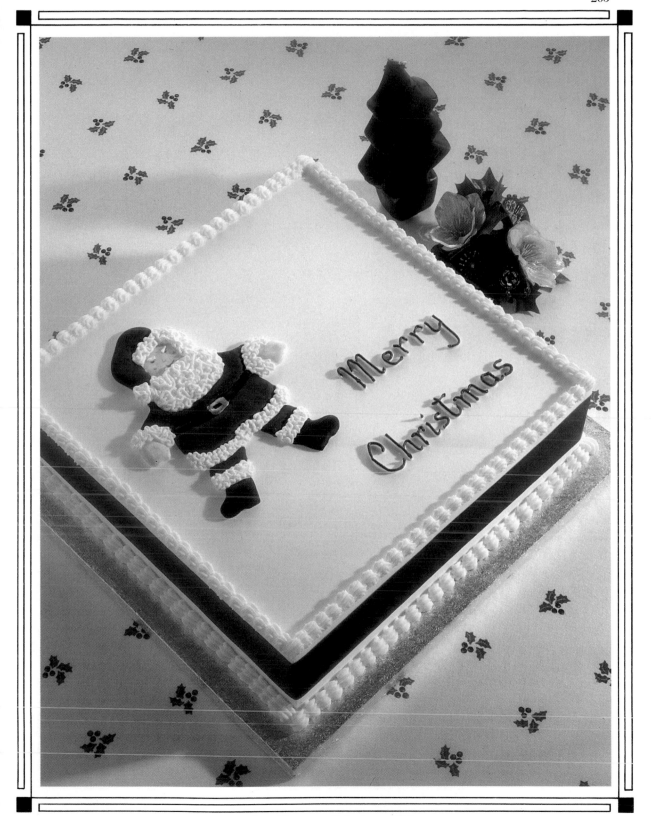

Father Christmas Cake (page 254)

Mini Christmas Cakes and Festive Log (both on page 255)

EMBROIDERY

This is used on the sides of the cake, instead of ribbon. Occasionally, a few motifs are brought on to the top of the cake in a limited design. For the best effect, the design is piped in a deeper shade or a contrasting colour to the main cake covering, for example white embroidery can be used on a base of blue flat icing.

THE PATTERN

Embroidery is best piped freehand. Tracing or pin-pricking an intricate design produces a mass of confusing holes. Copy lace borders or embroidery transfers and draw the design on a piece of paper cut to the same size as the area which is to be piped. Mark main areas, such as the beginning and end of sections, on the cake. The piping on the cake does not have to be exactly like the pattern and it does not have to be uniform on both sides of the cake.

A variety of simple designs can be used, for example petals, leaves, scrolls, 'S' and 'C' shapes, dots, beads, bows, birds and butterflies. Avoid piping straight lines.

THE ICING AND NOZZLES

Use a soft peak icing (page 157) and check the texture after adding any food colouring. Use a variety of plain writing nozzles to create the texture of the pattern, from no 00 to 0 and 1.

TO PIPE EMBROIDERY

Place the cake on a turntable or cake tin. Sit down to work so that the side of the cake is at eye level.

Hold the nozzle at an angle of 45 degrees to the cake. Use only light pressure, enough to maintain a steady stream of icing as you 'draw' on the cake. Remember to ease off the pressure before you pull away the nozzle, otherwise the icing will peak and the design may well be spoilt.

LACE WORK

Use a no 0 plain writing nozzle. Lace work is made up of small, delicate motifs which are piped on to waxed paper and allowed to dry. They are then lifted off and attached to the cake. The motifs can either be used on their own or with extension work (page 210).

THE PATTERN

Trace your chosen pattern. Use embroidery transfers, a wallpaper pattern or a piece of lace as a guide. Trace the pattern as for run-outs (page 212). You will need to pipe about twice as many patterns as you will need to allow for breakages. Trace the pattern ten or twelve times on card and move this along under the waxed paper as you complete the motifs.

THE ICING

This should be of a thinner consistency than for ordinary piping as it must flow smoothly through a fine hole and the joins should flow together as one. However, the icing must be thick enough to hold a good, clear shape.

TO PIPE THE LACE

Hold the nozzle at an angle of 45 degrees, using only sufficient pressure to enable a thin stream of icing to flow. Hold the nozzle close to the paper for greater control. Take care when joining icing to make sure the join is neat and free of any ugly peaks. Use a pin to move the edge of the icing, if necessary. Ensure that all loops are connected, otherwise they will be left behind when the lace is removed from the paper.

ATTACHING THE LACE TO THE CAKE

Leave the lace to dry for at least 24 hours. Use a palette knife or round-ended knife to lift the lace off the paper, moving it gently on the paper first. Pipe small dots or a thin line on to the cake where the lace is to be attached. Carefully hold the motif in position for a second on the wet icing to ensure that it is secure. The lace should be at an angle of 45 degrees to the surface of the cake. Even the most experienced cake decorator will have some breakages, so make sure that you have plenty of motifs at the ready. Any remaining motifs can be stored between layers of greaseproof paper in a box for future use.

Alternatively, instead of piping the wet icing on to the surface of the cake, it can be piped on to the lace, then pressed on to the cake as part of the motif.

MRS BEETON'S TIP When fine nozzles are used the icing tends to dry on the tip. Keep a clean, damp cloth handy and wipe the end of the nozzle occasionally to keep it clean and to keep the icing in the bag damp and free flowing.

Designs for Lace Work

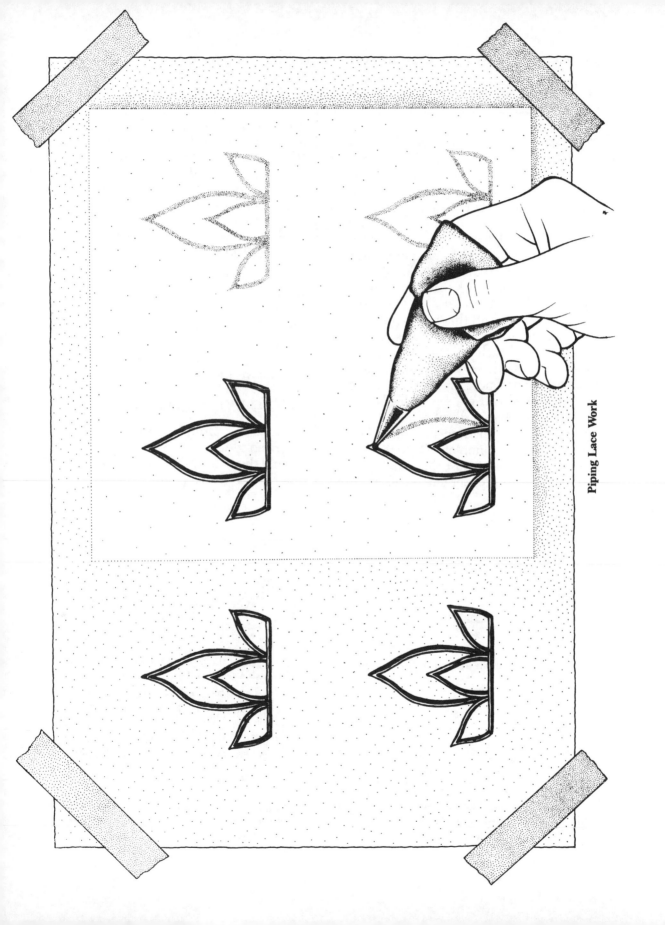

Piping Lace Work

EXTENSION WORK

This delicate piping is used round the side of the cake, near the base, and it stands out from the side of the cake. Allow plenty of time for each layer to dry before adding the next. All these designs require patience and skill, and plenty of time. Extension work is made up of bridge work – built up layers of plain piping in the shape required, usually scalloped – and curtain work. Curtain work is fine parallel lines of icing placed close together. The bottom edge of the design is often scalloped but the top edge may be scalloped or straight. The work is usually about 2.5 cm/1 inch in length and very close together. Extension work can either be brought down almost on to the board, or it can be finished above a row of shells or stars around the base of the cake. These decorations are piped on the cake when all the other icing is complete. Once the work is finished the cake must be handled with extreme care to prevent any breakages from occurring.

THE ICING AND NOZZLES

Two nozzles are used: no 2 for bridge work and a finer nozzle for curtains. Start with size 0 but progress to 00 and eventually 000 when you have mastered the technique.

Use a soft peak icing for the bridge work and a softer peak for the curtain work. Keep the nozzle clean while piping.

THE PATTERN

Cut a paper pattern to exactly fit the sides of the cake. Fold the paper, cut scallop shapes and mark them on to the cake by pricking or scratching the icing with a pin.

Mark a second pattern of scallops or a straight line pattern on the cake 2.5 cm/1 inch above the first marks.

PIPING EXTENSION WORK

Scallops or Bridge work Start with the larger nozzle (no 1 or 2) and pipe a thick line around the base of the cake where it joins the board. Alternatively, pipe a row of stars or shells here.

1 Pipe a row of shells around the base of the cake.

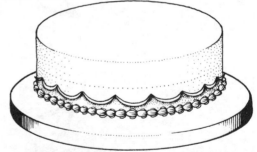

2 Mark out the top and bottom lines of the extension work and pipe the scallops.

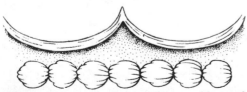

3 The scallops are built up with several lines of icing: this is known as bridge work.

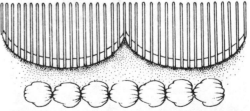

4 Fine threads of icing are piped from the line which marks the top of the extension work to the top of the scallops, or bridge work. This is known as the curtain.

Use a large plain nozzle and pipe the scallops by placing the nozzle on to the cake at the beginning of one scallop. Press out the icing and lift the nozzle, then move it along close to the cake so that a fine line of icing can be laid in position on the marked scallop. Ensure that the icing touches the cake all along the scallop otherwise it will weaken the next stage of the extension work. Continue piping all the scallops around the cake, then leave the icing to dry at least 15 minutes before piping a second line of icing on top of the first one. Continue to build up the scallops until the icing is five or six layers deep. Leave to dry overnight.

The Curtains Using the fine nozzle, start by placing a tiny blob of icing on the line marked above the scallops. Push out a fine thread of icing as you lift the nozzle and draw it downwards and outwards towards the bridgework on the scallop shape below. Tuck the end of the icing in just under the bridgework. Use a pin or fine paint brush to help, if necessary.

Continue piping these threads parallel to each other from the top line, down to the scallop shape. They should be so close together that there is no room for a thread between them. This work takes some time to complete and it should be piped in sections, starting with a fresh bag of icing and clean nozzle each time.

FINISHING THE EXTENSION WORK

Leave the work to dry overnight before neatening the edges with a row of small beads. Lace motifs can be added to create an elaborate finish along the top line.

TIPS FOR SUCCESS WITH DELICATE PIPING

■ When piping a lace design or any other very small motifs, always make many more than required to allow for breakages.

■ When piping delicate designs, always check that the icing is of the right consistency and practice piping one motif or shape so that you get the 'feel' of the icing before you start.

■ Always have a strong, well-made icing bag. If the bag feels as though it is about to break, then start afresh with a new bag and icing rather than ruin the icing.

■ Always leave delicate pieces of piped icing to dry thoroughly before attempting to remove them from the card. When piping extension work, always leave the layers of piping to dry thoroughly as directed.

■ When piping extension work on a cake, make sure that you have decided on the complete pattern for the decoration on the cake. Mark it clearly and accurately on the cake before you start.

■ Allow plenty of time for piping these delicate designs and make sure that you are standing or sitting in a comfortable position before you start.

■ Take great care when moving the finished cake as lace work and extension work are particularly delicate.

RUN-OUTS

Royal icing sets very hard and it can be used for quite delicate decorations, collars and plaques. A run-out consists of a shape which is piped on to waxed paper, then flooded with a softer icing and allowed to set. When hard, the shape is strong enough to lift off the paper and transfer to its position on the cake. Run-outs can be used on the sides of the cake where piping is difficult.

The run-out can be made in any shape – a club emblem, badge, numbers, letters and/or characters. They can be made in white icing and painted with food colouring when dry. Alternatively, the icing can be coloured first if not too many colours are required. Allow plenty of time to pipe the run-outs and let them dry thoroughly, preferably for up to a week. Make several as they are fragile and may break when handled.

THE DESIGNS

Choose simple designs that can be piped in sections. Trace shapes from Christmas and birthday cards, wrapping paper, gift tags, children's books and posters.

THE ICING AND NOZZLE

Outlines are piped with a no 1 plain writing nozzle. A well-made paper icing bag is required for the flooding. The icing should be of a soft peak consistency for the outlines. Add a little lemon juice or water to make a softer consistency for the flooding. For flooding, the consistency should be that of thick cream that slowly finds its own level; if the icing is too slack the run-outs will be thin and very fragile. Icing made with egg white gives a smoother surface than icing made with albumen. Designs that have several different colours are best piped in white and painted over when dry. This gives a stronger colour and is useful for figure run-outs such as Father Christmas. For less complicated designs, colour the icing first, remembering that only a tiny dot of colour is required.

Use a sharp, dark pencil to trace the design on to a piece of greaseproof paper. Reverse the paper and trace over the outline again. Turn the paper over and lay it on a piece of thin white card. Trace over the design once more and a faint mark will be transferred on to the card. Trace the design three or four more times over different parts of the card, then go over the images carefully so that they are quite clear.

Attach the card to a firm, flat, portable surface such as a large chopping board, upturned tray or large cake board. Use tape or drawing pins to keep the card firmly in place. Cover with a piece of waxed paper or non-stick baking parchment and secure it perfectly flat with tape or drawing pins at the corners. If the paper is crumpled or creased the run-outs will not dry flat.

PIPING RUN-OUTS

The designs are piped in sections, allowing each one to dry briefly before piping the next section. This creates run-outs of height; otherwise they would be flat and uninteresting. Divide the design into sections and start with sections that do not touch each other.

Using soft peak icing, hold the nozzle at an angle of 45 degrees to the paper at a suitable starting point on the design. Press out a thread of icing as you lift the nozzle, then lay the icing down on the pattern. Pipe all around the outline of one section, leaving no gaps.

Fill a strong paper icing bag with softer icing; snip off the end to make a small hole. Flood the outlined area by moving the bag backwards and forwards as the icing flows out. Keep the point of the bag under the icing until the area is covered and slightly domed. Use a pin or skewer to tease the icing into difficult corners. Tap the board gently on the table or run a palette knife quickly from side to side under the waxed paper if you have difficulty in making the icing flow.

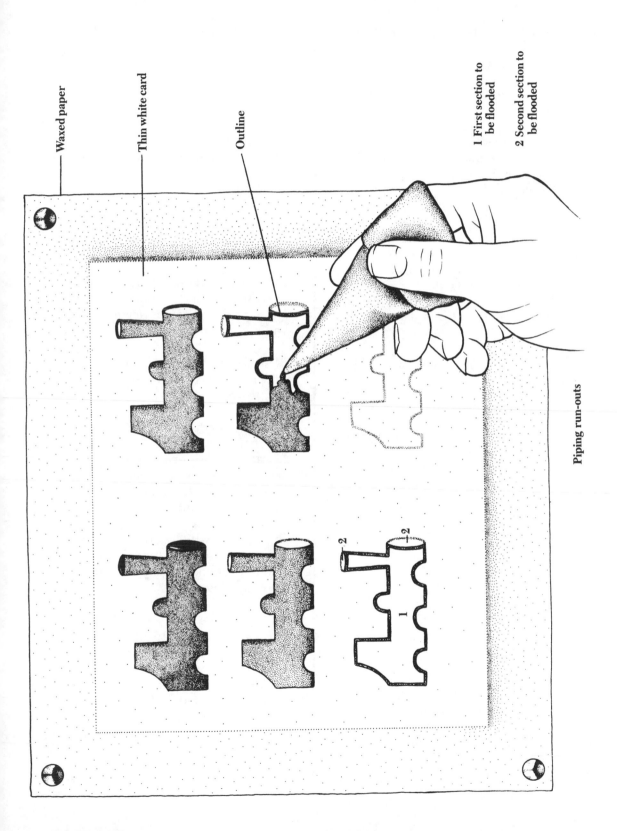

Waxed paper

Thin white card

Outline

1 First section to be flooded

2 Second section to be flooded

Piping run-outs

If any air bubbles appear, prick them with a pin.

The flooding should slightly bevel-out on to the outline to hide it but it should not flow over it. The exception is when the outline has been piped in a contrasting colour to give form to the design, for example, the shape of an arm which might otherwise be difficult to define. Fill the outline as full as possible as the icing tends to shrink on drying. Leave each section for about 20 minutes or more, before outlining and flooding the adjacent section.

For a shiny surface, the icing must be dried as quickly as possible. Place the run-out under a table lamp, if possible, for 10 minutes before placing it in a warm, dry atmosphere. An airing cupboard is ideal; the icing will not dry in a damp place.

TO REMOVE RUN-OUTS FROM THE PAPER

If several run-outs have been worked on one sheet of paper, it is a good idea to cut around each of them with a razor blade leaving a large margin of paper all around. With care, the paper can be peeled away from each run-out. Alternatively, use a palette knife to ease between the icing and the paper. Handle run-outs carefully – remember that some designs will have weak areas.

ATTACHING RUN-OUTS TO THE CAKE

Pipe a little royal icing on to the underside of the run-out and attach it to the cake. Do not press hard on the run-out once placed in position or it may crack.

SMALL DESIGNS

An alternative method to use for small run-outs is to use the same icing and nozzle for both the outline and the flooding. Make the outline in the same way, then fill the centre by pressing the icing out and moving the nozzle at an angle of 45 degrees very slowly in small circular movements. This method is only suitable for small designs as it takes a long time to fill and smooth the flooding.

> **MRS BEETON'S TIP** When you have mastered the technique of making run-outs, a one-off design can be run-out directly on to the surface of the cake.

TIPS FOR SUCCESS WITH RUNOUTS

■ Select a design that has distinct areas which can be flooded with icing. Do not attempt too intricate a design if you are a beginner.

■ Make sure that the pattern is clearly drawn and visible through the paper before you begin.

■ Make sure that both the pattern and the paper cover are secured to the board. Use pins or masking tape. Clear sticky tape does not come away easily and in trying to remove it you may break the run-out.

■ Decide which areas are to be flooded at the same time. Do not try to flood neighbouring sections that may flow together.

■ When one area of the run-out is flooded, leave it to dry completely before flooding a neighbouring area.

■ Make sure that the run-out is thoroughly dried before removing it from the paper.

DESIGNS USING STAR AND SHELL NOZZLES

The star nozzle is particularly versatile, as it can be used for piping stars, scrolls, ropes and shells and it makes a more delicate design than the shell nozzle which is thicker and uses a lot of icing. These nozzles are available in various sizes but the medium and small sizes are easier to use. The final size of the design will, however, be determined by the amount of pressure used when piping.

The icing should have the consistency of a medium peak (page 157). Practise on the table or a board first to determine the size of your design, especially if you are using coloured icing which tends to mark a base coat of white icing.

USING THE STAR NOZZLE

Stars Work directly over the cake, holding the icing bag at an angle of 90 degrees to the surface. Hold the end of the bag in closed fingers and try to use one hand only for piping the stars. Holding the nozzle just off the cake, squeeze the bag gently, then stop pressing before you lift up the nozzle. If you remove the nozzle while still pressing the star will end in a peak. For bigger stars, press out

more icing before removing the bag. Pipe the stars so that they are just touching each other. For an elaborate star border, using a writing nozzle, loop a fine thread of plain icing from the top of one star to the next.

Scrolls Hold the nozzle as for a star but maintain the pressure and twist the nozzle in an 'S' shape. Then release the pressure and pull the nozzle away quickly to make a thin tail. The scrolls can be joined up to form a continuous edging or they can be piped in alternate directions for a more decorative finish.

Rope Borders Keeping an even pressure on the bag and holding the nozzle at an angle of 45 degrees to the cake, press out a thick line of royal icing using a circular movement to form a cable or rope.

USING THE SHELL NOZZLE

Shells Hold the nozzle at an angle of 45 degrees to the cake and squeeze out a rounded shape, lifting the nozzle slightly and replacing it again in the same place, then releasing the pressure and pulling the nozzle away along the cake to form a tail. Start the next shell at the end of the preceding tail so that the rounded shell shape slightly overlaps the tail. Use the tip of a pointed knife to tuck the last tail into position if necessary.

Star

Rope

Scroll

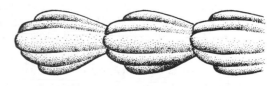

Shells

Basket Weave Icing

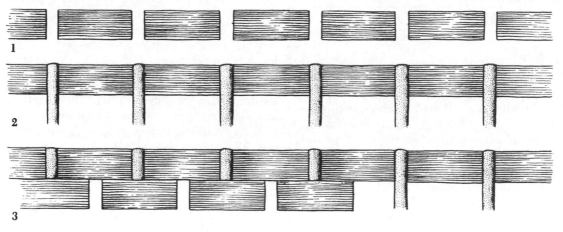

Alternative Method

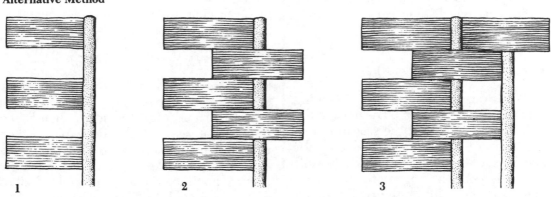

BASKET WEAVE ICING

This design can be piped in buttercream over a sponge cake, but the royal icing gives a neater effect. Allow plenty of time to pipe this design. The icing should be of a medium-peak consistency. For the best effect, use coloured icing. You will need a plain writing nozzle no 2 for the vertical lines and a basket or serrated ribbon nozzle for the horizontal piping. Have both nozzles fitted in separate bags of icing ready before you begin.

The design is often piped on the sides of the cake, so raise the cake so that it is at eye level by placing it on a turntable or cake tin.

Sit down for steady, controlled piping.

Start at the back of the cake with the serrated nozzle and pipe a 2.5 cm/1 inch long ribbon horizontally around the cake at the top edge. Leave a gap the same width as the ribbon and pipe another ribbon horizontally underneath the first, beginning and ending at the same place as the first. Repeat these parallel lines of piping, leaving a gap between each one until you reach the base of the cake.

Using the icing bag fitted with the plain nozzle, pipe a vertical line down the cake at the point where the ribbons end.

Using the serrated nozzle, pipe a second row of 2.5 cm/1 inch long ribbons over the vertical line and in between the first line of ribbons. Begin piping each ribbon parallel to the ribbon above and halfway along it. Now pipe another vertical line with the plain nozzle. Continue in this way all around the cake to build up the pattern. Finish the bottom and top edge of the cake with a shell border (page 215).

ALTERNATIVE METHOD

Alternatively, using exactly the same technique, the basket weave icing can be worked in horizontal rows. To do this pipe a line of 2.5 cm/1 inch ribbons, with a space between each, all around the cake. Next pipe the vertical, straight lines, then pipe another horizontal row of ribbons underneath. Continue building up the pattern in this way.

GARRETT FRILL

This is the frilled edge of a strip of sugar paste which is used to edge iced cakes or for making moulded flowers.

The sugar paste must be rolled out paper thin – a laminex board and rolling pin are very useful for this purpose to prevent the paste from sticking to the surface. Cover any paste which is not being used. Use only a very fine dusting of cornflour when rolling the paste, otherwise the paste will become dry and break easily. The edge of the rolled paste is stretched into a frill, using a cocktail stick or a wooden dowel.

PREPARING THE CAKE

Make a paper pattern to fit halfway around the sides of the cake. Fold the paper 2 or 3 times then mark and cut out a shallow curve. Open out the paper, transfer it to thin card and use a pin to scratch the design around the cake, about 2.5 cm/1 inch up from the base at the lowest point of the curve. Pipe a row of stars or shells around the lower edge of the cake or use a thin roll of paste to neaten the edge.

MAKING THE FRILL

Method 1 Roll out a small piece of paste, paper thin, and trim it to a strip measuring 2.5 cm/1 inch wide and 10 cm/4 inches long.

Lay a cocktail stick flat on the board, overlapping the sugar paste by about 1 cm/½ inch. Place your index finger on the stick at the edge of the paste, then firmly and quickly roll the stick backwards and forwards until the paste frills. Move the stick along the edge and continue until the whole strip is frilled. Dust the cocktail stick with a little cornflour occasionally.

Quickly brush the marked line on the cake with a damp brush – this is where the frill is to be attached. Place the unfrilled edge of the strip of paste on to the cake, holding it for a few seconds until it sticks. Gently lift up the edge of the frill with the blunt end of the brush. Repeat this process, all round the cake, overlapping the frill a little at each join.

Method 2 Use a 7.5 cm/3 inch Garrett frill cutter, or fluted cutter, to cut out thin circles of paste. Stamp out their centres with a 3.5 cm/1½ inch plain cutter.

Frill the edges of the rings of paste as in the previous method. Cut the ring and open it out. Alternatively, cut the ring in half to make smaller curves. Attach the frill as in the first method.

A second layer of frills can be attached to the cake once the first one is dry. To neaten the top edge of the frill, either prick it decoratively with a cocktail stick or pipe a row of small beads along it.

MRS BEETON'S TIP To strengthen the frill, knead a small piece of petal paste (pages 133 and 218) into the sugar paste before you begin.

MAKING MOULDED AND PIPED DECORATIONS

A variety of decorations can be made at home and, with practice, they can be far superior to the shop-bought alternatives. As well as moulded and piped flowers for formal cakes, this chapter shows how to make run-outs and colourful marzipan fruits or vegetables.

The choice of decorations that are added to a plain iced cake will depend on the type of icing used for covering the cake, as it is much easier to use the same icing rather than making up a totally different type. However, for very special occasions, when the decorations are made well in advance or even stored for future use, it is worth taking the trouble to create an elaborately designed cake which may be decorated with piped royal icing on a base of a softer, moulded icing.

One important factor to keep in mind is your own ability. Plan to make decorations which you are confident will turn out well. If this is your first or second attempt at cake decorating, it is safer and more sensible to follow some of the simpler techniques.

Within this chapter you will find instructions for making a variety of decorations, some easier than others. Allow yourself plenty of time and make more decorations than you need to finish the cake and you are unlikely to have a disaster. Indeed, you may be surpised at how successful you are.

MOULDING PASTES

A variety of decorations can be moulded using marzipan, sugar paste or petal paste.

WHITE MARZIPAN

This is smoother than almond paste and will absorb colours more readily. It is suitable for making figures, vegetables, fruits, leaves and larger flowers such as roses. The marzipan will dry if left in a dry, warm atmosphere but it will remain soft enough to eat. Use icing sugar for rolling it out and for moulding the pieces.

PETAL PASTE

This is a paste which is made specifically for modelling flowers and similar decorations. The paste sets hard and it is quite strong once it has set. However the decorations are usually too hard to eat. Use cornflour for rolling out and modelling.

SUGAR PASTE OR MOULDING ICING

These are easy to use and they dry hard but they are not as strong as petal paste. For a good compromise, knead a small piece of made-up petal paste (about the size of a walnut) into 225 g/8 oz sugar paste. Use cornflour for rolling out and modelling.

MATCHING COLOURS

When colouring the marzipan or paste remember to keep small balls of the coloured paste for matching up with any batches that may have to be made later. Keep the pieces of coloured paste wrapped in cling film inside a plastic bag or jar.

MRS BEETON'S TIP To avoid using too much cornflour when handling the paste, use a new, clean powder puff to dust the surface, rolling pin and hands with cornflour.

MOULDED LEAVES

There are several methods of making leaves; the following are all suitable for marzipan, petal paste or moulding icing.

Method 1 Roll out the paste thickly and use a leaf cutter to stamp out the leaves. Carefully peel away excess paste, then lift the leaves off with a palette knife and spread them out on non-stick baking parchment until dry.

Method 2 Roll out the paste thickly and cut it into diamond-shaped pieces of the required size. Either smooth the edges to form leaves or cut out small pieces around the leaf using a tiny plain cutter or the wide end of an icing nozzle.

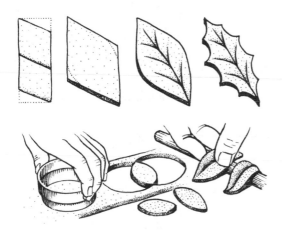

Method 3 Using a round plain cutter, stamp out a circle. Place the cutter three quarters of the way across the circle and cut again to give an oval-shaped leaf.

TO FINISH THE LEAVES

Use a small pointed knife to mark the veins on the leaves. Dry some of the leaves over a small rolling pin, empty foil roll or pencil so that they curve. Alternatively, place the leaves in a box lined with crumpled foil so that they dry into uneven shapes.

MOULDED FLOWERS

Roses and daisies are the easiest flowers to mould, but once you have mastered the techniques you will be able to create a variety of different flowers. Study real flowers (or use seed catalogues or other pictures as reference) for guidance. If you have real flowers to copy keep one in water just beside you. Carefully pull another one apart to study the shape of the petals and the way in which they are assembled. Small posies or miniature baskets of flowers can be made from Petal Paste (pages 133 and 218). The paste gives the moulded shapes strength; once dry they will keep indefinitely for permanent display. Shaped cutters are available for stamping out simple petal shapes but those that are moulded free-hand look more authentic.

The flowers can be made in white paste and painted with food colouring when dry or they can be moulded in a coloured paste in which case they should be tinted with extra colour when dry to make each flower individual. Marzipan is only suitable for the larger flowers such as roses, as it cannot be moulded as thinly as the other pastes.

DRYING THE FLOWERS

The flowers need to be supported as they dry – they can be placed on trays lined with non-stick baking parchment, in boxes lined with crumpled foil or rested in the holes of a wire cake cooling rack.

POINSETTIA

Using a deeply tinted red-coloured paste, cut large diamond leaf shapes from rolled out paste and leave them to dry over a rolling pin. Arrange the dried petals in a circle each slightly overlapping its neighbour. Make the stamen with piped icing or use small sugar cake decorations. Leave to dry on crumpled greaseproof paper.

SMALL DAISY

Take a small ball of white paste and shape it into a cone. Pinch the thin end into a stalk and ease out the other end with the fingertips (or use a modelling tool with a ball end) until it is thin and shaped like a shallow

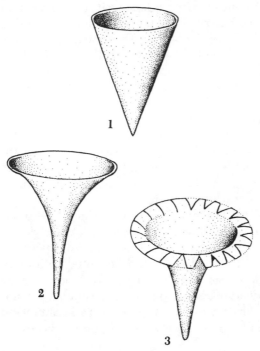

bowl. Snip all around the bowl at short intervals with scissors to make the petals. Prick the middle of the daisy to make the centre and leave to dry on crumpled paper. To finish, paint the centre yellow and tip some of the petals with pink.

LARGE DAISY

Make as for the small daisy but use a larger ball of paste and after cutting ten petals, snip each petal to a point with the scissors and curl them outwards to dry. Instead of pricking the centre for the stamen, mould a small ball of yellow paste, prick it with scissors and stick it into the centre of the

daisy by brushing the base with a dampened paint brush.

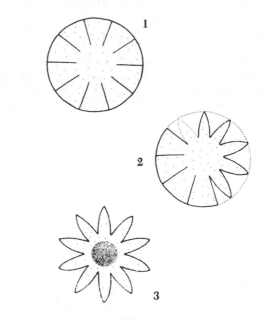

DOUBLE DAISY

Make two sets of petals as for the large daisy,

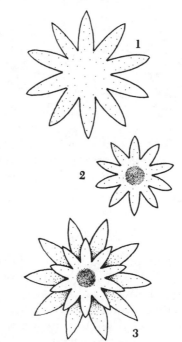

one slightly smaller than the other. Stick the smaller one inside the larger. Finish as for the large daisy.

AFRICAN VIOLET

Using violet-coloured paste, form a long thin cone and mould a large hole in the thicker

end with the blunt end of a pen or paint brush. Snip around to make fine petals and gently flatten and ease the petals outwards. Trim off the sharp corners of each petal, then mould each one into a very thin round-shaped petal. The petals should be almost spread out flat. Stick tiny balls of deep yellow paste in the centre for stamens.

ROSE

Mould a piece of paste the size of a pea into a cone and stand it pointing upwards on the table. Take another piece of paste the same size and hold it in the left hand. With the right thumb on top of the paste and the other fingers underneath, mould and pull the paste outwards into a very thin petal. Wrap the narrow end of the petal around the base of the cone. The tighter it is wrapped, the tighter the resulting bud:

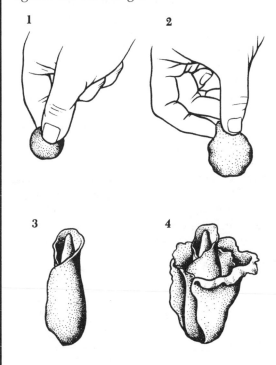

Repeat the process, making and wrapping more petals, each one slightly larger than the preceding one and wrapped more loosely around the bud. Gently roll the edge of the petals outwards. Vary the number of petals used to make flowers of different sizes, from buds through to fully opened specimens. Do not add too many petals or the shape will resemble a tightly packed cabbage rather than a loosely open rose! Trim the base off the rose to a slant and leave it to dry, supported on a tray or on crumpled foil.

It is best to make one rose at a time so that the petals readily stick to each other. If preferred, several roses can be shaped at once, in which case brush the base of each rose with a damp paint brush before moulding on a new petal.

CARNATION

The technique for making a carnation is the same as for making a Garret frill (page 217), where the edge of the paste is frilled with a wooden cocktail stick. Strengthen the moulding icing with a piece of petal paste.

The paste (marzipan is not suitable for this) is rolled paper-thin preferably using a laminex board and rolling pin.

The rolled-out paste is cut with a special carnation cutter or a small fluted pastry cutter about 4 cm/1½ inches in diameter. The carnation is built up from four circles. These can all be cut out together but remember to place cling film over any circles not being moulded.

Lightly dust a board with cornflour and roll out the paste as thinly as paper, picking it up and rotating it around as you roll it to prevent it from sticking. Cut out four circles, peel away excess paste and cover three of the circles with cling film.

With the pointed end of a knife, cut 5 mm/¼ inch slits at frequent intervals all around the remaining circle. Lay a cocktail stick flat on the surface with one pointed end overlapping the circle of paste between two slits. Use your index finger to roll the stick backwards and forwards until the edge of the paste frills and flutes between the slits. Frill the edge between all the slits in the same way, dusting the stick with cornflour, as necessary.

Fold the fluted circle into four and pinch the base together. Frill and fold two of the remaining circles in the same way. Flute the remaining circle but do not fold it. Pinch the three folded circles together and place them in the centre of the flat circle. Pinch the bases together. Brush the bases with a damp paint brush, if necessary, to ensure that they stick in the fourth circle to make the completed carnation. Leave the carnation to dry, supported in a wire rack.

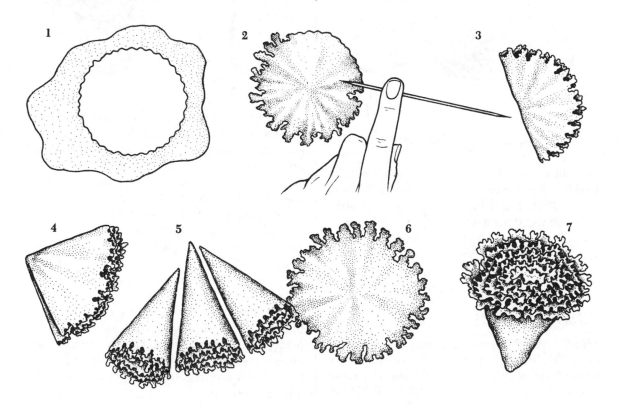

Dark Secrets Ring Cake (page 256)

Feathered Square (page 257) and Spider's Webs (page 258)

Sailing Yacht (page 257)

Teddy Bear (page 258) and Novelty Buns (page 261)

Shaping Daffodils

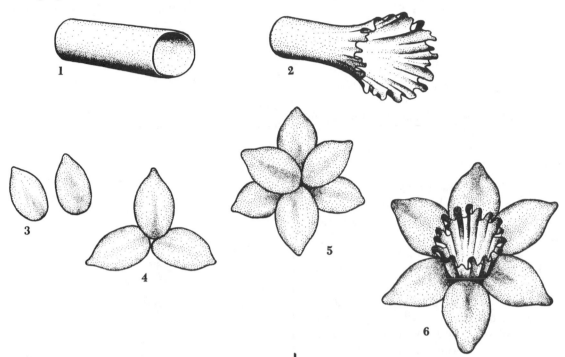

DAFFODIL

Daffodils can be made with marzipan or petal paste. Do not make them too large or they will flop or dwarf your other flowers. Allow several days for the flowers to dry. The daffodils are laid on the cake and the stalks added when they are in position.

Start each daffodil by shaping the trumpet: mould a small roll, about 2 cm/¾ inch long, from bright yellow paste. Insert the blunt end of a clean pencil into one end to make the hollow trumpet. Open out the end and thin the paste out with the fingers, then frill it with a cocktail stick (as for making a carnation, page 222). Cut a thin slice off the blunt end, then leave the trumpet to dry.

While the trumpet is drying, make the petals. If using marzipan, mould by hand to six petal shapes about 2.5 cm/1 inch long. They should be wider at the base than the tip. If using petal paste, roll it out thinly and cut out petal shapes. Arrange three petals, bases overlapping, to form a triangle, then place the other three on top, in between the first three. Lightly pinch the tips of the petals to soften the edge. Mould the petals over a crumpled ball of foil with the tips just touching the work surface so that they curl outwards. Pinch the centre of the petals together, gently moulding the paste into a small knob; this will be the position for the stalk. Leave to dry for 24 hours. Stick the trumpet inside the petals and lay the daffodil on crumpled foil.

To make the stamens, roll a tiny piece of white paste into a very thin roll and cut it into 2.5 cm/1 inch lengths. Place several together and put them into the trumpet. Add small blobs of yellow paste for tips, or pipe these in royal icing. Finish the daffodil by moulding two thin green leaves; wrapping them round the base of the flower, squeezing their ends together and bending them at right angles to the flower to form the beginning of the stalk. Arrange the dried daffodils on the cake and add rolls of green paste to represent stalks.

MOULDED FIGURES AND ANIMALS

These can be made with sugar paste or marzipan. The finished figures should be left to dry for up to seven days in a dry place. Protect them from dust by draping them loosely with greaseproof paper, allowing air to circulate around them.

SNOWMAN

If making several, knead colour into a small piece of paste; black for hats, eyes and buttons; a small orange piece for noses and a small red piece for scarves. Alternatively, if only making one or two, make the figure all in white and paint the colour on the features after twenty-four hours.

You will need 40 g/1½ oz marzipan or paste for each snowman, allowing 25 g/1 oz to mould into the body. Cut the remaining piece in half. Use one piece for the head, taking off a tiny piece to mould into a carrot-shaped nose.

Divide the final piece into three: use one piece to mould arms, one piece to mould into a floppy hat and roll the last piece into a thin sausage. Slightly flatten the sausage to make a scarf and cut both ends with scissors or a knife to make a fringe.

Assembling the Snowman Coat the body, head and arms in icing sugar. Arrange the body and arms in position, dampening them with a paint brush dipped in boiled water or alcohol. Attach the nose, scarf and hat.

DUCK

Use 25 g/1 oz of yellow marzipan or paste for each duck and mould three-quarters of it into a large tear-drop shape for the body.

Flick up the thin end to make the tail. Cut a tiny piece of paste from the remaining piece to make a beak. Flatten it out and cut it into a small diamond shape measuring not more than 5 mm/¼ inch at the widest point. Use the remaining paste to make a ball for the head and place it in position. Bend the beak in half, then insert it into position using the blunt end of a paint brush to push the middle of the beak into the head. Using scissors, cut a 'V' shaped slit on either side of the body to represent wings. Using white royal icing in an icing bag fitted with a plain writing nozzle, pipe beads for eyes or add tiny balls of paste. Leave to dry for 24 hours, then paint the beak bright yellow.

MARZIPAN FRUITS AND VEGETABLES

White marzipan is better than almond paste for moulding these fruits and vegetables because it is smoother and more pliable. It is also more suitable for tinting with food colouring. Study the real fruit or vegetable, or have it in front of you, to achieve the best result. Use icing sugar to dust your fingers while you work. Colour one small piece of marzipan yellow and another green as the two basic colours. To do this, knead the food colouring into the marzipan. Small pieces of these colours can be moulded into the remaining marzipan as required. Most fruits and vegetables are painted for optimum effect; this should be done 24 hours after shaping, when the marzipan has dried slightly.

Use cloves to represent the calyx and stalk on fruit. The fine side of a grater is used to simulate the rough skin of citrus fruits. Mould leaves out of marzipan. The fruit can also be half dipped in chocolate (page 235) or rolled in caster sugar. The marzipan can be moulded around a shelled hazelnut or raisin.

The finished fruits and vegetables may be used to decorate large or small cakes. They may also be packed in paper sweet cases and presented as a charming home-made gift.

FRUIT

Lemon Roll into a ball and ease out to a soft point at each end. Roll lightly on a fine grater.

Apple Roll into a ball, indent top and use a clove for the stalk. Streak with red food colouring.

Pear Gradually taper a ball into shape and put a clove in the narrow end for a stalk. Add another clove to the rounded end for a calyx. Streak with green food colouring.

Banana Shape into a curved sausage, tapering either end. Colour the tip brown and streak the middle with brown 'ripening' lines using a brown icing pen or food colouring, lightly applied with a brush.

Orange Use orange-coloured marzipan. Mould into a ball and roll on a fine grater.

Strawberry Shape into a ball then pinch out one end. Paint with red food colouring and sprinkle with caster sugar at once.

Cherries Shape small balls of red marzipan and add long marzipan stalks. These are the ideal shape in which to conceal a hazelnut or raisin.

Peaches Roll into a ball and indent the top, flattening the paste slightly. Brush with a hint of red food colouring.

VEGETABLES

Parsnips and Carrots Roll into a long cone shape. Mark ridges with a knife or paint these on using thin wisps of brown food colouring. Use orange marzipan for the carrot.

Baby Turnips Use white marzipan. Start with a ball and slightly flatten the top. Paint the top with streaks of purple food colouring and add marzipan leaves.

Mushrooms Cut out a small circle from pink marzipan, and a large piece of white marzipan. Cup the white over the pink, then mark the pink to represent the underside of a mushroom. Add a stalk.

Cauliflower Press lots of small balls of white marzipan together to represent the florets. Mould leaves from green marzipan and press them around the florets.

Peas Mould small green balls. Mould a thin, open pod and put the green balls in it.

Cabbages Make as for moulded roses (page 221), using green marzipan.

PIPED DECORATIONS

These are made with royal icing and are piped on to waxed paper. When dry they are quite brittle. They can be painted, tinted or sprinkled with lustre powder. They keep well for many months when stored between layers of greaseproof paper in a box. Always make many more than you need.

Success depends mainly on having the icing at the correct consistency. This should be firm peak and stiff enough to hold a clean, thin shape once piped. However, it must not be so stiff that your arm aches as you pipe or the icing bag bursts. Flowers are piped on to a special flower nail; you can make one of these by sticking a cork on to a short knitting needle. Some flowers, such as roses, are easier to make when piped around a cocktail stick.

PIPED ROSES

Nozzles Petal nozzles come in a variety of sizes but the smaller sizes are easier to use. The nozzle has a thin end which forms the top of the petal and a bulbous end for the petal base. Take care not to distort the thin end of the nozzle or let it get blocked with icing as this will spoil the piped edge of the petals. If you are left-handed, use an appropriate petal nozzle and reverse all the piping instructions.

Piping the roses This is a time-consuming task, so seat yourself at a comfortable height with the work surface – about elbow height is best. Have ready several cocktail sticks and a supply of waxed paper squares, about 2.5 x 2.5 cm/1 x 1 inch. Place two or three tablespoons of icing into a paper icing bag (page 138) fitted with a petal nozzle. Fold over the top of the bag so that when the top of the bag is held under the fingers, the thin part of the nozzle points upwards. Pierce a square of waxed paper on a cocktail stick positioning this half way down; the paper is used to remove the rose after it has been piped. Hold the stick in your left hand and pipe a strip of icing around the tip, rotating the stick anti-clockwise as you pipe. This forms the central bud.

Hold the nozzle at an angle of 45 degrees to the bud and start at the base of the bud. Squeeze out the icing, lifting up the nozzle and returning it almost immediately to the base of the bud about one-third of the way around. Rotate the stick slowly with the left hand so that the right hand moves up and down, *not* around.

Make two more petals around the bud, slightly overlapping each one at the base. Remember to lift the nozzle for a rounded edge to the petals. Add two or three slightly larger petals around the outside. Do not add too many petals or the rose will resemble a cabbage. Make rosebuds as well as blooms.

Tease the petals gently outwards with a dry paint brush, then slide the paper up the

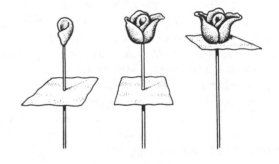

stick until it rests under the rose. Support the base of the rose with your thumb and push the paper off the stick. Make more roses in the same way, then leave the roses to dry for 48 hours. When dried, the roses can be painted and brushed with lustre, if you like.

Two-tone or Tinted Roses These can be made by placing a stream of icing in a contrasting colour down the inside edge of the icing bag when it is filled. Put this icing on the same side as the narrow end of the nozzle. As you pipe, the tips of the petals will be tinted with contrasting icing.

PIPED BLOSSOM

Fit the same nozzle as for piping roses but use a flower nail instead of a cocktail stick. Stick a piece of waxed paper on to the nail with a little icing. Hold the bag horizontally above the nail, with the bulbous end towards the centre. Slowly rotate the nail, squeeze the bag and pipe a petal that covers a quarter of a circle like a fan. Stop squeezing, lift the nozzle and pipe another four petals in the same way. Overlap the petals at the centre base until they are piped in a complete circle. Carefully remove the paper from the nail and leave the flower to dry for a few hours. Fill a paper icing bag fitted with a writing nozzle with yellow icing and pipe small yellow blobs in the centre for stamens.

PIPED LEAVES

Long feathery leaves can be piped directly on to the cake or on to a sheet of waxed paper or non-stick baking parchment.

Nozzles Special nozzles that resemble an inverted 'V' can be purchased. For piping a few leaves, the end of a paper icing bag can be cut to a 'V' shape. Renew the bag if the leaves begin to lose their definition.

Piping the Leaves Make a paper icing bag with a good point (page 138). Snip off either side of the point of the bag to make an inverted 'V' shape. The cuts should be between 3-5 mm/⅛-¼ inch in length from the tip to the side of the bag. The tip of the 'V' marks the vein in the leaf.

Place two tablespoons of green icing in the bag, fold down the end and hold it in the right hand with the point at an angle of 45 degrees to the paper. The index finger of the left hand can be used to steady the bag and to give slight pressure near the base of the bag, if necessary. Squeeze out the icing, then ease off the pressure and pull the bag away to draw the icing into a point. For a fuller leaf, quickly push the nozzle backwards and forwards as you squeeze before releasing the pressure.

PIPED BELLS

These must be left for at least 24 hours to dry completely. Use a plain no 2 or 3 writing nozzle on an icing bag filled with royal icing and pipe large beads about 1.5 cm/¾ inch across on to waxed paper or non-stick baking parchment. Leave to dry for several hours, then pipe a small bead on top and pull the nozzle away quickly to make a thin peak which should fall over to make a loop. Use a pin to tuck in the end of the loop. Leave the bells to dry for 24 hours, then carefully peel them away from the paper and leave them to dry on their sides for a further 24 hours. Carefully scrape away the soft icing inside each with the end of a small pointed knife. Arrange the bells in pairs on the cake.

TIPS FOR SUCCESS WITH PIPED DECORATIONS

■ Make sure that the icing bag is strong.

■ Check that the icing is of the right consistency by piping a sample shape.

■ Always make plenty of extra piped decorations to allow for breakages and so that only the best ones can be used on the cake.

■ Leave the piped decorations to dry completely before removing them from the paper.

Piping Bells

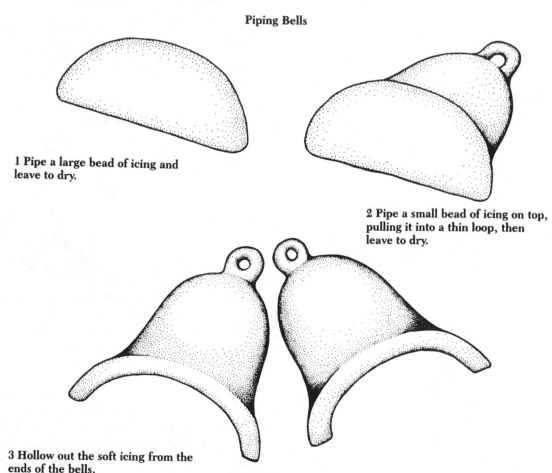

1 Pipe a large bead of icing and leave to dry.

2 Pipe a small bead of icing on top, pulling it into a thin loop, then leave to dry.

3 Hollow out the soft icing from the ends of the bells.

Piping Birds

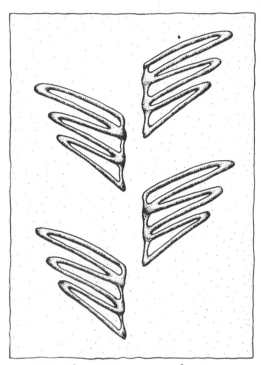

1 Pipe the wings on to waxed paper, making sure that all the feather shapes are joined at the base of the wing. Leave to dry.

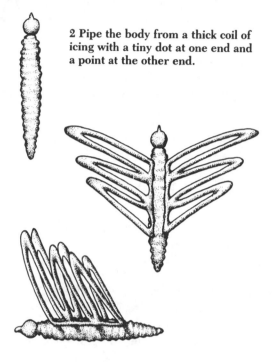

2 Pipe the body from a thick coil of icing with a tiny dot at one end and a point at the other end.

3 Place a wing on either side of the body and hold in place, or support, until firm. Leave to dry.

PIPED BIRDS

These are ideal for decorating christening and wedding cakes. The wings are piped on to waxed paper, then dried before being assembled on to the body.

The icing should be of a firm peak consistency. Use an icing bag fitted with a plain no 1 or 2 writing nozzle. Line a tray with waxed paper. Hold the nozzle at an angle of 45 degrees to the paper and squeeze the icing out into a thin thread, moving the nozzle quickly backwards and forwards to the right. Pipe an arched line about 2 cm/¾ inch long, then pipe back to the starting point. This forms the first feather of the wing. Make two more feathers immediately under the first, and joined at the base, each one slightly shorter than the preceding one. This makes one wing.

Pipe several more wings over the paper, then reverse the direction and pipe the left wings. Leave the wings to dry for 24 hours.

To Assemble the Birds When the wings are dry, ease them off the paper and place them on a saucer.

Using a bag fitted with a no 2 nozzle, pipe a thick body about 2 cm/¾ inch long. Squeeze out the icing and rotate the nozzle to form a coil of icing as you slowly pull it along. Narrow the icing to a point at one end for the tail. Place a wing on either side of the body and hold them in the icing for a few seconds to set. Alternatively, support the wings in position by placing cotton wool balls under them while they dry. Pipe a small bead for the head and quickly draw away the nozzle to make a beak. When dry, the birds can be stored in the same way as the flowers.

CHOCOLATE WORK

Dark and bitter, smooth and milky or pale and creamy – there are many types of chocolate available now and they can be put to a variety of uses. This chapter explains all about chocolate, from successful melting to creative ideas for piping, shaping and curling.

CHOCOLATE AND ITS USES

Chocolate is a blend of cocoa solids and cocoa butter to which varying quantities of vegetable fats, milk and sugar have been added. The quantity of added fat determines the hardness or softness of the chocolate.

A block of chocolate can be finely or coarsely grated, chopped, slivered and curled for decorating or coating the sides and tops of cakes.

Melted chocolate is malleable; it dries to a smooth, glossy film. It flavours and provides texture, as well as setting quality, to icings and fillings. Melted chocolate has many other uses: it can be poured over cakes or fruits or marzipan and nuts can be dipped in it. Chocolate leaves are made by coating real leaves. Chocolate curls, known as caraque, is a widely used decoration. Melted chocolate can also be set in a thin sheet, then cut into shapes, for example squares, triangles or shapes using cutters. The melted chocolate can also be piped in many ways.

Milk and Plain Chocolate Milk Chocolate has added milk products and is paler and softer in texture than plain chocolate which is darker and more brittle. The quantity of added sugar determines the sweetness. Milk chocolate contains more sugar than plain chocolate which is available as bitter, semi-sweet or plain.

Chocolate-flavoured Cake Covering This is not true chocolate. In this product the cocoa butter is replaced by other fats which make it more malleable. The resulting flavour is poor and the texture waxy. It is useful for inexpensive, everyday cakes but it should not be applied when a good result is required.

White Chocolate This is made from cocoa butter, sugar and milk and does not contain any of the cocoa solids or non-fat parts of the cocoa bean.

Carob This is manufactured from the pulp of the carob or locust bean to resemble chocolate in appearance. It is naturally sweeter than cocoa so less sugar is added; also, it is caffeine free. It is in powder form for cooking and in block form for eating. Carob can be used instead of chocolate for some of the following ideas but it is waxy in consistency and does not have such a glossy appearance.

STORING CHOCOLATE DECORATIONS

Store chocolate decorations in a cool, dry atmosphere for the shortest possible time, and no longer than seven to ten days. The chocolate will sweat if it is kept in a warm room. On very hot days keep the chocolate in the refrigerator but bring it to room temperature before melting it.

CHOCOLATE ICINGS AND DECORATIONS

Use a hard, plain dessert chocolate for the best flavour and texture. Do not be disappointed by its appearance; it will not have the same high gloss as commercial chocolates. Avoid handling the chocolate once it has set as fingermarks will readily show and the surface will become dull.

CHOPPING CHOCOLATE

Break the chocolate into pieces and place it on a chopping board. Use a sharp knife with a long blade and hold the tip of the knife on to the board with one hand. Pivot the blade, bringing it up and down with the other hand. Scrape the chocolate back to the centre of the board and continue until the pieces are even and quite small.

GRATING CHOCOLATE

Place the grater on a piece of greaseproof paper on a large plate or chopping board. Rub the block of chocolate on the coarse side of the grater. Use long, even strokes and keep your hands as cool as possible.

CHOCOLATE SLIVERS

Hold your hands under cold running water, then dry them. Hold the chocolate in the palm of the hand and shave off thin pieces of chocolate with a potato peeler, letting them fall on to a chilled plate or a sheet of greaseproof paper.

MELTING CHOCOLATE

Break up or roughly chop the chocolate and place it in a basin that fits over a saucepan. Place about 5 cm/2 inches of water in the pan and bring to the boil, then remove the pan from the heat and stand the basin over it. Leave for a few minutes, then stir the chocolate until it has melted and is smooth and glossy. If you leave the pan on the heat, the chocolate will overheat and white streaks may appear in it when it sets again.

DIPPING FOOD IN CHOCOLATE

Biscuits, choux buns, nuts, marzipan shapes, real leaves and fruits such as maraschino cherries, grapes, raisins, dates and slices of banana can all be dipped in melted chocolate. They can be part-dipped or fully dipped according to the effect required. Special dipping forks have two long prongs that are bent at the ends to stop the food falling off when dipped. Alternatively, use a corn-on-the-cob fork, cocktail stick or two fine skewers, one on either side of the food. For larger pieces of food such as choux buns, or hard foods such as almonds, it is best to use your fingers to dip the ingredients.

Melt the chocolate following the instructions left. For dipping food the consistency should be thick enough to coat the back of a spoon. If the chocolate is too thin, remove the basin from the pan and leave it to cool slightly, until the chocolate thickens. Keep the chocolate warm (over the saucepan of water), while you are working. If the chocolate becomes too thick, remove the basin, re-heat the water, then replace the basin. Stir the chocolate occasionally as you are dipping the food; this gives a glossy finish.

You will need a good depth of melted chocolate to dip food successfully; it should be at least 5 cm/2 inches deep. (When the chocolate becomes too shallow for successful dipping, do not discard it; stir the excess into buttercreams or similar icings to avoid wastage.)

Line a baking sheet or wire rack with a sheet of waxed paper or non-stick baking parchment. Have ready all the food to be dipped and start with firm items, such as nuts and marzipan. Finish with soft foods, such as fruits. Plunge the food into the chocolate to the depth required, then quickly withdraw at the same angle at which it was plunged. Do not rotate part-dipped food in the chocolate or the top line of chocolate will be uneven.

Gently shake the food to allow the excess chocolate to fall back into the basin, then place it on the prepared sheet or rack to dry.

TO DIP LEAVES

Use clean, dry leaves, such as rose leaves, and brush the underside of the leaf over the surface of the chocolate. Dry the leaves chocolate side uppermost, then carefully peel away the leaf, leaving the impression of the leaf on the chocolate.

PIPING CHOCOLATE

When adding chocolate decoration to the top of a cake, melted chocolate is difficult to pipe because it begins to set in the nozzle. Mixing a little icing sugar with it will make it more malleable; however this is not suitable for piping shapes that have to set hard.

25 g/1 oz icing sugar, sifted
100 g/4 oz chocolate, melted

Stir the icing sugar into the melted chocolate with a few drops of water to make a mixture of a thick piping consistency that drops from the spoon.

MRS BEETON'S TIP If using piping chocolate in large quantities to pipe shells around a cake, use sugar syrup (page 155) instead of icing sugar to soften the chocolate.

PIPING WITH CHOCOLATE

The chocolate should be of a thin flowing consistency. Very little pressure is required to pipe with chocolate as it should flow slowly out of the bag without any encouragement.

TO DRIZZLE CHOCOLATE OVER CAKES AND BISCUITS

Place 15 ml/1 tbsp of melted chocolate into a small paper icing bag. Snip off the end and quickly move the bag backwards and forwards over the cake or biscuit. Finish by lowering the bag and quickly withdrawing it.

TO PIPE MOTIFS AND SHAPES

Prepare the pattern and piping surface as for royal icing run-outs (page 212). Alternatively, work freehand on to the waxed paper. Make several paper icing bags out of non-stick baking parchment – greaseproof paper is not strong enough for chocolate work.

Place 30-45 ml/2-3 tbsp melted chocolate in an icing bag and snip off the end. Start with a fine hole until you have checked the size of the piping. It is a good idea to practise piping beads and buttons on the paper first. Hold the bag and pipe the shapes as for run-outs (page 212) and lace (page 208). Remember to make sure that all the lines of piping are joined somewhere in the design. Shapes may be filled in using a different coloured chocolate, such as milk chocolate or white chocolate with plain chocolate. Leave the shapes to dry hard before peeling them off the waxed paper.

TO PIPE CHOCOLATE SHELLS AROUND A CAKE

Prepare piping chocolate (left). Use a strong bag made from double non-stick baking parchment and fitted with a small star nozzle. Pipe a shell pattern quickly around the cake as for royal icing (page 215). This method can also be used to pipe around home-made Easter eggs.

Outlines to Pipe in Chocolate

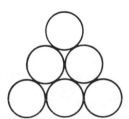

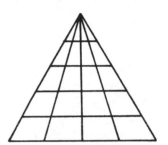

Designs to Pipe and Flood in Chocolate

TO MAKE CURLS, FRILLS AND SHAPES

Melted chocolate can be used to make a variety of different decorations without the need for piping. Here are a few examples: the key to success is to make sure that you use good quality chocolate and to leave the decorations to set firmly before using them.

CHOCOLATE CURLS OR SCROLLS (CARAQUE)

Whether you are making curls or frills the chocolate is prepared in the same way: pour melted chocolate over a clean, dry surface, such as a marble slab or a clean smooth area of work surface. Spread the chocolate backwards and forwards with a large palette knife until it is smooth, fairly thin and even. Leave to dry until almost set; do not allow the chocolate to set hard.

Hold a long, thin-bladed knife at an acute angle to the chocolate. Hold the top of the knife with the other hand and pull the knife towards you with a gentle sawing action, scraping off a thin layer of chocolate which should curl into a roll.

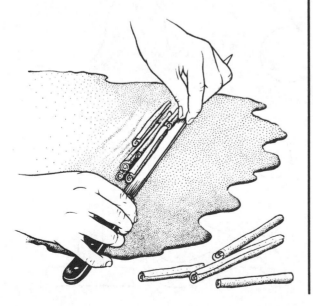

CHOCOLATE FRILLS

Starting at the edge of the chocolate, hold the tip of a small palette knife at an angle of 45 degrees or lower to the surface, and push the palette knife away from you. A thin layer of chocolate will frill as you push. Place the frills on waxed paper as you make them.

TO CUT CHOCOLATE SHAPES

Spread the melted chocolate on to waxed paper or non-stick baking parchment paper. Use petits fours cutters or small biscuit cutters, to stamp shapes out of the chocolate, cutting them as close together as possible. Leave to set hard before peeling away the paper. The excess chocolate can be finely chopped for decorations or melted for use in making more shapes.

TO CUT SQUARES, TRIANGLES OR WEDGES

Prepare a precise pattern, drawing a large square and dividing it up into smaller squares or triangles. Alternatively, draw a circle and divide it into equal wedges. In either case extend the lines beyond the square or circle so that when the pattern has been covered in chocolate, the ends of the lines will still be visible. Place the pattern under non-stick baking parchment as for royal icing run-outs (page 212).

Spread the melted chocolate over the marked shape and leave to set but not harden. Use a long-bladed knife and cut the chocolate into the shapes by holding the tip of the knife at one side of the chocolate and firmly lowering the handle so that the blade follows the cutting line. Leave the chocolate until firm, then carefully peel the shapes off the parchment.

CHOCOLATE CAKE COVERINGS

As well as chocolate-flavoured buttercreams and icings, here are two recipes for contrasting cake coverings. The Chocolate Velvet Cream recipe gives a soft and creamy, chocolate-flavoured covering that can be spread or piped on to the cake.

Alternatively, the Tipsy Chocolate Velvet is a rich, glossy and dark icing which is poured over the cake.

CHOCOLATE VELVET CREAM

150 ml/¼ pint double cream
100 g/4 oz chocolate, chopped

Combine the cream and chocolate in a small saucepan. Place over a low heat until the chocolate has melted. Continue to stir over the low heat for a further 5 minutes until the mixture is dark and creamy. Pour the cream into a bowl and chill for at least 1 hour.

Beat the cream for 5 minutes or beat it with a balloon whisk for about 10 minutes, until it has doubled in volume.

SUFFICIENT TO COVER THE TOP AND SIDES OF A 20 CM/8 INCH CAKE

TIPSY CHOCOLATE VELVET

75 g/3 oz chocolate, cut up
100 g/4 oz icing sugar, sifted
15 ml/1 tbsp dark rum
5 ml/1 tsp vegetable oil

Melt the chocolate with the 60 ml/4 tbsp water in a basin over a saucepan of hot water. Gradually beat in the icing sugar, rum and oil until the icing is smooth and coats the back of the spoon. Pour the icing over a cake and level the top and sides with a palette knife.

SUFFICIENT TO COAT THE TOP AND SIDES OF A 20 CM/8 INCH CAKE

VARIATIONS

ORANGE CHOCOLATE VELVET Use Grand Marnier instead of rum.

MOCHA VELVET Replace the rum and water with freshly made black coffee.

CAKE DESIGNS

This chapter offers a selection of ideas for elaborately decorated cakes as well as jolly novelty cakes. Plain cake recipes from the previous chapters can be used as a base or the recipes given here may be followed; however, the cake baked in a roasting tin (below) is most suitable for cutting into novelty shapes.

BASIC SPONGE CAKE

275 g/10 oz soft margarine
275 g/10 oz caster sugar
5 eggs, beaten
275 g/10 oz self-raising flour
7.5 ml/1½ tsp baking powder

Grease and line an oblong roasting tin measuring about 30 x 20 cm/12 x 8 inches or a 25 cm/10 inch square tin. Set the oven at 190°C/375°F/gas 5.

Place all the ingredients in a bowl. Add 15 ml/1 tbsp hot water and beat hard for 2 minutes if using an electric mixer or longer if beating by hand. The mixture should be light and creamy. It should have a soft dropping consistency.

Spoon the mixture into the prepared tin, making sure that it is spread well into the corners. Bake for 30-35 minutes until set and beginning to shrink from the sides of the tin. Turn the cake out on to a wire rack to cool.

MAKES ONE 30 x 20 CM/12 x 8 INCH CAKE OR ONE 25 CM/10 INCH SQUARE CAKE

VARIATIONS

SANDWICH CAKE Use 100 g/4 oz each of soft margarine, caster sugar and self-raising flour. Add 5 ml/1 tsp baking powder, 2 beaten eggs and a few drops of milk. Follow the method above but bake in two 18 cm/7 inch sandwich tins for 25-30 minutes.

CRYSTAL MADEIRA CAKE

225 g/8 oz butter, softened
225 g/8 oz caster sugar
grated rind and juice of 1 lemon
4 eggs, beaten
75 g/3 oz ground almonds
75 g/3 oz glacé cherries (red, green and
    yellow), chopped
75 g/3 oz crystallised ginger, chopped
75 g/3 oz crystallised pineapple, chopped
75 g/3 oz flaked almonds, chopped
350 g/12 oz self-raising flour

Line and grease a 25 cm/10 inch square tin. Set the oven at 180°C/350°F/gas 4.

Cream the butter, sugar and lemon rind in a mixing bowl, until light and fluffy, then beat in the eggs, a little at a time. Mix the ground almonds, cherries, ginger, pineapple and nuts together in a separate bowl, then fold the mixture into the cake, alternating with the flour until all the ingredients are incorporated. Add the lemon juice.

Spoon the mixture in the prepared tin, spreading it well into the corners. Bake for 1 hour or until the cake is firm on top and beginning to shrink from the sides. Leave to cool in the tin for 15 minutes, then turn the cake out on to a wire rack. Leave the paper on the cake.

MAKES ONE 25 CM/10 INCH SQUARE CAKE

INGREDIENTS FOR RICH FRUIT CAKE

ROUND SQUARE	15 cm/6 inch 13 cm/5 inch	18 cm/7 inch 15 cm/6 inch	20 cm/8 inch 18 cm/7 inch	23 cm/9 inch 20 cm/8 inch	25 cm/10 inch 23 cm/9 inch	28 cm/11 inch 25 cm/10 inch	30 cm/12 inch 28 cm/11 inch	33 cm/13 inch 30 cm/12 inch
Currants	225 g/8 oz	275 g/10 oz	400 g/14 oz	500 g/1 lb 2oz	575 g/1¼ lb	675 g/1½ lb	900 g/2 lb	1.25 kg/2½ lb
Raisins	100 g/4 oz	150 g/5 oz	200 g/7 oz	250 g/9 oz	300 g/11 oz	375 g/13 oz	450 g/1 lb	575 g/1¼ lb
Sultanas	100 g/4 oz	150 g/5 oz	200 g/7 oz	250 g/9 oz	300 g/11 oz	375 g/13 oz	450 g/1 lb	575 g/1¼ lb
Butter, softened	100 g/4 oz	150 g/5 oz	200 g/7 oz	250 g/9 oz	300 g/11 oz	375 g/13 oz	450 g/1 lb	575 g/1¼ lb
Moist dark brown sugar	100 g/4 oz	150 g/5 oz	200 g/7 oz	250 g/9 oz	300 g/11 oz	375 g/13 oz	450 g/1 lb	575 g/1¼ lb
Lemon, grated rind of	½	½	1	1	1½	1½	2	2
Almonds, shelled	25 g/1 oz	25 g/1 oz	40 g/1½ oz	65 g/2½ oz	75 g/3 oz	90 g/3½ oz	100 g/4 oz	100 g/4 oz
Citrus peel, chopped	25 g/1 oz	25 g/1 oz	40 g/1½ oz	65 g/2½ oz	75 g/3 oz	90 g/3½ oz	100 g/4 oz	100 g/4 oz
Glacé cherries	50 g/2 oz	50 g/2 oz	75 g/3 oz	90 g/3½ oz	100 g/4 oz	150 g/5 oz	175 g/6 oz	175 g/6 oz
Plain flour	100 g/4 oz	150 g/5 oz	200 g/7 oz	250 g/9 oz	300 g/11 oz	375 g/13 oz	450 g/1 lb	575 g/1¼ lb
Ground mixed spice	1.25 ml/¼ tsp	2.5 ml/½ tsp	2.5 ml/½ tsp	5 ml/1 tsp	5 ml/1 tsp	7.5 ml/1½ tsp	7.5 ml/1½ tsp	10 ml/2 tsp
Eggs, beaten	2	2	3	4	5	6	8	10
Black treacle	10 ml/2 tsp	10 ml/2 tsp	15 ml/1 tbsp	15 ml/1 tbsp	22.5 ml/4½ tsp	22.5 ml/4½ tsp	30 ml/2 tbsp	30 ml/2 tbsp

This chart provides an alternative to the recipe for the three-tiered wedding cake on page 82. It also gives quantities for cakes of different sizes.

Set the oven at 150°C/300°F/gas 2. Line and grease the appropriate tin. Mix the currants, raisins and sultanas. Cream the butter, sugar and lemon rind until very soft. Beat in the almonds and the citrus peel. Wash and dry the cherries, then roughly chop them and toss them with a little of the measured flour. Sift the remaining flour with the spice and toss a little with the mixed dried fruit. Beat the eggs and treacle into the creamed mixture, adding a spoonful of the flour occasionally to prevent the mixture curdling. Fold in the the remaining flour. Lastly fold in the fruit and the cherries.

Turn the mixture into the tin and smooth the top with the back of a wetted metal spoon, hollowing out the centre slightly. The cooking time depends on the size of the cake. The small cakes will take about 1½-2 hours, the cakes of between 20-23 cm/8-9 inches will need about 4-5 hours and the larger cakes take about 7-8 hours. Insert a clean metal skewer into the centre of the cake to test if it is cooked: it should come out clean when the cake is ready. If there is any sticky mixture on the skewer the cake is not cooked.

Leave the cake to cool in the tin for at least an hour, then transfer it to a wire rack to cool completely. Do not remove the lining paper. Wrap the cake, still in the lining paper, in fresh greaseproof paper and store it in an airtight tin.

WEDDING CAKES

Traditional tiered wedding cakes are covered in royal icing. However, sugar paste, a soft icing which is now very popular, can also be used on wedding cakes. The only minor drawback with using sugar paste is that the tiers have to be supported independently, otherwise the weight of the cake pushes the pillars into the sugar paste.

To ensure that a tiered cake looks in proportion when stacked, the size of the tiered cakes usually decreases by 5 cm/2 inches when there are three or more tiers. For a two-tier cake, the top cake may be 7.5 cm/3 inches smaller than the one below. When planning the cake, the height of any decoration on the top tier must also be considered. The cake at the base of a triple tier should be slightly deeper than the other cakes, this may be achieved by baking a 28 cm/11 inch cake quantity in a 25 cm/10 inch cake tin (see page 262).

CAKE BOARDS AND PILLARS

Cake Boards Always use drum boards for tiered cakes. The base board should be 5 cm/2 inches larger than the cake that stands upon it; the tiers above should have boards about 2.5 cm/1 inch larger than their cakes. If the cake is decorated with a Garrett frill or extension work, use a board which is 2.5 cm/1 inch larger than usual to protect the edging. Board edging or ribbon can be placed around the edges of the board. Upper cakes that are assembled directly on top of each other should be placed on thin cake cards exactly the same size as the iced cake.

Pillars Use four pillars for each tier, except for very small cakes or heart-shaped cakes when three pillars will be sufficient. Check that the pillars are all level. Make sure that the pillars are evenly positioned before assembling the tiers. It is a good idea to include the pillars on the base cake as part of the decoration design.

If the cake is covered with sugar paste, use special pillars with stakes that are pushed down through the cake to support the tiers. Alternatively, use hollow pillars and push a piece of wooden dowel through each pillar and the cake to the board. It is important to measure the length of dowel required accurately, otherwise the weight of the cake will rest on the pillars, rather than on the lengths of dowel. If the dowel rods are too long, or if they are uneven, the tiers will not be level.

TIMING

Making the Cakes The cakes should be made at least three months in advance. They should be wrapped in several layers of greaseproof paper, then in foil, and stored in a cool, dry place. *Do not* wrap cakes in cling film as they tend to sweat. Nor should cakes be wrapped directly in foil since the acid in the fruit would react with aluminium and the foil would disintegrate in particles on the surface of the cake.

The Almond Paste Use white almond paste and leave this to dry on the cake for at least 2 weeks. Cover the cake layers lightly with a clean tea-towel or greaseproof paper to protect them from dust.

The Icing Allow at least 2 weeks for the completed flat icing to dry before adding any piping and decoration.

Cutting the Cake The cake should be cut into pieces about 5 cm/2 inches by 2.5 cm/1 inch. Cut right across the cake, making large 2.5 cm/1 inch thick slices. Cut the slices into fingers. Remember that you will cut fewer pieces from a round cake than from a square one. If a large number of guests are to be entertained and lots of cake is to be posted out, it is a good idea to bake an additional large square cake and cover it with almond paste and icing. There is no need to add decorations, but the extra cake can then be cut up behind the scenes and served as required.

Number Six Cake (page 259) and Building Blocks (page 261)

Clown Cake (page 260)

Shortbread (page 286) and Jim-jams (page 289)

From the top: **Dover Biscuits and Jumbles** (both on page 288), and **Cinnamon Bars** (page 287)

THREE-TIERED WEDDING CAKE

Illustrated on page 129

The cake is covered in royal icing and decorated with garlands of piped roses in pastel shades. Instead of flowers, run-outs of hearts, bells, birds or the couple's initials can be used to decorate the sides of the cakes. The decoration on this cake can be used with the recipe for the wedding cake given in the previous section of the book (page 82).

3 square Rich Fruit Cakes (page 241), covered with Almond Paste (page 142) and flat iced with Royal Icing (page 156):
    1 x 25 cm/10 inch
    1 x 20 cm/8 inch
    1 x 15 cm/6 inch
about 800 g/1¾ lb Royal Icing (page 156) for piping

DECORATION

    240 piped roses (page 230):
        80 pastel pink
        80 pastel green
        80 cream
    (this number allows plenty of choice)
    piped green leaves (page 231)

NOZZLES

    plain writing nozzle no 1
    small star nozzle
    medium shell or star nozzle

All three cakes should be flat iced, on cake boards ready for decorating. Draw and cut out the following circles in thin white card: one 18 cm/7 inches in diameter, one 13 cm/5 inches in diameter and one 7.5 cm/3 inches in diameter. Divide each circle into four equal segments and cut out one quarter segment from each to use as a template.

Place the largest template on the corner of the bottom cake and gently scratch around the curved edge with a pin. Repeat with the remaining corners. Mark curves on the corners of the smaller cakes in the same way, each time using the appropriate sized template as guide.

Using an icing bag fitted with the plain nozzle, pipe double trellis work in royal icing over the marked corner areas of each cake. Neaten the trellis by piping a row of fine stars using a second bag fitted with the small star nozzle on the curved edges.

Cut paper patterns to fit one side of each cake. Fold the larger piece of paper into three and the second piece into two. Mark a line 1 cm/½ inch from the top and 1 cm/½ inch from the bottom of each folded pattern and along the pattern for the smallest cake. Draw around a tea cup or similar round object to make a curve between the lines on the patterns. Cut round the curve, open out the folded paper and transfer the patterns on to pieces of thin white card. The largest cake should have three scallops along its side, the middle cake two scallops and the smallest cake one curve only (page 262).

Position the patterns on the sides of the cakes and prick the scallop designs on to the icing with a pin or fine skewer.

Using an icing bag fitted with the medium shell or star nozzle, pipe a row of shells around the top and lower edges of the cakes. Stick the roses, in alternate colours along the marked pattern on the sides of the cake. Make sure you have flowers of the same colour at the top of each curve on each side of the cakes, so that all three tiers match. Position three or more roses on top of each cake between the trellis work and one rose in each corner on the shell edging. Place the green leaves at random between the roses.

ABOUT 120 PORTIONS

SINGLE-TIER WEDDING CAKE

Illustrated on page 130

If you do not want to attempt the complicated extension work on this cake, simply pipe a border of shells on the cake.

30 cm/12 inch Rich Fruit Cake (page 241), covered with Almond Paste (page 142)
Sugar Paste (page 158) tinted with cream colouring
450 g/1 lb royal icing (page 156) for piping

DECORATION

2 m/6½ feet x 5 mm/¼ inch cream ribbon
selection of frosted flowers (page 165)

NOZZLES

plain writing nozzles nos 2 and 0

The cake should be positioned on a 38 cm/ 15 inch round cake board. Using the no 0 nozzle pipe embroidery over the cake, leaving the centre area free, as shown in the photograph (page 130).

Place the ribbon around the cake and secure it at the back of the cake. Pipe extension work around the base of the cake, below the ribbon, omitting the initial line of shells (page 210). Neaten the top edge with a row of tiny beads. Leave the icing to dry.

The day before the wedding plan an arrangement of frosted flowers on a board, then carefully transfer it to the cake, taking care not to touch – and therefore damage – the extension work.

ABOUT 60 PORTIONS

CHRISTENING CAKES

These can be iced in royal icing or in sugar paste and the sugar paste can be used on a rich sponge cake instead of a fruit cake if preferred.

Traditionally, for a Christening, cakes were round and iced in blue for a boy and pink for a girl. Although this tradition is often followed, many new ideas are now used instead. For example, a cake baked in the shape of the initial letter of the child's name makes an interesting centrepiece. Cake tins in the shape of letters and numerals are available for hire from special cake decorating shops, some bakers and kitchen shops. Check that the tin will be available when you need it as most are only hired for 48 hours. This means you have to be ready to make and cook the cake to time. It is not a good idea to cut your own shape from fruit cakes, as once cut, the cake tends to dry more quickly.

CAKE TIN SIZES

Unless an initial tin comes with instructions and a guide to quantities, you will need to use the capacity test to work out the quantity of cake mixture to use. Measure the quantity of water needed to fill the tin, then pour this water into a round or square cake tin until you find one where the water equals the height of a cooked cake. Generally speaking, initial cakes look best if they are quite deep.

If the chosen tin comes as a 'form' without a base, you will have to measure it and do some guesswork!

GIRL'S CHRISTENING CAKE

Illustrated on page 147

Instead of a fruit cake, a Classic Madeira Cake mixture (page 85) can be used to make this cake, in which case it should not be covered with almond paste. The exact number of portions depends on the shape of the cake; remember that Madeira Cake is cut in larger pieces than fruit cake.

Rich Fruit Cake (page 241) baked in the shape of an initial and covered in Almond Paste (page 142)
Sugar Paste, allowing about 225 g/8 oz more than for a round or square cake (page 158)
450 g/1 lb Royal Icing (page 156), for piping

DECORATIONS

20 small piped pink roses (page 230)
1 m/3¼ feet pink ribbon

NOZZLES

plain writing nozzle no '0'
small star or shell nozzle

Roll out small strips of sugar paste to the same depth as the cake and use to cover the insides of any holes in the letter. In the cake illustrated on page 147, the triangle below the apex of the letter is covered in this way. Smooth the top edge of the paste so that it graduates smoothly into the top of the cake.

Measure across the widest part of the cake and add on twice the depth of the cake. Roll out the icing to fit this measurement and smooth it over the cake (see Mrs Beeton's Tip). It will take some time to smooth the paste evenly around all the corners but this is necessary in order to achieve a good result. Trim and smooth the icing as you go (page 181). Leave the cake to dry for 24 hours.

Measure the height and length of one long side of the cake and cut a paper pattern to fit. Draw a line 2.5 cm/1 inch up from the base of the pattern and repeat with the shortest side. Fold the long piece into three. Using a teacup or pastry cutter mark a curve to fit each paper, cut and open out the paper. Place the paper on the cake and prick out the curves with a pin. Repeat with one curve on the leg of the letter.

Use royal icing in an icing bag fitted with a plain nozzle no 0 and pipe a cornelli pattern (page 204) over the top of the cake and down into each curve.

Using a second bag, this time with the small star nozzle, pipe small stars around the curves to make a neat border for the cornelli icing. Pipe a row of shells around the base of the cake and place a rose on the side of the cake at each point where two curves meet.

Make a flamboyant bow with the ribbon and place it on the cake as shown in the photograph.

ABOUT 40 PORTIONS

VARIATION

For letters of the alphabet that have long curves, cut the paper pattern to fit and fold an appropriate number of times to make equal curves.

MRS BEETON'S TIP In the cases of shapes that are long and thin, roll the paste into a strip and gently ease this over the shape.

BOY'S CHRISTENING CAKE

Illustrated on page 148

White run-out trains puffing around the sides of a pale blue cake create a very effective design.

23 cm/9 inch square Rich Fruit Cake
(page 241), covered in Almond Paste
(page 142)
Sugar Paste (page 158) tinted with blue
food colouring
225 g/8 oz Royal Icing (page 156), for
piping
blue food colouring

NOZZLES

plain writing nozzle no 1 or 2
medium shell nozzle

DECORATIONS

train run-outs (page 265), consisting of 5
engines and 16 carriages
run-out letters (pages 212-4)

Cut out a 23 cm/9 inch square paper pattern and a 20 cm/8 inch square paper pattern. Centre the smaller square on top of the larger one and draw around it to mark a 20 cm/8 inch square within the 23 cm/9 inch square. Place the pattern on top of the cake and mark the inner square on to the icing by pricking pin holes fairly close together.

Place a little royal icing in an icing bag fitted with the plain writing nozzle and pipe a line along the square marked out on the cake (page 203). Pipe a second line of icing inside the first so that the lines are almost touching.

Attach the train run-outs to the sides of the cake with a little icing and pipe large beads for wheels and carriage links. Pipe a swirl of smoke from each funnel. Place the letters, and an engine, on top of the cake attaching them with a little icing.

Use a second icing bag, with the shell nozzle, to pipe a row of shells around the base of the cake. Leave all the icing to dry before moving the cake.

ABOUT 35 PORTIONS

SILVER OR GOLDEN ANNIVERSARY CAKE

Illustrated on page 149

25 cm/10 inch round Rich Fruit Cake
(page 241) covered in Almond Paste
(page 142) and Royal Icing (page 156)
225 g/8 oz Royal Icing (page 156) for
piping

NOZZLES

plain writing nozzle no 1
medium star nozzle

DECORATIONS

1 m/3¼ feet silver or gold sequin ribbon
'25' or '50' run-out (pages 212-4)
silver or gold food colouring
piped doves (page 233)

Position the run-out on the cake. Place a little royal icing in an icing bag fitted with the plain writing nozzle and pipe 'congratulations' underneath the run-out. When the icing is dry, brush the edges lightly with silver or gold colouring as shown in the photograph. Change to an icing bag fitted with the star nozzle and pipe a small row of stars along the top and bottom edges of the cake. Leave the icing to dry.

Attach the doves to the top of the cake with little beads of white royal icing (use the writing nozzle). Finish the cake with a ribbon.

ABOUT 35 PORTIONS

RUBY ANNIVERSARY CAKE

Illustrated on page 150

If time is short, the edge of this cake can be finished with a twisted rope of sugar paste instead of the frill. The design can be used for silver or gold anniversary cakes by changing the colour of the roses and ribbon.

25 cm/10 inch square Rich Fruit Cake (page 241) covered with Almond Paste (page 142) and Sugar Paste (page 158)
225 g/8 oz Sugar Paste (page 158) for frill
cornflour for dusting

DECORATIONS

moulded marzipan roses (page 221) or carnations (page 222), coloured deep red
1 m/3¼ feet deep red velvet narrow ribbon
deep red and gold food colouring

The cake must be placed on a 33 cm/13 inch square board. Use some of the extra sugar paste to make a Garrett frill and attach it to the base of the cake (page 217).

Roll out the remaining paste thickly and cut out four 5 cm/2 inch circles. Mould each into an oval and leave to dry for 24 hours on a non-stick surface dusted with cornflour. With a fine paint brush and red or gold food colouring, write '40' on each oval. Using a palette knife lift the plaques on to the cakes positioning one in each corner. Outline each plaque with a little gold colouring.

Arrange the flowers in the centre of the cake and add the narrow ribbon directly above the frill to neaten it.

ABOUT 40 PORTIONS

TWENTY-FIRST BIRTHDAY CAKE

Illustrated on page 167

25 cm/10 inch quantity Rich Fruit Cake (page 241), baked in a tin about 30 cm x 20 cm/12 x 8 inches and covered in Almond Paste (page 142)
1 kg/2¼ lb Sugar Paste (page 158)
225 g/8 oz Royal Icing (page 156) for piping
navy blue or marine food colouring

NOZZLES

plain writing nozzle no 1 or 2
shell nozzle

DECORATIONS

1 m/3¼ feet ribbon, 1 cm/½ inch wide
run-out '21' in blue (page 237)

The cake should be placed on a 35 x 25 cm/14 x 10 inch gold board. Cover it with the sugar paste (page 181), then insert the ribbon 2.5 cm/1 inch up from the base of the cake (page 199).

Cut out two paper rectangles, one 30 x 20 cm/12 x 8 inches, the other 25 x 15 cm/10 x 6 inches. Cut off the corners on the smaller rectangle (page 265). Lay the smaller rectangle on the larger one and draw around it. Place this pattern on the cake and mark it by pricking pin holes round it.

Using the plain writing nozzle, pipe a row of icing around the marked design. Set aside to dry. Colour a little of the remaining royal icing navy blue and, using the clean writing nozzle, pipe over the white. Change to a shell nozzle and pipe a row of white shells around the base. Fix the run-out '21' in the centre.

ABOUT 40 PORTIONS

MUSICAL NOTES BIRTHDAY CAKE

Illustrated on page 168

This cake is ideal for any birthday, particularly for an eighteenth celebration. Since it is made up of two cakes it is also a good idea for twins.

> two 15 cm/6 inch round Rich Fruit Cakes (page 241)
> 18 cm/7 inch square Rich Fruit Cake (page 241)
> 1.5 kg/3 lb Almond Paste (page 142)
> 1 kg/2 lb Royal Icing (page 156)
> black food colouring

NOZZLES

> small star nozzle
> plain writing nozzle no 1 or 2

Cut the square cake into two 5 cm/2 inch strips and one 7.5 cm/3 inch strip. Trim the round cakes as shown in the diagram on page 266. Cover all the cakes with almond paste (page 180).

Assemble the cake on the board, then remove the top cake only. Move the notes slightly apart, then cover them and the individual bar cake in smooth royal icing. When completely dry, slide the notes back together and place the bar cake back into position.

Colour the remaining royal icing black and place in an icing bag fitted with a small star nozzle. Pipe a small shell edging around the base and top edges of the cake.

Change to a bag fitted with the plain writing nozzle and pipe 'Happy Birthday' on the top bar. Pipe the appropriate number or name on the notes.

ABOUT 50 PORTIONS

BRUSH EMBROIDERY CAKES

Illustrated on page 169

Brush embroidery is painted directly on to the cake using a fine line of royal icing as the starting point.

Trace the pattern of the icing design from embroidery patterns, cards or other pictorial sources. Prick the shapes out on the cake. The cake covering must be dry before you do this. You may like to trace the flower or butterfly patterns on page 267. These are illustrated on finished cakes on page 169. The cakes are covered in sugar paste and finished with ribbons.

You will need about 30-45 ml/2-3 tbsp Royal Icing (page 156), made up to soft peak consistency. Stir in 1.25 ml/¼ tsp piping gel to prevent the icing from drying out too quickly (page 133). Divide the icing between two or three egg cups and colour as required. Place each colour in a paper icing bag without a nozzle.

Snip off the point from one of the icing bags and pipe an outline around one of the petals or wings. Dip a fine paint brush in water then wipe it across a clean sponge. Use the damp brush to gently pull the icing down the design using long firm strokes; work towards the centre of the flower or butterfly.

Build up the design by piping different shades of icing around the flower or wings. The piping must be completed in sections and each section allowed to dry before beginning the next. When dry, pipe in stalks or leaves and dust the pattern with petal dust or lustre.

When piping large areas, a double line of icing should be piped so that there is enough icing to pull across the area of the design.

HARVEST CAKE

Illustrated on page 187

The cake can either be covered in a thin layer of marzipan or almond paste and sugar paste; a sponge cake can be covered in buttercream. The basket weave piping is done in royal icing; however buttercream can also used.
The centre of the basket is filled with a selection of moulded marzipan fruits, vegetables and leaves (pages 229 and 219).

23 cm/9 inch round Rich Fruit Cake (page 241) covered in Marzipan (page 142) or Almond Paste (page 142) and Sugar Paste (page 158)
450 g/1 lb Royal Icing (page 156), tinted with yellow or cream food colouring

DECORATION

marzipan fruits, vegetables and leaves (pages 229 and 219)

NOZZLES

medium basket or ribbon nozzle
plain writing nozzle no 2
small shell or star nozzle

Centre the cake on a 28 cm/11 inch board. Cut out a 23 cm/9 inch circle of greaseproof paper and fold it in half. Draw a line parallel to the fold and 5 cm/2 inches away from it. Turn the paper over and draw another line 5 cm/2 inches from the fold. Open out the paper.

Place the pattern on top of the cake and mark the position of the two lines with a pin. Remove the pattern. Place some of the royal icing in an icing bag fitted with the basket nozzle and fill in the two end areas on top of the cake with basket weave piping (page 216). Change to an icing bag fitted with the writing nozzle and neaten the straight edges of the basket weave piping with a line of plain piping.

Pipe basket weave around the side of the cake. Using an icing bag fitted with the shell nozzle, neaten the top and bottom edges with a row of fine shells. Leave icing to dry.

Arrange the fruits, vegetables and leaves down the centre of the cake.

ABOUT 30 PORTIONS

EASTER CAKES

Illustrated on page 170

Yellow is associated with Easter and springtime and yellow almond paste or marzipan is traditionally used to cover Simnel and Easter cakes.

EASTER LOG

Cover a Swiss Roll (page 72) with yellow almond paste by first cutting out two circles to fit the ends and then enclosing in a large piece of almond paste extending slightly over the ends. Neaten the roll, then drizzle melted chocolate over the top. Decorate the board with green-coloured desiccated coconut (page 164), moulded marzipan ducks (page 228) and small Easter eggs or piped spring flowers.

EASTER CROWN

Colour almond paste green. Roll it out and cut a shape to cover the side only of a round cake (page 180). Before placing the almond paste in position around the cake, pattern it by pressing a meat hammer or grater over the surface. Coat the top of the cake in Apricot Glaze (page 140); sprinkle with chopped chocolate and lay the moulded marzipan daffodils (page 227) on top.

FATHER CHRISTMAS CAKE

Illustrated on page 205

Prepare and paint the run-out for this cake in advance, allowing it to dry before placing it on the cake. Leftover royal icing is used to pipe the beard and fur trimmings.

23 cm/9 inch square Rich Fruit Cake
  (page 241), covered in Almond Paste
  (page 142) and Royal Icing (page 156)
225 g/8 oz Royal Icing (page 156) for
  piping
red food colouring

NOZZLES

1 plain writing nozzle no 1
1 medium shell or star nozzle

DECORATION

run-out Father Christmas (page 270)
1.25 metres/4 feet red ribbon, about 4 cm/
  1½ inches wide

Place some of the extra royal icing in an icing bag fitted with the writing nozzle and pipe the greetings message (as shown in the photograph) on the cake. Top the Father Christmas run-out with Cornelli icing on the beard and trimmings. Leave to dry. Fit the shell nozzle on to a second bag of royal icing and pipe a border of shells or stars around the top and lower edge of the cake. Allow the icing to dry for several hours.

Stick the run-out in position and place the ribbon around the Father Christmas cake, securing it at the back.

Colour a little of the remaining royal icing red. Place it in an icing bag fitted with the clean writing nozzle and pipe directly over the white writing to highlight the greetings.

ABOUT 35-40 PORTIONS

BELL CAKE

Illustrated on page 188

Crystal Madeira Cake (page 240), baked
  in a roasting tin
Apricot Glaze (page 140)
1.25 kg/2½ lb Sugar Paste (page 158)
red and green food colourings

Trace and cut out the template (page 269) for the bell. Place the template on the cake and cut around the shape. Position the pieces on a 35 x 30 cm/14 x 12 inch board, sticking them together with apricot glaze. Brush more glaze over the whole cake. Use 900 g/2 lb of the sugar paste to cover the cake (page 181).

Divide and colour the remaining sugar paste as follows:
mould 50 g/2 oz into a clanger
colour 75 g/3 oz red
colour 75 g/3 oz green

Reserve a little red and green paste. Roll the remaining red paste into two ropes, each measuring 20 cm/8 inches long. Roll the remaining green paste into two similar ropes. Twist one green and one red rope lightly together and repeat with the other two ropes. Place the ropes across the lower half of the bell and join them in the middle in a decorative knot.

Shape the reserved red and green paste into a loop for the top of the bell. Place the clanger and loop in position.

ABOUT 60 PORTIONS

MINI CHRISTMAS CAKES

Illustrated on page 206

These small cakes make an ideal Christmas gift for anyone who lives alone.

20 cm/8 inch round quantity Rich Fruit
    Cake mixture (page 241)
Almond Paste (page 142)
Sugar Paste (page 158)

DECORATION

cut-out candle, holly and berries (page
    268, lower)
moulded snowman (page 228), without a
    scarf
red or orange icing pen or food colouring
red and green food colouring

You will need crimpers and a modelling tool to decorate these cakes. Use two 10 cm/ 4 inch round cake tins as containers to bake the rich fruit cake mixture. Alternatively, wash and dry two empty 822 g/1 lb 3 oz cans, for example fruit cans. Bake the cakes for about 1½ hours, leave them to cool and cover with almond paste and sugar paste.

Using the crimpers, mark around the top edge of one of the cakes (page 198). Roll out a thin rope of sugar paste and place it around the base of the cake, joining it at the back to make a neat edge.

Place the candle, holly and berries on the top of the cake. Use a dampened paint brush to moisten them if they are dry. If the cut-outs are freshly made, smooth them on to the cake and round off the corners. Leave the cake to dry.

Finish this first cake by painting or drawing short lines radiating out from the flame of the candle. Tie a ribbon around the side of the cake, if you like, securing the join at the back with a tiny piece of adhesive tape.

To decorate the second cake, use the modelling tool to mark around the top edge of the cake. Divide the remaining sugar paste in half and colour one portion red, the other green. Make the snowman's scarf by arranging two thin rolls of coloured paste side by side. Place the scarf around the snowman's neck.

Roll the remaining portions of coloured paste separately into two long rolls, twist these together lightly and place them around the lower edge of the cake. Make a decorative join at the front of the cake. Place the snowman on top of the cake.

ABOUT 10-12 PORTIONS EACH

FESTIVE LOG

Illustrated on page 206

Swiss Roll (page 72) or Chocolate Roll
    (page 73)
1 quantity American Frosting (page 152)

DECORATION

Chocolate leaves (page 236) or Marzipan
    leaves (page 219), dipped in chocolate
small piece of marzipan or moulding
    icing, coloured red and rolled into
    berries

Place the cake on a suitable board. Make up the frosting and quickly spread it over the cake, making sure it comes well down on each side. As the frosting begins to set, draw a fork or serrated scraper down the length of the cake. Swirl the icing on the ends of the cake into circles. Add the leaves and berries to complete the decoration.

ABOUT 10 PORTIONS

DARK SECRETS RING CAKE

Illustrated on page 223

An irresistible almond-flavoured cake, soaked in maraschino syrup and coated in dark chocolate. Maraschino cherries with stalks are available, bottled in syrup, from good food shops.

150 g/5 oz butter, softened
150 g/5 oz caster sugar
3 small eggs, beaten
200 g/7 oz self-raising flour
50 g/2 oz ground almonds
a little milk
75 ml/3 fl oz maraschino syrup (from a jar of cherries, or home-made syrup flavoured with the liqueur)
fat for greasing
flour for dusting

ICING AND DECORATION

one quantity Tipsy Chocolate Velvet (page 239), omitting the rum
icing sugar for dusting
half quantity Citrus Cheese Icing (page 171)
small star nozzle
three pairs of maraschino cherries, half dipped in plain chocolate (page 235)

Grease a 1.1 litre/2 pint capacity ring tin and dust it lightly with flour. Set the oven at 160°C/325°F/gas 3.

Cream the butter and sugar in a mixing bowl until pale and soft, then beat in the eggs, a little at a time. Fold in the flour and ground almonds, adding sufficient milk to give the mixture a soft, dropping consistency.

Spread the mixture into the prepared tin and stand it on a baking sheet. Bake the cake for 1-1¼ hours, until firm to the touch and beginning to shrink from the side of the tin.

Leave the cake to rest in the tin for 5 minutes, then turn it out on to a wire rack.

Wash and dry the mould and invert the cake back into it. Prick the cake all over with a skewer. Warm the maraschino syrup and drizzle it over the warm cake. Leave the cake to cool completely in the mould. When it is cold, invert the cake on to a piece of non-stick baking parchment on a wire rack or baking sheet. Pour the chocolate icing over the cake, using a palette knife to smooth the sides if it does not coat the cake evenly. Leave it to set, then trim the base of any excess chocolate and carefully transfer the cake to a plate. Dust with icing sugar.

Place the citrus cheese icing in an icing bag fitted with a star nozzle and pipe a row of small stars around the base of the cake. Decorate with the dipped cherries.

MRS BEETON'S TIP Instead of using the cherries for decoration, this rich ring cake can be varied by adding different decorations according to the season. For example frosted or moulded flowers may be used to decorate the cake for Easter. For a quick Christmas cake add holly leaves and berries instead of the cherries. For a fun birthday cake combine moulded flowers or shop-bought decorations with a ring of birthday candles on the top of the cake.

ABOUT 20 PORTIONS

FEATHERED SQUARE

Illustrated on page 224

A simply decorated square sponge cake – ideal as an impromptu birthday cake, for Mother's Day or just for a Sunday-tea treat!

25 cm/10 inch square Basic Sponge Cake
(page 240)
Buttercream (page 144) made with 175 g/
6 oz icing sugar

DECORATION

100 g/4 oz chopped pistachio nuts (or
chopped mixed nuts or desiccated
coconut, tinted green)
one quantity Glacé Icing (page 151)
green food colouring
small star nozzle
Piped Blossom (page 231) or bought
piped flowers

Cut the cake in half horizontally, then sandwich the cake layers together with about one third of the buttercream. Spread about half the remaining buttercream around the sides of the cake. Coat the sides in the chopped nuts or coconut and place the cake on a board or plate.

Colour half the glacé icing green, place white and green glacé icing in separate paper icing bags, then feather ice the top of the cake (page 193). Place the remaining buttercream in an icing bag fitted with a star nozzle and pipe small stars around the top and bottom edges of the cake. Decorate with piped blossom or bought piped flowers.

ABOUT 25 PORTIONS

SAILING YACHT

Illustrated on page 225

Basic Sponge Cake (page 240), baked in a
roasting tin
1 quantity Apricot Glaze (page 140)
575 g/1¼ lb Sugar Paste (page 158)
yellow, red and blue food colourings
1 quantity Glacé Icing (page 151)
a little icing sugar

Trace and cut out the template on page 271; place it on the cake and cut out the pieces. Arrange the cake pieces together to form a boat shape on a 35 cm/14 inch square cake board, using apricot glaze to stick them together. Brush the cake with glaze.

Halve the sugar paste and colour one half yellow. Remove a small piece from the white piece and colour it red. Cut a small piece of paste from the white portion – enough to form a thick rope 23 cm/9 inches long. Set this aside.

Roll out the remaining white paste to about 38 x 13 cm/15 x 5 inches and smooth it over the base part of the boat. Trim the excess paste from the edges of the cake.

Roll out the yellow paste to about 25 cm/ 10 inches square. Cut this diagonally, making one piece slightly larger than the other, then smooth it over the sails of the boat cake. Trim the edges. Shape a flag from the red paste and position it as shown in the photograph. Place the reserved white paste in position to represent a mast. Colour a little of the glacé icing red and pipe the name of the child on the boat.

Colour the remaining glacé icing blue, adding a little extra icing sugar to give the icing a stiff texture. Spread the icing roughly over the board to represent the sea.

ABOUT 25 PORTIONS

TEDDY BEAR

Illustrated on page 226

Basic Sponge Cake (page 240), baked in a
    roasting tin
Buttercream (page 144) made with 450 g/
    1 lb icing sugar
a little milk
50 g/2 oz Sugar Paste (page 158)
brown, black, blue and red food
    colourings
small savoy nozzle

Trace and cut out the template for the teddy bear (page 273). Place the template on the cake and cut around the shape. Place the cake pieces on a large board – at least 35 x 30 cm/14 x 12 inches – joining the paws and feet with a little of the buttercream.

Place 60 ml/4 tbsp of the remaining buttercream in a small bowl and slacken it with a little milk. Using a small palette knife, cover the whole cake, including the sides, with a thin layer of this soft buttercream.

Knead a little brown colouring into two thirds of the sugar paste, roll it out and use the template to cut out the teddy bear's paws, feet and ears. Remember to reverse the template for one paw and one foot. Press the sugar paste pieces lightly on the cake.

Colour one third of the remaining sugar paste black to make the nose. Half of the last portion of paste should be coloured blue to make the eyes and the remainder coloured red for ribbon.

Place one third of the buttercream in an icing bag fitted with a small savoy nozzle and pipe stars all over the cake, re-filling the bag as necessary. Do not press too hard or the stars will be too thick. Slacken the icing with a few drops of milk, if necessary, to make the stars softer. To finish the cake, place the paste eyes, nose and ribbon in position.

ABOUT 20 PORTIONS

SPIDER'S WEBS

Illustrated on page 224

Children will love these individual cakes, decorated to resemble spider's webs. They are especially good for Hallowe'en.

Basic Sponge Cake (page 240), baked in
    25 cm/10 inch square tin or in a
    roasting tin
200 g/7 oz bar plain chocolate
1 quantity Apricot Glaze (page 140)
1 quantity Glacé Icing (page 151)
blue food colouring

Set aside 50 g/2 oz of the chocolate and grate or finely chop the remainder. Sprinkle the grated or chopped chocolate on to a piece of greaseproof paper. Using a 5.5 cm/2¼ inch cutter, cut out 16 circles from the cake. Brush the sides of each piece of cake with apricot glaze, then coat them in the grated chocolate.

Place the reserved chocolate in a basin and melt it over a saucepan of hot water. Tint the glacé icing pale blue and ice the tops of the cakes. Immediately transfer the melted chocolate to a paper icing bag, snip the end and feather ice the cakes with chocolate (page 193). If you like, place a small piece of grated chocolate somewhere on the 'web' to represent a spider.

ABOUT 16 PORTIONS

NUMBER SIX CAKE

Illustrated on page 243

Cakes in the shape of numerals or letters can be baked in shaped cake tins which can be hired from cake decorating shops, kitchen shops or bakers. Alternatively, bake a basic round cake and follow the instructions for cutting the cake in the shape of the numeral.

20 cm/8 inch Basic Sponge Sandwich
    Cake (page 240)
1 quantity Apricot Glaze (page 140) or jam
900 g/2 lb Sugar Paste (page 158)
food colouring
moulded or piped flowers or moulded
    shapes or cut-outs (pages 219 and 230)

Sandwich the cake layers together with apricot glaze or jam. Trace and cut out the template for the numeral (page 272). Place the template on the cake and cut around the shapes. Cut the hole in the six using a 3 cm/1¼ inch cutter.

Assemble the pieces of cake on a 35 x 25 cm/14 x 10 inch board, sticking the pieces together with some of the apricot glaze or jam. Brush the cake with apricot glaze. Fill in any small gaps with pieces of sugar paste to make a smooth surface.

Reserve a small piece of sugar paste to make a plain rope for the base of the cake. Colour the remaining sugar paste in the colour of your choice, following the instructions on page 181.

Roll out a small piece of sugar paste to the same depth as the cake and use to cover the inside of the hole in the six. Smooth the paste edges over the top of the cake. Roll out the remaining paste to a piece large enough to cover the cake, lift it over and smooth it down, taking care to cut the paste at the hole.

Smooth the edges down to neaten them over the existing paste. Trim all excess paste as you go. Trim the edges.

Decorate the base of the cake with a fine rope shaped from the reserved sugar paste. Add the decorations to the top of the cake, as shown in the photograph.

> **MRS BEETON'S TIP** The basic sponge cake baked in a roasting tin can be cut up to make cakes in the shape of different numerals. First cut a piece of greaseproof paper to the same size as the cake. Draw the shape of the numeral on the paper, making the most economical use of the cake to avoid wastage. When you have decided exactly how to cut the cake and how the pieces will fit together to make the numeral, cut the shape out of paper and use this as a template for cutting the shape.

ABOUT 20 PORTIONS

CLOWN CAKE

Illustrated on page 244

This cheerful fellow is easily cut from a rectangular cake following the template.

Basic Sponge Cake (page 240), cooked in
  a roasting tin
Buttercream (page 144) made with 450 g/
  1 lb icing sugar
milk (see method)
225 g/8 oz Sugar Paste (page 158)
black, red, pink or flesh, green, yellow
  and brown food colourings

NOZZLES

small ribbon or basket nozzle
plain writing nozzle no 2

Trace the template (page 274). Place it on the cake and cut out the shapes. Place the main body pieces on a 50 x 30 cm/20 x 12 inch cake board and set the boots, hands, head and hat aside on a tray. Place 75 ml/5 tbsp of the buttercream in a small bowl and slacken it with a little milk. Spread it very thinly over all the pieces of cake, especially down the sides.

Divide the sugar paste in half, colouring one half pink.

Divide the remaining sugar paste in half and colour one piece black. Lastly divide the uncoloured sugar paste in half, colouring one piece red and the other green.

Roll out two thirds of the pink paste into an 18 cm/7 inch circle. Smooth this over the face and down the sides of the cake. Roll out the remaining pink paste to a rectangle measuring about 15 x 10 cm/6 x 4 inches and cut this in half lengthways. Smooth these pieces over the clown's hands.

Roll out the black paste into a rectangle measuring 15 x 10 cm/6 x 4 inches. Cut in half lengthways and smooth one piece over each boot. Place the pieces of cake that make up the head and hat into position.

Colour three-quarters of the remaining buttercream green. Colour 45 ml/3 tbsp of the second half brown and the remainder yellow.

Spread half the green buttercream over the lower half of the clown to represent trousers and cover his hat. Place the remainder in an icing bag fitted with the ribbon nozzle.

Spread the yellow buttercream liberally over the top half of the clown, swirling it with a knife. Place the boots and hands in position on the cake. Pipe a frill of green buttercream along the top and bottom of the trousers, on the sleeves, around the collar and around the hat. Using the same bag of buttercream, pipe a pair of braces from the trousers to the shoulders.

Put the brown buttercream in an icing bag fitted with a plain nozzle and pipe curly hair on to the clown.

Using the red sugar paste, roll out a large nose and a big mouth, then place them on the cake. Use the green sugar paste to make the small circles for eyes and the circles on the hat. Alternatively, use blue paste for eyes. Add large circles to represent shirt buttons.

ABOUT 20 PORTIONS

NOVELTY BUNS

Illustrated on page 226

Prepare colourful run-outs well in advance of making these cakes. If you prefer, make decorations by stamping shapes out of coloured sugar paste. For very small children, bake the cakes in small paper petits fours cases, and after icing top each with a sugar-coated chocolate bean or other suitable decoration.

double quantity Small Rich Cakes (page 45)
half quantity Quick Fondant (page 155)
food colouring
cut-outs or run-out shapes (pages 197 and 212)

Prepare and bake the cakes following the recipe instructions. Cool the cakes on a wire rack and trim off any tops that have peaked. Make up the fondant and pour a little over each bun until it finds its own level at the top of each paper case. Leave to dry, then decorate each cake with the novelty cut-out or run-out shapes as shown in the photograph on page 226

ABOUT 20 CAKES

BUILDING BLOCKS

Illustrated on page 243

These individual cakes are ideal for a child's birthday party. The sponge cake can be left plain or it can be split and filled with buttercream or jam if preferred.

Basic Sponge Cake (page 240) baked in a roasting tin
Apricot Glaze (page 140) to coat
1 kg/2¼ lb Sugar Paste (page 158)
4 different food colourings of your choice

Trim the edges of the cake and cut it into 4 cm/1½ inch squares. Brush the pieces of cake with apricot glaze and set aside.

Roll out 100 g/4 oz of the sugar paste thinly. Using small cutters or a fine pointed knife, cut out small letters to decorate the blocks. Re-roll the trimmings and cut out more letters. You will need about 175 letters.

Divide the remaining sugar paste into four and tint each quarter a different colour. Wrap three pieces in cling film and set aside. Roll out the fourth piece thinly and cut it into 10 cm/4 inch squares, re-rolling the scraps as necessary; you will need about eight or nine squares, depending on how many pieces of cake you have cut. Lay a square of the paste over one of the cakes and smooth it down over the corners. Trim off excess paste. Repeat with the remaining paste until all the squares are covered.

Place letters on the blocks, pressing one on each side, then leave to dry for a few hours.

ABOUT 35 BLOCKS

Three-tiered Wedding Cake

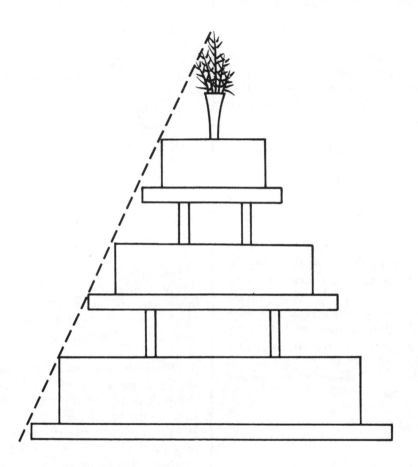

 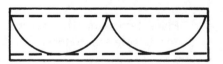 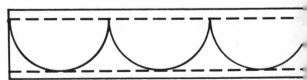

Melting Moments (page 291) and Almond Macaroons (page 295)

Flapjacks (page 294) and Ginger Snaps (page 292)

Boy's Christening Cake

Actual size

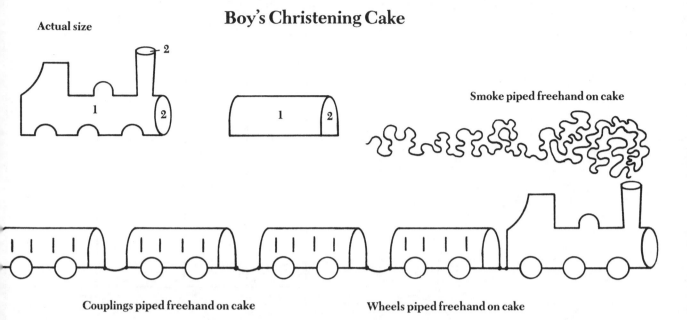

Smoke piped freehand on cake

Couplings piped freehand on cake

Wheels piped freehand on cake

Twenty-first Birthday Cake

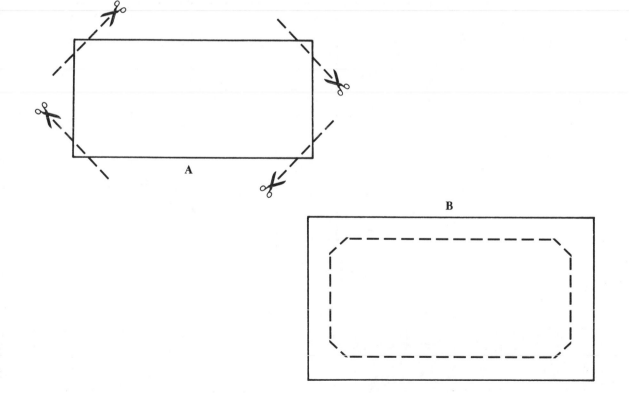

A

B

Musical Notes Birthday Cake

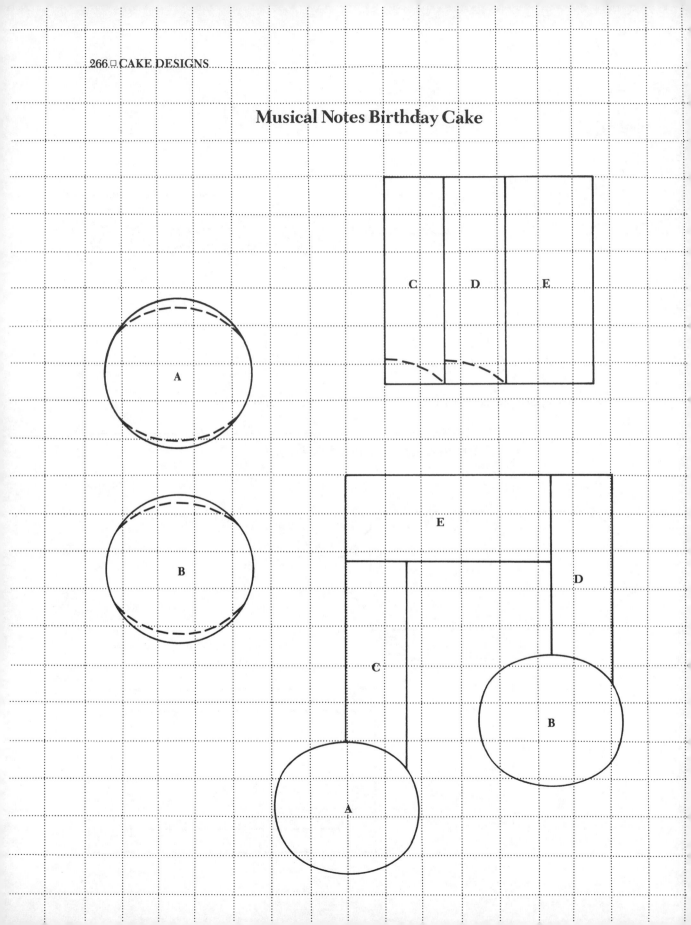

Designs for Brush Embroidery

Harvest Cake

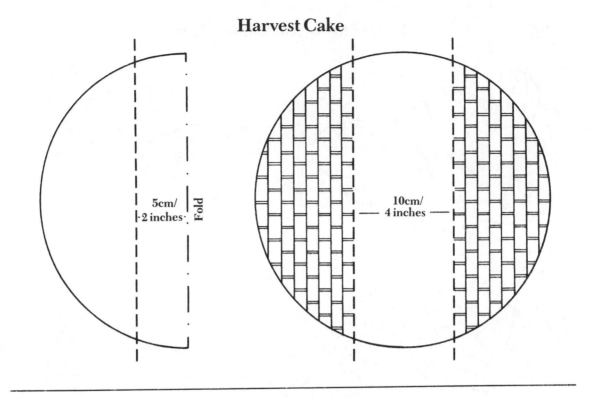

5cm/
2 inches

Fold

10cm/
4 inches

Mini Christmas Cakes

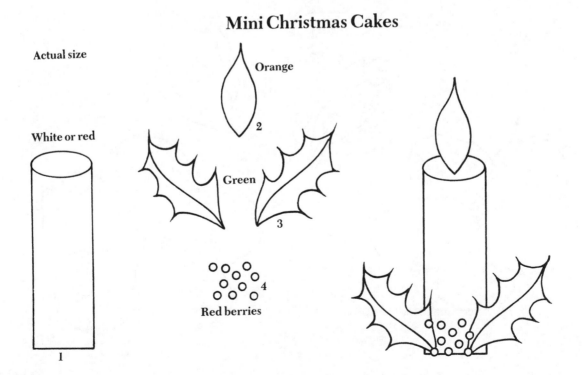

Actual size

Orange
2

White or red

Green
3

Red berries
4

1

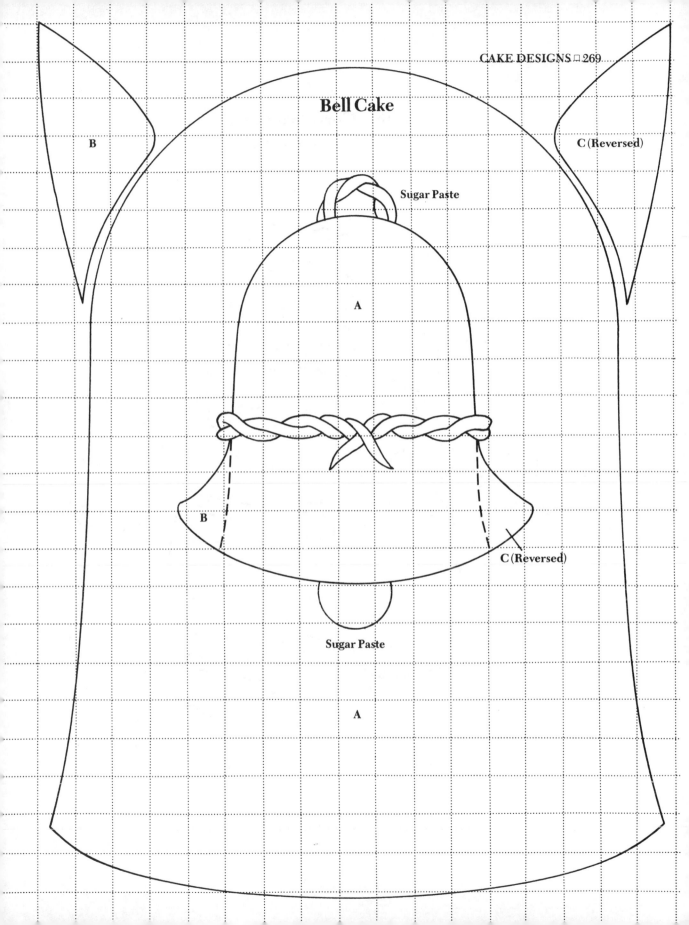

Bell Cake

B

C (Reversed)

Sugar Paste

A

B

C (Reversed)

Sugar Paste

A

Father Christmas Cake

Actual size for Christmas Cake

(Numbers represent order in which to pipe and flood sections).

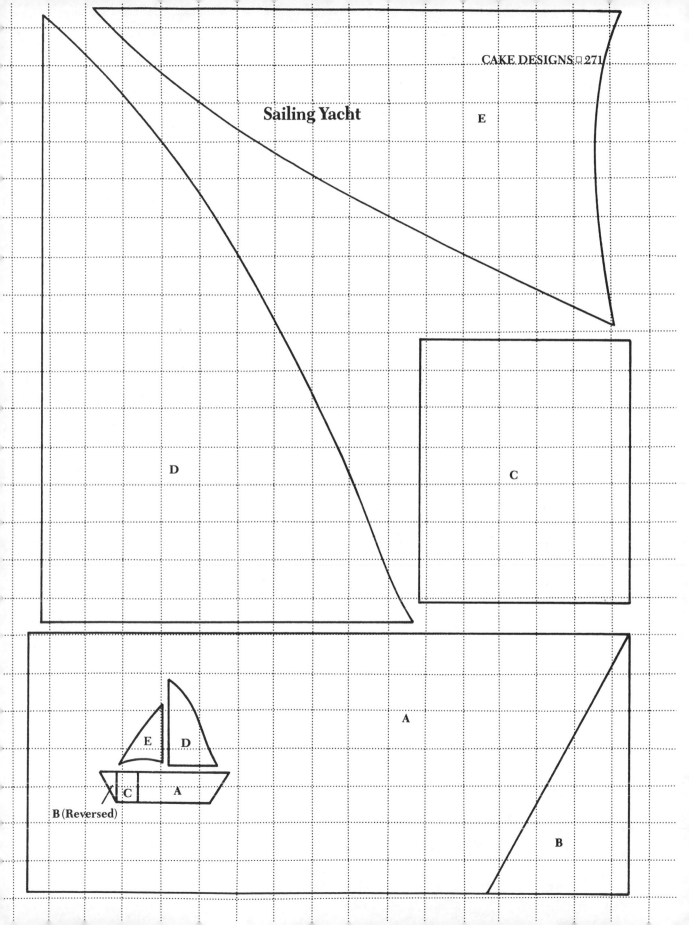

Sailing Yacht

E

D

C

A

B

E D

C A

B (Reversed)

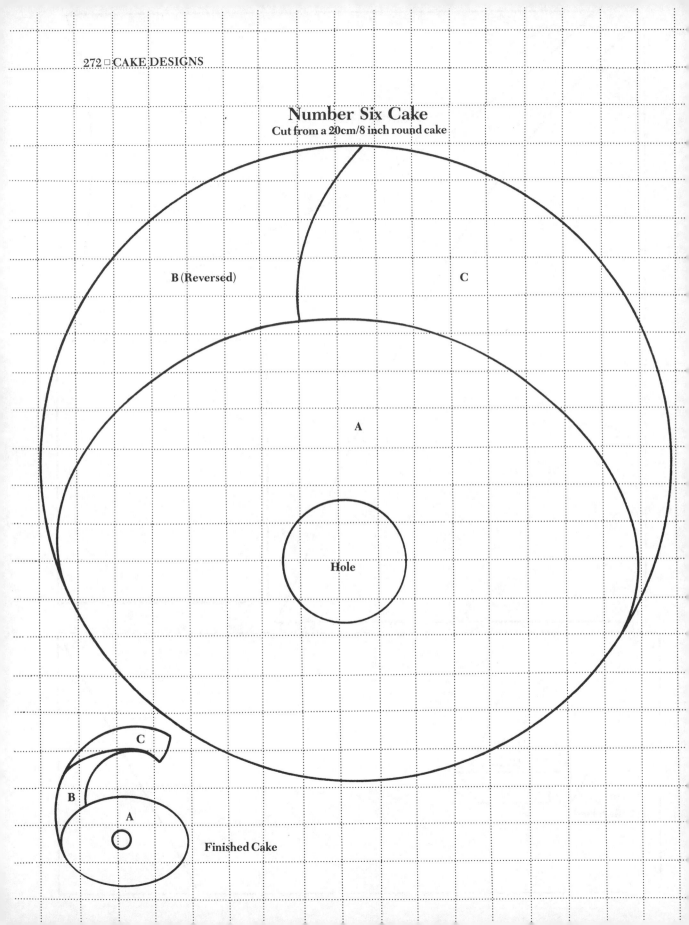

Number Six Cake
Cut from a 20cm/8 inch round cake

B (Reversed)

C

A

Hole

C

B

A

Finished Cake

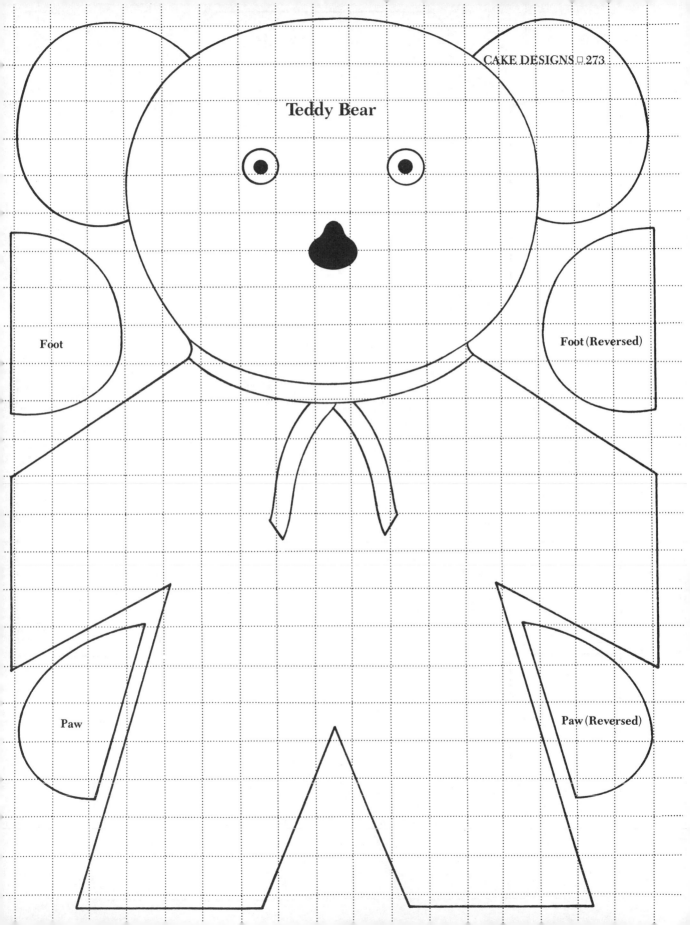

Teddy Bear

CAKE DESIGNS □ 273

Foot

Foot (Reversed)

Paw

Paw (Reversed)

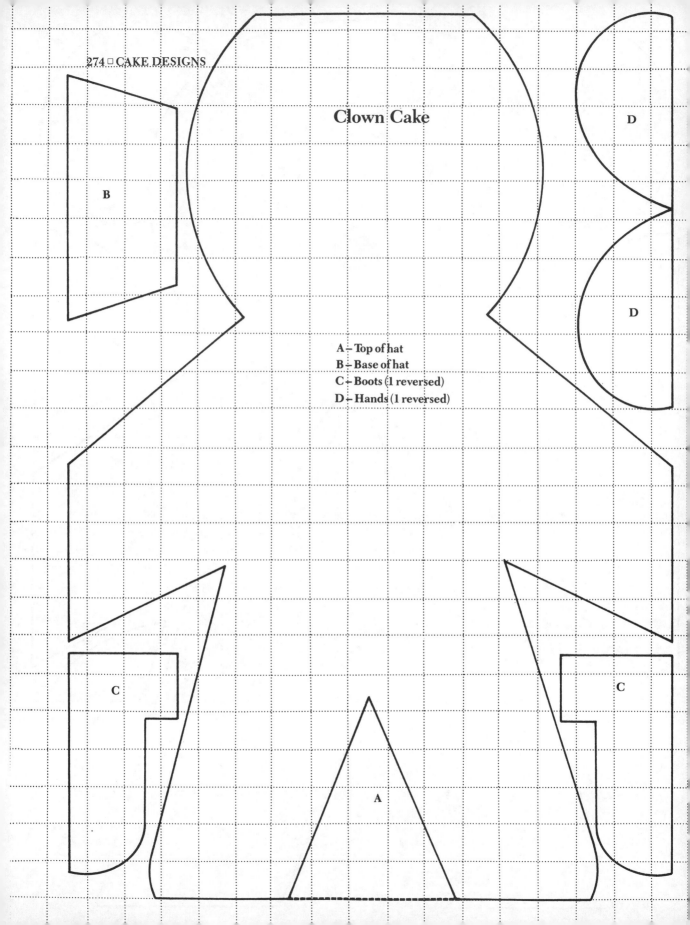

Clown Cake

B

D

D

A – Top of hat
B – Base of hat
C – Boots (1 reversed)
D – Hands (1 reversed)

C

C

A

CAKE BOARDS FOR NOVELTY CAKES

Finding a cake board for a large novelty cake can be a problem; however there are alternatives to a shop-bought cake board.

MAKING CAKE BOARDS

Decide on the size and shape of board required and cut out a paper pattern if necessary. For example, you will need a pattern if the board is to be cut in an unusual shape. Square or oblong shapes are the easiest to cover and they usually give the neatest results.

Cut out two or three thicknesses of stiff cardboard from old boxes. Select clean, undamaged card to make a good base. Cover the cardboard and tape the covering neatly in place underneath to hold the carboard layers together securely.

Instead of a cardboard base, a clean chopping board can be covered. For a very large cake, or for a cake that is particularly fragile, a length of laminated shelving can be covered to make a stable base.

COVERING MATERIALS

Cake decorating suppliers often sell the foil covering that is used on commercial cake boards. This is useful for re-covering used cake boards as well as for covering home-made boards. Ordinary cooking foil can be used to cover the boards and a decorative edging can be placed around the board to neaten it. Thick, white baking parchment also makes an attractive board covering for some cakes but a double thickness must be used and the edges should be very neat.

Wrapping papers that have a foil finish are ideal for covering cake boards. Select patterned papers with Christmas motifs or colourful designs to complement the cake. Board edging can be used or buy a length of narrow ribbon which matches the paper

covering and attach it neatly all around the edge of the board.

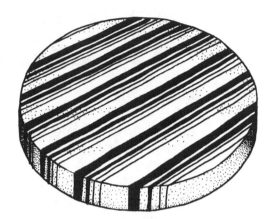

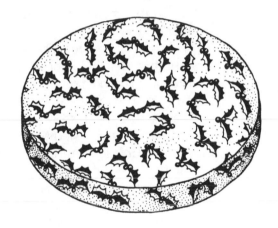

MAKING USE OF OLD CAKE BOARDS

Old cake boards can be re-covered or they can be used as a base on which to make run-outs. The drawn pattern for the run-out can be pinned to the board very successfully, then the completed icing can be left on the board until it has thoroughly dried.

BISCUITS

Home-made biscuits can be simple or elaborate but both types are far superior to the less expensive purchased varieties. Plain sweet biscuits can be made in large batches to store in an airtight jar, ready to perk up any mid-morning coffee break. More substantial biscuits may contain lots of good ingredients, such as dried fruit, oats and nuts, that justify their inclusion as part of the daily lunch box.

As well as the biscuits that are ideal for everyday nibbling, delicate specialities can be served for dessert and they are the perfect complement for smooth fruit fools or airy soufflés. Some of the more delicate biscuits may even play a role in dessert recipes; for example, home-made sponge finger biscuits can be used in charlottes and perfect unfilled brandy snaps make an impressive border for the sides of creamy gâteaux.

As well as sweet biscuits, this section includes recipes for savouries – cheese biscuits to serve with drinks or perfect oatcakes to accompany a good cheese. The plainest of savoury biscuits call for the simplest combination of flour, salt and water – the knack for success is to roll them thinly and bake them perfectly. The chapter of savoury recipes offers plenty of ideas for varying these old-fashioned plain bakes to make a variety of flavoursome, crunchy crackers.

Start by checking up on all the information at the front of the book – there you will find details relating to ingredients and general recipe know-how. In the opening pages to this section you will find additional guidance for making biscuits.

SPECIAL UTENSILS FOR BISCUIT MAKING

Take note of the general information given on baking utensils at the front of the book. Here are additional notes on the specialist equipment which is available for making biscuits. Remember, if you plan on baking large batches of biscuits, you will need to have several baking sheets at the ready.

Rolling Pins   Many types of biscuits have to be rolled out. Although a rolling pin is not an absolute essential (a clean, heavy bottle can be used to roll dough) it is considered to be a basic piece of kitchen equipment. There are many types available: wooden ones with different types of handles or ends, or more elaborate pins which can be filled with iced water to keep the dough cool as it is being rolled.

It is also possible to purchase pins which can be adjusted to roll the dough to different thicknesses. Patterned pins may produce a simple serrated design on the dough or they can be deeply marked into biscuit shapes, so that the biscuits are marked out as the dough is rolled.

Flour Dredger   A flour dredger is useful, but not essential, when rolling out dough. If you roll out pastry regularly, then it is worth investing in a good dredger – make sure you buy one which has a lid that screws firmly in place.

Cutters   There is an enormous variety of cutters available, either plastic or metal. The basics are round and square, plain or fluted. Other cutters come in all sorts of shapes and sizes – men or women shapes for cutting gingerbread, animal shapes, seasonal shapes, hearts, stars, birds or butterflies. Multi-sided cutters include several different shapes in one cutter.

Biscuit Press   These are syringes into which biscuit dough is placed to be pushed out through different shaped nozzles or discs straight on to the prepared baking sheet. The press works in the same way as an icing syringe and it may also be known as a 'cookie press'

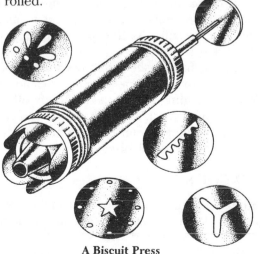

A Biscuit Press

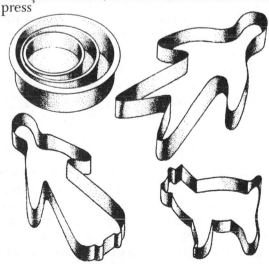

A Selection of Biscuit Cutters

BASIC METHODS AND TECHNIQUES FOR MAKING BISCUITS

The ingredients used for making biscuits are much the same as those for making cakes and the same applies to some of the basic methods that are involved.

RUBBED-IN BISCUITS

This is a simple method of making biscuit dough. The flour is sifted into a bowl and the fat is rubbed in. The proportion of fat to flour in biscuit mixtures of this type is smaller than in rubbed-in cake mixtures.

Once the fat has been incorporated other flavouring ingredients are added and liquid is used to bind the dough. The method is much the same as for making shortcrust pastry.

All the ingredients should be cool and the fat should be chilled. When rubbing the fat into the flour, lift the ingredients and rub them lightly between your fingertips. The liquid should be added carefully because the dough must not be too sticky or it will be difficult to roll.

This type of dough can be sweetened with sugar or it can be seasoned with salt. Various flavouring ingredients can be added, including spices, dried fruit, nuts or seeds.

CREAMED BISCUITS

The fat and sugar are creamed together until they are pale and soft, then the dry ingredients are worked in to make a biscuit dough. An egg yolk may be added to enrich the dough or other liquid may be used to moisten and bind particular combinations of ingredients.

Biscuits made by this method tend to be richer than those made by the rubbed-in method and this technique is used mainly for sweet biscuits. Before it is suitable for rolling, the dough should be chilled until it is firm.

This basic method is also used to make mixtures which are pushed through biscuit presses or they may be piped into shapes using large nozzles. The mixture is not chilled before shaping but it is chilled after shaping and before cooking.

MELTED METHOD

Some delicate biscuits are made by the melted method. The fat and sugar or other ingredients are gently heated until they are melted, then the flour is added together with selected flavourings. The mixture is very moist but not too runny.

Small amounts of mixture are cooked well apart on baking sheets. As it begins to heat, the mixture melts and spreads out to make very thin biscuits. As the cooking progresses the biscuits set.

A good baking sheet that does not stick is essential for this type of mixture and the knack of sliding the cooked biscuits off the sheet is made easier with practice. Non-stick baking parchment can be a useful aid when cooking this type of biscuit.

NO-COOK MIXTURES

Simple biscuits and cookies can be made without the necessity for cooking. A melted mixture is combined with other ingredients such as breakfast cereals, nuts and dried fruits. The mixture is set in the refrigerator, then cut into individual pieces.

REFRIGERATOR BISCUITS

These avoid the necessity for rolling out the dough. The dough is usually prepared by the creamed method, then it is shaped into a long roll, wrapped in plastic film and thoroughly chilled. When the dough is really firm it is cut into slices and these are placed on a prepared baking sheet and cooked.

The uncooked dough can be kept in the refrigerator for several days or up to a couple of weeks, depending on the ingredients used. A large quantity of dough can be prepared and slices cut off for baking as and when they are required.

ROLLING, CUTTING OR SHAPING

ROLLING

The rules that apply to pastry cookery should be remembered when rolling out biscuits. The dough should be chilled or allowed to rest before it is rolled. The work surface must be absolutely clean and dry and it should be dusted with a little flour. In some cases the recipe may suggest that cornflour or icing sugar is used instead.

When rolling the dough, work in one direction only, pushing the pin away from you. Keep the dough evenly thick, gently pressing the edges together if they begin to crack slightly. Lift the dough lightly occasionally, if necessary, and turn it round slightly to keep it dusted with flour underneath. This prevents it from sticking to the work surface. Do not turn the dough over.

Once the dough is rolled to the required thickness cut out the biscuits and transfer them to prepared baking sheets. Carefully stack the trimmings and re-roll them, pressing them together gently.

Using Cutters Metal cutters tend to be better than the plastic ones but both types

are adequate. Have a little mound of flour on the work surface, keeping it well away from the dough, otherwise it will get in the way when it comes to rolling out the trimmings. Dip the cutter first in the flour, then stamp out the shape in the dough. Do not twist the cutter as you press it into the dough. Cut all the shapes as near to each other as possible and keep stamping the cutter in the flour to prevent the dough from sticking to it. Use a palette knife or other round-bladed knife to slide underneath each of the biscuit shapes, leaving the trimmings in place on the work surface.

Piping and Using a Biscuit Press The consistency of the biscuit mixture must be just right for this method. It must be soft enough to pipe but if it is too warm, then it will become oily as it is pushed out on to the baking sheet.

Always place the shapes slightly apart on the baking sheet to allow for them to spread during cooking. When piping fingers, use a knife to cut a neat finish to the dough when the required length has been piped on to the baking sheet. When piping circles, one way to obtain a neat finish is to pipe a small star of mixture when the circle is completed.

Before cooking, the majority of shapes of this type should be chilled. When piping sponge fingers the opposite is true and the essence of success is in speed. The sponge mixture will run if it is allowed to stand and it should be piped quickly, pulling the nozzle end of the bag up sharply at the end of each biscuit.

Shaping with Spoons Soft biscuit mixtures can be dropped off spoons on to baking sheets. You will need two spoons: scoop up a small amount of mixture with one spoon, then use a second spoon to push it off cleanly on to the sheet.

Rolling Balls One of the easiest ways to shape biscuit dough and ideal for those doughs which are prepared by the creamed method. Take a small lump of mixture about the size of a walnut and roll it into a ball between the palms of your hands. Place the balls slightly apart on prepared baking sheets, then flatten them with a fork. Press down once or twice with the prongs of the fork to make a pattern of lines or a criss-cross design. Chill the biscuits before baking them.

Shaping a Roll for Slicing Press the dough together and roughly shape it into a roll. Wrap it in cling film, then carefully shape it into an even roll, neatening the ends by patting them flat. The dough is easier to shape when it is within the confines of the plastic wrapping. When the roll is well chilled check its shape again, rolling it and patting it gently.

Pressing into Tins Some biscuits, for example shortbread, are formed into a shape by pressing the mixture into a tin. The mixture must be unchilled and the tin should be greased. Place the dough in it and gradually press it out to fill the tin, making sure it is evenly thick all over. Use the back of your fingers and knuckles for this. Smooth the surface with your finger tips or a moistened palette knife. Mark the edges with a fork if you like and cut the dough into portions. It should be well chilled before cooking.

COOKING, COOLING AND STORING

The cooking time is crucial for many types of biscuit and a few extra minutes can be long enough to turn golden to black!

Once the biscuits are cooked leave them on the sheet for a few minutes unless the recipe states otherwise. Use a palette knife to slide each biscuit off the sheet and on to a rack to cool.

Very delicate mixtures may have to set slightly before they can be lifted off the sheet. Biscuits such as brandy snaps may be shaped after cooking, over a greased rolling pin or wooden spoon handle. Alternatively they may be formed into cups in greased patty tins. They should be left to cool completely before they are moved.

Once the biscuits are completely cool they can be stored in an airtight container – a tin, plastic container or bag which is firmly closed. Most biscuits keep very well in a cool dry place. Decorated biscuits do not keep well and those with soft creamy fillings should be eaten within a few hours of filling, although the unfilled biscuits can be stored successfully.

FREEZING

Biscuits freeze well, either cooked or as uncooked dough. The cooked biscuits should be stored in an airtight, rigid freezer container to protect them from being crushed.

Uncooked dough can be stored in a neat, lightly kneaded lump, ready to be rolled out. Alternatively it can be stored in a roll, as for refrigerator biscuits. The roll can be cut into slices and these can be re-shaped, interleaved with film, before freezing. This enables you to remove a few slices at a time for cooking. It is best to part-thaw the dough but it should not be allowed to thaw completely before cooking as it tends to become sticky.

Florentines (page 298) and Brandy Snaps (page 303)

Coffee Kisses and Catherine Wheels (both on page 304)

RUBBED-IN BISCUITS

This simple method may be used for making a wide variety of biscuits.

fat for greasing
200 g/7 oz plain flour
1.25 ml/¼ tsp salt
75-100 g/3-4 oz butter or margarine
50 g/2 oz caster sugar
5 ml/1 tsp baking powder
1 egg yolk
flour for rolling out

Grease 2 baking sheets. Set the oven at 180°C/350°F/gas 4.

In a mixing bowl, mix the flour and salt. Rub in the butter or margarine until the mixture resembles fine breadcrumbs, then stir in the sugar and baking powder. Bind to a stiff paste with the egg yolk.

Knead well and roll out to a thickness of just under 1 cm/½ inch on a lightly floured surface. Cut into rounds with a 5 cm/2 inch cutter. Re-roll and re-cut any trimmings.

Place the biscuits on the prepared baking sheets, pricking the top of each in several places. Bake for 12-15 minutes or until firm to the touch and pale golden brown. Leave to stand for a few minutes, then cool on wire rack.

MAKES 24 TO 26

VARIATIONS

PLAIN MOCHA BISCUITS Add 50 g/2 oz powdered drinking chocolate with the flour and 10 ml/2 tsp instant coffee dissolved in 7.5 ml/1½ tsp boiling water with the eggs.
PLAIN CINNAMON OR SPICE BISCUITS Add 5 ml/1 tsp ground cinnamon or mixed spice to the flour. When cold, sandwich the biscuits together in pairs with jam, and dredge with icing sugar.

PLAIN COCONUT BISCUITS Use 150 g/5 oz flour and 50 g/2 oz desiccated coconut. As soon as the biscuits are cooked, brush with warm Jam Glaze (see page 140) and sprinkle with coconut.

MRS BEETON'S TIP The technique of rubbing fat into flour, or mixed dry ingredients, is one which is used in many areas of cookery, so it is as well to get it right.

The aim when rubbing fat into flour is to combine both ingredients evenly, at the same time incorporating air into the mixture. The result is a dough, or mixture, which is light and airy; if the process of rubbing in is not successful, then the result can be a heavy, dense dough or mixture.

First make sure that all the ingredients are cool and that the fat is chilled. The mixing bowl and other utensils should also be cool; for example, do not use a bowl which is still warm from being washed in hot water. Make sure that your hands are perfectly clean and hold them under cold water if they are warm.

Cut the fat into small pieces – this can be done in the bowl with the flour, a technique sometimes known as 'cutting the fat into the flour'. Pick up pieces of fat and some flour with the tips of your fingers and rub them gently together. Let the mixture drop back into the bowl after one or two rubs. Do not allow the mixture to fall back into the palms of your hands but use just the fingertips. Lift the mixture quite high above the bowl as you rub it together to allow the air to lighten it. Do not over-rub the mixture or it will become sticky and heavy.

PLAIN BISCUITS

Home-made plain biscuits are quite inexpensive in their use of ingredients and they taste particularly good. The recipes in this chapter will ensure that the biscuit jar is always brimming over with variety, from buttery Shortbread to favourite Flapjacks.

SHORTBREAD

Illustrated on page 245

fat for greasing
100 g/4 oz plain flour
1.25 ml/¼ tsp salt
50 g/2 oz rice flour, ground rice or
    semolina
50 g/2 oz caster sugar
100 g/4 oz butter

Invert a baking sheet, then grease the surface now uppermost. Set the oven at 180°C/350°F/gas 4.

Mix all the ingredients in a mixing bowl. Rub in the butter until the mixture binds together to a dough. Shape into a large round about 1 cm/½ inch thick. Pinch up the edges to decorate. Place on the prepared baking sheet, and prick with a fork. Bake for 40-45 minutes. Cut into wedges while still warm.

MAKES 8 WEDGES

VARIATION

SHORTBREAD BISCUITS Roll out the dough on a lightly floured surface to a thickness of just under 1 cm/½ inch. Cut into rounds with a 5-6 cm/2-2½ inch cutter. Place on 1-2 greased baking sheets, allowing room for spreading. Prick the surface of each biscuit in several places with a fork. Bake for 15-20 minutes. Leave to stand for a few minutes, then cool on a wire rack.

SOYA FLOUR SHORTBREAD

fat for greasing
flour for dusting
125 g/4½ oz plain flour
25 g/1 oz soya flour
100 g/4 oz butter
50 g/2 oz caster sugar

Grease and flour a baking sheet and the inside of a 15 cm/6 inch flan ring. Set the oven at 140-150°C/275-300°F/gas 1-2. Mix the plain and soya flours in a mixing bowl. Rub in the butter until the mixture resembles fine breadcrumbs. Mix in the sugar, and knead the dough until it forms a single mass. Place the ring on the prepared baking sheet, and press the shortbread dough into it in an even layer. Prick the centre of the dough deeply with a fork.

Bake for 45-50 minutes or until very lightly coloured. Leave for 5 minutes. Mark into 6 wedges and leave to cool completely. When cold, remove the flan ring and cut into sections as marked.

MAKES 6 WEDGES

MRS BEETON'S TIP Soya flour has a high protein content. It is also high in fat, which is why a cool oven is always recommended for baking: a higher oven temperature would cause the shortbread to overbrown.

WHOLEMEAL ORANGE SHORTBREAD

Zesty orange rind contrasts well with the wholemeal flour in this recipe, adding a lively note of flavour to complement the wholemeal texture.

fat for greasing
175 g/6 oz butter
75 g/3 oz caster sugar
grated rind of 1 orange
225 g/8 oz wholemeal flour
caster sugar to sprinkle

Base-line and grease a 20 cm/8 inch round sandwich tin. Set the oven at 150°C/300°F/gas 2.

Cream the butter and sugar together until very soft, pale and fluffy. It is important that the creamed mixture is very light. Beat in the orange rind, then work in the flour to make a soft dough.

Lightly knead the dough together in the bowl, then press it into the prepared tin. Prick the shortbread all over with a fork and mark the edges with the fork. Chill the shortbread for at least 15 minutes, preferably for 30 minutes.

Bake the shortbread for 40-50 minutes, until firm and lightly browned on top. Cut into wedges at once but do not remove from the tin. Sprinkle with caster sugar while hot. Leave the shortbread in the tin until it is firm enough to lift out. This will take about 15 minutes. Carefully remove the first wedge by easing the point of a knife all round it; the remaining wedges are easily lifted out of the tin.

Cool on a wire rack and store in an airtight container once cooled.

MAKES 8 WEDGES

CINNAMON BARS

Illustrated on page 246

fat for greasing
175 g/6 oz plain flour
5 ml/1 tsp ground cinnamon
50 g/2 oz caster sugar
100 g/4 oz butter
25 g/1 oz flaked almonds
15 ml/1 tbsp granulated sugar

Grease a 20 x 30 cm/8 x 12 inch Swiss roll tin. Set the oven at 180°C/350°F/gas 4.

Sift the flour and 2.5 ml/½ tsp of the cinnamon into a mixing bowl and add the caster sugar. Rub in the butter until the mixture resembles fine breadcrumbs and work into a soft dough. Press the mixture into the prepared tin. Flatten and level the surface, then sprinkle with the flaked almonds, granulated sugar and remaining cinnamon.

Bake for 15-20 minutes until golden-brown. Cut into bars or fingers while still warm.

MAKES ABOUT 20

MRS BEETON'S TIP For a look that children will love, substitute coloured sugar granules (sometimes called coffee sugar) for the granulated sugar in the topping. Omit the cinnamon.

JUMBLES

Illustrated on page 246

fat for greasing
50 g/2 oz plain flour
pinch of salt
50 g/2 oz caster sugar
40 g/1½ oz butter or margarine
10 ml/2 tsp beaten egg
flour for rolling out

Grease 2 baking sheets. Set the oven at 160°C/325°F/gas 3.

Mix the flour, salt and sugar in a mixing bowl, then lightly rub in the butter or margarine until the mixture resembles coarse breadcrumbs. Stir in the egg and mix to a soft dough. Roll out with the hands on a floured surface to a long sausage shape about 2 cm/¾ inch thick. Divide into 20 pieces, and roll each into a 7.5 cm/3 inch long sausage.

Form each piece into an 'S' shape and place well apart on the prepared baking sheets. Bake for 12-15 minutes. Leave the Jumbles to stand for a few minutes, then cool on a wire rack.

MAKES ABOUT 20

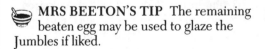 **MRS BEETON'S TIP** The remaining beaten egg may be used to glaze the Jumbles if liked.

DOVER BISCUITS

Illustrated on page 246

fat for greasing
200 g/7 oz plain flour
1.25 ml/¼ tsp salt
2.5 ml/½ tsp ground cinnamon
50 g/2 oz currants
100-150 g/4-5 oz butter or margarine
100-150 g/4-5 oz caster sugar
1 egg, separated
flour for rolling out
caster sugar for topping

Thoroughly grease 2-3 baking sheets. Set the oven at 180°C/350°F/gas 4. Mix the flour, salt and cinnamon in a bowl, then add the currants and stir to coat thoroughly.

In a mixing bowl, beat the butter or margarine until soft, add the sugar and continue to beat until light and fluffy. Beat in the egg yolk, reserving the white. Fold in the flour mixture, first using a knife and then the fingers.

Knead the biscuit dough lightly on a floured surface, then roll out to a thickness of 5 mm/¼ inch. Cut into rounds with a 6 cm/2½ inch cutter. Re-roll and re-cut any trimmings.

Place the biscuits on the prepared baking sheets, pricking the top of each in several places. Bake for 10 minutes, then remove from the oven and add the topping: brush the biscuits with beaten egg white and sprinkle with caster sugar. Return to the oven and bake for 5 minutes more. Leave to stand for 5 minutes, then cool on a wire rack.

MAKES 26 TO 30

SMILES

Children love these cheerful-looking biscuits and enjoy adding the smiles to the basic shapes.

fat for greasing
200 g/7 oz plain flour
1.25 ml/¼ tsp salt
grated rind of 1 orange
100 g/4 oz butter or margarine
100 g/4 oz caster sugar
1 egg yolk
flour for rolling out

TOPPING
12-15 jellied orange and lemon slices

Thoroughly grease 2 large baking sheets. Set the oven at 180°C/350°F/gas 4. Mix the flour, salt and orange rind in a bowl.

In a mixing bowl, beat the butter or margarine until soft, add the sugar and continue to beat until light and fluffy. Beat in the egg yolk. Fold in the flour mixture, first using a knife and then the fingers.

Knead the biscuit dough lightly on a floured surface, then roll out to a thickness of 5 mm/¼ inch. Cut the dough into rounds with a 7.5 cm/3 inch cutter. Re-roll and re-cut any trimmings.

Place the biscuits on the prepared baking sheets. Using a sharp knife dipped in hot water, trim the orange and lemon slices to emphasize the smile shapes. Press one smile on to each biscuit. Use the jelly slice trimmings to make 'eyes', if liked.

Bake for 12-15 minutes. Leave to stand for 5 minutes, then cool on a wire rack.

MAKES 12 TO 15

JIM-JAMS

Illustrated on page 245

fat for greasing
150 g/5 oz plain flour
50 g/2 oz ground almonds
1.25 ml/¼ tsp salt
100 g/4 oz butter or margarine
100 g/4 oz caster sugar
1 egg yolk
flour for rolling
strawberry jam for filling
sifted icing sugar for dredging

Thoroughly grease 2-3 baking sheets. Set the oven at 180°C/350°F/gas 4. Mix the flour, ground almonds and salt in a bowl.

In a mixing bowl, beat the butter or margarine until soft, add the sugar and continue to beat until light and fluffy. Beat in the egg yolk. Fold in the flour mixture, first using a knife and then the fingers.

Knead the biscuit dough lightly on a floured surface, then roll out to a thickness of 5 mm/¼ inch. Cut the dough into rounds with a 6 cm/2½ inch cutter. Re-roll and re-cut any trimmings.

Place the biscuits on the prepared baking sheets, pricking the top of each in several places. Bake for 12-15 minutes, until golden. Leave to stand for 5 minutes, then cool on a wire rack.

When quite cold, sandwich the biscuits together in pairs with strawberry jam and dredge with icing sugar, if liked.

MAKES 26 TO 30

COCONUT CIRCLES

fat for greasing
100 g/4 oz butter or margarine
100 g/4 oz caster sugar
1 egg yolk plus a little egg white if needed
150 g/5 oz self-raising flour or 150 g/5 oz
    plain flour and 5 ml/1 tsp baking
    powder
pinch of salt
50 g/2 oz desiccated coconut
flour for rolling out
egg white for glazing
desiccated coconut for dusting

Grease 2-3 baking sheets. Set the oven at 160°C/325°F/gas 3.

Cream the butter or margarine with the sugar in a mixing bowl until light and fluffy. Beat in the egg yolk, then beat in the flour, salt, and coconut, adding a little of the egg white reserved for glazing if necessary, to bind together.

Roll out the dough to a thickness of 5 mm/ ¼ inch on a floured board and cut into rounds with a 5-6 cm/2-2½ inch cutter. Prick the biscuits and brush with lightly beaten egg white. Sprinkle with coconut. Place on the prepared baking sheets and bake for 15-20 minutes. Let stand for a few minutes, then cool on a wire rack.

MAKES 28 TO 30

> ☀ **MICROWAVE TIP** If biscuits become soft on keeping, firm them in batches of 6-8 in the microwave for 10-20 seconds on High. Allow them to stand for 1-2 minutes.

AFTER DINNER BISCUITS

Serving the biscuits as a dessert is an American custom which is gaining popularity here with those who enjoy ending a meal on a sweet note, but do not relish a substantial pudding.

fat for greasing
100 g/4 oz butter
200 g/7 oz plain flour
100 g/4 oz caster sugar
3 eggs
2.5 ml/½ tsp of any of the following
    flavourings: ground ginger, ground
    cinnamon, grated lemon rind or a few
    drops of lemon essence

Lightly grease 2-3 baking sheets. Set the oven at 160°C/325°F/gas 3.

Cream the butter in a mixing bowl. Add the flour gradually, beating well after each addition. Beat in the sugar, eggs, and flavouring.

Place tablespoons of the mixture, well apart, on the prepared baking sheets; flatten the biscuits slightly, and bake for about 15 minutes. Cool on the baking sheets.

MAKES 30 TO 36

GINGER SQUARES

fat for greasing
200 g/7 oz plain flour
1.25 ml/¼ tsp salt
10 ml/2 tsp ground ginger
75 g/3 oz butter or margarine
50 g/2 oz sugar
75 g/3 oz golden syrup
2 eggs, beaten
flour for rolling out

Grease a large baking sheet. Set the oven at 180°C/350°F/gas 4. Sift the flour, salt, and ginger into a bowl.

In a mixing bowl, cream the butter or margarine with the sugar and syrup. Add the dry ingredients and work enough beaten egg into the mixture to make a stiff dough.

Roll out the dough to a thickness of 5 mm/ ¼ inch. Cut into squares using a plain 6 cm/ 2½ inch or 7.5 cm/3 inch cutter. Place on the prepared baking sheet and bake for about 15-20 minutes. Leave to stand for a few minutes, then transfer the biscuits to a wire rack.

MAKES ABOUT 16

🥄 **MRS BEETON'S TIP** If liked, the biscuits may be decorated before baking with small pieces of crystallised ginger.

MELTING MOMENTS

Illustrated on page 263

fat for greasing
100 g/4 oz margarine or half margarine and half blended white vegetable fat
75 g/3 oz caster sugar
30 ml/2 tbsp beaten egg
125 g/4½ oz self-raising flour
pinch of salt
rolled oats for coating
4-5 glacé cherries, quartered

Grease 2 baking sheets. Set the oven at 180°C/350°F/gas 4.

In a mixing bowl, cream the margarine or mixed fats and sugar until pale and fluffy. Add the egg with a little flour and beat again. Stir in the remaining flour with the salt, mix well, then shape the mixture into 16-20 balls with the hands.

Place the rolled oats on a sheet of greaseproof paper and toss the balls in them to coat them evenly all over. Space the balls on the prepared baking sheets. Place a small piece of glacé cherry in the centre of each.

Bake for about 20 minutes until pale golden-brown. Leave to stand for a few minutes on the baking sheets, then cool on a wire rack.

MAKES 16 TO 20

VARIATION

CUSTARD TREATS Substitute 40 g/1½ oz of the flour with custard powder for a deliciously creamy biscuit with a rich buttery colour. Omit the rolled oats coating.

DIGESTIVE BISCUITS

fat for greasing
75 g/3 oz wholemeal flour
25 g/1 oz plain white flour
25 g/1 oz fine or medium oatmeal
2.5 ml/½ tsp baking powder
1.25 ml/¼ tsp salt
15 ml/1 tbsp soft light brown sugar
50 g/2 oz butter or margarine
30 ml/2 tbsp milk
flour for rolling out

Grease a baking sheet. Set the oven at 180°C/350°F/gas 4. Mix all the dry ingredients in a mixing bowl, sifting the sugar if it is lumpy. Rub in the butter or margarine until the mixture binds together and mix to a pliable dough with the milk.

Knead the biscuit dough lightly on a floured board and roll out to a thickness of just under 5 mm/¼ inch. Cut into rounds with a 6 cm/2½ inch round cutter, place on the prepared baking sheet and prick with a fork. Bake for 15 minutes or until golden brown. Leave to stand for a few minutes, then cool on a wire rack.

MAKES ABOUT 12

GINGER SNAPS

Illustrated on page 264

fat for greasing
200 g/7 oz self-raising flour
pinch of salt
5 ml/1 tsp ground ginger
100 g/4 oz soft light brown sugar
75 g/3 oz margarine
100 g/4 oz golden syrup
1 egg, beaten

Thoroughly grease several baking sheets. Set the oven at 160°C/325°F/gas 3. Sift together the flour, salt and ginger. Stir in the sugar.

Melt the margarine with the syrup in a large heavy-bottomed saucepan. When the fat has melted, add the dry ingredients and beaten egg alternately and beat until smooth and thick.

Using 2 teaspoons, place rounds of the mixture on to the prepared baking sheets, allowing plenty of room for spreading. Bake for 15 minutes. Leave to stand for a few minutes, then cool on a wire rack.

MAKES ABOUT 56

MRS BEETON'S TIP If the biscuit mixture has to stand before baking – perhaps because a shortage of baking sheets makes it necessary to batch-bake – it will thicken. When this happens, simply shape the biscuit mixture into small balls and bake as above.

CRUNCHIES

fat for greasing
100 g/4 oz margarine
125 g/4½ oz rolled oats
75 g/3 oz demerara sugar

Grease a 28 x 18 cm/11 x 7 inch baking tin. Set the oven at 190°C/375°F/gas 5.

Melt the margarine in a large saucepan and stir in the oats and the sugar. Press into the prepared tin and bake for 15-20 minutes. Cut into squares or strips while warm, and leave in the tin until cool.

MAKES ABOUT 20

> **MRS BEETON'S TIP** Coconut makes a good addition to these biscuits. Substitute desiccated coconut for 50 g/2 oz of the oats.

PIPED ALMOND RINGS

Illustrated on page 263

fat for greasing
175 g/6 oz butter
100 g/4 oz caster sugar
1 egg, beaten
225 g/8 oz self-raising flour
50 g/2 oz ground almonds
1-2 drops vanilla essence
about 10 ml/4 tsp milk

Thoroughly grease 1-2 baking sheets. In a mixing bowl, cream the butter and sugar until light and fluffy. Add the beaten egg, beating thoroughly and adding a little of the flour if the mixture begins to curdle. Blend in the remaining flour and ground almonds gradually. Add the vanilla essence and enough milk to give a piping consistency. Leave the mixture to stand for about 20 minutes in a cool place.

Set the oven at 200°C/400°F/gas 6. Put the biscuit mixture into a piping bag fitted with a medium star nozzle, and pipe small rings on to the prepared baking sheets. Bake for 10 minutes or until golden. Leave to stand for a few minutes, then cool on a wire rack.

MAKES ABOUT 24

> **MRS BEETON'S TIP** An oil well is a useful aid when greasing baking sheets. The device consists of a clear spill-resistant oil reservoir with a built-in brush.

FLAPJACKS

Illustrated on page 264

fat for greasing
50 g/2 oz margarine
50 g/2 oz soft light brown sugar
30 ml/2 tbsp golden syrup
100 g/4 oz rolled oats

Grease a 28 x 18 cm/11 x 7 inch baking tin. Set the oven at 160°C/325°F/gas 3. Melt the margarine in a large saucepan. Add the sugar and syrup, and warm gently. Do not boil. Remove from the heat and stir in the oats.

Press into the prepared tin, then bake for 25 minutes or until firm. Cut into fingers while still warm and leave in the tin to cool.

MAKES ABOUT 20

VARIATIONS

SULTANA FLAPJACKS Add 50 g/2 oz of sultanas to the basic mixture, stirring them in with the oats.
SESAME FLAPJACKS Sesame seeds contribute their own, distinct flavour to this traditional recipe. Press the flapjack mixture into the tin, then sprinkle a layer of sesame seeds over the top and press them down well with the back of a spoon. Do not use roasted sesame seeds.
HONEY FLAPJACKS Use clear honey instead of the golden syrup and continue as in the main recipe.

APPLE AND WALNUT FLAPJACKS

Tart eating apples and roughly chopped walnuts turn a batch of simple flapjacks into a special treat.

fat for greasing
75 g/3 oz margarine
75 g/3 oz soft light brown sugar
30 ml/2 tbsp clear honey
2 tart eating apples, peeled, cored and diced
100 g/4 oz walnuts, chopped
50 g/2 oz raisins
100 g/4 oz rolled oats

Grease a 28 x 18 cm/11 x 7 inch baking tin. Set the oven at 160°C/325°F/gas 3. Melt the margarine with the sugar and honey in a large saucepan over low heat. Stir the mixture occasionally.

Off the heat, add the apples, walnuts and raisins to the melted mixture. Stir well, then add the oats and mix thoroughly. Press the mixture into the prepared tin and bake for 25 minutes, or until golden brown and firm.

Leave the flapjacks to cool in the tin, cutting them into fingers while still warm.

MAKES ABOUT 20

MRS BEETON'S TIP Muesli can be used to make the flapjacks instead of the rolled oats. For best results use a variety which is not over-sweetened or enriched with milk powder. The combination of fruits and nuts in the cereal makes an excellent flapjack mixture.

TEATIME TREATS

These biscuits are extra special in different ways – perfect for a coffee party or teatime gathering. Some, such as brandy snaps, have a lace-like delicacy while others are crunchy and nutty, or short and creamy – a selection to suit all tastes.

SPONGE FINGERS

Speed is the secret ingredient of successful sponge fingers. Do not allow the mixture to stand before baking or it will collapse, resulting in solid rather than spongy biscuits.

fat for greasing
caster sugar for dusting
3 eggs, separated
100 g/4 oz caster sugar
100 g/4 oz plain flour
pinch of salt

Grease 18 sponge finger tins and dust with caster sugar. Set the oven at 160°C/325°F/gas 3. In a bowl, beat the egg yolks with the sugar until pale and thick. Sift the flour with the salt into a second bowl. Fold half the flour into the egg mixture very lightly.

In a clean, dry bowl, whisk the egg whites until stiff. Fold very lightly into the yolk mixture with the rest of the flour. Half fill the prepared tins and bake for 12 minutes. Leave to cool slightly before removing from the tins and cooling completely on a wire rack.

MAKES 18

ALMOND MACAROONS

fat for greasing
2 egg whites
150 g/5 oz caster sugar
100 g/4 oz ground almonds
10 ml/2 tsp ground rice
split almonds or halved glacé cherries

Grease 2 baking sheets and cover with rice paper. Set the oven at 160°C/325°F/gas 3.

In a clean dry bowl, whisk the egg whites until frothy but not stiff enough to form peaks. Stir in the sugar, ground almonds, and ground rice. Beat with a wooden spoon until thick and white.

Put small spoonfuls of the mixture 5 cm/ 2 inches apart on the prepared baking sheets or pipe them on. Place a split almond or halved glacé cherry on each macaroon and bake for 20 minutes or until pale fawn in colour. Cool slightly on the baking sheets, then finish cooling on wire racks.

VARIATION

RATAFIAS Ratafias are used in trifles, to decorate desserts, and as petits fours. Follow the recipe above, but reduce the size of the biscuits so that when cooked they are only 2 cm/¾ inch in diameter. Omit the split almond or cherry topping.

ALMOND AND RASPBERRY FINGERS

fat for greasing
150 g/5 oz plain flour
50 g/2 oz ground almonds
1.25 ml/¼ tsp salt
75-100 g/3-4 oz butter or margarine
50 g/2 oz caster sugar
5 ml/1 tsp baking powder
1 egg yolk
flour for rolling out

TOPPING
1 egg white
75 g/3 oz icing sugar
50 g/2 oz slivered almonds
about 60 ml/4 tbsp seedless raspberry
    preserve

Grease a 28 x 18 cm/11 x 7 inch baking sheet. Set the oven at 180°C/350°F/gas 4.

Combine the flour, ground almonds and salt in a mixing bowl. Rub in the butter or margarine, then stir in the sugar and baking powder. Bind to a stiff dough with the egg yolk, adding a little water if necessary. Knead well and pat or roll out to fit the prepared baking sheet. Pinch up the edges all around. Bake for 15 minutes.

Meanwhile make the topping. In a clean, dry bowl, whisk the egg white to stiff peaks, then fold in the sugar and almonds. Remove the baking sheet from the oven and spread the biscuit base with raspberry preserve.

Spread the topping over the preserve and return the baking sheet to the oven for 7-10 minutes until the meringue topping is set and lightly browned. Cut into fingers while still warm, then cool on a wire rack.

MAKES ABOUT 14

> **MRS BEETON'S TIP** Do not worry if some of the preserve combines with the meringue mixture when it is spread on to the biscuit. The ripple effect is not unattractive and the recipe still works perfectly.

ALMOND FAVOURS

fat for greasing
150 g/5 oz plain flour
50 g/2 oz ground almonds
1.25 ml/¼ tsp salt
100 g/4 oz butter or margarine
100 g/4 oz caster sugar
1 egg yolk
flour for rolling
smooth apricot jam for filling
icing sugar for dredging (optional)

Thoroughly grease 2-3 baking sheets. Set the oven at 180°C/350°F/gas 4. Mix the flour, ground almonds and salt in a bowl.

In a mixing bowl, beat the butter or margarine until soft, add the sugar and continue to beat until light and fluffy. Beat in the egg yolk. Fold in the flour mixture, first using a knife and then the fingers.

Knead the biscuit dough lightly on a floured surface, then roll out to a thickness of 5 mm/¼ inch. Cut into rounds with a 6 cm/2½ inch biscuit cutter. Re-roll and re-cut any trimmings.

Place the biscuits on the prepared baking sheets, pricking the top of each in several places. Bake for 15-20 minutes, until golden. Leave to stand for 5 minutes, then cool on a wire rack. When cold, sandwich the biscuits together with apricot jam and dredge with caster sugar, if liked.

MAKES 13 TO 15

MERINGUES

This basic meringue mixture – Swiss or Chantilly meringue – may be used for a wide variety of dishes, from individual meringues of various sizes to shells, cases and toppings. Provided the cooked meringues are dried out thoroughly, they will keep for 1-2 weeks in an airtight tin.

4 egg whites
pinch of salt
200 g/7 oz caster sugar, plus extra for
    dusting
1.25 ml/¼ tsp baking powder (optional)
whipped cream to fill (optional)

Line a baking sheet with oiled greaseproof paper or with non-stick baking parchment. Set the oven at 110°C/225°F/gas ¼.

Combine the egg whites and salt in a mixing bowl and whisk until the whites are very stiff and standing in points. They must be completely dry or the meringues will break down in baking. Gradually add half the caster sugar, 15 ml/1 tablespoon at a time, whisking after each addition until stiff. If the sugar is not thoroughly blended in it will form droplets of syrup which will brown, spoiling the appearance of the meringues and making them difficult to remove from the paper.

When half the sugar has been whisked in, sprinkle the rest over the surface of the mixture and, using a metal spoon, fold it in very lightly with the baking powder, if used. Put the meringue mixture into a piping bag fitted with a large nozzle and pipe into rounds on the paper. Alternatively, shape the mixture using two wet tablespoons. Take up a spoonful of the mixture and smooth it with a palette knife, bringing it up into a ridge in the centre. Slide it out with the other spoon on to the prepared baking sheet, with the ridge on top.

Dust the meringues lightly with caster sugar, then dry off in the oven for 3-4 hours, until they are firm and crisp but still white. If the meringues begin to brown, prop the oven door open a little. When they are crisp on the outside, lift the meringues carefully off the sheet, using a palette knife. Turn them on to their sides and return to the oven until the bases are dry. Cool on a wire rack and, if liked, sandwich them together with whipped cream. Filled meringues should be served within 1 hour or they will soften.

MAKES 24 TO 30 MEDIUM MERINGUES

VARIATIONS

MERINGUE FINGERS Pipe the meringue mixture into fingers instead of shaping rounds. Dip one end of each meringue in melted chocolate when cool, then leave to set on wax paper. Alternatively, sandwich the fingers together with whipped cream and coat the top of each with melted chocolate.

MERINGUE PETITS FOURS Make half the quantity of mixture. Pipe very small meringues and dry out as in the main recipe, for about 2-3 hours. Set the meringues on small circles of almond paste, attaching them with warmed apricot jam. Alternatively, sandwich them in pairs with whipped cream.

MRS BEETON'S TIP It is vital that the egg whites have been separated with great care. The fat in even a trace of egg yolk would prevent the whites from whisking properly. For the same reason, the bowl and whisk must be dry and absolutely clean and grease-free.

NUTTY MERINGUES

oil for greasing, if required
100 g/4 oz icing sugar
2 egg whites
few drops of almond or vanilla essence
50 g/2 oz almonds, walnuts or hazelnuts,
    blanched and finely chopped

Line two 20 x 25 cm/8 x 12 inch baking sheets with oiled greaseproof paper, rice paper or non-stick baking parchment. Set the oven at 150°C/300°F/gas 2.

Sift the icing sugar into a bowl. Add the egg whites and stand the bowl over a saucepan of hot water. Whisk the mixture until it clings stiffly to the whisk. Add a few drops of almond or vanilla essence and stir in the nuts.

Put in small rough heaps on the prepared baking sheets and bake for 20-30 minutes until the meringues are crisp outside, soft inside and lightly coloured. Cool on the baking sheets.

MAKES 10 TO 12

FLORENTINES

Illustrated on page 281

oil for greasing
25 g/1 oz glacé cherries, chopped
100 g/4 oz cut mixed peel, finely chopped
50 g/2 oz flaked almonds
100 g/4 oz chopped almonds
25 g/1 oz sultanas
100 g/4 oz butter or margarine
100 g/4 oz caster sugar
30 ml/2 tbsp double cream
100 g/4 oz plain or couverture chocolate

Line 3 or 4 baking sheets with oiled greaseproof paper. Set the oven at 180°C/350°F/gas 4.

In a bowl, mix the cherries and mixed peel with the flaked and chopped almonds and the sultanas. Melt the butter or margarine in a small saucepan, add the sugar and boil for 1 minute. Remove from the heat and stir in the fruit and nuts. Whip the cream in a separate bowl, then fold it in.

Place small spoonfuls of the mixture on to the prepared baking sheets, leaving room for spreading. Bake for 8-10 minutes. After the biscuits have been cooking for about 5 minutes, neaten the edges by drawing them together with a plain biscuit cutter. Leave the cooked biscuits on the baking sheets to firm up slightly before transferring to a wire rack to cool completely.

To finish, melt the chocolate in a bowl over hot water and use to coat the flat underside of each biscuit. Mark into wavy lines with a fork as the chocolate cools.

MAKES 20 TO 24

Orange Peanut Butter Biscuits (page 306) and Nut Clusters (page 307)

300

Cheese Butterflies (page 308), Cheese Straws (page 309) and Anchovy Appetisers (page 313)

From the middle of the basket, outwards: **Caraway Crackers and Oatcakes (both on page 311), and Crisp Crackers (page 310)**

From the top: **German Spice Biscuits (page 314), Chocolate-tipped Cinnamon Stars (page 318), Snowmen (page 316) and Anzacs (page 314)**

BRANDY SNAPS

Illustrated on page 281

These traditional treats make a popular addition to a buffet table or may be served as a tempting dessert. Fill them at the last moment with fresh whipped cream or Confectioners' Custard (see page 162). Use either a small spoon or a piping bag fitted with a large star or rose nozzle.

fat for greasing
50 g/2 oz plain flour
5 ml/1 tsp ground ginger
50 g/2 oz margarine
50 g/2 oz soft dark brown sugar
30 ml/2 tbsp golden syrup
10 ml/2 tsp grated lemon rind
5 ml/1 tsp lemon juice

Grease two or three 20 x 25 cm/8 x 10 inch baking sheets. Also grease the handles of several wooden spoons, standing them upside down in a jar until required. Set the oven at 180°C/350°F/gas 4.

Sift the flour and ginger into a bowl. Melt the margarine in a saucepan. Add the sugar and syrup and warm gently, but do not allow to become hot. Remove from the heat and add the sifted ingredients with the lemon rind and juice. Mix well.

Put small spoonfuls of the mixture on to the prepared baking sheets, spacing well apart to allow for spreading. Do not put more than 6 spoonfuls on a baking sheet. Bake for 8-10 minutes.

Remove from the oven and leave to cool for a few seconds until the edges begin to firm. Lift one of the biscuits with a palette knife and roll loosely around the greased handle of one of the wooden spoons. Allow to cool before removing the spoon handle. Repeat with the remaining biscuits.

MAKES 14 TO 18

VERSATILE BRANDY SNAPS

The difficult part of making brandy snaps is removing them from the baking sheet and sure success only comes with practice. The knack is to test a corner of one brandy snap every few seconds until the mixture is set just enough to be lifted off the sheet and shaped. Once you have mastered the technique you will be able to put the brandy snaps to many uses. For example, try some of the suggestions below.

BRANDY SNAP CUPS Instead of rolling the cooked biscuits, mould them into greased patty tins. Leave until completely cool, then lift the cups out of the tins. For larger cups, mould the biscuits over oranges. The cooled cups can be filled with fresh fruit salad or ice cream and served as a splendid summer dessert.

BRANDY SNAP GATEAU Spread the sides of a sponge cake with whipped cream, then lightly press rolled brandy snaps all round the cake. Tie a ribbon round the cake to keep the biscuit edge firmly in place.

BRANDY SNAP PETITS FOURS Make small brandy snaps by baking tiny amounts of the mixture and wrapping them round a wooden spoon handle when hot. Use a small star nozzle to fill the tiny brandy snaps with whipped cream just before they are served with a selection of other petits fours.

> **MRS BEETON'S TIP** If the biscuits begin to harden before they may be rolled, return the baking sheet to the oven for a minute or two to soften them.

CATHERINE WHEELS

Illustrated on page 282

fat for greasing
150 g/5 oz plain flour
1.25 ml/¼ tsp salt
5 ml/1 tsp baking powder
75 g/3 oz butter
75 g/3 oz caster sugar
few drops of vanilla essence
5 ml/1 tsp cocoa
flour for rolling out

Grease 2 baking sheets. Sift the flour, salt and baking powder into a mixing bowl. Rub in the butter until the mixture resembles fine breadcrumbs, then stir in the sugar. Add the vanilla essence, then bind to a pliable dough, using about 15-30 ml/1-2 tbsp water.

Divide the dough in half. Return one half to the mixing bowl. Sprinkle the cocoa over the top and work it in evenly, using a fork. Roll out the plain dough on a lightly floured surface to a rectangle measuring 18 x 23 cm/ 7 x 9 inches. Set aside. Roll out the chocolate dough to the same size and place it on top of the plain piece (see Mrs Beeton's Tip). Roll up both pieces from a long side, like a Swiss roll, keeping the join underneath. Chill. Set the oven at 180°C/350°F/gas 4.

Cut the chilled dough roll into slices 1 cm/ ½ inch thick. Reshape into neat rounds with the hands, and place well apart on the prepared baking sheets. Bake for 15-20 minutes until the plain part of each Catherine Wheel is golden brown. Cool.

MAKES 24

> 🥣 **MRS BEETON'S TIP** To prevent the Catherine Wheels from unravelling when sliced, use a rolling pin to press the plain and chocolate rectangles together before rolling up.

COFFEE KISSES

Illustrated on page 282

fat for greasing
150 g/5 oz self-raising flour
75 g/3 oz butter or margarine
50 g/2 oz caster sugar
1 egg yolk
5 ml/1 tsp liquid coffee essence

FILLING
Coffee Buttercream (pages 144 and 145)
Icing sugar for dusting (optional)

Grease 2 baking sheets. Set the oven at 190°C/375°F/gas 5. Sift the flour into a mixing bowl. Rub in the butter or margarine until the mixture resembles fine bread-crumbs then stir in the sugar. Mix the egg yolk with the coffee essence in a cup. Use this to bind the dry ingredients together to a stiff dough.

Roll the dough into balls, each about the size of a walnut, and place, well apart, on the prepared baking sheets. Bake for 10 minutes, then cool on a wire rack.

Use the coffee buttercream to sandwich the biscuits together in pairs. If liked, dust with icing sugar.

MAKES ABOUT 12

WINE BISCUITS

225 g/8 oz plain flour
1.25 ml/¼ tsp salt
1.25 ml/¼ tsp ground cloves
5 ml/1 tsp ground cinnamon
2.5 ml/½ tsp ground ginger
2.5 ml/½ tsp bicarbonate of soda
100 g/4 oz butter
150 g/5 oz caster sugar
50 g/2 oz ground almonds
30 ml/2 tbsp beaten egg
30 ml/2 tbsp white wine
fat for greasing
flour for rolling out
halved almonds (optional)

Sift the flour, salt, spices and soda into a mixing bowl. Rub in the butter until the mixture resembles fine breadcrumbs and add the sugar and ground almonds. In a bowl, mix the egg with the wine. Add to the dry ingredients and mix to a stiff dough. Leave to stand for several hours or overnight.

Grease 3-4 baking sheets. Set the oven at 220°C/425°F/gas 7. Roll out the dough on a lightly floured surface to a thickness of 3 mm/⅛ inch. Cut into rounds with a 5 cm/ 2 inch cutter and put these, well apart, on the prepared baking sheets. Place half an almond on each biscuit, if liked. Bake for 10 minutes. Cool slightly on the sheets, then complete cooling on wire racks.

MAKES ABOUT 60

BOURBON BISCUITS

fat for greasing
50 g/2 oz butter or margarine
50 g/2 oz caster sugar
15 ml/1 tbsp golden syrup
100 g/4 oz plain flour
15 g/½ oz cocoa
2.5 ml/½ tsp bicarbonate of soda
flour for rolling out

FILLING
50 g/2 oz butter or margarine
75 g/3 oz icing sugar, sifted
15 ml/1 tbsp cocoa
5 ml/1 tsp coffee essence or 2.5 ml/½ tsp
    instant coffee dissolved in 5 ml/1 tsp
    boiling water and cooled

Line and grease a baking sheet. Set the oven at 160°C/325°F/gas 3.

In a mixing bowl, cream the butter or margarine with the sugar very thoroughly; beat in the syrup. Sift the flour, cocoa and bicarbonate of soda into a second bowl, mix well, then work into the creamed mixture to make a stiff dough. Knead well, and roll out on a lightly floured surface into an oblong strip about 13 x 23 cm/5 x 9 inches and 5 mm/ ¼ inch thick. Cut in half to form two 6 cm/ 2½ inch wide rectangles. Place on the prepared baking sheet and bake for 15-20 minutes. Cut into equal-sized fingers while still warm. Cool on a wire rack.

Prepare the filling. In a bowl, beat the butter or margarine until soft, then add the sugar, cocoa, and coffee. Beat until smooth. Sandwich the cooled fingers in pairs with the filling.

MAKES 14 TO 16

NAPOLEON'S HATS

fat for greasing
50 g/2 oz margarine
50 g/2 oz caster sugar
30 ml/2 tbsp beaten egg
100 g/4 oz plain flour
2.5 ml/½ tsp baking powder
pinch of salt
flour for rolling out

ALMOND PASTE
    50 g/2 oz ground almonds
    50 g/2 oz caster sugar
    20 ml/4 tsp beaten egg

DECORATION (optional)
    Glacé Icing (page 151)
        using 25 g/1 oz icing sugar
    food colouring (see method)

Grease a baking sheet. Set the oven at 180°C/350°F/gas 4. Cream the margarine in a mixing bowl with the sugar until light and fluffy. Beat in the egg. In a second bowl, sift the flour, baking powder and salt, and work into the creamed mixture. Knead well and roll out on a lightly floured surface to a thickness of 5 mm/¼ inch. Cut into rounds with a 7.5 cm/3 inch plain cutter, making 12 biscuits.

Make the almond paste. Mix the almonds and sugar in a bowl. Add 10 ml/2 tsp beaten egg and work to a paste. Divide the paste into 12 pieces and roll each into a ball. Place one in the centre of each biscuit. Place the remaining 10 ml/2 tsp beaten egg in a cup and mix with 5 ml/1 tsp water. Brush the edges of the biscuits with the egg and water mixture and fold into a hat shape by lifting and pinching the edge of each biscuit at 2 points spaced equally apart. Place the 'hats' on the prepared baking sheet and bake for 25 minutes. Cool on the baking sheet.

When the 'hats' are cold, a little glacé icing can be put on the almond paste, to give them white or coloured 'crowns'.

MAKES 12

ORANGE PEANUT BUTTER BISCUITS

Illustrated on page 299

100 g/4 oz margarine
100 g/4 oz smooth peanut butter
65 g/2½ oz caster sugar
75 g/3 oz soft light brown sugar
5 ml/1 tbsp grated orange rind
1 egg, beaten
2.5 ml/½ tsp vanilla essence
125 g/4½ oz plain flour
2.5 ml/½ tsp bicarbonate of soda
2.5 ml/½ tsp salt

Line 2-3 baking sheets with non-stick baking parchment. In a mixing bowl, cream the margarine and peanut butter with the caster and brown sugars until light and fluffy. Stir in the orange rind. In a cup, mix the egg with the vanilla essence, and stir it into the creamed mixture.

Sift the flour, bicarbonate of soda and salt into a second bowl. Add to the creamed mixture, and mix thoroughly to form a dough. Chill the dough.

Set the oven at 180°C/350°F/gas 4. Shape the biscuit dough into 2 cm/¾ inch balls. Lay them well apart on the prepared baking sheets. Flatten the balls slightly with the palm of the hand. Bake for 15-20 minutes. Leave on the sheets to firm up, then cool on a wire rack.

MAKES ABOUT 36

NUT CLUSTERS

Illustrated on page 299

50 g/2 oz soft margarine
50 g/2 oz sugar
30 ml/2 tbsp beaten egg
2.5 ml/½ tsp vanilla essence
50 g/2 oz plain flour
pinch of salt
1.25 ml/¼ tsp bicarbonate of soda
50 g/2 oz seedless raisins
50 g/2 oz salted peanuts

Set the oven at 190°C/375°F/gas 5. In a mixing bowl beat the margarine and sugar until light and fluffy. Beat in the egg and vanilla essence.

Sift the flour, salt and bicarbonate of soda into a second bowl and beat them into the creamed mixture in 3 portions, mixing well after each addition. Stir in the raisins and nuts. Place small spoonfuls on 1 or 2 ungreased baking sheets and bake for 9 minutes. Cool on the baking sheets.

MAKES 20 TO 24

PRINCESS PAIRS

fat for greasing
100 g/4 oz butter or margarine
25 g/1 oz caster sugar
pinch of salt
100 g/4 oz self-raising flour
grated rind of ½ orange

FILLING
Orange Buttercream (pages 144 and 145),
using 25 g/1 oz butter

Grease 2 baking sheets. Set the oven at 180°C/350°F/gas 4. In a mixing bowl, cream the butter or margarine with the sugar. Work in the salt, flour and orange rind. Put the mixture in a piping bag fitted with a large star nozzle, and pipe 9 cm/3½ inch lengths on to the prepared baking sheets, making 20 biscuits. Bake for 15 minutes. Cool on the sheets. When cool, sandwich together in pairs with the buttercream.

MAKES 10

RING O' ROSES

fat for greasing
100 g/4 oz margarine
50 g/2 oz caster sugar
1 egg yolk
100 g/4 oz plain flour
flour for rolling out

ALMOND TOPPING
1 egg white
75 g/3 oz caster sugar
50 g/2 oz ground almonds

DECORATION
60 ml/4 tbsp red jam or jelly

Grease a baking sheet. Set the oven at 180°C/350°F/gas 4. In a mixing bowl, cream the margarine and sugar thoroughly. Work in the egg yolk and then the flour to form a dough. On a lightly floured surface, knead well, then roll out to a thickness of 5 mm/¼ inch. Cut into 4 cm/1½ inch rounds. Place on the prepared baking sheet.

Make the almond topping. In a bowl, whisk the egg white until frothy, then stir in the caster sugar and the ground almonds. Using a piping bag fitted with a plain nozzle, pipe a circle of the almond mixture around the edge of each biscuit. Bake for 15 minutes then cool on the baking sheet. When cold, fill the centres of the biscuits with jam or jelly.

MAKES 12

SAVOURY BISCUITS AND CRACKERS

Here you will find recipes that Mrs Beeton considered to be the most wholesome of the class of unfermented breads. Crisp and light or deliciously savoury, their value today is as accompaniments for cheese or as mouthwatering cocktail snacks.

CHEESE BUTTERFLIES

Illustrated on page 300

fat for greasing
100 g/4 oz plain flour
pinch of mustard powder
pinch of salt
pinch of cayenne pepper
75 g/3 oz butter
75 g/3 oz grated Parmesan cheese
1 egg yolk
flour for rolling out

TOPPING
100 g/4 oz full-fat soft cheese
few drops of anchovy essence
few drops of red food colouring

Grease 2 baking sheets. Set the oven at 200°C/400°F/gas 6.

Sift the flour, mustard, salt and cayenne into a bowl. In a mixing bowl, cream the butter until soft and white, then add the flour mixture with the cheese. Stir in the egg yolk and enough cold water to form a stiff dough.

Roll out on a lightly floured surface to a thickness of about 3 mm/⅛ inch and cut into rounds about 6 cm/1½ inches in diameter. Cut half the rounds across the centre to make 'wings'.

With a palette knife, lift both the whole rounds and the 'wings' on to the prepared baking sheets and bake for 10 minutes. Cool on the baking sheets.

Meanwhile make the topping. Put the soft cheese in a bowl and cream until soft with a fork, adding the anchovy essence for flavour and just enough of the red food colouring to tint the mixture a pale pink. Transfer the topping to a piping bag fitted with a shell nozzle.

When the biscuits are quite cold, pipe a line of cheese across the centre of each full round and press the straight edges of two half-rounds into the cheese to make them stand up like wings.

MAKES 12 TO 18

VARIATIONS

Use the basic recipe for the biscuits to make a variety of different-flavoured cocktail snacks. This is achieved by varying the flavour of the cream cheese which is piped on to the biscuits.

PARMESAN AND PINE NUT Add a little grated Parmesan cheese to the cream cheese and omit the anchovy essence and colouring. Sprinkle toasted pine nuts down the middle of the cheese when the wings are in place.

TOMATO AND OLIVE Leave out the anchovy essence and colouring, then flavour the cream cheese with a little tomato purée and add a little lemon juice, to taste. Top the butterflies with a few pieces of black olive once the wings are in place.

CHEESE STRAWS

Illustrated on page 300

fat for greasing
100 g/4 oz plain flour
pinch of mustard powder
pinch of salt
pinch of cayenne pepper
75 g/3 oz butter
75 g/3 oz grated Parmesan cheese
1 egg yolk
flour for rolling out

Grease 4 baking sheets. Set the oven at 200°C/400°F/gas 6.

Sift the flour, mustard, salt and cayenne into a bowl. In a mixing bowl, cream the butter until soft and white, then add the flour mixture with the cheese. Stir in the egg yolk and enough cold water to form a stiff dough.

Roll out on a lightly floured surface to a thickness of about 5 mm/¼ inch and cut into fingers, each measuring about 10 x 1 cm/4 x ½ inch. From the pastry trimmings make several rings, each about 4 cm/1½ inches in diameter.

With a palette knife, transfer both rings and straws to the prepared baking sheets and bake for 8-10 minutes or until lightly browned and crisp. Cool on the baking sheets.

To serve, fit a few straws through each ring and lay the bundles in the centre of a plate with any remaining straws criss-crossed around them.

MAKES 48 TO 60

> **MRS BEETON'S TIP** For a decorative effect, the straws may be twisted, corkscrew-fashion.

HOT PEPPER CHEESES

When freshly cooked, these savouries are inclined to crumble and break easily. For this reason it is best to allow them to cool completely, then reheat gently until warm.

fat for greasing
200 g/7 oz plain flour
200 g/7 oz butter
200 g/7 oz Lancashire cheese, grated
few drops of hot pepper sauce
1.25 ml/¼ tsp salt
flour for rolling out

Grease 4 baking sheets. Sift the flour into a mixing bowl. Rub in the butter until the mixture resembles fine breadcrumbs. Add the cheese and seasonings. Work the mixture thoroughly by hand to make a smooth dough. Use a few drops of water if necessary, but the dough will be shorter and richer without it. Chill for 30 minutes.

Meanwhile, set the oven at 180°C/350°F/gas 4. Roll out the dough on a floured surface to a thickness of 5 mm/¼ inch. Cut into rounds or shapes.

With a palette knife, transfer the shapes to the prepared baking sheets and bake for 10-12 minutes or until lightly browned and crisp. Cool on the baking sheets.

MAKES 40 TO 50

> **MRS BEETON'S TIP** When cutting out the cheese dough it is best to stick to regular shapes such as rounds, crescents, squares or stars. The mixture is so short that any thin projections on the biscuits are likely to break off.

CHEESE MERINGUES

2 egg whites
50 g/2 oz finely grated Parmesan cheese
pinch of salt
pinch of cayenne pepper
oil for deep frying
grated Parmesan cheese and cayenne
    pepper for sprinkling

In a clean dry bowl, whisk the egg whites until stiff peaks form. Lightly fold in the cheese and seasonings.

Heat the oil to 180-190°C/350-375°F or until a cube of bread added to the oil browns in 30 seconds. Using a rounded spoon, gently lower puffs of the mixture into the hot oil or fat (see Mrs Beeton's Tip). Fry the puffs until golden brown, then carefully remove with a slotted spoon and drain thoroughly on absorbent kitchen paper. Serve warm, sprinkled with Parmesan and cayenne.

MAKES 14 TO 16

MRS BEETON'S TIP If preferred, the cheese meringue mixture may be put into a piping bag with a large nozzle. Squeeze out the meringue into the hot oil, cutting off small lengths with a sharp knife. Proceed as in the recipe above.

CRISP CRACKERS

Illustrated on page 301

These plain crackers are the ideal accompaniment for cheese. If you use very small cutters to cut the dough, then the crackers can be used as a base for making little canapés – top them with piped smooth pâté or cream cheese, olives and parsley.

fat for greasing
225 g/8 oz plain flour
2.5 ml/½ tsp salt
about 100 ml/4 fl oz milk
1 egg yolk, beaten

Grease 2 baking sheets. Set the oven at 180°C/350°F/gas 4. Sift the flour and salt into a bowl, then make a well in the middle and add about half the milk. Add the egg yolk to the milk and gradually work in the flour to make a firm dough, adding more milk as necessary.

Turn the dough out on to a lightly floured surface and knead it briefly until it is perfectly smooth. Divide the piece of dough in half and wrap one piece in cling film to prevent it from drying out while you roll out the other piece.

Roll out the dough very thinly and use a 7.5 cm/3 inch round cutter to stamp out crackers. Gather up the trimmings and re-roll them. Place the crackers on the prepared baking sheets and bake them for 12-18 minutes, until they are golden. Transfer the crackers to a wire rack to cool.

MAKES ABOUT 24

CARAWAY CRACKERS

Illustrated on page 301

Originally, these simple biscuits were sweetened with 50 g/2 oz caster sugar but the flavour of the caraway seeds makes such an excellent savoury cracker that the sugar is omitted in this recipe. However, if you particularly like the flavour of caraway you may like to try the old recipe and add the sugar to the flour. If you are making the savoury crackers try using brown flour instead of white.

fat for greasing
50 g/2 oz butter
225 g/8 oz plain flour
15 g/¼ oz caraway seeds
good pinch of salt
1 egg, beaten
milk to glaze

Grease 2 baking sheets. Set the oven at 180°C/350°F/gas 4. Place the butter in a small bowl and beat it until it is very soft. Gradually beat in the flour, caraway seeds and salt until the ingredients are thoroughly mixed.

Add the beaten egg and mix well to make a firm dough. Knead the dough briefly on a floured surface, then roll it out thinly and cut out 5 cm/2 inch circles.

Place the crackers on the baking sheets and brush them with a little milk, then bake them for about 12-15 minutes. Transfer the crackers to a wire rack to cool.

MAKES ABOUT 30

OATCAKES

Illustrated on page 301

fat for greasing
50 g/2 oz bacon fat or dripping
100 g/4 oz medium oatmeal
1.25 ml/¼ tsp salt
1.25 ml/¼ tsp bicarbonate of soda
fine oatmeal for rolling out

Grease 2 baking sheets. Set the oven at 160°C/325°F/gas 3.

Melt the bacon fat or dripping in a large saucepan. Remove from the heat and stir in the dry ingredients, then add enough boiling water to make a stiff dough.

When cool enough to handle, knead the dough thoroughly, then roll out on a surface dusted with fine oatmeal, to a thickness of 5 mm/¼ inch. Cut into wedge-shaped pieces and transfer to the prepared baking sheets. Bake for 20-30 minutes. Cool on a wire rack.

MAKES ABOUT 16

RUSKS

This is an old Suffolk recipe for simple, dry biscuits which are made from a yeasted bread dough. The original recipe used fresh yeast but this version takes advantage of easy-blend yeast.

fat for greasing
225 g/8 oz strong plain flour
15 g/½ oz easy-blend dried yeast
25 g/1 oz sugar
2.5 ml/½ tsp salt
25 g/1 oz butter
75 ml/3 fl oz milk
1 egg, beaten
flour for kneading

Grease a large baking sheet. Set the oven at 220°C/425°F/gas 7.

Place the flour, yeast, sugar and salt in a mixing bowl. Stir the ingredients together, then make a well in the middle. In a small saucepan, heat the butter and milk together very gently until the butter has melted, then remove the pan from the heat and leave the liquid to cool until warm.

Pour the milk mixture into the well in the dry ingredients, add the beaten egg and stir well. Gradually stir in the flour mixture to make a firm dough. Turn the dough out on to a lightly floured surface and knead thoroughly until smooth and elastic. The dough should be kneaded for about 10 minutes.

Place the dough in a clean, lightly floured bowl and cover it with a clean cloth. Set the dough to rise in a warm place until it has doubled in bulk. This may take up to 1½ hours in a warm room.

Lightly knead the dough again, then divide it into six portions. Shape each portion of dough into an oblong roll measuring about 13 cm/5 inches in length. Place the rolls on the baking sheet and bake them for about 15-20 minutes, or until they are evenly golden.

Remove the rolls from the oven and reduce the temperature to 180°C/350°F/gas 4. Using a clean tea-towel to protect your hand, split each roll in half lengthways to make a slim rusk. Place them back on the baking sheet, cut side uppermost, and cook for a further 30-40 minutes, or until they are crisp and lightly browned on the cut side. The rusks are ready when they are quite dry.

Leave the rusks to cool on a wire rack, then transfer them to an airtight container.

MAKES 12

SIMPLE CRISPIES

fat for greasing
225 g/8 oz plain flour
good pinch of salt
150 ml/¼ pint milk
25 g/1 oz butter

Grease 2 baking sheets. Set the oven at 190°C/375°F/gas 5. Sift the flour and salt into a bowl, then make a well in the middle.

Heat the milk and butter in a small saucepan until the butter has dissolved, then pour the mixture into the well in the flour. Gradually work the flour into the milk to make a stiff dough, Knead the dough briefly until it is smooth, then roll it out thinly and cut out 7.5 cm/3 inch crackers.

Place the crackers on the baking sheets and bake them for 6-10 minutes, or until they are golden. Transfer the crackers to a wire rack to cool.

MAKES ABOUT 30

ANCHOVY APPETISERS

Illustrated on page 300

fat for greasing
75 g/3 oz plain flour
40 g/1½ oz butter or margarine
1 egg yolk
few drops of anchovy essence
flour for rolling out

ANCHOVY CREAM
1 (50 g/2 oz) can anchovy fillets, drained
1 egg, hard-boiled (yolk only)
25 g/1 oz butter
pinch of cayenne pepper
45 ml/3 tbsp double cream
few drops of red food colouring

Grease 2 baking sheets. Set the oven at 200°C/400°F/gas 6.

Sift the flour into a mixing bowl and rub in the butter or margarine until the mixture resembles fine breadcrumbs. Add the egg yolk, anchovy essence and enough water to mix to a stiff dough. Roll out thinly on a lightly floured surface and cut into rounds about 2.5-4 cm/1-1½ inches in diameter.

Place on the prepared baking sheets and bake for about 12 minutes until crisp. Cool for a few minutes on the sheets, then transfer to wire racks to cool completely.

Make the anchovy cream. Put the anchovies in a bowl and pound with the yolk of the hard-boiled egg and the butter until smooth, adding a little cayenne for seasoning. In a second bowl, whip the cream until fairly stiff, then fold it into the anchovy mixture. Add the colouring until the mixture is pale pink. Transfer it to a piping bag fitted with a star nozzle and pipe rosettes of anchovy cream on to the biscuits.

MAKES 12

CHESHIRE CHIPS

fat for greasing
50 g/2 oz plain flour
50 g/2 oz butter
50 g/2 oz Cheshire cheese, grated
50 g/2 oz soft white breadcrumbs
1.25 ml/¼ tsp cayenne pepper
1.25 ml/¼ tsp salt
flour for rolling out

Grease 4 baking sheets. Sift the flour into a mixing bowl. Rub in the butter until the mixture resembles fine breadcrumbs. Add the cheese, breadcrumbs and seasonings. Work the mixture thoroughly by hand to make a smooth dough. Chill for 30 minutes.

Meanwhile, set the oven at 180°C/350°F/gas 4. Roll out the dough on a floured surface to a thickness of 5 mm/¼ inch. Cut into thin chips, each measuring about 3 mm x 5 cm/⅛ inch x 2 inches.

With a palette knife, transfer the chips to the prepared baking sheets and bake for 7-10 minutes or until lightly browned and crisp. Cool on the baking sheets.

MAKES 48 TO 60

BISCUITS FROM MANY COUNTRIES

Short and snappy, rich and spicy, the small selection of recipes in this chapter includes some of the best-known biscuits from all corners of the world. As well as everyday biscuits, the chapter includes some fun-to-make biscuits for the Christmas season.

ANZACS

Illustrated on page 302

These Australian specialities became popular during the first world war, when they were often sent to the Anzacs – soldiers of the Australia, New Zealand Army Corps.

fat for greasing
75 g/3 oz rolled oats
100 g/4 oz plain flour
150 g/5 oz sugar
50 g/2 oz desiccated coconut
100 g/4 oz butter
15 ml/1 tbsp golden syrup
7.5 ml/1½ tsp bicarbonate of soda

Grease 2 baking sheets. Set the oven at 160°C/325°F/gas 3. Mix the rolled oats, flour, sugar and coconut in a bowl. In a saucepan, melt the butter and syrup gently. Meanwhile put 30 ml/2 tbsp boiling water in a small bowl, add the bicarbonate of soda and stir until dissolved. Add to the melted mixture and stir into the dry ingredients.

Spoon scant tablespoons of the mixture on to the prepared baking sheets, leaving plenty of space between them. Bake for 20 minutes. Cool on the baking sheets.

MAKES ABOUT 36

GERMAN SPICE BISCUITS

Illustrated on page 302

fat for greasing
100 g/4 oz plain flour
50 g/2 oz caster sugar
1.25 ml/¼ tsp mixed spice
75 g/3 oz margarine
flour for rolling out

Grease a baking sheet. Set the oven at 160°C/325°F/gas 3.

Mix the flour, sugar and spice in a mixing bowl. Rub in the margarine until the mixture binds together and forms a pliable dough.

Roll out on a floured board to a thickness of 5 mm/¼ inch and cut into rounds with a 6 cm/2½ inch round cutter. Place on the prepared baking sheet. Bake for about 20 minutes until very pale gold in colour. Leave to stand for a few minutes, then cool on a wire rack.

MAKES ABOUT 12

MRS BEETON'S TIP A glass makes a good biscuit cutter. Dip it in flour before use to prevent the dough from sticking to the rim.

LEBKUCHEN

The dough for these traditional biscuits is easier to handle if it is made in advance and stored overnight in the refrigerator.

350 g/12 oz honey
575 g/1¼ lb plain flour
1.25 ml/¼ tsp salt
2.5 ml/½ tsp bicarbonate of soda
5 ml/1 tsp ground cloves
7.5 ml/1½ tsp ground cinnamon
7.5 ml/1½ tsp grated nutmeg
2.5 ml/½ tsp ground allspice
grated rind of 1 lemon
100 g/4 oz cut mixed peel, finely chopped
2 eggs
175 g/6 oz soft light brown sugar
15 ml/1 tbsp lemon juice
225 g/8 oz blanched almonds, finely chopped
fat for greasing
100 g/4 oz icing sugar for glaze

Warm the honey in a small saucepan until runny. Sift the flour, salt, bicarbonate of soda and spices into a bowl. Add the grated lemon rind and mixed peel and mix well.

In a mixing bowl, whisk the eggs with the sugar until light and fluffy. Add the lemon juice and honey and mix well, then stir in the flour mixture and nuts. Mix to a soft dough. The mixture will still be sticky. Leave it in the bowl in the refrigerator for 1 hour until it becomes more manageable, then knead lightly, wrap in cling film and refrigerate overnight.

Next day, grease 3 or 4 baking sheets. Set the oven at 190°C/375°F/gas 5. Roll out half the dough on a floured surface to a thickness of 5 mm/¼ inch, returning the remaining dough to the refrigerator. Cut into shapes, using heart, star or round cutters. Place on the prepared baking sheets. Repeat with the remaining dough, re-rolling and re-cutting any trimmings.

Bake for 13-15 minutes. Meanwhile make a thin glaze by mixing the icing sugar in a small bowl with 15-30 ml/1-2 tbsp water.

Cool the biscuits for a few minutes on the baking sheets, then transfer to a wire rack set over a plate. Drizzle the glaze over the warm biscuits, then cool completely.

MAKES ABOUT 72

MRS BEETON'S TIP Lebkuchen should be soft and chewy. To achieve this, store the glazed biscuits for 1-2 weeks in a sealed tin to which a slice of apple has been added, before eating.

KOURABIEDES

Many a traveller has returned from a Greek holiday with a box of these melt-in-the-mouth biscuits as a souvenir.

450 g/1 lb plain flour
450 g/1 lb unsalted butter
150 g/5 oz icing sugar
1 egg yolk
30 ml/2 tbsp brandy
extra icing sugar for coating

Grease 2-3 baking sheets. Set the oven at 180°C/350°F/gas 4. Sift the flour into a bowl.

In a mixing bowl, cream the butter with 30 ml/2 tbsp of the icing sugar until light and fluffy. Gradually beat in the remaining icing sugar and the egg yolk. Still beating, add the brandy.

Stir in 100 g/4 oz of the flour and mix well, then fold in the remaining flour, first using a knife and then the fingers, to make a soft dough.

Using a teaspoon, scoop up a little of the dough. Use a second teaspoon to transfer the dough to one of the prepared baking sheets. Repeat with the remaining dough, making the heaps about 5 cm/2 inches apart to allow for spreading.

Bake for 12-15 minutes or until pale gold in colour. Cool on the baking sheets, then sift over enough icing sugar to give each biscuit a generous coating.

MAKES ABOUT 56

🥄 MRS BEETON'S TIP Kourabiedes need careful handling if they are not to break. If making them as a gift, pack them in plenty of tissue paper in a rigid container.

SNOWMEN

Illustrated on page 302

Hang these American favourites on to your tree for a special Christmas treat. You will require a snowman template: on a piece of heavy cardboard, arrange a 7.5 cm/3 inch biscuit cutter with a 5 cm/2 inch cutter on top to create a snowman shape. Draw round the shape, overlapping the cutters slightly to give a wide neck, and adding a top hat if liked. Cut out the template.

fat for greasing
225 g/8 oz plain flour
45 ml/3 tbsp cocoa
5 ml/1 tsp bicarbonate of soda
50 g/2 oz margarine
100 g/4 oz golden syrup
75 g/3 oz soft light brown sugar
1 egg, beaten

DECORATION
white Glacé Icing (see page 151)
chocolate chips
glacé cherries
jelly diamonds
Chocolate Glacé Icing (see page 151)
(optional)

Grease 3-4 baking sheets. Set the oven at 180°C/350°F/gas 4. Mix the flour, cocoa and bicarbonate of soda in a mixing bowl.

Melt the margarine in a large saucepan. Add the syrup and sugar and warm gently, but do not allow to become hot. Remove from the heat.

Add the melted mixture to the dry ingredients with the beaten egg, and mix to a dough. Wrap in cling film and refrigerate for 1-2 hours.

Roll out the dough on a floured surface to a thickness of 5 mm/¼ inch. Using the template and a sharp knife, carefully cut out snowmen, re-rolling and re-cutting any trimmings. Use a straw to make a small hole in each snowman, near the top of the head or hat.

Transfer the snowmen to the prepared baking sheets and bake for 12-15 minutes until firm to the touch. Cool the biscuits on the baking sheets for a few minutes, then transfer the biscuits carefully to wire racks to cool completely.

When cold, thread a length of fine string or thick cotton through each snowman. Ice each with white glacé icing and decorate as appropriate, using chocolate chips for eyes and small pieces of glacé cherry for mouths. Jelly diamonds make excellent coat buttons. If the snowmen have been given hats, these may be iced in a different colour, using chocolate glacé icing, perhaps.

MAKES ABOUT 8

> **MRS BEETON'S TIP** Children love to decorate these biscuits. Let them loose with a tub each of glacé cherries, jelly diamonds, sugar strands, chocolate chips and chocolate vermicelli and they will be happy for hours.

*P*FEFFERNÜSSE

The secret of making these spicy biscuits is to give the flavours time to develop. Make the dough 2-3 days before baking.

350 g/12 oz plain flour
5 ml/1 tsp baking powder
1.25 ml/¼ tsp ground cloves
5 ml/1 tsp ground cinnamon
1.25 ml/¼ tsp grated nutmeg
1.25 ml/¼ tsp freshly ground black pepper
50 g/2 oz butter
225 g/8 oz golden syrup
100 g/4 oz soft light brown sugar
fat for greasing

Mix the flour, baking powder and spices in a mixing bowl. Melt the butter, syrup and sugar in a large saucepan. Do not allow the mixture to become hot. Remove from the heat as soon as the syrup and butter have melted.

Add the melted mixture to the dry ingredients and mix to a dough. Wrap in cling film and refrigerate for 2-3 days.

Grease 3-4 baking sheets. Set the oven at 200°C/400°F/gas 6. Pinch off small portions of the dough – about 10 ml/2 tsp at a time – and roll each to a small ball. Place on the prepared baking sheets, allowing room for spreading.

Bake for 10-12 minutes until golden brown. Cool the biscuits for a few minutes on the baking sheets, then transfer to wire racks to cool completely.

MAKES 30 TO 36

> **MICROWAVE TIP** If the chilled dough is too stiff to work, soften it for 2 minutes on Defrost.

CHOCOLATE-TIPPED CINNAMON STARS

Illustrated on page 302

Canadians created these delicious edible Christmas decorations.

fat for greasing
350 g/12 oz plain flour
5 ml/1 tsp bicarbonate of soda
10 ml/2 tsp ground cinnamon
2.5 ml/½ tsp ground ginger
150 g/5 oz butter
100 g/4 oz sugar
100 g/4 oz honey
1 egg yolk
30 ml/2 tbsp milk
flour for rolling out
150 g/5 oz dark chocolate, broken into
    squares, to decorate

Thoroughly grease 3-4 baking sheets. Set the oven at 180°C/350°F/gas 4. Mix the flour, bicarbonate of soda and spices in a bowl.

In a mixing bowl, beat the butter until soft, add the sugar and continue to beat until light and fluffy. Beat in the honey and egg yolk, then the milk. Fold in the flour mixture.

Knead the biscuit dough lightly on a floured surface, then roll out to a thickness of 3 mm/⅛ inch. Cut into stars with a 5 cm/2 inch star-shaped biscuit cutter. Using a straw, make a small hole in each star. The hole should be on a point, but not too near the edge. Transfer the biscuits to the prepared baking sheets.

Bake for about 8 minutes, until golden brown. Cool for a few minutes on the baking sheets, then transfer to wire racks.

Melt the chocolate with 15 ml/1 tbsp water in a saucepan over low heat. Brush the tips of each star generously with chocolate, then place on a wire rack until the chocolate has set. This process may be speeded up if the biscuits are chilled in the refrigerator.

When the chocolate is firm, thread a length of ribbon through each biscuit and hang on the Christmas tree.

MAKES ABOUT 60

CHOCOLATE CHIP COOKIES

America's contribution to the biscuit barrel.

fat for greasing
150 g/5 oz plain flour
1.25 ml/¼ tsp salt
2.5 ml/½ tsp bicarbonate of soda
100 g/4 oz butter or margarine
50 g/2 oz caster sugar
50 g/2 oz soft light brown sugar
1 egg, beaten
2.5 ml/½ tsp vanilla essence
75 g/3 oz chocolate chips

Thoroughly grease 2-3 baking sheets. Set the oven at 180°C/350°F/gas 4. Mix the flour, salt and bicarbonate of soda in a bowl.

Beat the butter or margarine until soft, add the sugars and continue to beat until light and fluffy. Beat in the egg and vanilla essence. Stir in the flour and chocolate chips.

Using a teaspoon, scoop up a little of the dough. Use a second teaspoon to transfer the dough to one of the prepared baking sheets. Repeat with the remaining dough, making the heaps about 5 cm/2 inches apart.

Bake the biscuits for 10-12 minutes, until golden. Leave to stand for 5 minutes, then cool on a wire rack.

MAKES 26-30

Rich Chocolate Slices (page 324) and Date and Walnut Nibbles (page 322)

Christmas Squares (page 326) and Date Surprises (page 322)

NO BAKE BISCUITS

A short chapter of simple biscuits that can all be prepared without involving baking. They are quick to make, good to eat and the majority of recipes are ideal for inexpensive surprise treats. These are also the recipes for children to make.

CANADIAN CRISPIES

100 g/4 oz plain chocolate
50 g/2 oz crisp rice cereal
25 g/1 oz seedless raisins or sultanas

Break the chocolate into small pieces and put it in a bowl over hot (not boiling) water until it melts completely. Stir in the cereal and the dried fruit. Place in rough heaps in paper cases and leave to cool and set.

MAKES 12 TO 14

☼ **MICROWAVE TIP** The chocolate may be melted in a shallow bowl on High for 1-2 minutes. Add the remaining ingredients and mix well. Drop in clusters on greaseproof paper or cool in paper cases as suggested above.

DATE SURPRISES

Illustrated on page 320

100 g/4 oz butter or margarine
150 g/5 oz sugar
1.25 ml/¼ tsp salt
200 g/7 oz dates, stoned and chopped
1 egg
1.25 ml/¼ tsp vanilla essence
15 ml/1 tbsp milk
50-100 g/2-4 oz crisp rice cereal
desiccated coconut for coating

Combine the butter or margarine, sugar, salt and dates in a heavy-bottomed saucepan and bring to the boil over moderate heat. Cook for 3 minutes, stirring all the time, then remove from the heat.

In a bowl, beat the egg with the vanilla essence and milk. Stir into the date mixture, return to very low heat and cook for 3 minutes, stirring vigorously. Off the heat, stir in the cereal. Return the mixture to the bowl and allow to cool, then chill until firm.

When quite cold, roll the mixture into balls. Spread the coconut on greaseproof paper and roll the date balls in it until coated. Serve in small paper cases, if liked.

MAKES 24 TO 30

BANANA RAISIN BARS

Mashed bananas add a pleasing flavour to these unusual, fruity bars. They are best kept in the refrigerator. Eat within a couple of days.

oil for greasing
60 ml/4 tbsp thick honey
100 g/4 oz unsalted butter
100 g/4 oz raisins
grated rind of 1 orange
225 g/8 oz digestive biscuits, crushed
2 bananas, mashed
100 g/4 oz hazelnuts, chopped and toasted

Grease an 18 cm/7 inch square tin. Place the honey, butter, raisins and orange rind in a small saucepan. Set the pan over low heat and warm the ingredients gently until the butter and honey are melted together and the raisins slightly plumped.

Meanwhile, place the crushed biscuits in a bowl. Remove the pan from the heat and pour the melted mixture over the biscuits, stirring all the time. When the biscuits are thoroughly coated in the melted ingredients, stir in the bananas and cream the mixture lightly to combine all the ingredients thoroughly.

Turn the mixture into the prepared tin and spread it evenly, smoothing the top with the back of a spoon. Sprinkle the nuts over the surface and chill the mixture until it is firm. Cut the mixture into twelve bars and ease them gently out of the tin.

MAKES 12

MRS BEETON'S TIP To crush biscuits, place them in a polythene bag and close the end with a plastic tie, leaving a little space for air to escape. Use a rolling pin to crush the biscuits, taking care not to burst the bag.

DATE AND WALNUT NIBBLES

Illustrated on page 319

These spicy little sweet nibbles are particularly good with mulled wine or to complement a glass of sweet sherry, or any similar refreshment.

75 g/3 oz butter
60 ml/4 tbsp thick honey
5 ml/1 tsp ground mixed spice
225 g/8 oz cooking dates, chopped
225 g/8 oz walnuts, chopped
175 g/6 oz gingernut biscuits, crushed
juice of ½ orange
about 24 walnut halves

Cream the butter and honey together until well combined and soft. Beat in the spice, then mix in the dates, walnuts and ginger biscuit crumbs. Add just enough orange juice to bind all the ingredients together.

If necessary, chill the mixture until it is firm enough to shape into balls. Lay a sheet of waxed paper on a baking sheet. Roll the mixture into balls which are slightly larger than walnuts, then place them on the baking sheet and flatten each one slightly with a fork. Press a walnut half on each nibble and chill until firm. The nibbles can be served in paper cake cases if you like.

MAKES ABOUT 24

TOFFEE FRUIT CRUNCH

oil for greasing
225 g/8 oz plain toffees
100 g/4 oz butter
50 g/2 oz cut mixed peel
100 g/4 oz sultanas
100 g/4 oz walnuts, chopped
100 g/4 oz unsweetened puffed rice
    breakfast cereal

Grease a 23 x 33 cm/9 x 13 inch Swiss roll tin. Place the toffees and butter in a large saucepan and heat them very gently, stirring frequently, until they are melted and well combined.

Remove the pan from the heat and add the mixed peel, sultanas and walnuts. Stir in the breakfast cereal, making sure it is well coated in the melted mixture. Try to avoid crushing the breakfast cereal.

Turn the mixture into the tin and spread it out thinly and lightly. Leave it to cool, then chill the mixture until it is quite firm. Cut the mixture into fingers or squares and carefully ease them out of the tin.

MAKES ABOUT 24

> **MRS BEETON'S TIP** If you like, cut the mixture into fingers and half dip them in melted chocolate, then leave them to set on greased waxed paper.

MUESLI MUNCHIES

Use good-quality muesli, full of fruit and nuts, to make these chocolate-coated snacks.

50 g/2 oz butter
30 ml/2 tbsp golden syrup
225 g/8 oz plain chocolate
100 g/4 oz glacé cherries, chopped
175 g/6 oz muesli

Set out 15 paper cake cases on a baking sheet. Melt the butter, syrup and chocolate in a bowl over a saucepan of hot, not boiling, water. Stir well to make sure all the ingredients are combined, then remove the bowl from the heat and stir in the cherries and muesli.

Make sure the cherries and muesli are well coated in chocolate, then divide the mixture between the paper cake cases. Leave the munchies in a cool place until set.

MAKES 15

RICH CHOCOLATE SLICES

Illustrated on page 319

Melted chocolate is used to bind crushed biscuits and chopped toasted hazelnuts in this recipe. The mixture is shaped into a roll, then sliced. It tastes excellent, particularly with coffee.

100 g/4 oz plain chocolate
50 g/2 oz butter
60 ml/4 tbsp golden syrup
60 ml/4 tbsp brandy or orange juice
225 g/8 oz chopped hazelnuts, toasted
225 g/8 oz digestive biscuits, crushed
100 g/4 oz ready-to-eat dried apricots,
    chopped

Place the chocolate, butter and syrup in a bowl. Set the bowl over a pan of hot, not boiling, water and stir the ingredients occasionally until the chocolate and butter are melted and combined.

Add the brandy or orange juice, nuts, biscuits and apricots. Pound the ingredients together with a wooden spoon until they are thoroughly combined, then chill the mixture until it is firm enough to shape; this should only take about 30 minutes.

Lay a piece of cling film on the work surface and spoon the mixture on to it, in a mound about 20 cm/8 inches long. Carefully lift the sides of the film around over the mixture and screw the ends to seal it in. Shape the mixture in the film until it forms a neat roll. As you shape the roll, pat the ends to prevent the mixture from becoming too long and thin. Chill the roll thoroughly, preferably overnight. Use a damp knife to cut the roll into thin slices.

MAKES ABOUT 20

COFFEE TRUFFLE FINGERS

A rich sweet delicacy that can only be described as a cross between a biscuit and a confection. Sponge fingers form the base; these may be bought or home-made.

150 ml/¼ pint double cream
15 ml/1 tbsp instant coffee
225 g/8 oz milk chocolate
12-15 sponge fingers
a little icing sugar

Pour the cream into a small saucepan and add the instant coffee. Heat the mixture gently until the cream boils, then remove the pan from the heat and allow the cream mixture to cool until it is hand-hot.

Break the chocolate into squares and place them in a basin over a saucepan of hot, not boiling, water. Stir the chocolate occasionally until it has melted, then remove the basin from the pan. Pour the cream mixture into the chocolate, stirring all the time, then leave the mixture to cool, stirring occasionally.

When the mixture cools and begins to thicken, beat it hard or use an electric beater to whip it until it is very creamy and light. Chill the whipped mixture until it is firm enough to pipe. The mixture should have formed a thick paste but it should not be allowed to become hard.

Fit a piping bag with a fairly large star nozzle and put the truffle mixture into it. Pipe lines of truffle mixture down the sponge fingers and dust them lightly with a little icing sugar. Chill until firm. To pipe the truffle mixture successfully, keep your hands as cool as possible by placing them under cold running water. If your hands are very warm they will melt the mixture as you hold the piping bag.

MAKES ABOUT 20

CREAM CHEESE FINGERS

Either low fat soft cheese or the richer full fat soft cheese can be used to make these unusual sweet fingers.

100 g/4 oz white chocolate
100 g/4 oz ground almonds
225 g/8 oz full fat soft cream cheese
grated rind of ½ lemon
225 g/8 oz ready-to-eat apricots, finely
    chopped
30 ml/2 tbsp thick honey
50 g/2 oz flaked almonds, toasted

Line the base of an 18 cm/7 inch square tin with waxed paper, putting the waxed side uppermost. Break the chocolate into squares and place them in a basin. Set the basin over a saucepan of hot, not boiling, water until the chocolate has melted.

In a mixing bowl, mix the ground almonds with the cheese, then add the lemon rind, apricots and honey. Beat the mixture to combine all the ingredients thoroughly. Lastly, stir in the melted chocolate.

Turn the mixture into the prepared tin and spread it out evenly. Sprinkle the toasted almonds over the mixture, pressing them down to make an even covering. Chill the mixture until firm, for several hours or overnight.

Cut the mixture in half, then cut each half into 2.5 cm/1 inch wide fingers. Serve at once or keep the fingers chilled until they are to be served.

MAKES 14

SPICY COCONUT CRUNCHIES

A quick alternative to coconut pyramids. Children making these should be supervised when using the grill.

1 egg white, lightly whisked
100 g/4 oz desiccated coconut
grated rind of ½ orange
5 ml/1 tsp ground cinnamon
30 ml/2 tbsp golden syrup
oil for greasing

In a mixing bowl, whisk the egg white until it is just frothy. Add the coconut and orange rind, then sprinkle in the cinnamon. Trickle the syrup over the mixture and stir all the ingredients together until they are totally combined.

Lightly grease a baking sheet. Shape the mixture into 12 small balls; to do this wet your hands lightly and press the ingredients together firmly. Place the balls of mixture on the baking sheet and flatten them slightly with the finger tips, then place the crunchies under the grill and cook slowly until golden on top.

Turn the crunchies and brown the second side. Watch the biscuits all the time they cook to make sure that they do not begin to burn. Leave for 10 minutes. Transfer the crunchies to a wire rack to cool.

MAKES 12

CHOCOLATE PEANUT CUPS

60 ml/4 tbsp crunchy peanut butter
100 g/4 oz plain chocolate
50 g/2 oz butter
30 ml/2 tbsp golden syrup
100 g/4 oz unsweetened breakfast cereal,
    for example puffed rice or cornflakes

Place the peanut butter, chocolate, butter and golden syrup in a basin over a saucepan of hot water. Stir the mixture occasionally until it melts and is thoroughly combined.

Meanwhile set out 20 paper cake cases on a baking sheet. When all the melted ingredients are well mixed, remove the bowl from the pan and stir in the breakfast cereal. Do not crush the cereal. Spoon the mixture into the paper cases; leave in a cool place until set.

MAKES 20

PRALINE FINGERS

10 sponge fingers
100 g/4 oz apricot jam, warmed
100 g/4 oz marzipan
100 g/4 oz sugar
50 g/2 oz blanched almonds, roughly
    chopped

Place the sponge fingers on a baking sheet and brush them with a little apricot jam. Divide the marzipan into ten pieces and shape each piece into a roll slightly shorter than the sponge fingers. Flatten each marzipan roll slightly and place one on top of each sponge finger.

In a small saucepan, gently heat the sugar with 60 ml/4 tbsp water until the sugar dissolves, then continue to cook the syrup until it turns golden. Remove the pan from the heat and stir in the nuts. Using a metal spoon, pour a little of this praline along each of the sponge fingers. Set aside until cold.

MAKES 10

CHRISTMAS SQUARES

Illustrated on page 320

100 g/4 oz sultanas
100 g/4 oz glacé cherries, chopped
100 g/4 oz cut mixed peel
100 g/4 oz dried figs or dates, chopped
grated rind of 1 orange
60 ml/4 tbsp rum, brandy or sherry
225 g/8 oz plain chocolate
100 g/4 oz butter
100 g/4 oz marzipan, cut into small pieces
100 g/4 oz almond macaroons or digestive
    biscuits, coarsely crushed

Place the sultanas, cherries, peel, figs or dates and orange rind in a bowl and sprinkle the rum or sherry over them. Mix lightly, cover and leave to stand for at least 2 hours, preferably overnight.

Line a 20 cm/8 inch square tin with rice paper. Break the chocolate into squares and place them in a bowl with the butter. Stand the bowl over a saucepan of hot water and stir the chocolate mixture occasionally until it has completely melted. Remove the bowl from the pan and mix in the soaked fruit with any juices. Add the marzipan and crushed biscuits and mix very lightly, trying not to break up the pieces of marzipan.

Turn the mixture into the prepared tin and chill until set. Cut the set mixture into 16 squares and gently ease them out of the tin. The rice paper base is edible.

MAKES 16

GLOSSARY

All the terms, techniques and ingredients that are used throughout this book are discussed in detail within the relevant chapter or in the introduction. This glossary can be used for quick reference, perhaps to check up on the meaning of a term.

All-in-one method A method of mixing cakes in one stage only, by combining all the ingredients in a bowl and beating them together. The fat used should be soft margarine, or softened butter or block margarine, and additional raising agent is required. Except for small quantities, it is usual to use an electric whisk or food mixer to combine the ingredients. Also known as the one-stage method.

Almond essence Very strong almond flavouring, measured in drops.

Angelica The green stems of a plant, candied and used in cakes or biscuits, or as a decoration. The plant grows easily in Britain and it can be candied at home, although this is a long, slow process.

Bake To cook by dry heat in the oven.

Beat To combine foods, using a firm, quick motion which slightly lifts and turns the food, so incorporating air. It is commonly used for batters and soft mixtures, and a wooden spoon or electric whisk is used. The mixture is 'hit' with the flat front (or back) of the spoon as it is pushed quickly through the mixture; then lifted slightly and taken back to the starting point before being pushed through the mixture again.

Bind To add moist ingredients or liquid to a dry mixture to make all the ingredients adhere to each other. Enough liquid is added to ensure that the mixture can be gathered together into one, fairly firm, mass. The term is not used when a large quantity of liquid is added to make a very soft mixture.

Blanch To cover food with, or immerse food in, boiling water, or to bring food to the boil in water, then drain and cool it quickly. This technique is used for various reasons – to preserve flavour and colour in foods that are to be frozen, to remove peel or skin, or to par-cook food. Nuts are blanched to remove their skins.

Blend To gently combine ingredients without overmixing them. Alternatively, this term is used for processing food in a blender.

Chill To cool food. This is usually carried out by placing the food in the refrigerator. Alternatively, the container of food can be immersed in a bowl of iced water. A quick method of chilling is to put the food in the freezer for a short period of time. Chilling is carried out on food which is at room temperature; hot food is cooled before it is chilled.

Chocolate cake covering An inexpensive alternative to couverture or dessert chocolate. This is useful for day-to-day cooking but its flavour cannot be compared to dessert chocolate.

Cinnamon A sweet spice, widely used in baked goods. It is the bark of a tree and is available as cinnamon sticks, which are rolled thin slivers of the spice, or ground to a fine, brown powder.

Coat To cover food with an outer coating. This can be a coating to protect foods such as fish or meat before cooking. In baking the term is applied to the use of icings and chocolate, where cakes or biscuits are covered with an even coating of one of these toppings.

Cocoa Seeds of the cocoa tree, dried,

partially fermented and roasted. They are ground to a fine powder for use as a flavouring. Cocoa is unsweetened, dark and strongly flavoured. It must not be confused with drinking chocolate which is a sweetened mixture, flavoured with cocoa.

Cochineal Natural food colouring which gives a pink, or dark pink-red colour to food. It will not give a true red colour.

Coffee Roasted coffee beans are available whole or ground. Instant coffee is the most common source of coffee flavouring for cakes and biscuits. Fresh coffee essence can be made by cooling and straining very strong fresh coffee.

Couverture Cooking chocolate which has a high cocoa fat content, giving an excellent flavour and glossy finish.

Cream This is a term used for combining ingredients, in baking usually fat and sugar. A circular motion is used and the edge of a wooden spoon cuts through the ingredients. The aim when creaming ingredients is to make them soft and light in texture by incorporating air. When fat and sugar are creamed together, the mixture gradually becomes pale in colour, soft and fluffy in texture. An electric food mixer can be used or ingredients can be creamed in a food processor.

Dariole moulds Small, straight-sided tins which are sometimes known as castle tins.

Dredge To sprinkle a fairly thick, even coating of sugar or flour over food or the work surface. If a cake is dredged with icing sugar, then it should be evenly covered in a thick coating. A sieve, sugar sifter or flour dredger (or shaker) is used to give a fine, even result.

Dust To sprinkle food or a surface with a fine, even coating of sugar or flour. Unlike dredging, dusting means that a very fine sprinkling of the dry ingredient should be evenly distributed over the surface without completely covering it.

Fold in To incorporate an ingredient into a very light mixture without knocking out any of the air. A large metal spoon is used and the mixture is gently lifted, then folded over the ingredient which has been added to it. The spoon should follow a figure of eight movement: the edge of the spoon cuts through the mixture, then the bowl of the spoon is turned to lift the mixture over in a diagonal movement. The spoon is then pushed back to the starting point. It is most important that a stirring movement is avoided as this will knock the air out of the mixture. Dry ingredients, such as flour and sugar, are folded into moist mixtures, such as whisked egg whites, beaten eggs or creamed fat and sugar. Melted fat or other liquids can be folded into light mixtures. The process of folding in should be quick, gentle and involve the minimum of 'mixing'.

Fondant A traditional icing which is made by boiling sugar and water to the soft ball stage. The mixture is then 'worked' or made pliable as it cools by turning it with the flat blade of a palette knife until it forms a soft malleable paste. Reheated and thinned, this is then poured over the cake.

Frosting The American term for 'icing'. Frosting is a soft creamy icing made by whisking egg whites and sugar over hot water.

Gâteau This term is used for creamy, light layer cakes, often filled or decorated with fruit. Instead of sponge cake, the base can be meringue (see also page 160).

Genoese sponge A light sponge cake, made by the whisked method, enriched with melted butter.

Glycerine This is an alcohol which is one of the ingredients used to make soap. It is a clear syrup which has a certain use as a sugar substitute or for softening mixtures. It is not widely used and should not be used in large quantities.

Knead This technique is most often used to make bread dough. One end of the dough is lifted and pulled over the middle of the piece of dough, then it is pushed back with the knuckles. As well as yeasted doughs, biscuit doughs are sometimes 'kneaded gently' but this is not a fierce movement.

When the term is applied to pastry or biscuit dough, then the fingertips are used to pull the dough, rolling it slightly and moving the hand in towards the middle of the piece of dough. Then the flat of the hand is used to lightly push the dough outwards, again slightly rolling it. This method is a combination of flattening and rolling, then pushing the dough back up again. The movement should be very light and quick, just enough to make sure that the biscuit dough is smooth.

Mocha The term used for the flavour of coffee and chocolate in combination.

Nutmeg Large, round, very hard seed of a tree. It is grated and used in sweet and savoury cooking. Available as whole nutmegs or ready grated. This is another sweet spice.

Pare To very thinly peel the rind or skin from a fruit or vegetable. The rind of citrus fruits is pared, then cut into fine strips and cooked in boiling water to be used as a decoration.

Rice Paper Rice paper has no connection with rice – it comes from a plant. It is very thin, brittle, opaque and edible. It is used as a base for mixtures such as macaroons.

Rub-in This is the term used for combining fat with dry ingredients such as flour. The fat is cut into small pieces and added to the flour. The fingertips are used to lift a portion of the dry ingredients and the fat is rubbed very lightly with the flour. As the ingredients are rubbed together, they are allowed to fall back into the bowl. The process of lifting the

ingredients before and during rubbing incorporates air into the mixture. It is important that just the fingertips are used and that the hands are kept cool.

Sieve A metal or nylon fine mesh through which ingredients are passed. To sieve food means to press the food through the mesh, usually using a spoon. This term is applied to moist ingredients which are sieved to reduce them to a purée or to break down any unwanted lumps.

Sift A sieve or sifter (a container with a holed lid) is used for this purpose. Dry ingredients are shaken through the sieve, either by tapping the side of the utensil or by pressing them through with the back of a spoon. If sugar is sifted over a cake, then the sieve should be tapped gently to give a fine even sprinkling. If icing sugar or flour are sifted before they are used, they can be pushed through with a spoon.

Strain A liquid mixture is strained through a sieve to remove all unwanted solids. The liquid is the part which is retained; the food which is strained out of it may be discarded or it may be separated for another purpose.

Vanilla A flavouring ingredient which is widely used in baking.

Vanilla sugar Caster sugar which has been flavoured with a vanilla pod.

Whip The term used for whisking double cream or whipping cream.

Whisk An implement used for whisking food. Many types of whisks are available, for example, wire balloon whisks, spring whisks, rotary whisks or electric whisks. Egg whites and liquids are whisked and the result is much lighter than for mixtures which are beaten using a wooden spoon.

Zest The oils that 'spit' from citrus rind. The zest of a fruit rind is obtained by rubbing a lump of sugar over it. The sugar absorbs the oils, and therefore the flavour, of the rind.

INDEX